Lives of the Laureates

Lives of the Laureates

Twenty-three Nobel Economists

sixth edition

Edited by Roger W. Spencer and David A. Macpherson

The MIT Press
Cambridge, Massachusetts
London, England

MIT Press books may be purchased at special quantity discounts for business or sales promotional use. For information, please email special_sales@mitpress.mit.edu.

This book was set in Sabon by Toppan Best-set Premedia Limited. Printed and bound in the United States of America.

Library of Congress Cataloging-in-Publication Data

Lives of the laureates : twenty-three Nobel economists / edited by Roger W. Spencer and David A. Macpherson. — Sixth edition.
    pages cm
Includes bibliographical references.
ISBN 978-0-262-02796-0 (hardcover : alk. paper)
1. Economists—Biography. 2. Nobel Prizes. I. Spencer, Roger W. II. Macpherson, David A., 1960–
HB76.L58 2014
330.092′2—dc23
[B]
2014009829

10 9 8 7 6 5 4 3 2 1

Contents

Introduction to the Sixth Edition

This book consists of autobiographical accounts of the careers of twenty-three people who have three qualities in common. First, they are all economists. Second, each of them has been awarded the Alfred Nobel Memorial Prize in Economic Science. Third, each traveled to San Antonio, Texas, to deliver his story in person at Trinity University.

The Nobel Prize in Economics was not created by Alfred Nobel himself. In 1901 his will established prizes in physics, chemistry, medicine or physiology, literature, and peace. He wished to reward specific achievements rather than outstanding persons. In the case of the natural sciences, the awards were to be given for "discoveries," "inventions," and "improvements." In 1968 the Central Bank of Sweden, in connection with its tercentenary celebration, initiated a new award, the Central Bank of Sweden Prize in Economic Science in Memory of Alfred Nobel. This prize was to be granted in conformity with the standards that governed the awarding of the original Nobel Prizes. According to the rules established by the Central Bank of Sweden, the "prize shall be awarded annually to a person who has carried out a work in economic science of the eminent significance expressed in the will of Alfred Nobel."[1]

The idea for a series of autobiographical lectures by Nobel laureates in economics was that of William Breit, who spent a good part of his academic career studying, teaching, and writing about the lives and ideas of leading contemporary U.S. economists.[2] His abiding interest in the relationship between biography and the creative process led naturally to the thought of providing a forum in which outstanding economists would express in their own words, in any way that seemed congenial, a personal memoir under the general rubric "my evolution as an economist." At the very least, such a forum would preserve part of the rich record of accomplishment that helped to shape the direction and character of economic science in the post–World War II era. But the larger purpose was to provide important source material for a theory of scientific discovery.

Little is known about the process by which original ideas germinate and are eventually accepted by one's peers. To what extent is the substance of scientific work in social science a reflection of the lives of those who produced it? What is the role of influential teachers and colleagues? To what degree are the problems to which these thinkers addressed themselves a result of their own backgrounds, and of the economic and social problems of their times? What forces were most responsible for leading them to their insights? In short, what is it that enables an individual to discover something that seizes and holds the attention of a large segment of a scientific community? To help answer such questions was the major rationale behind the series.

But whom should we invite? It was clear that budgetary and time constraints would limit the number of invitations, and so the roster was restricted in the following ways: only economists who served on the faculties of U.S. universities at the time the Nobel Prize was awarded would be included, and the roster would represent as many different facets of economics in terms of types of contributions, specific areas, methods of analysis, and ideological differences as possible. In 1983, when the program was being planned, there were twelve Nobel Prize winners who met the first criterion, though one was too ill to travel. A difficult winnowing process in accordance with the second criterion narrowed the final list to eight. Only one invitee declined to participate.

The autobiographical lectures that made up the first edition of this volume were presented at Trinity University during the 1984–85 year. The success of the project encouraged then Trinity University president Ronald Calgaard to allow the series to continue.

During the three years immediately following the end of the original series, a trio of Americans was honored with the Alfred Nobel Memorial Prize in Economic Science: Franco Modigliani of MIT in 1985, James M. Buchanan of George Mason University in 1986, and Robert M. Solow of MIT in 1987. Each of them accepted the request to present a lecture in which he would chart the route that led him to the highest accolade a scholar can receive. These lectures were included in the second edition of *Lives of the Laureates,* published in 1990.

As more Nobel Prize winners accepted the invitation to speak at Trinity, a third edition was published in 1995, a fourth in 2004, and a fifth in 2009. The sixth edition of *Lives of the Laureates* includes four new lectures, by Eric Maskin (co-recipient in 2007), Joseph Stiglitz (co-recipient in 2001), Paul Krugman (2008), and Peter Diamond (co-recipient in 2010).

To make room in a single volume for these additions, the publisher determined that four lectures from earlier editions had to be dropped. The four are the lectures of W. Arthur Lewis, Ronald H. Coase, John C. Harsanyi, and Clive W. J. Granger. It is anticipated that as the number of Nobel Prize lectures delivered at Trinity University continues to grow, some future edition can be produced in two volumes, which would permit the deleted lectures to be restored.

For many of the laureates, the assignment has been a difficult one. There is an understandable reluctance to give a public talk about one's own intellectual contributions. As one of the invitees put it, "I do not know that I could keep it between the Scylla of false modesty and the Charybdis of boastfulness, and I am afraid I would find the whole business rather stressful." Moreover, most of their work in its professional formulation was technical in nature, difficult to understand by those not trained as economists. Yet each was being asked to make his contribution accessible to a lay audience at a public lecture open to the whole community. This provided greater difficulties for some than for others. Paul A. Samuelson's and Kenneth J. Arrow's scientific contributions are largely in the domain of mathematical economics. Lawrence R. Klein and James J. Heckman, among others, made heavy use of statistical techniques and econometrics. All the Nobel economists express themselves in the technical vocabulary of their discipline.

Yet in each instance, as the reader of these pages will discover, the speaker managed to convey the nature and significance of his contributions. (The essays in this book are in the order in which they were presented in the Trinity lecture series.) It is hard to imagine a less painful way of grasping the essentials of Arrow's impossibility theorem than hearing it (or reading about it) in his own words. And is there anywhere a more clearly presented conception of what goes into econometric model building than is to be found in Klein's essay? George J. Stigler's masterful explanation of his information theory is lucid and accessible to almost everyone with an interest in this fruitful innovation. The recent Nobel laureates follow in this trend. Indeed, each participant achieved the goal of clarity without sacrificing inherently difficult content.

The visit of each of the Nobel laureates was an unqualified success. The audiences were large and appreciative. Some of the laureates traveled considerable distances to attend. Each economist met with students and faculty informally. At small receptions, at restaurants, over coffee, and at dinners in private homes, students and faculty were able to talk with some of the most highly regarded economists of the twentieth and twenty-first centuries. Notwithstanding their formidable reputations as scholars and, in some cases, strong personalities, their modesty impressed all who came into contact with them. An important side benefit of the lecture series was the lesson that some of the most illustrious figures of modern economics are human after all.

Looking back over these lectures, one is struck by the many currents in the stream of modern economics. The reader will find that paths cross in unexpected ways, that disparate thinkers were often influenced by the same teachers, and that serendipity, in addition to perseverance and hard work, plays a role in the successful creation of scientific knowledge. Equally significant, these autobiographical essays reveal psychological truths—perhaps hidden from the subjects themselves—that an especially perceptive reader may discern. Taken as a whole, they provide a comprehensive picture of the diversity, richness, and profundity that are the hallmarks of contemporary economic thought.

Apart from an afterword by the editors, this edition of *Lives of the Laureates* ends with Peter Diamond's lecture, delivered in April 2013. The Trinity University series, however, is an ongoing enterprise. Readers who would like to follow subsequent presentations in the series can visit our website at http://www.trinity.edu/nobel. The site offers a chronology of lectures in the series, plus selected quotations from each laureate's presentation at Trinity University.

Notes

1. For an authoritative discussion of the history, purpose, and qualifications for the Nobel Prize in Economics by one of the members of the Prize Committee, see Assar Lindbeck, "The Prize in Economics Science in Memory of Alfred Nobel," *Journal of Economic Literature* 23 (March 1985): 37–56.

2. See William Breit, "Biography and the Making of Economic Worlds," *Southern Economic Journal* 53 (April 1987): 823–833.

Acknowledgments

This edition of *Lives of the Laureates* is dedicated to William Breit (1933–2011). Bill arrived at Trinity University in 1983 after years of academic success at the University of Virginia and Louisiana State University. Charged by Ronald Calgaard, then president of Trinity University, to enhance the Economics Department's national reputation, Bill advanced the concept of a lecture series by Nobel laureates who would address the topic "my evolution as an economist." The edited lectures were to be made available to the public by way of a book he envisioned with the title *Lives of the Laureates*. Both lectures and the book, through multiple editions, have been well received.

Bill, who served as senior editor of the first five editions, elevated the Trinity Economics Department's image in other ways. His many academic publications, particularly in the fields of antitrust and the history of economic thought, helped establish his scholarly reputation. In a different arena, the three lively economics mystery novels he wrote with his friend Ken Elzinga (published under the pseudonym Marshall Jevons) enlightened generations of students who might otherwise have thought economics a boring subject.

Bill also introduced a distinguished visitor program at Trinity. He enticed a number of top economists in the profession to spend a semester with the Economics Department's students and faculty. One of them, Walter Adams, past president of Michigan State University, so enjoyed the experience that he returned each spring semester for nearly a decade. Visitors, department economists, and his many friends delighted in Bill's sense of humor, storytelling capacity, creative nature, and joie de vivre.

In addition to Bill, we extend our thanks to the three Trinity University presidents who have generously supported the Nobel series endeavor since its inception. They are Ronald Calgaard (economist), John Brazil (English faculty), and the current president (and economist) Dennis

Ahlburg. The precedent initiated by President Calgaard in hosting a dinner at his campus home prior to each lecture has been graciously continued by his successors. The dinner is a perfect prologue to each Nobel economist's public lecture.

For this edition, as for the previous ones, we owe much to colleagues in the Department of Economics at Trinity University for their enthusiasm and cooperation. Special mention should be made of former colleague Barry T. Hirsch, now of Georgia State University, co-editor of the fourth and fifth editions of this title. It is a pleasure to acknowledge a debt to our assistants, Rande Spector, Blanca Kirkman, and Gabriela Cantu Couvillion, for their skillful management of the many tasks and arrangements that accompany such an enterprise. We would also like to recognize the important contributions of the MIT Press staff members Deborah Cantor-Adams, Jane Macdonald, Emily Taber, and Yasuyo Iguchi.

Roger W. Spencer
David A. Macpherson

Lawrence R. Klein

In studying the development of great economists and trying to understand why economic thinking takes particular directions, it has always
seemed fruitful to me to look at the interaction, often one-way, between
the prevailing situation of the economy and developing tendencies in
economic thought. This has been most noticeable in macroeconomics but
is also the case in the whole of economics. A primary example, which is
closely tied up with my own development, is the emergence of Keynesian
economics to deal with the problems of the 1920s and '30s, especially
the Great Depression. Keynes was intensely interested in the problems
of the day and tried to develop an economic theory that would deal with
these problems. It was long in coming. His career got a large impetus
from the Treaty of Versailles, then the problems of the gold standard in
England, inflation after World War I, unemployment, and the world collapse after 1929.

For our university catalog, all professors are being asked to write
a sentence or three about why they entered their respective fields.
I entered economics because, as a youth of the Depression, I wanted
intensely to have some understanding of what was going on around me.
It was psychologically difficult to grow up during the Depression. It
was easy to become discouraged about economic life and did not give
one, at eighteen or twenty years, the feeling that there were boundless
opportunities just waiting for exploitation. The young people of the
past two or three decades have had nuclear war to worry about, but
they have also had feelings of abundant opportunities if peace could be
preserved.

But I was blessed with something else, that just happened. I was carrying around in my head the feeling that mathematics could be used in
the analysis of economic problems. I spent most of my undergraduate
time in either mathematics or economics classes. I was not a creative

mathematician or any kind of a match for *wunderkinder*; I saw that readily enough in math competitions. But I was fascinated by university-level mathematics and had some hunches about applications of mathematics to economics, say, to the expression for demand curves and the estimation of revenues. It was a great surprise for me to go into the U.C. Berkeley library and find journals for a whole budding subject, carried out at an advanced level, handling problems that were far more complicated than anything that I had thought about.

My undergraduate advisers gave me no encouragement to study mathematics along with economics; I went my own way and took the best of Berkeley in the early 1940s—first-class departments in economics, mathematics, and mathematical statistics. Of course, one can go back to high school or, in my case, junior college and find roots; there are some indeed, but my professional beginnings were in the Berkeley that existed just before World War II and the scholarship I won to MIT. There I met the dazzling *wunderkind* Paul Samuelson. When I was browsing in the Berkeley library and came across early issues of *Econometrica*, Samuelson's contributions caught my eye. When I got an opportunity to go to MIT, it was the possibility of working with Samuelson that confirmed all my choices. I was attached to him as a graduate assistant from the outset, and I tried to maximize my contact with him, picking up insights that he scattered on every encounter.

Working with Samuelson, who was at the forefront of interpreting Keynesian theory for teaching and policy application, I was put immediately in the midst of two challenging contests—one to gain acceptance for a way of thinking about macroeconomics and another to gain acceptance for a methodology in economics, namely, the mathematical method. Later, both challenges were to be overcome, but for ten or twenty years opposition was fierce.

Once Samuelson's *Economics* became a widely used text in first courses in the subject, Keynesian economics was firmly embedded. There was no turning back from that achievement. The successive student generations turned more toward the mathematical approach in graduate school, and they taught or did research in this vein. That eventually established the mathematical method, first in the United States, then in Europe, Japan, India, and other centers. Much of the foundation was built in Europe, and many of the American masters at mathematical economics were immigrants, but Samuelson, Friedman, and others gave it a native-born American flavor, and the approach truly caught on in this country.

The MIT years were, for me, a start in the professional field of economics, and my first position after leaving graduate school was with the Cowles Commission at the University of Chicago. Being just twenty-four years old when I started work there, I was almost in the position of having another chance at graduate school. As in many scientific fields of study, I was essentially a postdoctoral fellow.

A truly exceptional group of people was assembled in Chicago during the late 1940s. I doubt that such a group could ever be put together again in economics. From our closely knit group, four Nobel laureates have emerged, and two others came from the next bunching of Cowles researchers—partly at Chicago and partly at Yale. We worked as a team and focused on a single problem—to put together an econometric model of the American economy (a second attempt after Tinbergen's of the 1930s)—using the best of statistical theory, economic theory, and available data. After about four or five years of intensive research built up around this theme, the team dispersed to new openings in academic life. The effort was kept alive through my own research, and many of the brilliant people of our group went on to do their work in quite different branches of economics—Koopmans in activity analysis, Arrow in general equilibrium theory, Simon in decision analysis, Anderson in statistics, Marschak in the theory of organization, and so on.

In our attempts to bring together econometric methods and Keynesian analysis of the macroeconomy we felt quite confident. In the field of postwar planning we imagined that we had the well-being of the economy right in the palms of our hands. Over the coming decade we accomplished much more by way of model building and using than we ever thought possible in our wildest dreams of postwar America, but it was never good enough. We built systems that evolved from our teamwork at the Cowles Commission, and they have become part of the standard tool kit of economists. They play a very big role, but they do not dominate the policy process. They take a leadership role in forecasting, but they are not the sole survivors in the forecasting derby.

Scientists at Chicago were, secretively, carrying out more significant team research than we economists at the Cowles Commission. Because the director of the Cowles Commission was an old friend (from Europe of the two previous decades) of Leo Szilard, a leader among the scientists, we had a great deal of interaction. Szilard, one of the cleverest people of this century, dabbled in amateur economics. He constructed parlor games of the macroeconomy to demonstrate a scheme of monetary control that he thought would lead the world to a cycle-free existence. He taught us a lot about the strategy of intellectual research and the blending of politics and science. Many of us interacted with him and also with the amazing John von Neumann, who frequently visited Chicago on his way to Los Alamos. In those days, a trip across country involved changing trains in Chicago. Another visitor who had a profound influence on everyone at Cowles was Abraham Wald, the mathematical statistician from Columbia University.

The next phase of my career was to become more internationally minded. These days, some of us travel all over the world every month; European trips are almost routine. But when I left the Cowles Commission in 1947, I set out on an ocean voyage to Europe, after a summer's research activity in Ottawa putting together the first model of the Canadian economy. That project has survived many generations and gave birth to an active professional community in Canada that still functions on an expanded level.

Visits to centers of economic and econometric research throughout Europe were part of my education. I learned a great deal about the world, but was more attracted by the liveliness of the development of our subject in America. Seeing Europe dig out from the postwar rubble was a learning experience, and it opened many professional relationships that remain active. It certainly had a major impact on my own career development. Before the war Cambridge, England, and London were the centers of economic thinking that shaped the world. Traveling fellows gravitated there for study. America had begun to compete, but from 1946 onward the magnet was the United States. Students came from all over to do their work in America. This was true in many fields and has not changed appreciably in the last forty years.

In that seasoning year abroad I made contact with the true Keynesians, the Cambridge group who worked directly with Keynes. I never met Keynes himself, but I got good insight into the group's thinking from Kahn, Joan Robinson, and Sraffa. I also met Kaldor and Stone on that trip. The interesting thing to me was that my teacher, Paul Samuelson, had inferred all that there was to know about this group without ever having been there. People in Cambridge remarked about this to me.

I had come to Europe for the first time only months ahead of Paul Samuelson and met him on his first stop—Norway—where I was spending most of the year abroad, learning from Frisch. Samuelson had just published *Economics* and was enjoying an early enthusiastic acceptance. He toured Western Europe just as I was completing my year there.

A problem with the interpretation of the Keynesian system was the influence of wealth on savings. In the literature of macroeconomics this became known as the Pigou effect, although Pigou had written about it more in terms of liquid assets rather than total wealth. People had emerged from the war with large holdings of liquid assets (especially government savings bonds), so it was a popular and important subject to investigate.

I had returned from Europe to join the National Bureau of Economic Research under the leadership of Arthur Burns. There I worked on production function estimation, focusing on the railroad sector, but after one year I worked jointly on a project with the Survey Research Center of the University of Michigan and the National Bureau of Economic Research to use the Surveys of Consumer Finance to throw more light on saving behavior, especially with respect to the Pigou effect.

One line of economic research that emerged after World War II was the one I was following in econometrics, particularly macroeconometrics. But survey research flourished during the war, as a tool to help government plan civilian activity in a way that would aid the military effort. One of the primary groups, located in the Department of Agriculture during the war, set up academic ties and formed the Institute for Social Research at the University of Michigan, Ann Arbor. I felt comfortable working with this statistical team. Also the cross-disciplinary attitude intrigued me. I learned a great deal about the interfaces between economics on the one hand and psychology, sociology, and other disciplines on the other.

At the Survey Research Center I learned a great deal about household behavior and techniques for measuring it. The work was based on samples of human populations consisting of a few thousand cases for each study. This initiated me into the realm of large-scale data processing, done by punched cards and electromechanical machines. Electronic computers were in existence but were not yet being used for most economic or social problems.

After I came to Michigan, where I was teaching econometrics on a small scale, but mainly concerned with survey research, I received some money from the Ford Foundation, which suddenly had found it necessary for tax purposes to make large grants of money available to several universities. Few people in the economics department had any ideas about how to spend the sum that was to be allocated to them. I then established the Research Seminar in Quantitative Economics, assembled some research students, and went back to econometric model building—restarting the research begun at the Cowles Commission.

One of those research students was Arthur Goldberger. He and I put together a new model of the U.S. economy called the Klein–Goldberger model. It streamlined the models built at the Cowles Commission, used some of the survey findings, and set about forecasting the economy on a regular basis.

Colin Clark, the intrepid Australian statistical economist, set us up for a great success. In the pages of the influential *Manchester Guardian*, which came my way in the weekly world edition, he observed that the winding down of the Korean War would possibly cause a large-scale recession. He frightened people about the most fearsome economic event of our time—a 1929-style collapse as a result of a cumulative downward spiral.

I looked at our model results for forecasts for 1953–54 and concluded that it did not look like 1929 again. I wrote a paper with Arthur Goldberger for the *Guardian* and was delighted to find that they would publish it, in large display accompanied by an intriguing David Low cartoon.

In a piecemeal fashion the statistical work on the Klein–Goldberger model made use of the computer for parts of the computations connected with model estimation. For solution of the model we set aside a day or two of laborious hand calculation with a desktop machine. A large-scale digital computer was installed at Michigan, and we started a project for automatic model solution—simulation, if you like—but it was not quite brought to fruition before I was to leave Ann Arbor.

In the McCarthy era I left Michigan for the peace and academic freedom of Oxford, where I joined the Institute of Statistics and worked on the British Savings Surveys, patterned after the Michigan Surveys. While at Oxford I went back to model building, this time for Great Britain. My friend of twenty-five subsequent years, Professor Sir James Ball, attended my lectures on econometrics at Oxford and worked with me on the Oxford model. Some progress was made in using the computer at Oxford for more of the numerical work, but again it was not for model solution.

In 1958 I returned to America and took up a professorship at Pennsylvania, where I admired the position of the president, provost, and deans on the serious matter of academic freedom. From the beginning of my tenure at Pennsylvania and the Wharton School, I set out again to build a model of the American economy. This time I turned to quarterly data and, encouraged by my survey experience in England and

Michigan, I used some *expectations* magnitudes. I started the first generation of a series of Wharton models.

The Wharton models shifted to a quarterly time frame, to emphasize interest in short-run business cycle movements, used more data on survey anticipations, and stated all the accounting identities in current prices. This last change corrected a defect in the specification of the Klein–Goldberger model. The first version of this new model was used for forecasting the American economy, and projections were sent round to economist members of the Kennedy administration, who voiced disbelief in the optimistic forecasts—recovery from the 1960–61 recession. Within a few years I was to turn my attention to a new approach, and I abandoned further work on this first version, but I turned over complete files, consisting of data listings and equations, together with a trained assistant to the Department of Commerce. They had asked me for help in starting a model-building project there. This evolved, with the help of other Pennsylvania Ph.D. products, into what is now the OBE model (Office of Business Economics, Department of Commerce). This model has taken off into its own life and is a distinguished member of the American family of models, but its roots are the first Wharton model.

At this stage I went in two research directions, each of which had a fundamental impact on my own professional development. The Committee on Economic Stability of the Social Science Research Council planned, in 1959, the creation of a new, enlarged, short-run forecasting model. I was one of the principal investigators of that project and played a role in designing a cooperative approach to model building, namely, assignment of a specialist to each sector of the economy. I undertook, together with other members of the steering committee, to fashion it into a consistent whole. In general, we had a model that was composed of the best practice in each department, and it functioned as a whole. But the real advances that emerged from this joint effort were (1) a detailed monetary sector that drew on Federal Reserve talent and was the forerunner of important monetary sectors in many subsequent models, thus repairing a defect of the Klein–Goldberger model; (2) an explicit input–output sector of interindustry flows that was tied consistently with the traditional macro models of final demand and income determination; (3) the preparation of a *databank* for the systematic accounting of all the data used in the system; and (4) automation of the computing for the project with a remarkable breakthrough in the ability to solve large systems of nonlinear dynamic equations. Other features of the research on this joint project have been outstanding and are documented in three project volumes, especially the final one.[1]

After the Social Science Research Council started the cooperative project, it was transferred to the Brookings Institution and became known as the Brookings model. In its cooperative set-up, we consulted many participants on its progress, development, and use. This was particularly striking in the case of computation. We struggled hard with the computer aspects among a group at the University of Pennsylvania (helped a great deal by our innovative young Ph.D. candidates, who prepared many of the first-generation computer programs for econometrics), a group at Brookings, and a group at MIT. I devised a clumsy algorithm at Pennsylvania; a suggestion by E. Kuh at MIT to G. Fromm at Brookings provided the essential link. When they communicated their findings about Gauss iteration methods, we tested them in Philadelphia and immediately switched to what has become a worldwide standard for solving large dynamic systems in economics. From the early days of computer application at Michigan, model simulation had been an obstacle to efficient model application, but once we saw the key principle, we were able to harness the computer for generations to come.

The SSRC–Brookings model was but one line of development, away from the first Wharton model. The second was to develop an entirely new model for a different kind of use—commercial forecasting. I secured a small sum from the Rockefeller Foundation for the construction of the first Wharton model. We then established a research unit at the Wharton School for general quantitative studies in economics, financed by the Ford Foundation and National Science Foundation. But I could see that these sources of support were temporary and would run out during the mid-1960s.

Meanwhile, several major corporations had independently approached me for help in their efforts at econometric model building to assist their economic research departments. I accordingly proposed to five core companies that we build one model for them at the Wharton School and provide forecasts in exchange for support of our research program in econometrics.

Michael Evans joined the Pennsylvania faculty in 1963 and participated in our new forecasting venture with the private sector. He brought with him a separate model that he had developed in his dissertation research at Brown University. At first, we prepared two forecasts, one from his model and one from the original Wharton model. After a short period a combined model was built, fused from the two, and this was the first to be published in a series of Wharton volumes.

The Wharton Econometric Forecasting Unit thrived. From five supporting participants in 1963 it expanded into a separate nonprofit corporation in 1969 (wholly owned by the University of Pennsylvania). It was sold in 1980 to a publishing corporation and was acquired by a French computer company in 1983. Both Data Resources, Inc., and Chase Econometrics took up commercial forecasting after 1969, and an entire new industry was born. It now has many competing firms and does business in the hundreds of millions of dollars.

With the growth of new centers of activity with models and support systems, it was natural to phase out the old Brookings Model Project. It had served its purpose and was superseded by the expanded commercial modeling systems and some fresh academic ventures.

During the 1960s the computer was finally harnessed for the needs of econometrics; it had first been used for scientific, engineering, and largescale data processing (such as censuses). During this decade all those complicated calculations that we had contemplated during the development years of econometrics at the Cowles Commission became possible. I spent a great deal of time with student collaborators and IBM researchers working on nonlinear problems associated with maximum likelihood and other methods of statistical estimation, but we also perfected the simulation techniques that grew out of Brookings model research activities. We pioneered two developments that took econometric methods one step further: the presentation of results in standard national accounting form that were readily understood by users of econometric analysis and the use of time sharing. Data banking and perfection of time sharing were carried much further on a "user-friendly" basis for Data Resources, Inc., but the Wharton team had time-sharing facilities before DRI was founded. Computer developments were only started in the 1960s. They flowered in the next decade and became available to a large army of researchers and students throughout the world.

In addition to the standard uses of the computer for data management, statistical inference, applications (mainly simulation), and presentation of results in easy-to-read tables and graphs, many deep research techniques were developed, starting as early as the late 1950s. These were based on stochastic simulations, which involved the disturbance of dynamic model solution by properly drawn random errors. This research was pioneered by Irma Adelman in studying dynamic properties of the Klein–Goldberger model and by Harvey Wagner in constructing Monte Carlo experiments to test statistical techniques in econometrics.[2]

The Wharton team did not use these methods first, but we used them to good advantage to learn a great deal about the cyclical and inference properties of our family of models. Some large-scale stochastic simulations of the Brookings model had already advanced the use of computer-based experimental techniques, and we drew upon this fund of information. In this extended research effort, we learned to understand the various response characteristics of large-scale models—multipliers, sensitivities to parameter shift, and long-term trends of the system. The total computer effort of mechanizing the operation of large-scale models meant that the Wharton team was able to respond quickly and informatively to such major events as President Nixon's new economic policy, the oil embargo, and the fall of the Shah's government in Iran.

During my long stay at Pennsylvania several related efforts were conceived and executed in addition to the build-up of the Wharton models and their various applications to forecasting and macroeconomic analysis. Soon after I arrived, I became involved in a venture with two colleagues in Japan, professors Michio Morishima and Shinichi Ichimura, both of whom I had known in either England or the United States. We collaborated in the founding of a new scholarly journal, the *International Economic Review*. There were two principal objectives: to foster the development of modern (Anglo-American) economics in Japan and to take the burden off *Econometrica*, which had a large backlog of unpublished articles. In looking back at that venture, I would say that it made a contribution to the development of modern economics in Japan, although that might have happened anyway. We probably helped the transformation. We probably did not relieve the pressure on *Econometrica*, except temporarily, and we joined many other new journals in a virtual explosion of article preparation and the opening up of new periodicals. At any rate, the *International Economic Review* still stands as a collegial collaboration between Osaka University and the University of Pennsylvania, of almost twenty-five years' duration, and is now self-sustaining. In the founding years inexpensive Japanese printing, beautiful rice paper, and support from the Kansai Economic Federation made publication of the review possible. Those features are gone, but the review has a healthy existence. The establishment of the review and other relationships took me to Japan in 1960 and on many subsequent occasions. In this connection, I prepared a model of the Japanese economy with

Yoichi Shinkai and participated in a model project at Osaka University. Over the years, many Japanese models have rendered these efforts obsolete, but the research on Japan, together with the previous econometric research on the United Kingdom, directed my interest toward international model building.

In 1966 researchers at the DuPont company in Wilmington asked me to supply three models of developing countries where the company was involved in direct investment. Accordingly, I assembled a research team among the students of the economic research unit of Pennsylvania's economics department and prepared models for Argentina, Brazil, and Mexico. The company, as agreed, made their proprietary use of these models, but the system, complete with databases and equations, were, as agreed in advance, in the public domain. The research scholar for Mexico, Abel Beltrán del Rio, went with me to Monterrey in the summer of 1969. There we obtained a commitment from private companies for research support for elaboration and replicated use of the Mexican model in forecasting, policy, and scenario analysis of the economy. Within Wharton Econometrics we formed DIEMEX (Department de Investigaciones Econometricos de México). From a base of a few private-sector supporters in Monterrey and Mexico City in 1969 this has evolved into a self-sustaining system with some 150 supporters—U.S. companies, Mexican government agencies, international organizations, and others. What interests me most in this success is that the same technologies for model preparation, computer use, presentation of model results, and contributions to decision making in the private and public sectors could be fully transferred from our base in Philadelphia to a developing country. This is a prize case, but similar efforts have worked in many other parts of the world as well.

Starting with Latin America, I was able to foster model-building efforts in many developing countries. There are many models in the Far East, some in Africa, and some in the Middle East. Data deficiency has always been a problem, but that is gradually being overcome, and now practically the entire developing world is being modeled. Some of our best students had gone to various U.N. groups to work on problems of economic development among the emerging countries. I took on a consulting agreement in the mid-1960s with a group in UNCTAD to help them build models of LDCs in order to estimate capital needs for growth.

Parallel with model building for developing countries, a related effort directed at socialist or centrally planned economies was also initiated.

The developing country models were deliberately structured to reveal some of the unique characteristics of these areas. They were not simply copies of models in the style of the neoclassical Keynesian synthesis that were being built for each of the industrial democracies (OECD countries); they had unique supply-side features, specialized foreign trade characteristics, distributional aspects, and demographic aspects plainly displayed. I had long been fascinated by the challenging problem of modeling the centrally planned economy, with its controlled markets and plan targets. In the summer of 1970, on the occasion of a lecture in Vienna at the Institute for Advanced Studies, I discussed these problems with economists in Bratislava who had contacted me in the United States. I continued these discussions during that summer in Novosibirsk and Budapest.

Finally, in 1973 I collaborated with my colleagues in Sovietology on a project to model the U.S.S.R. SOVMOD I and succeeding generations grew from that effort. In discussions and formal presentations, this model was put before Soviet economists, and I believe that by now we have a better understanding of that country's economic system. Visiting scholars from Bratislava, Budapest, Łodz, Novosibirsk, Moscow, and Beijing have, over a period of more than ten years, contributed to our appreciation of the fundamental differences in structure between the Western market economy and the Eastern command economy.

The modeling of the pieces—different OECD countries, some LDCs and some CPEs—set the stage for the next step, namely, the modeling of the international system. In a meeting of the SSRC Committee on Economic Stability and Growth in 1967 I suggested that we approach the growing international problem through a cooperative project designed, to some extent, along the lines of the SSRC—Brookings model project. Country representatives would take the place of sector representatives, and we could put together a consistent system of the leading economic centers of the world economy. The SSRC committee had earlier hoped to see such an effort undertaken by the OECD. We held a meeting in London in 1967 under the intriguing title "Is the Business Cycle Obsolete?" We, fortunately, recognized the continuing presence of the cycle, but were not successful in starting research on model building for analysis of the international problem at that conference. We did, however, establish some lasting contacts at that meeting that served us well for later developments.

With a small grant from the Ford Foundation, Bert Hickman, Aaron Gordon, and I assembled a group of international model builders from leading OECD countries in summer 1968 at Stanford, where I was giving some class lectures. We decided to launch a new project to model the international transmission mechanism. Initial support came from the International Monetary Fund, with active participation of Rudolf Rhomberg, and from the National Science Foundation.

This was truly a group endeavor. Many individual model builders from different countries and many specialists in international economics convened at formative meetings, realizing that there was a researchable project but not knowing exactly how to go about it. Through the dynamics of group discussion and person-to-person analysis, we finally decided on some procedures and goals. Out of that effort we spawned project LINK—*The International Linkage of National Economic Models.*[3] More than fifteen years later the project is still functioning and trying to break new ground.

At an early stage we recognized that the developing countries and the socialist countries would play an increasingly important role in the world economy. Although the main interest at the IMF was the analysis of OECD countries, the U.N. supporters of the project continuously pressed for attention to the role of the LDC and CPE areas. The project has grown from a system of thirteen OECD countries, four regions of developing countries, and one region of socialist countries to an enlarged system of seventy-two country/area groups comprising each of the OECD countries, most large developing countries individually, and most large socialist countries individually. That is the most ambitious coordinating task for model building that has ever been undertaken, and we are in the midst of putting all the pieces together now in Philadelphia. Each separate piece exists.

During the fifteen-year period of development we have succeeded in allowing for floating exchange rates, coping with oil price changes, adding country detail, introducing primary commodities, streamlining the enormous computational program, and tackling many policy problems through scenario analysis. Analysis of capital flows, coordination of policies among countries, and methods of optimal control are high on the present research agenda.

The computer, as one can easily see, has played a large role in my involvement with econometric research and application, but that part of the story is not yet finished. Interesting new developments are on the horizon. I am now involved in three research directions: (1) Use of the microcomputer for conventional econometrics. This involves collapsing the size of systems to fit limited, tabletop capacities, but these limitations are steadily disappearing. Some studies, especially of developing countries, are necessarily compact, small enough to fit the present generation of microcomputers. (2) Cooperative computing, whereby conventional computers are linked in a network for simultaneous computation; the LINK system is an ideal trial case. (3) Use of the supercomputer to accommodate the ever-increasing demands of the expanding LINK system, now consisting of more than 15,000 dynamic nonlinear equations.

Just as the Brookings model gave way to improved versions at the various commercial econometric centers, official agencies and some individual university centers, there is a possibility that project LINK could be eclipsed. The Federal Reserve System has their own multicountry model, as does the OECD, Japan's Economic Planning Agency, the Common Market, and Wharton Econometrics. What seemed chancy and questionable in 1968 has become an often duplicated reality for analysis of the world economy.

When I went to Eastern Europe and the U.S.S.R. in 1970, embryonic groups were starting up activity in econometric model building. I helped, where possible, and had many trainees at either the University of Pennsylvania or Wharton Econometrics. The same thing was true of activities in the developing countries. The case of the People's Republic of China is somewhat different. After the renormalization of relationships in 1978, I led a team of economists sponsored by the National Academy of Sciences, in fall 1979, to try to establish scholarly contacts. As a follow-up to that visit I organized, privately, with the Chinese Academy of Social Sciences, a summer workshop in econometrics in 1980. Also, visiting scholars from China have come to Philadelphia. Progress is limited but promising toward the preparation of a China model, maintained in the PRC, for LINK. We already have our own version of a China model built by Laurence Lau of Stanford University. A repeat visit in 1984 continued in the vein of teaching econometric method and trying to encourage participation in Project LINK. Similar workshops and efforts for LINK-compatible model building were undertaken in Taiwan during 1982 and1983. Meetings with economists in Manila (Asian Development Bank and Philippine Institute for Development Studies), Bangkok (U.N. Economic and Social Commission for Asia and the Pacific), and New Delhi (Delhi University) are furthering the effort to have good LINK models for the whole Far East.

This account of forty years' research activity in economics and econometrics has avoided the political or the popular side. In 1976 I served as Jimmy Carter's coordinator of his economic task force. During his administration I tried to be helpful in various White House economic matters. I gave similar assistance to Milton Shapp, the governor of Pennsylvania, and W. Wilson Goode, the mayor of Philadelphia. All these private ventures contributed enormously to my own education. They taught me a bit about handling the media, about public appearances, and about the trade-offs between economic and political considerations. That experience was very interesting and I am glad that I did it, but I feel most comfortable in academia, doing the things I have described in this essay.

As for popularizing, I continue to write a periodic column for the Los Angeles *Times* and have had my stints at *Newsweek*, *Business Week*, and *Le Nouvel Observateur*. The *Manchester Guardian* in 1954 took my every word and table and published it as is. The same is true in my continuing relationship with the Los Angeles *Times*, but I feel the same way about other popular excursions into the media that I feel about politics. The trade-offs with what I believe to be good economics are not acceptable, and I feel more comfortable writing in the scholarly domain.

Notes

1. *The Brookings Quarterly Econometric Model of the United States*, eds. J. Duesenberry, G. Fromm, L. Klein, and E. Kuh (Chicago: Rand McNally, 1965); *The Brookings Model: Some Further Results*, eds. J. Duesenberry, G. Fromm, L. Klein, and E. Kuh (Chicago: Rand McNally, 1969); *The Brookings Model: Perspectives and Recent Developments*, eds. G. Fromm and L. Klein (Amsterdam: North-Holland, 1975).

2. Irma and Frank Adelman, "The Dynamic Properties of the Klein-Goldberger Model," *Econometrica* 27 (October 1959): 596–625; H. Wagner, "A Monte Carlo Study of Estimates of Simultaneous Linear Structural Equations," *Econometrica* 26 (January 1958): 117–133.

3. The evolution of project LINK is spelled out in three volumes and updated by some descriptive articles. See R. J. Ball, *The International Linkage of National Economic Models*, J. Waelbroeck, *The Models of Project LINK*, J. Sawyer, *Modeling the International Transmission Mechanism* (Amsterdam: North-Holland, 1973, 1976, 1979); B. G. Hickman and L. R. Klein, "A Decade of Research by Project LINK," *ITEMS*, Social Science Research Council, N.Y. (December 1979), 49–56; L. R. Klein, Peter Pauly, and Pascal Voisin, "The World Economy—A Global Model," *Perspectives in Computing* 2 (May 1982): 4–17.

Lawrence R. Klein

Awarded Nobel Prize in 1980. Lecture presented October 25, 1984.

Dates of Birth and Death

September 14, 1920; October 20, 2013

Academic Degrees

B.A., University of California, Berkeley, 1942
Ph.D., Massachusetts Institute of Technology, 1944

Academic Affiliations

Lecturer in Economics, University of Michigan, 1950–54
Senior Research Officer, Oxford University Institute of Statistics, 1954–55
Reader in Econometrics, Oxford University Institute of Statistics, 1956–58
Professor of Economics, University of Pennsylvania, 1958–64
Visiting Professor, Osaka University, summer 1960
University Professor of Economics, University of Pennsylvania, 1964–67
Benjamin Franklin Professor, University of Pennsylvania, 1968–85
Benjamin Franklin Professor, Emeritus, University of Pennsylvania, 1985–2013
Distinguished Visiting Professor, City University of New York, 1962–63, 1982
Visiting Professor, The Hebrew University of Jerusalem, 1964
Visiting Professor, Princeton University, spring 1966
Ford Visiting Professor, University of California, Berkeley, 1968
Visiting Professor, Stanford University, summer 1968
Visiting Professor, Institute for Advanced Studies, Vienna, summer 1970, winter 1974
Visiting Professor, University of Copenhagen, spring 1974

Selected Books

The Keynesian Revolution, 1947, 1966
A Textbook of Econometrics, 1953, 1974
An Econometric Model of the United States, 1929–1952, 1955 (with A. S. Goldberger)
The Brookings Quarterly Econometric Model of the United States, 1965 (with J. Duesenberry, G. Fromm, and E. Kuh)
Econometric Models as Guides for Decision Making, 1981

Kenneth J. Arrow

Studying oneself is not the most comfortable of enterprises. One is caught between the desire to show oneself in the best possible light and the fear of claiming more than one's due. I shall endeavor to follow the precept of that eminent seeker after truth, Sherlock Holmes, on perhaps the only occasion on which he was accused of excessive modesty. "'My dear Watson,' said he, 'I cannot agree with those who rank modesty among the virtues. To the logician all things should be seen exactly as they are, and to underestimate one's self is as much a departure from truth as to exaggerate one's own powers'" ("The Greek Interpreter").

An individual examining himself cannot claim omniscience. I cannot really claim to know all the forces impinging on my life, personal or intellectual. Indeed, as will be seen, there are some elements in the development of my ideas and interests that I cannot now reconstruct. On occasion, on rereading an old scholarly paper of mine, I have realized that my mental recollection was in some degree in error. In effect, the speakers in this series are asked to be historians and biographers of themselves; and like all historians and biographers, they can occasionally make mistakes. Recollection can be taken as reliable when it can be checked against the documentary record. Otherwise, it is imperfectly reliable evidence, though of a kind to which the speaker, such as myself, has unique access.

I have always had an interest in the history of economic thought. In the last few years I have been giving a course in this subject. One question I have been facing is the relative importance of different factors in the development of new ideas. One might suppose, for example, that the personal histories and class backgrounds of economists would be important factors. Yet that does not seem to be the case. Among the great economists of the nineteenth century, David Ricardo was a highly successful businessman, a stock-exchange speculator to be exact, while John

Stuart Mill was brought up to be an intellectual by an exacting father. Yet their economic theories were very similar indeed. Of course, access to education is important in intellectual development, and far more so today as economics, like all the natural and social sciences, has become a profession. Further, individual talents and interests may well govern which particular aspects of economics are studied and what techniques are used. But there is no evidence that the personality of an economist plays any significant role in the new concepts that he or she introduces to the subject.

I will therefore be brief in sketching my biography. My family, on both sides, were immigrants who arrived in this country about 1900 and settled in New York. My parents were born abroad but came here as infants, so they were effectively first-generation Americans. My father's family was very poor, my mother's hardworking and moderately successful shopkeepers. Both were very intelligent. My mother completed high school, my father college. My father was unusually successful in business when young, and the first ten years of my life were spent in a household that was comfortable and, more important for me, had many good books. Later, my father lost everything in the Great Depression, and we were very poor for about ten years.

I was early regarded as having unusual intellectual capacity. I was an omnivorous reader, and I added to that a desire to systematize my understanding. As a result, history, for example, was not merely a set of dates and colorful stories; I could understand it as a sequence in which one event flowed out of another. This sense of order crystallized during my high-school and college years into a predominant interest in mathematics and mathematical logic.

My primary and secondary schools were on the whole good. When it came to college, my family's poverty constrained me to attend the City College, which was then a completely free college opportunity that New York City had offered since 1847. I was far from the only able student in the same economic position, so the quality of the students was high. The faculty, which was generally competent and occasionally better, was stimulated to hold the students to high standards, and I learned a good deal. Fear of unemployment led me to supplement my abstract interests in mathematics and logic with preparation for several alternative practical pursuits, among them high-school teaching, actuarial work, and statistics. It was the study of statistics that turned out to shape my economics career in a decisive way.

By following obscure references in footnotes, I learned about the then rapidly developing field of mathematical statistics, which gave a theoretical foundation to statistical practice and led to profound changes in it. When at college graduation, in 1940, I found there were still no jobs available in high-school teaching, I decided to enter graduate studies in statistics. There were then no separate departments of statistics and few places where mathematical statistics was taught. I enrolled at Columbia University to study with a great statistician, Harold Hotelling. Hotelling had his official position in the department of economics and had written a small number of important papers in economic theory. When I took his course in mathematical economics, I realized I had found my niche.

I received strong moral support from Hotelling and indeed from the whole economics department, somewhat surprisingly, as apart from Hotelling, economic theory was not well regarded by them. The emphasis was almost entirely on empirical and institutional analyses. The department's support was expressed in the most tangible and necessary way— good scholarships. As a result I learned economic theory as I had learned so much else, by reading. In my case at least, I believe this self-education was much better than any lectures I could have attended anywhere. The use of mathematics in economics had had a long history, but it was then still confined to a small group. By reading selectively, I could choose my teachers, and I chose them well.

I was an excellent student, but I was doubtful that I was capable of genuine originality. This concern was concentrated on the choice of topic for a Ph.D. dissertation. There were many possibilities for an acceptable dissertation, but I felt that I had to justify the expectations of my teachers and for that matter of myself by doing something out of the ordinary. This responsibility was crushing rather than inspiring. Four years of military service, though interesting in itself, served further to delay my coming to grips with my aspirations. Finally, a series of abortive research ideas, each of which seemed to be more of a distraction than a help, culminated in my first major accomplishment, known as the theory of social choice.

I will go into some detail about the genesis of this contribution of mine because it displays the interaction between the state of economic thinking in general and my own special talents and background. It differs in one significant way from the other areas of my research, which I will discuss later. The question was essentially a new one, on which there had been virtually no previous analysis. The others had been discussed to some extent in the literature, and my role was to bring new analytic methods or new insights. In social choice theory, I was almost completely the creator of the questions as well as some answers.

It had been argued by the more advanced economic theorists that economic behavior in all contexts was essentially rational choice among a limited set of alternatives. The household chooses among collections of different kinds of goods. The collections available to it are those that it can afford to buy at the prevailing prices and with the income available to it. A firm chooses among alternative ways of producing a given output and also chooses among different output levels. To say that choice is rational was interpreted by these theorists, such as Hotelling, John Hicks, and Paul Samuelson, as meaning that the alternatives can be ranked or ordered by the chooser. From any given range of alternatives, say, the technically feasible production processes or the collections of commodities available to a household within its budget limits, the choosing agent selects the highest-ranking alternative available.

To say that alternatives are ordered in preference has a very definite meaning. First, it means that any two alternatives can be compared. The chooser prefers one or the other or possibly is indifferent between them. Second, and this is somewhat more subtle, there is a consistency in the ordering of alternatives. Let us imagine three alternatives labeled A, B, and C. If A is preferred to B and B to C, we would want to insist that A is preferred to C. This property is referred to as *transitivity*.

Though this formulation of choice had been originated for use in economic analysis, it was clearly applicable to choice in other domains. Hotelling, John von Neumann, Oskar Morgenstern, and Joseph Schumpeter had already suggested some applications to political choice, the choice of candidates for election or of legislative proposals. Voting could be regarded as a method by which individuals' preferences for candidates or legislative proposals could be combined or aggregated to make a social choice.

The question first came to me in an economic context. I had observed that large corporations were not individuals but were supposed (in theory, at least) to reflect the will of their many stockholders. To be sure, they all had a common aim, to maximize profits. But profits depend on the future, and the stockholders might well have different expectations as to future conditions. Suppose the corporation has to choose among alternative directions for investment. Each stockholder orders the different investment policies by the profit he or she expects. But because different stockholders have different expectations, they may well have different orderings of investment policies. My first thought was the obvious one suggested by the formal rules of corporate voting. If there are two investment policies, call them A and B, that one chosen is the one that commands a majority of the shares.

But in almost any real case, there are many more than two possible investment policies. For simplicity, suppose there are three, A, B, and C. The idea that seemed natural to me was to choose the one that would get a majority over each of the other two. To put it another way, since the policy is that of the corporation, we might want to say that the corporation can order all investment policies and choose the best. But since the corporation merely reflects its stockholders, the ordering by the corporation should be constructed from the orderings of the individual stockholders. We might say that the corporation prefers one policy to another if a majority of the shares are voted for the first as against the second.

But now I found an unpleasant surprise. It was perfectly possible that A has a majority against B, and B against C, but that C has a majority against A, not A against C. In other words, majority voting does not always have the property that I have just called transitivity.

To see how this can happen, let me take an election example. Suppose there are three candidates, Adams, Black, and Clark, and three voters. Voter 1 prefers Adams to Black and Black to Clark. We will suppose that each voter has a transitive ordering, so voter 1 will prefer Adams to Clark. Suppose voter 2 prefers Black to Clark and Clark to Adams, and therefore Black to Adams, while voter 3 prefers Clark to Adams and Adams to Black. Then voters 1 and 3 prefer Adams to Black, so that Adams is chosen over Black by the group. Similarly, Black receives a majority over Clark through voters 1 and 2. Transitivity would require that Adams be chosen over Clark in the election. But in fact voters 2 and 3 prefer Clark to Adams. This intransitivity is sometimes called the paradox of voting. Of course, the intransitivity need not arise; it depends on what the voters' preferences are. The point is that the system of pairwise majority voting cannot be guaranteed to produce an ordering by society as a whole.

The observation struck me as one that must have been made by others, and indeed I wondered if I had heard it somewhere. I still don't know whether I did or not. In any case the effect was rather to cause me to drop the whole matter and study something else.

About a year later my thoughts recurred to the question of voting, without any intention on my part. I realized that under certain special but not totally unnatural conditions on the voters' preferences, the paradox I had found earlier could not occur. This I thought worth writing about. But when I started to do so, I picked up a journal and found the same idea in an article by an English economist, Duncan Black. The result that Black and I had found could have been thought of any time in the last one hundred and fifty years. That two of us came to it at virtually the same time is an occurrence for which I have no explanation.

Priority in discovery is the spur to science, and being anticipated was correspondingly frustrating. I again dropped the study of voting for what I took to be less fascinating but more significant topics, on which I made little progress. But a few months later I was asked a chance question that gave the problem sufficient significance to justify a reawakened interest. The then new theory of games was being applied to military and diplomatic conflict. In this application, nations were being regarded as rational actors. How could this be justified when nations are aggregated of individuals with different preference orderings? My earlier results, I realized, taught me that one could not always derive a preference ordering for a nation from the preference orderings of its citizens by using majority voting to compare one alternative with another.

This left open the possibility that there were other ways of aggregating individual preference orderings to form a social ordering, that is, a way of choosing among alternatives that has the property of transitivity. A few weeks of intensive thought made the answer clear.

Given any method of aggregating individual preference orderings to yield a social choice that satisfies a few very natural conditions, there will always be some individual preference orderings that will cause the social choice to be intransitive, as in the example given.

My studies in logic helped to formulate the question in a clear way, which stripped it of unnecessary complications. But I did not use the concepts of mathematical logic in any deep way.

This result quickly attracted attention. One by-product was that I learned from several correspondents of what previous literature there was. The paradox of majority voting had indeed been discovered before—in fact, by the French author the Marquis du Condorcet in *1785*! But there was not a continuous literature. There were some ingenious unpublished proposals for conducting certain elections at Oxford about 1860, based on the possibility of paradox. They were circulated by a mathematician named Charles L. Dodgson. Dodgson also wrote an adventure tale for the daughter of one of his colleagues, Alice Lidell, which he published under a pseudonym, Lewis Carroll. The only significant published paper on social choice had appeared in 1882 in an Australian journal, hardly everyday reading matter. I know few if any interesting research topics that have had such a spotty and intermittent history.

The subsequent record is very different. The literature has exploded. A recent survey, not intended to be complete, listed more than six hundred references. A journal devoted entirely to social choice theory and related issues has been started.

Social choice is a topic in which there was little direct relation to past work, although the connection with parallel developments in the theory of economic choice was important. I would like to discuss two further contributions of mine, which illustrate different relations to current economic theory and to the world of economic reality.

The first of the two is the study of what is known as general equilibrium theory. This is an elaboration of the simple but not easily understood point that in an economic system everything affects everything else. Let me illustrate. The price of oil became very low in the 1930s because of discoveries in Texas and the Persian Gulf area. Homeowners shifted in great numbers from coal to oil for home heating, thereby decreasing the demand for coal and employment in the coal mines. Refineries expanded, so more workers were employed there. There was as well a demand for refinery equipment, a complicated example of chemical processes. This in turn induced demands for skilled chemical engineers and for more steel. Gasoline was cheaper, so that more automobiles were bought and used. Tourist areas accessible by road but not by railroad began to flourish, while railroads decayed. Each of these changes in turn induced other changes, and some of these in turn reacted on the demand for and supply of oil.

The economic lesson of this story is that the demand for any one product depends on the prices of all products, including the prices of labor and capital services, which we usually call wages and profits. Similarly, the supply of any product or of labor or capital depends on the prices of all commodities. What determines what prices will prevail? The usual hypothesis in economics is that of equilibrium. The prices are those that cause supply to equal demand in every market. This hypothesis, like many others in economics and indeed in the natural sciences, is certainly not precisely true. But it is a useful approximation, and those who disregard it completely are much further from the truth than are those who exaggerate the prevalence of equilibrium.

The general equilibrium theory, or perhaps vision, of the economy was first stated in full-fledged form by a French economist, Leon Walras, in 1874. But it was hard to use as a tool of analysis and too difficult for economists with little mathematical training to understand. Only in the 1930s did interest revive, especially through the masterful exposition and development by John Hicks, with whom I had the honor of sharing the Nobel Prize in 1972.

But there was an unresolved analytic issue, recognized by at least some. General equilibrium theory asserts that the prices of all commodities are determined as the solution of a large number of equations, those that state the equality of supply and demand on each market. Did these equations necessarily have a solution at all? If not, the general equilibrium theory could not always be true. Indeed, some work by German economists about 1932 suggested the possibility that the equations need not have a meaningful solution. A Viennese banker named Karl Schlesinger, who had studied economics in the university and continued to follow developments in the subject, recognized that the apparent difficulties rested on a subtle misunderstanding and felt that the existence of general equilibrium could be demonstrated. He hired a young mathematician, Abraham Wald, to work on the problem. Wald came up with a proof of existence under certain conditions not easy to interpret; indeed, in light of later work, they were much too stringent. Even so, the proof was difficult.

The heavy tread of history breaks in on the story. Schlesinger would not believe that Austria could fall to Hitler; when it did, he committed suicide. Wald did succeed in leaving and came to the United States, where he shifted his interests to mathematical statistics. He was one of my teachers at Columbia. I came to learn, I do not know how, of the unsolved or only partially solved problem of the existence of general equilibrium. But when I asked Wald about his work on the question, he merely said that it was a very difficult problem. Coming from him, whose mathematical powers were certainly greater than mine, the statement was discouraging.

As frequently happens in the history of science, however, help came from developments in other fields. The theory of games was in a process of rapid development. One theorem, proved by a mathematician named John Nash, struck me as being parallel in many ways to the existence problem for competitive equilibrium. By borrowing and adapting the mathematical tools used by Nash, I was able to state very generally the conditions under which the equations defining general equilibrium had a solution.

There was more than mathematics involved, though. It was necessary to state the general equilibrium system much more explicitly. As Schlesinger had already shown in part, the exact assumptions that were made needed clarification, and much was learned in the process.

As you may see from this account, the existence proof was based on general theoretical progress in economics and in mathematics, and I was certainly not the only one with access to it. Indeed, while writing up my results, I learned that Gerard Debreu, the Nobel laureate in economic sciences for 1983, had independently come to essentially the same results. We decided to publish the results jointly. Just before our paper appeared, there was one by a third economist, Lionel McKenzie, along similar though not identical lines.

Multiple discoveries are in fact very common in science and for much the same reason. Developments in related fields with different motivation help one to understand a difficult problem better. Since these developments are public knowledge, many scholars can take advantage of them. It is pleasant to the ego to be first or among the first with a new discovery. However, in this case at least, the evidence is clear that the development of general equilibrium theory would have gone on quite as it did without me.

I may add that, despite their abstract and mathematical sound, existence theorems in general equilibrium theory have turned out to be very useful. They certainly stimulated many more applications of general equilibrium theory to particular economic problems. They gave a greater understanding of what may be termed "general equilibrium thinking," that is, recognizing that a particular economic change will have remote repercussions that may be more significant than the initial change. More directly, Herbert Scarf showed that the method of proof could be adapted to find a way of actually calculating the solutions to general equilibrium systems. The method has been used to study a variety of policy problems: tariffs, corporate income taxation, changes in welfare measures, and economic development in a number of developing countries.

The third contribution I would like to discuss is drawing the economic implications of differences in information among economic agents. My sustained interest arose from considering a practical problem, the organization of medical care, but the ground had been prepared by my studies in mathematical statistics, some of my earlier theoretical work on the economics of risk bearing, and some developments by others of these topics. My contribution here, unlike the first two examples, has been not so much a specific and well-defined technical accomplishment as a point of view that has served to reorient economic theory.

The general equilibrium theory, like most economic theory up to about 1950, assumed that the economic agents operated under certainty. That is, the households, firms, investors, and so forth knew correctly the consequences of their actions or, in some versions, at least acted as if they did. Thus, producers were assumed to know what outputs they would get for given inputs. Investors would know what prices would prevail in the future for the goods they were planning to sell.

I don't mean to imply that economists were so foolish as not to recognize that the economic world was uncertain or that economic agents didn't realize that this was the case. Indeed, some literature clearly showed that much economic behavior could only be explained by assuming that economic agents were well aware of uncertainty; for example, investors held diversified portfolios and bought insurance. However, a general formulation that would permit integration with standard economic theory and in particular with general equilibrium theory was lacking. I was able to work out such a formulation, which introduced the concept of contingent contracts, contracts for delivery of goods or money contingent on the occurrence of any possible state of affairs. In effect, I postulated the existence of insurance against all conceivable risks. My rather sketchy paper was greatly enriched and extended by Gerard Debreu. The idea was simplicity itself and yet novel.

It has become a standard tool of analysis, in this case rather more than I intended. I considered the theory of contingent contracts as a sketch of an ideal system to which the methods of risk bearing and risk shifting in the real world were to be compared. It was clear enough empirically that the world did not have nearly as many possibilities for trading risks as my model would have predicted. I did not, however, have at first a particularly good explanation for the discrepancy.

A considerable insight came a few years later. I was asked by the Ford Foundation to take a theorist's view of the economics of medical care. I first surveyed the empirical literature on the subject. My theoretical perspective suggested that there was inadequate insurance against the very large financial risks. Indeed, insurance coverage, both governmental and private, has expanded greatly since then. But I soon realized that there were obstacles to the achievement of full insurance. Insurance against health expenditures creates an incentive to spend more freely than is desirable.

Was there a general theoretical principle behind this? The concept of insurance against uncertainties did not fully reflect the actual situation, namely, that different individuals may have different uncertainties. The person insured knows more about his or her state of health than the insurer. The fact that individuals have informational differences is a key element in any economic system, not just in health insurance.

To take a very different example, consider tenant farming. If the land-lord hired someone to work his or her farm, the farm worker would have limited incentives to work to full capacity, since the worker's income is assured. The owner could indeed direct the worker if fully informed about what the worker was doing. But his information can be obtained only by costly supervision. In its absence, the two parties will have different information, and production will be inefficient. The other extreme alternative is to rent the farm at a fixed fee. Then indeed incentives to the worker (or, in this case, tenant) are very strong. But farming is a risky business, and poor farmers at least may not be able to bear the uncertainty. Hence, the compromise of sharecropping arose. It dulls incentives, but not completely, and it shares risks, but not completely. Similarly, most health insurance policies have a coinsurance feature, so that risks are partially shared, while the patient still has some incentive to economize.

The theme may be stated without elaboration. Informational differences pervade the economy and have given rise to both inefficiencies and contractual arrangements and informal understandings to protect the less informed. My own contributions here were conceptual rather than technical, and the present theory is the result of many hands.

I have tried to present, as clearly as I can, the genesis of some of my researches. They have all been related to the present state of thinking by others. The field of science, indeed, the whole world of human society, is a cooperative one. At each moment, we are competing, whether for academic honors or business success. But the background, and what makes society an engine of progress, is a whole set of successes and even failures from which we all have learned.

Kenneth J. Arrow

Awarded Nobel Prize in 1972. Lecture presented November 5, 1984.

Date of Birth

August 23, 1921

Academic Degrees

B.S., City College, New York, 1940
M.A., Columbia University, 1941
Ph.D., Columbia University, 1951

Academic Affiliations

Assistant Professor of Economics, University of Chicago, 1948–49
Acting Assistant Professor of Economics and Statistics, Stanford University, 1949–50
Associate Professor of Economics and Statistics, Stanford University, 1950–53
Executive Head, Department of Economics, Stanford University, 1953–56
Professor of Economics, Statistics, and Operations Research, Stanford University, 1953–68
Visiting Professor of Economics, Massachusetts Institute of Technology, fall 1966
Fellow, Churchill College (Cambridge), 1963–64, 1970, 1973
Professor of Economics, Harvard University, 1968–74
James Bryant Conant University Professor, Harvard University, 1974–79
Joan Kenney Professor of Economics and Professor of Operations Research, Stanford University, 1979–91
Joan Kenney Professor of Economics and Professor of Operations Research, Emeritus, Stanford University, 1991–present

Selected Books

Social Choice and Individual Values, 1951, 1963
Studies in the Mathematical Theory of Inventory and Production, 1958 (with S. Karlin and H. Scarf)
Public Investment, the Rate of Return, and Optimal Fiscal Policy, 1970 (with M. Kurz)
Essays in the Theory of Risk-Bearing, 1971
The Limits of Organization, 1974
Collected Papers of Kenneth J. Arrow, Volumes 1–6, 1983–1985

Paul A. Samuelson

Economics in My Time

The last five or six decades have seen American economics come of age
and then become the dominant center of world political economy. When
I began the study of economics back in 1932 on the University of
Chicago Midway, economics was literary economics. A few original
spirits—such as Harold Hotelling, Ragnar Frisch, and R. G. D. Allen—
used mathematical symbols; but, if their experiences were like my early
ones, learned journals rationed pretty severely acceptance of anything
involving the calculus. Such esoteric animals as matrices were never seen
in the social science zoos. At most a few chaste determinants were admitted to our Augean stables.

Do I seem to be describing Eden, a paradise to which many would
like to return in revulsion against the symbolic pus-pimples that disfigure
not only the pages of *Econometrica* but also the *Economic Journal* and
the *American Economic Review*?

Don't believe it. Like Tobacco Road, the old economics was strewn
with rusty monstrosities of logic inherited from the past, its soil generated few stalks of vigorous new science, and the correspondence between
the terrain of the real world and the maps of the economics textbook
and treatises was neither smooth nor even one-to-one.

The Great Takeoff

Yes, 1932 was a great time to be born as an economist. The sleeping
beauty of political economy was waiting for the enlivening kiss of new
methods, new paradigms, new hired hands, and new problems. Science
is a parasite: the greater the patient population the better the advance
in physiology and pathology; and out of pathology arises therapy.

The year 1932 was the trough of the Great Depression, and from its rotten soil was belatedly begot the new subject that today we call macroeconomics.

Do I refer to the Keynesian revolution? Of course I do. But people are wrong to associate with that name the particular policies and ideologies found fifty years ago in the writings of John Maynard Keynes, Alvin Hansen, Joan Robinson, Abba Lerner, and Michael Kalecki. The New Classical School, through the quills of Robert Lucas, Tom Sargent, and Robert Barro, reverse those Keynesian doctrines 180 degrees. Nevertheless, the present-day equations found in monetarism, eclectic mainstream Keynesianism, or rational expectationism are a galaxy removed from what were in Walras and Marshall—or in Frank Knight and Jacob Viner, my great neoclassical teachers in Chicago. The macromethodology innovated by Keynes's 1936 *General Theory* constitutes both the 1985 swords that slash at Keynesianism and the shields that defend mainstream macroeconomics.

So far I have been talking about the internal logic and development of economics as a science. It has been an inside-the-seminar-room survey of the subject, where of course the observations of the economic world have been brought into that seminar room. As a result of outside influences the period from 1932 to 1975 was a favorable one for economists like me, in that it was an epoch of tremendous university expansion and job opportunity. If one can borrow from the vulgar terminology of economic science fiction, my generation of economic activity was buoyed along by the great wave of a Kondratieff expansion.

The New Deal and welfare state created a vast new market for economists in government. Then came the war, which was carried on by armaments, cannon fodder, and economists: when the business cycle was put into hibernation by the wartime command economy, whenever problems of quantitative resource allocation ran out, economists could chance their arm on the new science of operations research, a game at which only the rare brilliant physicist could beat the run-of-the-mill economists.

Then came the postwar boom in education. Where there had been in 1935 only a few strong centers for economic research—Harvard, Chicago, Columbia, and a few others—now everywhere in the land there grew up excellent graduate departments. No longer did one wait to be made a full professor at forty-five; the typical new Shangri-La in the firmament of postwar economics was created by an activist department chairman, given the go-ahead signal by his administration to go out and hire hotshot stars at twice his own salary. Like beardless colonels in the wartime air corps, thirty-year-old full professors deigned to grace prestigious academic chairs.

Pax Americanus

The sheer number of American economists gave them unfair advantage over economists abroad. In addition, Hitler gave us even before the war the cream of the continental crop. Just as Chicago is the biggest Polish city after Warsaw, and New York the greatest Swedish city after Stockholm, America obtained practically the whole of the Austrian school in economics. Along with such names as Einstein, von Neumann, and Fermi go such American economist names as Koopmans, Leontief, Schumpeter, Marschak, Haberler, Kuznets, and many others. Later, as strength draws to itself strength, there began to appear in the American lineup the names of Hurwicz, Debreu, Theil, Bhagwati, Coase, Fischer, and many others.

Again and again I have seen in recent decades the tremendous stimulus that top postdoctoral scholars from abroad have received from a year's sojourn in the States, hopping on the grand tour from Cambridge to Stanford. They go back home fired up to change the old world. For half a decade their reprints keep coming. Then, almost in accordance with some second law of thermodynamics, the Schumpeterian burst subsides.

Evidently science itself is not subject to the law of constant returns to scale. The book of Matthew applies: To him who hath shall be given. Unfair? you say. Well, as Jack Kennedy observed: Who said life is fair?

Life at the Top

I have seen economists grow in public esteem and in pecuniary demand. Surveys have shown that the highest-paid scientists, physical and biological scientists as well as economists, are not to be found in private industry but rather in the university—perhaps in-and-out of the universities would put it more accurately. I don't know scholars who have agents. But some do have lecture bureaus. And being a public member on corporate boards has become a new way of life.

It is a heady experience to advise the Prince on a sabbatical tour of duty in Washington. Newspaper columnists from academia, serendipitously, acquire the omniscience they need for the job.

"And gladly teach" used to refer to the lecture hall and seminar table, but now includes telling congressional committees there is no free lunch and telling TV audiences to buy cheap and sell dear.

Trees do not grow to the sky. Every Kondratieff wave has its inflection point. The 1932–1965 expansion in economists' prestige and self-esteem has been followed by some leaner years. We have become more humble and, as Churchill said, we have much to be humble about. Economists have not been able to agree on a good cure for stagflation. That disillusions noneconomists. And, to tell the truth, it punctures our own self-complacency. We shop around for new paradigms the way alchemists prospect for new philosophers' stone. Just because a National Bureau paper is silly does not mean it is uninteresting. Just because it is profound does not mean that it is admired.

Mea Culpa

So far I have been talking about economics. The title of this series, "My Evolution as an Economist," suggests that I should be talking about *me*. Mr. Dooley said that Theodore Roosevelt was going to write a book about the Spanish-American War called *Me and Cuba*. It would begin with Teddy's tribute, "My black sergeant was the bravest man I ever knew. He followed me up San Juan Hill."

I can claim that in talking about modern economics I am talking about me. My finger has been in every pie. I once claimed to be the last generalist in economics, writing about and teaching such diverse subjects as international trade and econometrics, economic theory and business cycles, demography and labor economics, finance and monopolistic competition, history of doctrines and locational economics. Kilroy, having been there, must share the guilt. (Goethe wrote that there was no crime he ever heard of that he didn't feel capable of committing. Bob Solow's reaction was that Goethe flattered himself. And perhaps what I called "crime" is a mistranslation of what Goethe meant only as "error.")

Here is my worst error. Do you remember the infamous wrong prediction by economists that after World War II there would be mass unemployment? I was not part of the multi-agency team that produced the official 1945 forecast of doomsday. But, if you look at the yellowing files of the *New Republic,* you will find a well-written article by this humble servant that involves a large squared forecasting error on the downward side. My friend and mentor, Alvin Hansen, who believed in a postwar restocking boom, could have taught me better. And so could Sumner Slichter and a host of Keynesians and non-Keynesians.

I reproach myself for a gross error. But I would reproach myself more if I had persisted in an error after observations revealed it clearly to be that. I made a deal of money in the late 1940s on the bull side, ignoring Satchel Paige's advice to Lot's wife, "Never look back." Rather I would advocate Samuelson's Law: "Always look back. You may learn something from your residuals. Usually one's forecasts are not so good as one remembers them; the difference may be instructive." The dictum "If you must forecast, forecast often," is neither a joke nor a confession of impotence. It is a recognition of the primacy of brute fact over pretty theory. That part of the future that cannot be related to the present's past is precisely what science cannot hope to capture. Fortunately, there is plenty of work for science to do, plenty of scientific tasks not yet done.

Other Testimonies

I shall not shirk talking more specifically about my own development as a scholar and scientist. But, as I do not believe in the kind of elegant variation that follows "he said," by "he averred," and then by "vouchsafed the speaker," I shall not try to duplicate some earlier autobiographical writings. Peppered through many of the technical articles in the four volumes of my *Collected Scientific Papers* are various personal reminiscences. But the richest vein of this kind of ore will be found in, first, my 1968 presidential address before the World Congress of the International Economic Association. It is cunningly entitled "The Way of an Economist," ambivalent words denoting both the economic road traveled and the personal style of the Siegfried traversing that road. Similarly, today in speaking of "Economics in My Time," I also mean economics in my own peculiar rhythms and style.

A second source is my "Economics in a Golden Age: A Personal Memoir," which appeared in the Daedalus book Gerald Holton edited, *The Twentieth Century Sciences: Studies in the Biography of Ideas* (New York: W. W. Norton, 1972).

A third source, one whose title was imposed on me, is *My Lifetime Philosophy*. This appeared in the series for students of *The American Economist* 27 (1983): 5–12, and in the fifth volume of *Collected Scientific Papers of Paul A. Samuelson* (2000).

The Scientist Delineated

Here briefly, in the third person for objectivity, is the superficial outline of my scientific career.

PAS has already been incredibly lucky throughout his lifetime, overpaid and underworked. A bright youngster, favored by admiring parents, he shone at school until the high-school years when he became an underachiever. The calendar lies in naming May 15, 1915, as his time of birth. Truly he was born on the morning of January 2, 1932, at the University of Chicago.

He was made for academic life. An A student at Chicago and an A+ one at Harvard, PAS wandered by chance into economics. Economics turned out to be made for him as the Darwinian genes from generations of commercial ancestors encountered their teleological destiny.

Every honor he aspired to came his way, and came early. He got the undergraduate social science medal his undergraduate year. Just when commencement loomed near, the Social Science Research Council created a new experimental fellowship program in economics, whose first award supported him handsomely at Harvard. Having drawn from Chicago giants like Knight, Viner, Henry Schultz, Henry Simons, Paul Douglas, John U. Nef, and Lloyd Mints, he levitated to Harvard Yard to learn from Joseph Schumpeter, Wassily Leontief, Edwin Bidwell Wilson, Gottfried Haberler, Edward Chamberlin, and Alvin Hansen. Before his SSRC fellowship gave out, he overcame the opposition of the Society of Fellows to economics and rode on the shoulders of Vilfredo Pareto into the sacred circle of Junior Fellows. The philosopher Willard van Orman Quine, the mathematician Garrett Birkhoff, the double-Nobel physicist John Bardeen, the chemists Bright Wilson and Robert Woodward, the polymath Harry T. Levine were his companions in arms in the Society of Fellows. There he hit his stride and began to turn out articles faster than the journals could absorb such quasi-mathematical stuff.

It is not true that PAS began life as a physicist or mathematician. Well into his undergraduate course he discerned that mathematics was to revolutionize modern economics. Proceeding to learn mathematics, PAS still remembers how a Lagrange multiplier first swam into his ken and how, with a wild surmise, it gave him independent discovery of the Edgeworth-Stackelberg asymmetric solution for duopoly—an insight that has kept him immune to the false charms of Nash–Cournot purported solutions.

His *Foundations of Economic Analysis,* written mostly as a Junior Fellow but usable later for the Ph.D. union card, won the David A. Wells Prize at Harvard. Later, in 1947, it helped him receive the first John Bates Clark Medal of the American Economic Association, awarded for scholarly promise before the age of forty. Its quality was thrice blessed: later still it contributed to his 1970 Nobel Prize in economics, the second time that fabricated (or "forged") honor was awarded and the first time to an American.

Hegira down the River

If PAS was born as a child his freshman year at Chicago, he was born a second time as a man that October 1940 day he succumbed to a call from MIT. MIT's force met no detectable Harvard resistance, so the movable object moved. It was the best thing that could have happened to PAS. A boy must always remain a boy in his father's house. On his own acres a man can build his own mansion and after 1941 PAS, along with magnificent colleagues, was able to help build up what became recognized as a leading world center for economics. Living well is the best revenge, Hemingway's crowd used to say; but, in sober truth, the example of MIT's Norbert Wiener, who in his days of fame still brooded over his ejection from Harvard Yard, led PAS ever to cherish his Harvard connections and labor for the greater glory of Cambridge and Middlesex County.

Peer recognition came early and often: from the American Academy of Arts and Sciences, the National Academy, the American Philosophical Society, and the British Academy. Just as it is the first million that is the hardest, one honor leads to another. After the first dozen honorary degrees, all it takes is longevity to double the number. The first such degree—from Chicago, alma mater and basilica of a church he no longer believed in—PAS found most touching. When Harvard honored a prophet in his own country, he also liked that.

Vice-presidencies and presidencies in professional societies came his way: the Econometric Society, the American Economic Association, the International Economic Association. As yet there is no Galaxy Political Economy Club.

A scholar at a new place for economic study like MIT receives plenty of offers from all over the world. PAS revealed a preference to be an immovable object, and when made an institute professor in 1966, with magnificent research opportunities and optional teaching duties, he in effect returned to the womb of a perpetual junior fellowship. Having arrived in paradise, he stayed there.

But not without excursions to the outside. Many a tutorial he gave to congressional committees. Often when he became a consultant to a federal agency, that precipitated its demise. The U.S. Treasury and the Federal Reserve Board did, however, survive his academic counsels. Murmuring that the United States is too precious to be turned over exclusively to big-picture thinkers like John Kenneth Galbraith and Walt Whitman Rostow, PAS gave economic tutorial to Adlai Stevenson and Averell Harriman; and worked his way as adviser to Senator J. F. Kennedy, candidate Kennedy, and president-elect Kennedy. Moses-like PAS did not pass into the promised land beyond the Potomac, but as an *eminence grise* he had the fun of backing the poker hands of such magnificent Joshuas as Walter Heller, James Tobin, and Kermit Gordon at the Kennedy Council of Economic Advisers.

What can the good fairies give the man who has everything? George Stigler, referring to Samuelson's 1947 *Foundations* and his newly published 1948 best-selling textbook *Economics,* introduced him with the words, "Samuelson, having achieved fame, now seeks fortune." Soon the smoke of burning mortgage could be sniffed in Belmont, Massachusetts. More than this, J. K. Galbraith's prophesy in a *Fortune* review, that a new generation would receive its economics from *Economics,* turned out to be right on the mark. PAS was heard to mutter complacently, "Let those who will write the nation's laws if I can write its textbooks." Being denounced by William Buckley for blaspheming God and man at Yale, the textbook took on a new aura of respectability and sales soared all over the world.

A quarter of a century ago the author of *Economics* commented on the new layer of fame that accrues to a scholar who writes a best-seller, stating modestly,

Writing a beginning textbook is hard work. But its rewards have been tremendous—and I do not mean simply pecuniary rewards. Contact with hundreds of thousands of minds of a whole generation is an experience like no other that a scholar will ever meet. And writing down what we economists know about economics has been truly an exciting experience. I can only hope that some of this excitement will rub off on the reader.

By Joy Possessed

Stop! Enough is enough. Of such *Who's Who* boilerplate, enough is too much. What has been described above could be said of many a successful go-getter. A West Pointer who hated soldiering might settle for a Faustian bargain in which promotions and blue ribbons compensate for a wasted life.

The reward that has counted for me in scholarship and science is the marvelous hunt through enchanted forests. I began to write articles for publication before I was twenty-one. I have never stopped. I hope never to stop. When Harry Johnson died, he had eighteen papers in proof. That is dying with your boots on! (Even for Harry, who never did things by halves or held down to the golden mean, eighteen was overdoing it.)

My mind is ever toying with economic ideas and relationships. Great novelists and poets have reported occasional abandonment by their muse. The well runs dry, permanently or on occasion. Mine has been a better luck. As I have written elsewhere, there is a vast inventory of topics and problems floating in the back of my mind. More perhaps than I shall ever have occasion to write up for publication. A result that I notice in statistical mechanics may someday help resolve a problem in finance.

Like a gravid spouse I achieve the release of publication. Have I published too much? Others must form their judgment on this. Speaking for myself, in my heart of hearts I have regretted almost no chapter, article, note, or footnote my quill has penned. And I have rued many an excision forced on me by editors of only finite patience or self-imposed for reasons of space and aesthetic measure.

Perhaps this betrays the lack of taste that marks the gourmand and not the gourmet? I hope not. I certainly sympathize with the view expressed in the following conversation of the classicist-poet A. E. Housman. A friend asked him why he was not including in a collection of his writings on Latin a certain item: "Don't you think it good?" "I think it good," Housman replied, "but not good enough for me." And not infrequently when I read some scholar's latest work, I have asked of Robert Solow what G. H. Hardy asked of J. E. Littlewood: "Why would a man who could write such an article do so?"

The able scholar with writer's block elevates by the mere passage of time the standards each future work must hurdle. It is easy to write a letter every day, but when you have not done so for five years, there is really nothing to report.

Repeatedly I have denied the great-man or great-work notion of science. Every drop helps, the old farmer said, as he spat into the pond. One does the best one can on the most pressing problem that presents. And, if after you have done so, your next moves are down a trajectory of diminishing returns, then still it is optimal to follow the rule of doing the best that there is to do. Besides, at any time a Schumpeterian innovation or Darwinian mutation may occur to you, plucking the violin string of increasing return.

Between Mozart and Brahms, I'm for Mozart. I am thankful for the precious gold pieces Pierro Sraffa left us. But economics would be the better if he had also blessed us all with some dozens of rubies and pearls. And, as I remember his eloquent but sad eyes, one wonders whether he would not have been the happier man if—as William James puts it—he had been born with a bottle of champagne to his credit. Maynard Keynes, who suffered from no writer's cramp, when asked at the end of his life what he'd have done different if he had it all over to do, replied, "I'd have drunk more champagne."

Earlier I confessed to having always been overpaid and underworked. Even good friends might agree with the first of these adjectives, but several will protest at the second, perhaps protesting, "Come off it, you work all the time, weekends and during vacations and, if legend holds, often during the reveries of the midnight hours." True enough. It is precisely my point though that working out economic analysis is play, not work. I am notorious for shirking tasks I hate to do. I minimize administrative duties, displaying an incompetence in their performance that chokes off additional assignments. Like Dennis Robertson, I always wash the forks last in the realization that should an atomic holocaust be imminent there may never be a need to do them.

If I am required to fill out an elaborate questionnaire, that liability is likely to stimulate me to write a new model in the theory of trade or in population genetics. Anything to put off the evil day of duty.

Remembered Kisses

Novels about painters, musicians, poets, or scientists notoriously fail to convey what they do in the working hours of the week. Come to think of it, novels about allegedly great business tycoons similarly fail to capture what it is precisely that they do.

Therefore, speaking to an audience of economists, I should be more specific and describe some particular acts of scientific gestation. How did I first notice the problem? When did a breakthrough occur? What were the steps of development? And how, in retrospect, was the pattern of knowledge affected by the research?

But where to begin? I toyed with the experiment of describing the big ledger that, for a year like 1983, served as a partial diary of research doodlings. Thus, the January 1 entry might be jottings on how to devise a numerical example of a linear programming system that violates a crude version of the Le Chatelier principle in economics. This never got published. Yet. It refers back to work done in 1949, and indeed in 1937, when I was a student at E. B. Wilson's knee—or perhaps shoulder. One might then trace in the daybook a return on January 2 and 3 to the problem, and perhaps discern how it modulates into a related problem.

Suffice it to say that, in the course of a year, there will be a half a hundred such finger exercises. But it would be misleading to believe that my 1983 research is well described, or even sampled, by the chance items that happen to get jotted down in one bedside journal. Therefore, I had better reserve for another and longer day detailed discussion of how some familiar result was conceived and came into being. (The impatient reader can be referred for a sample to my 1982 contribution to the Jørgen Gelting Festschrift, which I entitled "A Chapter in the History of Ramsey's Optimal Feasible Taxation and Optimal Public Utility Prices.")

Chasing the Bitch Goddess of Success

Let me close with a few remarks on the motivations and rewards of scientists. Scientists are as avaricious and competitive as Smithian businessmen. The coin they seek is not apples, nuts, and yachts; nor is it the coin itself, or power as that term is ordinarily used. Scholars seek fame. The fame they seek, as I noted in my 1961 American Economic Association presidential address, is fame with their peers—the other scientists whom they respect and whose respect they strive for. The sociologist Robert K. Merton has documented what I call this dirty little secret in his book *The Sociology of Science*.

I am no exception. Abraham Lincoln's law partner and biographer William Herndon observed that there was always a little clock of ambition ticking in the bosom of honest and whimsical Abe. No celebrity as a *Newsweek* columnist, no millions of clever-begotten speculative gains, no power as the Svengali or Rasputin to the prince and president could count as a pennyweight in my balance of worth against the prospect of recognition for having contributed to the empire of science.

Once I asked my friend the statistician Harold Freeman, "Harold, if the Devil came to you with the bargain that, in exchange for your immortal soul, he'd give you a brilliant theorem, would you do it?" "No," he replied, "but I would for an inequality." I like that answer. The day I proved that no one could be more than 60,000 standard deviations dumber than the mean, that Samuelson inequality made my day. The fact that subsequent writers have both generalized beyond it and discovered antecedents of it in earlier writings has not altered my pleasure in it. For that is the way of science, and sufficient to the day is the increment to the house of science that day brings.

Being precocious, I got an early start. Unconsciously and consciously, I was a young man in a hurry because I felt that the limited life span of my male ancestors tolled the knell for me. My father died young when I was twenty-three. I was supposed to resemble him, and the effect on me was especially traumatic. What I was to do I would have to do early, is what I thought. Actually, modern science granted me respite. Heredity, always, is modifiable by environment. Whatever the reason, I have been granted bouncing good health, a factor given too little weight in allocating merit to scientists and in explaining their achievements. A respected friend of mine, sometimes unfairly marked down as an under-achiever, has been subject all his life to debilitating migraines. I say he is the meritorious one for having, as the Bible says, used his pound so judiciously.

There is another aspect to early, full (even overfull) recognition. It relaxes you. Why fret about priorities when, in the time you might spend in recriminations and turf claiming, you can dip your hook into the waters and be pulling out other pretty fish?

I long ago enunciated the doctrine that scholars work for their self-esteem, in the sense of what they all agree to judge meritorious. However, once your need for glory in the eyes of others has been somewhat appeased, you become free to work for your own approval. The job you will think well done is the one that brings true bliss. Perhaps part of this involves the faith that what one craftsman will like, so will eventually the rest.

There was never a time when I didn't strive to please myself. There have been those who thought that my fooling around with thermody-namics was an attempt to inflate the scientific validity of economics; even perhaps to snow the hoi polloi of economists who naturally can't judge intricacies of physics. Actually, such methodological excursions, if any-thing, put a tax on reputation rather than enhancing it. So what? Taxes are the price we pay for civilization. Such work is fun. And I perceive it adds to the depth and breadth of human knowledge.

At a deeper level one works not just to gain fame and esteem with colleagues. Not just to please oneself and enjoy the fun of the chase. At a deeper level the antagonist of Dr. A. B. Physiologist is not some rival physician at Göttingen or Oxford. The opponent is cancer. So at bottom is it with the economist. There is an objective reality out there that we are trying to understand, hard as that task may be. If ever a person becomes sick to death of faculty intrigue and professional infighting, if ever one sees democracy and civilization crumbling around one, always one can retreat to that objective study of reality. The complex numbers do not dissemble and even for toothache there is no better anodyne than five fast rounds with the puzzler of the business cycle or the intricacies of the theory of control.

I mean this literally and can illustrate what I mean by a true story. The late Voss Neisser, a refugee economist who graced the New School for Social Research, once told me what a relief it was in those grim days of Hitler's march toward power to grapple with the problem of the determining of Walrasian competitive equilibrium. I understood perfectly and agreed completely.

Someone asked me whether I enjoyed getting the Nobel Prize. I thought before answering. "Yes," I replied, "few things in life bring undiluted pleasure, but this one actually did." The honor was a pleasant surprise and came early, but not so early as to worry even me. Friends whose opinions I valued were pleased. If there were contrary opinions, I was too obtuse to be aware of them. My family enjoyed the Stockholm hoopla. Some colleagues in science have looked back with pain at the public interviews and turmoil that took them out of their laboratories. I bore up well and discovered that it takes only a few days of dependence upon one's own chauffeur to develop an addiction.

Indian Summer

Sociologists of science study how the Nobel award affects a scholar. Do the laureates go into an era of depressed fertility? Do they write fewer or more joint papers, and more often list their names first or list them last? Does citing of them accelerate? What is the propensity to change fields—for a physicist to tackle the problem of the brain, for a chemist to become an expert on peace or the minimum wage?

To me it was a case where my cup runneth over—almost. The last vestiges of guilt disappeared when I chose to go off the main turnpike of my discipline of economics: to explore R. A. Fisher's notion of survival value, or Clerk Maxwell's image of a Demon who cheats the second law of thermodynamics of its certainty. I still monitor business trends and the latest fads like a hawk. I still write articles in the many different provinces of political economy. But the last generalist no longer feels it

necessary to keep on top of—I mean try to keep on top of—all the litera-
tures of economics.

As I veer toward the traditional three score and ten, how do I feel
about it? Goethe, who like Wagner and Verdi had a great long run, wrote
that the difference between age and youth was that in youth, when you
called on it, it was always there in response. By contrast, only on the
best good days could the octogenarian attain the peak performance. To
myself, I am sixty-nine going on twenty-five. All the days seem as good
as ever. But, as the lyricist says and reason insists, the stock of what's left
of the good times must shrink as you reach September.

Paul A. Samuelson
Awarded Nobel Prize in 1970. Lecture presented February 6, 1985.

Dates of Birth and Death
May 15, 1915; December 13, 2009

Academic Degrees
B.A., University of Chicago, 1935
M.A., Harvard University, 1936
Ph.D., Harvard University, 1941

Academic Affiliations
Assistant Professor of Economics, Massachusetts Institute of Technology, 1940
Associate Professor of Economics, Massachusetts Institute of Technology, 1944
Professor of International Economic Relations, Fletcher School of Law and Diplomacy, Tufts University, 1945
Professor of Economics, Massachusetts Institute of Technology, 1947
Institute Professor, Massachusetts Institute of Technology, 1966–86
Institute Professor, Emeritus, Massachusetts Institute of Technology, 1986–2009
Vernon F. Taylor Visiting Distinguished Professor, Trinity University, 1989

Selected Books
Foundations of Economic Analysis, 1947, 1983
Economics, 1948, 2001 (17th ed., with W. Nordhaus)
Linear Programming and Economic Analysis, 1958, 1987 (with R. Dorfman and R. M. Solow)
The Collected Scientific Papers of Paul A. Samuelson, Vols. 1–5, 1966–2000

Milton Friedman

The topic assigned to me was "My Evolution as an Economist." I am sure, however, that some questions about the Nobel Prize hold greater interest for at least some of you than my evolution as an economist—in particular, how to get a Nobel Prize in economics. So, as an empirical scientist, I decided to investigate statistically what an economist has to do to get a Nobel Prize.

As most of you may know, the economics award is relatively recent. It was established by the Central Bank of Sweden in 1968 to commemorate its three-hundredth anniversary. So far, twenty-two people have received the Nobel award in economics. Not one of them has been female—so, to judge only from the past, the most important thing to do if you want to be a Nobel laureate is to be male. I hasten to add that the absence of females is not, I believe, attributable to male chauvinist bias on the part of the Swedish Nobel Committee. I believe that the economics profession as a whole would have been nearly unanimous that, during the period in question, only one female candidate met the relevant standards—the English economist Joan Robinson, who has since died. The failure of the Nobel Committee to award her a prize may well have reflected bias but not sex bias. The economists here will understand what I am talking about.

A second requirement is to be a U.S. citizen. Twelve of the twenty-two recipients of the Nobel Prize were from the United States, four from the United Kingdom, two from Sweden, and one each from four other countries. This generalization is less clear-cut than the first because the population of the United States is more than three times as large as Britain, but the number of Nobel recipients only three times as large. So on a per-capita basis, Britain has a better record than we have.

A third generalization is, at least to me, the most interesting statistical result. Of the twelve Americans who have won the Nobel Prize in economics, nine either studied or taught at the University of Chicago. So the next lesson is to go to the University of Chicago. And I may say, in addition to those nine, one other, Friedrich Hayek, also taught at the University of Chicago for ten years. However, I have classified him as an Austrian rather than an American in my compilation. Beyond that, the statistics won't go, and that's all the advice I can give to potential Nobel laureates.

The most memorable feature of receiving a Nobel award is the week in Sweden in early December during which the formal ceremonies are held. It seemed to my wife and me when we were there that all of Sweden spends that week doing nothing but paying attention to the Nobel ceremonies. One party or affair succeeds another. The week culminates in a feast and a dance at which each laureate is required to give a toast lasting not more than three minutes to an already tipsy audience. I thought you might like to hear part of the toast that I gave in 1976. I will leave out the pleasantries that began it and ended it and give just the central part:

My science is a latecomer, the Prize in Economic Sciences in Memory of Alfred Nobel having been established only in 1968 by the Central Bank of Sweden to celebrate its tercentenary. That circumstance does, I admit, leave me with something of a conflict of interest. As some of you may know, my monetary studies have led me to the conclusion that central banks could profitably be replaced by computers geared to provide a steady rate of growth in the quantity of money. Fortunately, for me personally, and for a select group of fellow economists, that conclusion has had no practical impact—else there would have been no Central Bank of Sweden to have established the award I am honored to receive. Should I draw the moral that sometimes to fail is to succeed? Whether I do or not, I suspect some economists may.

Delighted as I am with the award, I must confess that the past eight weeks [this was in December 1976] have impressed on me that not only is there no free lunch, there is no free prize. It is a tribute to the worldwide repute of the Nobel awards that the announcement of an award converts its recipient into an instant expert on all and sundry, and unleashes hordes of ravenous newsmen and photographers from journals and TV stations around the world. I myself have been asked my opinion on everything from a cure for the common cold to the market value of a letter signed by John F. Kennedy. Needless to say, the attention is flattering but also corrupting. Somehow, we badly need an antidote for both the inflated attention granted a Nobel laureate in areas outside his competence and the inflated ego each of us is in so much danger of acquiring. My own field suggests an obvious antidote: competition through the establishment of many more such awards. But a product that has been so successful is not easy to displace. Hence, I suspect that our inflated egos are safe for a good long time to come.

To turn to the suggested autobiographical subject matter, as I have thought back over my own life experience and that of others, I have been enormously impressed by the role that pure chance plays in determining our life history. I was reminded of some famous lines of Robert Frost:

Two roads diverged in a yellow wood,
And sorry I could not travel both
I took the one less traveled by,
And that has made all the difference.

As I recalled my own experience and development, I was impressed by the series of lucky accidents that determined the road I traveled. The first, and surely the most important, was the lucky accident that I was born in the United States. Both my parents were born in Carpatho-Ruthenia, which when they emigrated to the United States was part of Austro-Hungary, later, part of Czechoslovakia, currently, part of the Soviet Union. Both came to the United States as teenagers; they met and married in this country. If they had stayed at home, had nonetheless married one another, and had the same children, I would today be a citizen of the Soviet Union and not of the United States. That was surely pure accident, as it is for most residents of the United States, who like myself are the descendants of people who came to this country as immigrants one or two or three generations ago. As with my parents, most of them brought little with them except their hands and their mouths.

The second major lucky accident was a high-school teacher I had as a sophomore. His field was political science—or civics, as it was called then—but he had a great love for geometry. The course I took from him in Euclidean geometry instilled in me a love and respect for and interest in mathematics that has remained with me ever since. I shall never forget his using the proof of the Pythagorean theorem (the theorem that the sum of the squares of the two sides of a right triangle equals the square of the hypotenuse) as an occasion to quote the last lines of Keats's *Ode on a Grecian Urn*, "Beauty is truth, truth beauty—that is all / Ye know on earth, / and all ye need to know."

A third event, or rather series of chance events, occurred during my college career. As Bill Breit told you, I went to Rutgers University, which today is a mega-university, a mammoth state university. In 1928, when I entered Rutgers, it was a small private college, though the process of converting it to a state university was already in its early stages, in the form of a system of competitive scholarships, tenable at Rutgers and funded by the state of New Jersey. I managed to win one of those scholarships, which relieved me of having to pay tuition to go to college.

My parents, like so many immigrants of that time, were very poor. We never had a family income that by today's standards would have put us above the poverty level. In addition, my father died when I was a senior in high school. However, thanks to the state scholarship plus the usual combination of such jobs as waiting on tables, clerking in stores, and working in the summer, I was well able to pay my own way through college—and indeed ended up with a small nest egg that helped meet the expenses of my first year of graduate study.

Because of my interest in math, I planned to major in mathematics. I was very innocent and the only occupation I knew of that used mathematics was being an insurance actuary, so that was my intended career. The actuarial profession is a highly specialized profession, which has an association that conducts a series of examinations that a budding actuary must pass to become a fellow and to become established in the profession. As an undergraduate, I took some of those exams. I passed a couple and failed a couple—the only exams I can remember ever failing.

By accident, I also took some courses in economics, and that is where the Goddess of Chance entered the picture, because the Rutgers economics faculty included two extraordinary teachers who had a major impact on my life. One was Arthur F. Burns, who many years later became chairman of the Federal Reserve System and is currently our ambassador to West Germany. When I first studied under him, more than fifty years ago, Arthur was in the process of writing his doctoral dissertation. Then, and in my later contacts with him, he instilled a passion for scientific integrity and for accuracy and care that has had a major effect on my scientific work. The other teacher who changed my life was Homer Jones, who was teaching at Rutgers to earn a living while working on a doctoral degree at the University of Chicago. Both are still among my closest friends a half-century later.

Homer later went on to become a vice-president in charge of research at the Federal Reserve Bank of St. Louis. In that capacity he has had a major influence on the spread of interest and knowledge about money in the United States. The publications of the Federal Reserve Bank of St. Louis are unquestionably cited more frequently in the scientific literature than those of any of the other eleven Federal Reserve banks; that is entirely attributable to Homer.

If not for my good fortune in encountering those two extraordinary people, my life would have been radically different, which brings me to the fourth accident. When I finished college I still didn't know whether

I wanted to continue in mathematics or economics. Like all youngsters who need financial assistance, I applied to a number of universities for fellowships or scholarships. In the 1930s the kind of assistance a student could get was much less generous than it is these days—it was a different world altogether. I was lucky enough to receive two offers of tuition scholarships, one in applied mathematics from Brown University and one in economics from the University of Chicago. The offer from Chicago undoubtedly came because Homer Jones intervened on my behalf with Frank Knight, who was his teacher at Chicago.

It was close to a toss of a coin that determined which offer I accepted. If I had gone to Brown, I would have become an applied mathematician. Having chosen Chicago, I became an economist. As Frost said, "Two roads diverged in a yellow wood." I cannot say I took the less traveled one, but the one I took determined the whole course of my life.

The reason I chose as I did was not only, perhaps not even primarily, the intellectual appeal of economics. Neither was it simply the influence of Homer and Arthur, though that was important. It was at least as much the times. I graduated from college in 1932, when the United States was at the bottom of the deepest depression in its history before or since. The dominant problem of the time was economics. How to get out of the Depression? How to reduce unemployment? What explained the paradox of great need on the one hand and unused resources on the other? Under the circumstances, becoming an economist seemed more relevant to the burning issues of the day than becoming an applied mathematician or an actuary.

The first quarter I was at Chicago, the fall of 1932, one course, with Jacob Viner, who was a great teacher, had a major effect on both my professional and personal life. Professionally, Viner's course in theory opened up a new world. He made me realize that economic theory was a coherent, logical whole that held together, that it didn't consist simply of a set of disjointed propositions. That course was unquestionably the greatest intellectual experience of my life.

In addition, it so happened that a fellow classmate was a beautiful young lady by the name of Rose Director. Because Viner seated people alphabetically, she sat next to me, and that too has shaped my whole life. We were married some years later and some forty-seven years later are still in that happy state. Again, consider the role of pure chance. Rose grew up in Portland, Oregon. I grew up in a small town in New Jersey. We met in an economics classroom in Chicago. Hardly something that could have been planned by anybody.

Other faculty members at Chicago included Frank Knight, Henry Simons, Lloyd Mints, Paul Douglas, and Henry Schultz. Economists will recognize their names; the rest of you will not. They were an extraordinarily talented and varied group of eminent economists. The graduate students were equally outstanding there—indeed one of them in addition to Rose is in this audience, Kenneth Boulding. I formed the view at that time, and have never seen reason to alter it since, that students don't learn from professors but from fellow students. The real function of a professor is to provide topics for bull sessions.

To continue with my own experience, Henry Schultz, who taught statistics and mathematical economics at Chicago, was a close friend of Harold Hotelling, a mathematical economist and statistician at Columbia, and recommended me to him. As a result, I was awarded a fellowship to Columbia. So after spending one year at Chicago I went to Columbia the next year.

Harold Hotelling gave me the same kind of feeling for mathematical statistics that Viner had for economic theory. In addition, Wesley C. Mitchell introduced me to both the institutional approach to economic theory and the various attempts to explain the business cycle, and John Maurice Clark, to his own inimitable combination of pure theory and social and institutional detail. At Columbia, too, the graduate students were a remarkably able group, some of whom have remained lifelong friends.

As a result of my experience, I concluded that, at least in the midthirties, the ideal combination for a budding economist was a year of study at Chicago, which emphasized theory, and a year of study at Columbia, which emphasized institutional influences and empirical work.

The following year I returned to Chicago as a research assistant for Henry Schultz, and once again chance was good to me. Two fellow graduate students happened to be George Stigler and W. Allen Wallis.

George Stigler is also a Nobel laureate and a fellow lecturer in this series. He still teaches at the University of Chicago. George was and is a delight and a treasure as a friend and an intellectual influence. No economist has either a more lively and original mind or a better writing style. His writings are almost unique in the economic literature for their combination of economic content, humor, and literary quality. Few economists have germinated so many new ideas and so profoundly influenced the course of economic research. Allen Wallis went on to be dean of the business school at the University of Chicago, then chancellor of the University of Rochester, and is currently undersecretary of state for economic affairs. Allen and George remain among Rose's and my closest friends and both have had a continuing influence on my own professional work.

The combination of influences stemming from Chicago and Columbia—the one heavy on theory, the other heavy on statistical and empirical evidence—has shaped my scientific work, essentially all of which has been characterized by a mixture of theory and fact—of theory and attempts to test the implications of the theory. I refer to "scientific work" to distinguish it from Rose's and my writings for the general public: *Capitalism and Freedom, Free to Choose,* and *Tyranny of the Status Quo.*

My doctoral dissertation grew out of a study I worked on under Simon Kuznets, another American Nobel laureate. Simon was then at the National Bureau of Economic Research. He hired me to work with him on a project growing out of data on professional incomes that he had collected in the course of constructing the initial Department of Commerce estimates of national income. The end result was a book Simon and I collaborated on entitled *Income from Independent Professional Practice.* The core of the book is the use of the economic theory of distribution to explain and interpret the data on the incomes of various professions. The book was finished just before World War II, but was not published until after the war because of a controversy about one of its findings. That finding had to do with the effect of the monopolistic position of the American Medical Association on the incomes of physicians—not exactly a topic that has lost interest over the subsequent forty-odd years. Similarly, a later book, *The Theory of the Consumption Function,* had the same characteristics of combining theory and empirical evidence, and that is also true of the various books I've written alone or in collaboration with Anna J. Schwartz on money.

Another major influence on my scientific work was the experience during World War II. The first two years of that war—1941–1943—I spent at the U.S. Treasury as an economist in the division dealing with taxes. Indeed, Rose has never forgiven me for the part I played in devising and developing withholding at source for the income tax. There is no doubt that it would not have been possible to collect the amount of taxes imposed during World War II without withholding taxes at source. But it is also true that the existence of withholding has made it possible for taxes to be higher after the war than they otherwise could have been. So I have a good deal of sympathy with the view that, however necessary withholding may have been for wartime purposes, its existence has had some negative effects in the postwar period. Those two years in Washington gave me a liberal education in how policy is and is not made in Washington—a most valuable experience. Fortunately, I escaped before I caught Potomac Fever, a deadly disease for someone whose primary interest is scientific.

The second two years of the war—1943–1945—I spent as a mathematical statistician at the Statistical Research Group of the Division of War Research of Columbia University. It had been set up to provide statistical assistance to the military services and to other groups engaged in war research. It was a subsidiary of the wartime-created Office of Scientific Research and Development. Harold Hotelling was its intellectual sponsor and Allen Wallis its executive director. That experience exposed me to physical scientists from a wide range of fields with whom I would otherwise never have had much contact. It also required me to apply statistical techniques to noneconomic data. Surprisingly, perhaps, it turned out that social scientists were often more useful than physical scientists in doing operational research that involved interpreting the results of battlefield experience. The reason is simple: social scientists are used to working with bad data and the wartime data were all very bad. Physical scientists are used to working with accurate data generated by controlled experiments. Many of them were at a loss as how to handle the data generated by experience in the field.

One episode from that period has contributed greatly to my long-term skepticism about economic forecasts and especially about econometric forecasts based on complex multiple regressions. One project for which we provided statistical assistance was the development of high-temperature alloys for use as the lining of jet engines and as blades of turbo superchargers—alloys mostly made of chrome, nickel, and other metals. The efficiency of jet engines and of gas turbines depends critically on the temperature at which they can operate. Raising the temperature a bit increases substantially the efficiency of the turbine, turbo supercharger, or jet engine. Experimentation was being carried on at MIT, Battelle Laboratory in Pittsburgh, and elsewhere. Our group advised on the statistical design of experiments and analyzed much of the resulting data. At one point in the course of doing so, I computed a multiple regression from a substantial body of data relating the strength of an alloy at various temperatures to its composition. My hope was that I could use the equations that I fitted to the data to determine the composition that would give the best result. On paper, my results were splendid. The equations fitted very well and they suggested that a hitherto untried alloy would be far stronger than any existing alloy. The crucial test was to hang a heavy weight on a specimen of the alloy, put it in an oven heated to a high and stable temperature, and measure how long it took for it to break. The best of the alloys at that time were breaking at about ten or twenty hours; my equations predicted that the new alloys would last some two hundred hours. Really astounding results!

A great advantage of the physical sciences over economics is that is possible to test such a prediction promptly. It is not necessary to wait ten years until experience generates new evidence, as is necessary with economic forecasts. So I phoned the metallurgist we were working with at MIT and asked him to cook up a couple of alloys according to my specifications and test them. In order to keep track of them, we had to name them. I had enough confidence in my equations to call them F1 and F2 but not enough to tell the metallurgist what breaking time the equations predicted. That caution proved wise, because the first one of those alloys broke in about two hours and the second one in about three. Ever since, I've been very skeptical of the economic forecasts that people like myself and others make by using multiple regression equations.

In my final comments, let me shift to a different aspect of the Nobel Prize in economics. As some of you may know, the establishment of a Nobel Prize in economics has been criticized on the grounds that economics is not a science. One of the severest critics has been Gunnar Myrdal, the Swedish economist who was awarded the Nobel Prize jointly with Friedrich Hayek. That was an alloy of a very peculiar kind—left and right. Myrdal accepted the prize, but subsequently he had second thoughts and wrote a series of articles condemning the prize and expressing regret that he had accepted it. Economics, he said, is not a science in the same sense as physics or chemistry or biology.

I believe that Myrdal is wrong. It is important to distinguish between the scientific work that economists do and the other things that economists do. Economists are members of a community as well as scientists. We do not spend 100 percent of our lives on our purely scientific work, and neither, of course, do physicists or chemists. In principle, I believe that economics has a scientific component no different in character from the scientific component of physics or chemistry or any of the other physical sciences. True, as those who believe otherwise often stress, the physicist can conduct controlled experiments and the economist cannot. But that is hardly sufficient ground to deny the scientific character of economics. Meteorology is a recognized science in which controlled experiments are seldom possible, and there are many other scientific fields that are equally limited. Economists may seldom be able to conduct controlled experiments—although some are possible and have been done—but uncontrolled experience often throws up data that are the equivalent of a controlled experiment. To give you a simple example, it would be hard to devise a better controlled experiment for comparing different economic systems than the experience provided by East Germany and West Germany: two nations that formerly were one, occupied by people of the same background, the same culture, and the same genetic inheritance, torn apart by the accident of war. On one side of the Berlin Wall is a relatively free economic system; on the other side, a collectivist society. Similar controlled experiments are provided by Red China and Taiwan or Hong Kong, and by North and South Korea.

No so-called controlled experiment is truly completely controlled. Two situations can differ in an infinite number of ways. It is impossible to control for all of them. Hence, I do not believe that there is any difference in principle between so-called controlled experiments and so-called uncontrolled experience or between the possibility of doing scientific work in economics and in physics. In physics no less than in economics, it is important to distinguish between what people do in their scientific capacity and what they do as citizens. Consider the argument that is now raging about Star Wars, the strategic defense initiative. Some physicists issue manifestos opposing Star Wars; other physicists issue manifestos supporting Star Wars. Clearly, those manifestos do not reflect simply agreed scientific knowledge, but in large measure reflect the personal values, judgments about political events, and so on of the physicists. Their scientific competence or contribution should not be judged by such statements. It should be judged by their scientific work. The same thing, I believe, is true of economists.

To return to my own experience, I have been active in public policy. I have tried to influence public policy. I have spoken and written about issues of policy. In doing so, however, I have not been acting in my scientific capacity but in my capacity as a citizen, an informed one, I hope. I believe that what I know as an economist helps me to form better judgments about some issues than I could without that knowledge. But fundamentally, my scientific work should not be judged by my activities in public policy.

In introducing me, Bill Breit referred to my wanting to be judged by my peers. The episode he referred to occurred in a parking lot in Detroit. The morning on which it was announced that I had been awarded the

Nobel Prize, I had agreed to go to Michigan to barnstorm on behalf of a proposed amendment to the state constitution requiring a balanced budget and limiting spending. I had to leave Chicago very early. In Detroit I was picked up at the airport by some of the people running the Michigan campaign and taken to the Detroit Press Club, for a press conference before we started our day of barnstorming. When we got to the parking lot of the press club, we were astonished to see how many reporters and TV people were there, and I remarked that I was amazed that the attempt to get an amendment was receiving so much attention. As I stepped out of the car, a reporter stuck a microphone in my face and said, "What do you think about getting the prize?" I said, "What prize?" He said, "The Nobel Prize." Naturally, I expressed my pleasure at the information. The reporter then said, "Do you regard this as the pinnacle of your career?" or something to that effect, and I said no. I said I was more interested in what my fellow economists would say about my work fifty years from now than about what seven Swedes might say about my work now.

When I was barnstorming that state, I wasn't doing it as a scientist; I was doing it as a citizen deeply concerned about a public issue. Similarly, when I engage in activities to promote a federal constitutional amendment to balance the budget and limit spending, I'm doing so as a citizen. The public has the impression that economists never agree. They have the impression that if three economists are in a room they will get at least four opinions. That is false. If scientific issues are separated from policy and value issues, there is widespread agreement among economists whatever their political views. Over and over again I have been in a group that includes both economists and practitioners of other disciplines. Let a discussion start about almost anything and, in ten minutes or so, you will find all the economists on the same side against all the rest—whether the economists are on the left or on the right or in the middle.

I have great doubts about whether Nobel Prizes as a whole do any good, but I believe that such doubts apply equally to Nobel Prizes in physics as to Nobel Prizes in economics.

I have wandered over much terrain and I am not sure that I have explained my evolution as an economist. Let me only say in closing that my life as an economist has been the source of much pleasure and satisfaction. It's a fascinating discipline. What makes it most fascinating is that its fundamental principles are so simple that they can be written on one page, that anybody can understand them, and yet that very few do.

Milton Friedman
Awarded Nobel Prize in 1976. Lecture presented March 21, 1985.

Dates of Birth and Death
July 31, 1912; November 16, 2006

Academic Degrees
B.A., Rutgers University, 1932
M.A., University of Chicago, 1933
Ph.D., Columbia University, 1946

Academic Affiliations
Part-time Lecturer, Columbia University, 1937–40
Visiting Professor of Economics, University of Wisconsin, 1940–41
Associate Professor of Economics and Business Administration, University
  of Minnesota, 1945–46
Associate Professor of Economics, 1946–48, Professor of Economics
  1948–63, Paul Snowden Russell Distinguished Service Professor of
  Economics 1963–82, University of Chicago
Visiting Fulbright Lecturer, Cambridge University, 1953–54
Wesley Clair Mitchell Visiting Research Professor, Columbia University,
  1964–65
Visiting Professor, UCLA, winter quarter, 1967
Visiting Professor, University of Hawaii, winter quarter, 1972
Senior Research Fellow, Hoover Institute (Stanford), 1977–2006

Selected Books
Essays in Positive Economics, 1953
A Theory of the Consumption Function, 1957
Capitalism and Freedom, 1962, 2002
Price Theory: A Provisional Text, 1962, 1976
A Monetary History of the United States, 1867–1960, 1963 (with Anna
  J. Schwartz)

George J. Stigler

It is a good rule that a scientist has only one chance to become successful in influencing his science, and that is when he influences his contemporaries. If he is not heeded by his contemporaries, he has lost his chance:
brilliant work that is exhumed by a later generation may make the
neglected scientist famous, but it will not have made him important.
Gossen was a genius, but nothing in the development of utility theory is
different for his having lived. Cournot was a genius, and perhaps a bit
of his work rubbed off on Edgeworth and later writers on oligopoly, but
the theory of the subject dates from the 1880s, not from when he published it in 1838.

Contemporary fame does not ensure lasting fame—the leaders of what
prove to be scientific fads recede from even the histories of the science.
Today a young economist will not know that a stagnation thesis concerning the American economy was widely discussed in the late 1930s,
and Alvin Hansen's name will never regain its onetime prominence.
Even Edward Chamberlin's theory of monopolistic competition, it is
now clear, failed to initiate a fundamentally new direction of economic
theorizing.

So scientific creativity—successful, lasting creativity—must be recognized at the time or it becomes a personal rather than a social achievement. This series of lectures is presented by economists who have met
at least the requirement that their work has been recognized by contemporaries. A later age will separate the fundamental from the faddish
contributions.

The conditions for creativity in economics have changed in one absolutely basic respect in the last hundred years or so. Until as late as the
1870s or 1880s it was possible for an amateur to become an influential
economist; today it is almost inconceivable that major contributions
could come from a noneconomist. The knowledge of economics possessed

by Adam Smith, or David Ricardo, or even Leon Walras and Francis Edgeworth, was self-taught: they had not received formal training in the subject. In more or less modern times the only influential noneconomists I can name are Ramsey, Hotelling, and von Neumann; of course, each was a highly trained mathematician, and all date back forty or more years.

So to understand the conditions under which modern work in economics has emerged, one must look at the conditions of training and work of the modern scholar. Those conditions are no substitute for creativity, but they have become an indispensable condition for creativity to be exercised. I turn, therefore, to a semi-autobiographical sketch of my own life in economics, with primary attention to how the conditions of training and work influence the problems and methods of economic research.

Some Autobiography

I grew up in Seattle, attended schools there through a BBA degree at the University of Washington, proceeded to an MBA on the downtown Chicago campus of Northwestern University, spent one more year dodging unemployment at the University of Washington, and then went to the University of Chicago to get a Ph.D. That breathless sentence covers twenty-two years, on which I shall elaborate a bit. My father and mother migrated to the United States from Bavaria and Hungary, respectively. My father, whose skills as a brewer were devalued by Prohibition, went into the business of buying, repairing, and reselling residential property in Seattle during its depressed 1920s as well as the 1930s. I was a fully relaxed student before college days, a voracious and promiscuous reader but not a strong scholar.

At the University of Washington I did very well in classes, but usually chose the wrong classes. Lacking good judgment as well as guidance from my parents, whose formal education had been modest, I took innumerable "applied" business courses and a good deal of political science, but nothing in mathematics or the physical sciences. I was unknowingly providing proof of a proposition I have come to believe: that undergraduate training is to graduate training perhaps as 1 is to 8 in the acquisition of a research-level mastery of a field. Washington had some respectable economists but none who was at the first level.

Northwestern University began to open my eyes. I took, again, too many applied courses, this time chiefly in urban land economics. I studied with one able and stimulating economist, Coleman Woodbury, and he did as much as anyone to arouse my interest in scholarship as a career. But the University of Chicago was receiving pretty close to a tabula rasa in 1933, when I enrolled. Not that I knew it: twenty-two is not an age of humility.

There I met and got to know three economists I still consider to be outstanding: Frank Knight and Henry Simons, and a year later, on his return from the U.S. Treasury, Jacob Viner.

Knight was both a great and an absurd teacher. The absurdity was documented by his utterly disorganized teaching, with constant change of subject and yet insistent repetition of arguments. In the course on the history of economics he was interested mostly in the seamy side of religious history, but got great relish out of emphasizing the perversities and blunders of Ricardo and other historic figures in economics. His greatness is attested best by the fact that almost all of the students were much influenced by him. He communicated beyond any possible confusion the message that intellectual inquiry was a sacred calling, excruciatingly difficult for even the best of scholars to pursue with complete fidelity to truth and evidence.

Henry Simons was Frank Knight's disciple, but his example was enough to teach us that a disciple may have an independent mind, an ambivalent attitude toward some of his master's beliefs, and a wholly different goal in life. Simons believed that in the 1930s the world was at a crisis of historic magnitude: the survival of freedom and the economic viability of the Western world were at stake. With a wider perspective, Knight believed that the history of man was a history of social folly; the then-current crises were grave, but had equally grave precedents and would be handled as badly as they had been previously. Simons believed with all his heart that the crisis of the 1930s had to be handled well or the basic values of civilization would be lost, and he dedicated his life to that task.

One thing that Knight and Simons both succeeded in teaching me, and in fact over-taught, was that great reputation and high office deserve little respect in scientific work. We were told to listen to the argument and look at the evidence, but ignore the position, degrees, and age of the speaker. This studied irreverence toward authority had a special slant: contemporary ideas were to be treated even more skeptically than those of earlier periods. I didn't realize this distinction at the time because it was implicit rather than explicit. We were taught by example that Ricardo's errors and Marshall's foibles deserved more careful and thorough attention than the nonsense or froth of the day. One can make a case for the greater respect for earlier economists on the basis of the fact that their work had stood the test of time, but that case was not made explicitly.

When Viner returned to Chicago the next year we met a very different type of scholar: immensely erudite, rigorous and systematic in his instruction. Viner was the founder of the Chicago tradition of detailed training in neoclassical microeconomics, including training in its application to real problems. Viner filled the class of Economics 301 with a respect bordering on terror. I still recall the time when he asked a student to list the factors determining the elasticity of demand for a commodity. The student began well enough but soon put the conditions of supply in the list of determinants of demand elasticity. Viner calmly said, "Mr. X, you do not belong in this class." This remark produced a suitable tension in the rest of us. Yet outside the classroom he was kind and helpful, and my appreciation of him has risen steadily over time.

Among the very able people I met in Chicago were several students, and of course we knew each other in a way one could not know the professors. My special friends were Milton Friedman and Allen Wallis. It did not take long to recognize Milton's talents: he was logical, perceptive, quick to understand one's arguments—and quick to find their weaknesses. Friedman has surely exercised one of the major intellectual influences upon me throughout my life.

Allen Wallis was so competent and systematic that we soon predicted, to his annoyance, that he would become a university president. A year later Paul Samuelson appeared as a senior in some of our graduate classes, and we had no difficulty in recognizing his quality. The give-and-take among us students (a group that included Kenneth Boulding and Sune Carlson) was the first experience I had of constant exchanges in a circle of first-class minds, and I acquired a lifelong taste for it.

I wrote my dissertation in the history of economic thought under Knight. He was the soul of kindness and generosity in dealing with me, then and forever after, but in retrospect there was a fly in the ointment. He was so strong-minded and so critical a student of the literature that it was a good many years before I could read the economic classics through my eyes instead of his. I have never brought myself to read through my doctoral dissertation, Production and Distribution Theories: The Formative Period, because I knew I would be embarrassed by both its Knightian excesses and its immaturity.

So when I left Chicago in 1936 to begin teaching at Iowa State College, I had acquired a light smattering of mathematics, a partial command of price theory, a fondness for intellectual history, and an irreverence toward prevailing ideas bordering on congenital skepticism. In retrospect a most modest intellectual arsenal.

Iowa and Minnesota and Later

At times I found myself in the midst of a group of vigorous young economists, who were being brought together by Theodore W. Schultz. I still remember my first class, in economic principles. I had prepared the first few weeks of the course in outline, so I entered the class with confidence. Forty minutes later I had covered all the material in my outline, and there remained ten minutes, not to mention ten and a half weeks, still to go! I wish I could state that eventually I encountered the problem so often reported by colleagues, of never being able to cover all the material, but I never reached this utopia of knowledge or loquacity.

I spent most of my spare time at Ames finishing my doctoral thesis, and I received my Ph.D. in the spring of the second year. I had a number of excellent colleagues and students at Ames, but before I was well settled in, Frederic Garver invited me to come to Minnesota, and I accepted.

My closest colleagues at Minnesota were Garver, Francis Boddy, and Arthur Marget. Alvin Hansen had just gone to Harvard and indeed it was largely his classes, but not his rank or salary, that I had inherited. It was rumored that my main rival had been Oskar Morgenstern; if that was true, I have fantasized that if he had been chosen I might have become the junior author of the theory of games!

By 1942 the outbreak of war led to a general retrenchment of academic life, and I took a sustained leave of absence from Minnesota, first to the National Bureau of Economic Research. I was hired to study the service industries as part of a program of studies of the trend of the output, employment, and productivity in the American economy. I and my associates collected an awful lot of numbers and published some monographs on such exotic fields as domestic science, education, trade, and (later) scientific personnel. These works were mostly quantitative, with mildly analytical skeletons, as when I made the first productivity measures relating output to an index of *all* inputs.

At the bureau I got to know Arthur Burns, Solomon Fabricant, and Geoffrey Moore. From them, and even more from Milton Friedman, I became persuaded of the importance of empirical evidence in the appraisal of economic theories; that is a theme to which I will return later. From the bureau I went to the Statistical Research Group at Columbia University, where statistical analysis was being used on military problems. The director was Allen Wallis, and the senior figures included Harold Hotelling, Milton Friedman, Jacob Wolfowitz, and, among other statisticians, L. J. Savage and Abraham Wald. I learned a little statistics there, and I did not seriously delay our nation's victory.

Near the end of the war I returned to Minnesota, and a year later Milton Friedman joined us. The reunion, alas, was brief, for a year later Friedman went to Chicago, and I to Brown. (I may mention that in 1946 I was offered a Chicago professorship, but managed to alienate the president, Ernest Colwell, in an interview and was vetoed. Thereby I probably hastened Friedman's return to Chicago by a year, and can claim some credit for helping found the new Chicago school.) And a year after that, I went to Columbia University, where Albert Hart, William Vickrey, and I taught the graduate theory course. I also assumed the teaching of industrial organization and the history of economics. Columbia then, as now, had a strong department, which included Arthur F. Burns, Carl Shoup, Ragnar Nurkse, and others. And that speedy journey brings me back to Chicago in 1958.

Back to Chicago

I was returning to an economics community in a stage of high prosperity. Friedman was an ascendant figure in world economics: his Consumption Function had revolutionized the statistical analysis of economic data, and his work on monetarism constituted the major attack on the ruling Keynesian doctrine. Modern labor economics was being fashioned by Gregg Lewis and by a recent Chicago Ph.D. already at Columbia, Gary Becker, and his colleague Jacob Mincer. Theodore Schultz was well into his work on the economics of education as well as continuing his influential work on economic growth. Arnold Harberger was making fundamental studies in public finance and developing a major role through both his work and his students in economic development.

My main work was to be in industrial organization. I already had Reuben Kessel and Lester Telser as colleagues, and to my great delight Ronald Coase joined us three years later. The main influence on me, however, was Aaron Director, with whom I had formed a close friendship at the first meeting of the Mt. Pelerin Society in 1947. Aaron was and is a paragon of all collegial virtues. He has a strong, independent mind and he has thought deeply on many questions, dissecting widely accepted and comfortable ideas to reveal their essential superficiality and frequent inconsistencies. He was in the law school, teaching primarily the antitrust course with Edward H. Levi, so his primary work was in antitrust economics.

I cannot recount the number of times in which Director's always courteous questioning led me either to change my views or to seek evidence to reinforce their relevance and weight. If we had been in Greece, I'm sure I would have called him Socrates. His questioning of McGee had already led to John's famous article on predatory pricing, his questioning of Telser soon contributed to Lester's famous article on resale price maintenance, and his questioning of Ward Bowman and Meyer Burstein and George Hilton led to their articles on price discrimination and the metering of demand. Concluding that Director would never write, later I was provoked to present one of his ideas with the title, "Director's Law of Income Redistribution."

A Digression on Research and Originality

There is good reason for believing that economics is a social science in quite another sense from the indisputable one that it concerns itself with mankind in social relationships. It appears also to be a social science in the literal sense that it is a science in which it is difficult to do creative work if one is not in a congenial intellectual environment.

Consider the fact that two of the premier nations of Western Europe, France and Germany, have made on the whole rather minor contributions to the evolution of modern economic analysis. They are nations with long histories of preeminence in mathematics and with great periods in physics, chemistry, and astronomy. Therefore we cannot ascribe their minor roles in economics to lack of powerful scientific capacities. Nor can we easily believe that these nations were sufficiently different in their social or economic or political systems from that of Great Britain so that they should have less reason to be interested in political economy.

Consider again the fact that economics has been characterized by periods of intense scientific progress and controversy, periods that have often lasted for several generations. Cambridge University was the scene of such activity, almost without a break, from 1890 to 1940, and Vienna has a similar history beginning twenty years earlier and also ending in the thirties. Or consider Chicago, which has been the home of similarly intense activity in economics from the 1930s to the present. These periods of sustained scientific enterprise must have some elements of a chain reaction. Indeed, the very notion of a Cambridge or Austrian or Chicago school implies the existence of more than one gifted person with a temporary coterie of disciples.

I will be told, most properly, that von Thünen and Gossen or Cournot were hardly minor economic theorists, just to cite examples from the Germany and France that I have said made rather minor contributions to economics. They were theorists of great creativity, but, as I argued earlier, they did not have any influence upon their contemporaries. The main reason, at least in the case of the two Germans, must have been their intellectual isolation. That isolation allowed von Thünen to spend prodigious energies on the attempt to discover the formula for a God-given fair wage, a will-of-the-wisp that he asked to have engraved on his tombstone ($\sqrt{ap}$). Gossen's book gets its ferocious difficulty not from the inherent complexity of his analysis but from its cryptic, crabbed, unmotivated exposition. Able colleagues would have helped to harness these geniuses. Cournot's book was in one respect similar: despite its splendid lucidity, it was written in a language of mathematics that no important contemporary economist was prepared to speak.

If scientific work is a social activity, discovery is surely not. The discovery of a new theory or a new dimension of an existing theory is an act of creativity that is most imperfectly understood, at least by me. We have little understanding of why Jevons and Gossen discovered marginal utility theory, rather than John Stuart Mill and Senior—certainly the latter two possessed the ingredients and the ability. I have given the explanation for the adoption of the utility theory by the profession that it only became useful as economics became a formalized study of academicians in the latter part of the nineteenth century. [1]Even if this is correct it does not explain how a young assayer in the mint in Sydney, Australia, or an unsuccessful minor civil servant in Germany came upon the idea.

Something can perhaps be said about the sources of new ideas in economics. I believe that we can usually divide new economic ideas into two classes: those that arise out of the critical examination of the ideas of other economists, and those that seek directly to explain some body of empirical phenomena. The classes are not sharply exclusive because the ideas of other economists are presumably directed ultimately to the explanation of real phenomena and therefore are a conduit to those phenomena. Nevertheless, the classification has some value, I believe.

Consider two greats of the late Victorian period, Walras and Marshall. Walras sought to construct a consistent theoretical structure to describe the nature of an enterprise economy. Almost nothing in that elegant structure was calculated to explain any observable behavior, except only the phenomenon of negatively sloping demand curves—and even that was not demonstrated.

Marshall, on the other hand, was concerned to explain the role of time in the formation of prices and the allocation of resources, and this is the central contribution of his Principles. He also made many improvements on predecessors' theories, a striking example being the identification of those elements of land (namely, its spatial relations and annuity of weather) that really constitute Ricardo's original and indestructible properties of the soil. Nevertheless, his eyes were mainly on economic phenomena to be explained, not on predecessors to be corrected.

It is worth pursuing Marshall's two kinds of work a step further. The influence of time was illustrated by a host of persuasive everyday examples, and this was proof enough to make market and short and long-run normal prices a part of the standard theory of economics. The redefinition of land was elegant, for it isolated the proper empirical content of Ricardian land, but it had no effect upon subsequent economics. I attribute this, at least proximately, to Marshall's failure to show that this concept of land had interesting empirical or policy implications.

On my reckoning, the immediate stimulation to advances in economics has overwhelmingly been the attempt to improve on other economists' work. This was the primary source of stimulation for Ricardo, Mill, Edgeworth, Pigou, and most modern economists. Grappling directly with real phenomena is less popular, as well it might be, for the phenomena appear disorderly and poorly enumerated. Yet in addition to Marshall I would put much of the work of Smith, Keynes, and Friedman in this tradition.

For quite a few thousand years most new or unfamiliar ideas must have been wrong: if they were not, the task of being a well-educated scholar would be quite overwhelming. Many "new" ideas are not new at all, only unfamiliar, and most new or unfamiliar ideas are mistaken or infertile.

This raises the question of how a science adopts a new idea, which returns us to the social element in scientific work. Even the new ideas that are eventually judged by many to be good ideas are not often easily absorbed by a discipline. New ideas look at new things or look at familiar things in a new perspective, and their fertility and usefulness are not self-evident. They carry no label or halo that certifies their value, and the claims of their inventors are no different from the claims of the inventors of poor ideas.

A successful innovator therefore finds his work only half done when he has developed a new idea. Indeed the fraction is probably less than half, since the criticisms and misunderstandings his idea encounters will force him to work further on it. He will have to show how it can be developed further, how it is applicable in interesting ways, and how its weaknesses can be patched up. He will be much assisted in all this work if he can enlist a few fervent disciples. Not only may they help in developing the theory, but they can engage in a variety of controversies, which are the best of ways in which to publicize the idea.

If the discoverer lacks the energy or position to pursue the new idea, it is likely to lie fallow. A host of creative ideas—not only those of Cournot and Gossen but some of those of successful economists like Edgeworth and Pareto—required decades to become subjects of active investigation. In passing, I may remark that I have usually moved on to another subject fairly soon after working on one, and as I read the history of science that is a failing.

My Work

Much the most important contribution I have made to economics is information theory. It could have originated in the attempt to generalize economic theories that usually assumed that economic actors had complete knowledge of their markets and technology. But it did not: my discomfort was with a theory that did not account for the fact that almost every product or service will have a distribution of prices, not a unique price, at a given time.

My own observations, partly of price data in antitrust areas, confirmed the existence of a variety of prices of a reasonably homogeneous good. The most obvious available explanation, product differentiation of Chamberlin's sort, seemed inappropriate to markets in automobiles of a given model at retail, bituminous coal, and the like. The apparent near-homogeneity of the products aside, there appeared to be no interesting empirical predictions derivable from monopolistic competition theory as to the extent of price dispersion, its changes over time, and the factors that led to the dispersion.

It occurred to me that it was the expensiveness of knowledge that sustained price differences. Search is never free and often expensive. To visit eight or ten automobile dealers in my search for a given automobile could cost a day plus transportation costs. To visit a second supermarket could require twenty minutes, and the average value of twenty minutes to an American adult is perhaps three dollars.

From the theory of search for the lowest price by a buyer or the highest price by a seller, we can deduce many corollaries. Clearly, the price dispersion relative to the average price will be less the more the buyer spends on it, because the costs of search do not go up as fast as the value of the commodity purchased. The dispersion of prices of automobiles relative to their average price will be lower than that of prices of microwave ovens. Again, knowledge decays gradually with the passage of time, so we expect goods bought frequently to have less price dispersion than infrequently purchased goods of equal value. The amount of search varies with the length of time one lives in a community, so tourists on average pay more for things than natives do.

I applied the theory to the labor markets and it shed light on a variety of the observed wage patterns. Information has other dimensions besides price, so I made a wholly different application of information to the problem of colluding oligopolists, where the central problem is to detect departures from the collusive agreement. Here I invoked observable quantities, not unobservable genuine transaction prices, to detect surreptitious competitive behavior. I also made an attempt to view the functions of advertising in this light, in contrast to the tradition of economists' hostility to advertising.

I must confess that I did not imagine the variety of informational problems in economics that would emerge in the next two decades. For a time it seemed essential to have the phrase "asymmetrical information" in the title of every journal article. Yet the subject is far from exhausted, and I have recently returned to the problem of political information.

I was not led to the economics of information by the previous literature; indeed that previous literature was virtually nonexistent. Only later did I realize that a suggestive treatment resided in Charles Babbage's discussion of what he called the verification of prices.

My work in the theory of economic regulation has a different but related intellectual history. Starting in the early 1960s, I made a series of studies of the actual effects of several public regulatory policies: state utility commission regulation of electric utility rates; SEC regulation of new stock issues; and the antitrust laws. I made these studies because I was skeptical of the prevailing practice in economics of treating the prescriptions of law as actual practice. My findings were often surprising: the regulation of electric utilities did not help residential users; the regulation of new stock issues did not help the widows and orphans who bought these issues.

Only slowly, I should say inexcusably slowly, did I come to the most obvious of questions: why do we get public regulation? I attempted to answer the question by looking at costs and benefits to the various parties. This approach was highly incompatible with the ruling approach in political science. There the introduction of a regulatory policy simply represented the response of the legislature to an aroused public demand for protection of the public interest. The demand of the public, in turn, was due to the existence and growth of some social evil, perhaps called to public attention by vigorous reformers. This "public interest" theory did very poorly in explaining protective tariffs or the farm program and had nothing to say about the dates at which policies were initiated: why was the social security system begun in the 1930s rather than the 1890s or the 1950s?

My work on regulation was much more closely related to that of others than was my work on information. Anthony Downs, James Buchanan, and Gordon Tullock had made large beginnings in the application of economic logic to politics, and my style of approach differed primarily in its strong empirical orientation.

These are examples of my theoretical work directed to the explanation of observed phenomena, with little or no relationship to the work of other economists. It is instructive to look also at a problem I worked on that emerged directly from the literature.

The determination of the efficient sizes of business enterprises is an interesting example. Economists sought to establish the most efficient size of enterprise in any industry by one of three methods: (1) a direct comparison of observed costs of enterprises of different sizes; (2) a direct comparison of rates of return on investment of enterprises of different sizes; and (3) an estimation of cost functions on the basis of technological information. Each of these methods encounters severe problems, always of data and often of logic.

I sought an answer by resorting to a sort of Darwinian approach, which had already been employed in a related manner by Alchian. My argument was essentially this: if I wish to know whether a tiger or a panther is the stronger animal, I put them in the same cage and return after a few hours. Similarly, by seeing the sizes to which firms competing in an industry were tending, I could deduce the efficient sizes—a method called the survivor technique.

The method seems obvious and, I later found, had antecedents as illustrious as John Stuart Mill, but for a considerable time the method encountered substantial opposition. The National Bureau of Economic Research, where it was written, did not wish to publish it, perhaps because it was too controversial.

There is no reliable way to discover something new: if there were, it would infallibly be discovered. It seems evident to me that Friedman's splendid theory of consumption function arose out of puzzles displayed by observable data, and Arrow's splendid impossibility theorem arose out of profound thought about the process of social decision making.

Conclusion

I should warn you, although I confess I should have done so at the outset rather than at the conclusion of this lecture, that I am a strong supporter of the view that a knowledge of the life of a scholar is more often a source of misunderstanding than of enlightenment about his work. Obviously, my arguments for this view have not been convincing, or Professor Breit would not have organized this lecture series.

The reason that this biographical approach—it bears the oppressive name of prosopography—is misleading is that its devotees usually pick out of a scholar's life some circumstance or event that they find explains a given theory. To give you real and absurd examples, one historian said life on a small island led Malthus to fear overpopulation; another said John Stuart Mill could not be original because he wrote his Principles in less than two years.

I am not prepared to say that one's work is independent of one's life. Possibly if I had gone to Harvard instead of Chicago, I would have been a believer in monopolistic competition, a student of input–output tables, or a member of the Mason school of industrial organization. But I do not attach high probabilities to these possibilities. I am no longer a faithful follower, although I am still an admirer, of Frank Knight and Henry Simons: each person has a mind-style of his own, and eventually it asserts itself. This does not mean that we are immune to our environment, but it does argue for me that environmental influences will be subtle.

I not only believe this to be true but also I hope that it is true: the prospects for scientific progress would be bleak if we could train our students to become truly faithful disciples. If you understand my scientific work better for having heard me, I shall be both pleased and envious.

Note

1. "The Adoption of the Marginal Utility Theory," reprinted in G. J. Stigler, *The Economist as Preacher* (Chicago: University of Chicago Press, 1982), 72–85.

George J. Stigler

Awarded Nobel Prize in 1982. Lecture presented April 17, 1985.

Dates of Birth and Death

January 17, 1911; December 1, 1991

Academic Degrees

B.B.A., University of Washington, 1931
M.B.A., Northwestern University, 1932
Ph.D., University of Chicago, 1938

Academic Affiliations

Assistant Professor, Iowa State, 1936–38
Assistant, Associate, and Full Professor, University of Minnesota, 1938–46
Professor, Brown University, 1946–47
Professor, Columbia University, 1947–58
Charles R. Walgreen Distinguished Service Professor of American Institutions, University of Chicago, 1958–81
Director, Center for the Study of the Economy and the State, University of Chicago, 1981–91

Selected Books

Production and Distribution Theories, 1941, 1994
The Theory of Price, 1946, 1987
Essays in the History of Economics, 1965
The Organization of Industry, 1968, 1983
The Citizen and the State: Essays on Regulation, 1975

James Tobin

Beginning with Keynes at Harvard

Rare is the child, I suspect, who wants to grow up to be an economist, or a professor. I grew up in a university town and went to a university-run high school, where most of my friends were faculty kids. I was so unfailing an A student that it was boring even to me. But I don't recall thinking of an academic career. I liked journalism, my father's occupation; I had put out "newspapers" of my own from age six. I thought of law; I loved to argue, and beginning in my teens I was fascinated by politics. I guess I knew that there was economics at the university, but I didn't know what the subject really was. Of course, economic issues were always coming up in classes on history and government—civics, in those days. I expected economics to be among the social science courses I would someday take in college, probably part of the pre-law curriculum.

I grew up happily assuming I would go to college in my hometown, to the University of Illinois. One month before I was scheduled to enroll as a freshman, I was offered and accepted a Conant Prize Fellowship at Harvard. I should explain how this happened. My father, a learned man, a voracious reader, the biggest customer of the Champaign Public Library, discovered in the *New York Times* that Harvard was offering two of these new fellowships in each of five midwestern states. President Conant wanted to broaden the geographical and social base of Harvard College. Having nothing to lose, I accepted my father's suggestion that I apply. University High School, it turned out, had without even trying prepared me superbly for the obligatory College Board exams. Uni High graduates only thirty to thirty-five persons a year, but it has three Nobels to its credit and, once I had broken the ice, many national scholarships.

Thus James Bryant Conant, Louis Michael Tobin, and University High School changed my life and career. Illinois was and is a great university. But I doubt that it would have led me into economics. For several reasons, Harvard did.

Harvard was the leading academic center of economics in North America at the time; only Columbia and Chicago were close competitors. Both its senior and junior faculty were outstanding. Two previous Nobel laureates in economics were active and influential members of the community when I was a student, Wassily Leontief on the faculty and Paul Samuelson as a Junior Fellow, a graduate student free of formal academic requirements. Of the senior faculty of the 1930s, Joseph Schumpeter would have been a sure bet for a Nobel, Alvin Hansen, Edward Chamberlin, and Gottfried Haberler likely choices. Haberler, still active, remains a possibility. Naturally, Harvard attracted remarkably talented graduate students. That able undergraduates might go on to scholarly careers was taken for granted.

When I arrived at Harvard, I knew I would want to major—at Harvard the word is *concentrate*—in one of the social sciences or possibly in mathematics. By the end of freshman year I was leaning to economics. But I hadn't yet taken any. In those days even Ec A, the introductory course, was considered too hard for freshmen. As a sophomore all of eighteen years old, I began Ec A in a section taught by Spencer Pollard, an advanced graduate student specializing in labor economics and writing a dissertation on John L. Lewis and the United Mine Workers.

Pollard was also my tutor. A Harvard undergraduate, besides taking four courses, met regularly, usually singly, with a tutor in his field of concentration, generally a faculty member or graduate student associated with the student's residential house. Tutorial was not graded. It was modeled, like the house system itself, on Oxford and Cambridge. Pollard suggested that we devote our sessions to "this new book from England." He had recently been over there and judged from the stir the book was creating even before publication that it was important. The book was *The General Theory of Employment, Interest and Money* by John Maynard Keynes, published in 1936.

Pollard was no respecter of academic conventions; that I was only an Ec A student meant nothing to him. I was too young, and too ready to assume that teacher knows best, to know that I knew too little to read the book. So I read it, and Pollard and I talked about it as we went through it. Cutting my teeth on *The General Theory,* I was hooked on economics.

Like many other economists of my vintage, I was attracted to the field for two reasons. One was that economic theory is a fascinating intellectual challenge, on the order of mathematics or chess. I liked analytics and logical argument. I thought algebra was the most eye-opening school experience between the three Rs and college.

The other reason was the obvious relevance of economics to understanding and perhaps overcoming the Great Depression and all the frightening political developments associated with it throughout the world. I did not personally suffer deprivations during the depression. But my parents made me very conscious of the political and economic problems of the times. My father was a well-informed and thoughtful political liberal. My mother was a social worker, recalled to her career by the emergency; she was dealing with cases of unemployment and poverty every day.

The second motivation, I observe, gave our generation of economists different interests and priorities from subsequent cohorts dominated by those attracted to the subject more exclusively by the appeal of its puzzles to their quantitative aptitudes and interests.

Thanks to Keynes, economics offered me the best of both worlds. I was fascinated by his theoretical duel with the orthodox classical economists. Keynes's uprising against encrusted error was an appealing crusade for youth. The truth would make us free, and fully employed too. I was already an ardent and uncritical New Dealer, much concerned about the depression, unemployment, and poverty. According to Keynesian theory, Roosevelt's devaluation of the dollar and deficit spending were sound economics after all.

By sheer application, unconstrained by the need to unlearn anything, I came to know Keynes's new book sooner and better than many of my elders at Harvard. Keynes was the founder of what later came to be known as macroeconomics, what his young associate Joan Robinson called at the time "the theory of output as a whole," a phrase I found strikingly apt. The contrast was with the theory of output and price in particular markets or sectors. This—what we now call "micro"—was the main stuff of the theory course we economics concentrators took after Ec A. I liked the methodology of the new subject, modeling the whole economy by a system of simultaneous equations; by now I had calculus to add to my algebra. J. R. Hicks and others showed, more clearly than Keynes himself, how the essentials of *The General Theory,* and it differences from classical theory, could be expressed and analyzed in such models.

Harvard was becoming the beachhead for the Keynesian invasion of the new world. The senior faculty was mostly hostile. A group of them had not long before published a book quite critical of Roosevelt's recovery program. Seymour Harris, an early convert to Keynes, was an exception, especially important to undergraduates like myself, in whom he took a paternal interest. Harris was an academic entrepreneur. He opened the pages of the *Review of Economics and Statistics,* of which he was editor, and the halls of Dunster House, of which he was senior tutor, to lively debates on economic theory and policy.

The younger faculty and the graduate student teaching fellows were enthusiastic about Keynes's book. Their reasons were similar to my own but better informed. A popular tract by seven of them, *An Economic Program for American Democracy,* preached the new gospel with a left-wing slant.

Most important of all was the arrival of Alvin Hansen to fill the new Littauer chair in political economy. Hansen, aged fifty, came to Harvard from the University of Minnesota the same year I was beginning economics. He had previously been critical of Keynes and had indeed published a lukewarm review of *The General Theory.* He changed his mind 180 degrees, a rare event for scholars of any age, especially if their previous views are in print. Hansen became the leading apostle of Keynesian theory and policy in America. His fiscal policy seminar was the focus of research, theoretical and applied, in Keynesian economics. Visitors from the Washington firing lines mixed with local students and faculty; I had the feeling that history was being made in that room. For undergraduates the immediate payoff was that Hansen taught us macroeconomics, though under the course rubric Money and Banking. Hansen was a true hero to me, and in later years he was to be a real friend also.

I wrote my senior honors thesis on what I perceived to be the central theoretical issue between Keynes and the classical economists he was attacking. The orthodox position was that prices move to clear markets, rising to eliminate excesses of demand over supply and falling to eliminate excess supplies. Applied to the labor market, this meant that reductions of wages would get rid of unemployment. Excess supply of labor could not be a permanent equilibrium. Unless wage cuts are prevented by law or by monopolistic trade unions, competition for jobs will lower wages and in turn restore or create jobs for the unemployed. This was just an application of the central thesis of orthodox economics, the Invisible Hand proposition of Adam Smith. Individual agents are selfish and myopic. They respond in their own interest to the market signals locally available to them. Their actions miraculously turn out for the best for the society as a whole. Competition brings this miracle about.

Keynes's heresy was to deny that this mechanism could be counted on to eliminate involuntary unemployment. He didn't say just that the mechanism was slow and needed help from government policy. He said it might not work at all. Instead, the economy would be stuck in an underemployment equilibrium. Orthodox economists thought they could prove that free competitive markets allocate resources efficiently. In saying that willing and productive workers can't get jobs, Keynes was indicting the market system for a massive failure. After all, there is no greater inefficiency than to leave productive resources idle.

My honors thesis found fault with Keynes's logic. That may seem surprising. But I didn't think Keynes needed to insist on so sweeping a theoretical victory on his opponents' home court. His practical message was just as important whether unemployment was an incident of prolonged disequilibrium or of equilibrium. My first professional publication (1941) was an article in the *Quarterly Journal of Economics* based on my senior thesis; the *QJE* is, of course, edited and published at Harvard. The issue is very much alive today. It has also remained an interest of mine, a subject on which I have published several other papers, including my 1971 presidential address to the American Economic Association (1972).

Tools of the Trade, Theoretical and Statistical

By graduation time in 1939 I had forgotten about law and drifted into the natural decision, to become a professional economist. Harvard has a way of keeping its own: my fellowship was extended and I went on to graduate school. The transition was easy; I had taken courses with graduate students while I was a senior. Now I needed to pick up some tools of the trade. One was formal mathematical economic theory, and another was statistics and econometrics. Harvard was just beginning to catch up to the state of these two arts.

I see in retrospect that our professors left most of our education to us. They expected us to teach ourselves and learn from each other, and we did. They treated us as adult partners in scholarly endeavor, not as apprentices. I am afraid our graduate programs today try too hard to convey a definite and vast body of material and to test how well students master what we know. I wrote my undergraduate thesis under the nominal supervision of my senior-year tutor, Professor Edward

Chamberlin. He said he knew nothing about my subject and left me on my own. Our tutorial sessions were nonetheless interesting; we argued about Catholic agrarianism, his vision of economic utopia. The faculty adviser for my doctoral dissertation in 1946–47 was, by my choice, Professor Schumpeter, one of the truly great economists, indeed social scientists, of the century. He had no use for Keynes and little for my topic, the consumption function. He read what I wrote and made helpful suggestions, but mostly he kept hands off. When I saw him, we talked of many other things, to my lasting benefit.

The theory we were taught was largely in the Anglo-American tradition, in which mathematical argument was subordinated to verbal and graphical exposition and relegated to footnotes. The great book was *Principles of Economics* by Alfred Marshall, Keynes's own mentor in the other Cambridge. Markets were analyzed mostly one at a time—*partial* equilibrium analysis. Little rigorous attempt was made to describe a *general* equilibrium of the system as a whole, with many commodities, many consumers and producers, many markets interconnected with each other.

Mathematical models of general equilibrium were a stronger tradition in continental Europe, to which the French-Swiss economist Leon Walras had made the seminal contribution in 1870. Though F. Y. Edgeworth at Oxford and Irving Fisher at Yale had written in the same vein, they had not greatly influenced the main line of English-language economics from Adam Smith to David Ricardo to John Stuart Mill to Marshall. But in the late 1930s and 1940s the mathematical general equilibrium approach was coming into vogue, thanks to J. R. Hicks and R. G. D. Allen in Britain and Wassily Leontief and Paul Samuelson at Harvard. Joseph Schumpeter fostered this development, believing that Walras had provided economics its "magna charta," even though his own theory of the dynamics of capitalism was wholly different.

I liked the general equilibrium approach; that was one of the great appeals of macroeconomics. But those models of output as a whole were small enough and specific enough to understand and manipulate. I have never been an aficionado of formal mathematical general equilibrium theory, which is so pure and general as to be virtually devoid of interesting operational conclusions. Moreover, I have come to think that its elegance gives many economic theorists today an exaggerated presumptive faith that free competitive markets work for the best. I did use the approach in some articles in the late 1940s on the theory of rationing, all but one of them in collaboration with Hendrik Houthakker.

In statistics and econometrics Harvard was further behind the times. The professors who taught economic statistics were idiosyncratic in the methods they used and quite suspicious of methods based in mathematical statistical theory. Until the 1950s Harvard was pretty much untouched by the developments in Europe led by Ragnar Frisch and Jan Tinbergen or those in the United States at the Cowles Commission. Students like me, who were interested in formal statistical theory, took refuge in the mathematics department. For econometrics we squeezed as much as possible from a seminar on statistical demand functions offered by a European visitor, Hans Staehle. We also discovered that regressions, though scorned by professors Crum and Frickey, were alive and well under the aegis of Professor John D. Black's program in agricultural economics. In the basement of Littauer Center we could use his electromechanical or manual Marchands and Monroes.

I did just that for my second published paper (1942), originally written for Edward S. Mason's seminar in spring semester 1941, on how to use statistical forecasts in defense planning; my example was estimation of civilian demands for steel. The paper was one reason Mason recommended me for a job in Washington with the civilian supply division of the nascent Office of Price Administration and Civilian Supply. So I left Harvard in May 1941, having completed all the requirements for the Ph.D. except the dissertation. I would not return until February 1946. After nine months of helping to ration scarce materials, I went in the Navy and served as a line officer on a destroyer until Christmas 1945.

Statistics and econometrics were important in my research after the war. In my doctoral dissertation (1947) on the determinants of household consumption and saving, I tried to marry "cross-section" data from family budget surveys with aggregate time series, the better to estimate effects of income, wealth, and other variables. In a later study of food demand (1950), I refined the method. This, along with my empirical and theoretical work on rationing, took place in England in 1949–50, at Richard Stone's Department of Applied Economics in Cambridge. I hoped that cross-section observations could resolve the ambiguities of statistical inference based on time series alone. Later my interest in cross-section and panel data led me to the work of the Michigan Survey Research Center, where I spent a fruitful semester with George Katona, James Morgan, and Lawrence Klein in 1953.

My work on data of this type led me to propose a new statistical method, which became known as Tobit analysis (1958). Probit analysis, which originated in biology, estimates how the probabilities of positive or negative responses to treatment depend on observed characteristics of the organism and the treatment. In economic applications, Yes responses often vary in intensity; for example, most families in a sample would report No when asked if they bought a car last year, while those who answer Yes spent varying amounts of money on a car. My technique would use both Yes-No and quantitative information in seeking the determinants of car purchases.

The label Tobit was perhaps more appropriate than Arthur Goldberger thought when he introduced it in his textbook. Perhaps not. My main claim to fame, a discovery enjoyed by generations of my students, is that, thinly disguised as a midshipman named Tobit, I make a fleeting appearance in Herman Wouk's novel *The Caine Mutiny*. Wouk and I attended the same quick Naval Reserve officers' training school at Columbia in spring 1942, and so did Willy, the hero of the novel.

Innovative and seminal work in mathematical economics and econometrics took place at the Cowles Commission for Research in Economics in the years 1944–54. The commission was then affiliated with the University of Chicago. Its research output over that period is one of the most fruitful achievements in the history of organized scientific inquiry. The leaders were Jacob Marschak and Tjalling Koopmans; Koopmans was awarded a Nobel Prize for his contributions to the theory of resource allocation, including linear programming, during this period. The remarkable teams Marschak and Koopmans assembled included two of the previous speakers in this series at Trinity, Arrow and Klein, and two other Nobel laureates, Simon and Debreu.

When I was a graduate student at Harvard after the war, I stood in awe of the Cowles Commission and of Marschak and Koopmans. I came to know them at meetings of the Econometric Society. For the December 1947 meeting in Chicago I was asked to be a discussant of a paper by Marschak. I didn't get the paper until a few days before the meeting, indeed a day or so before Christmas. I worked hard on the paper—neglecting my wife, Betty, pregnant with our first child, and holiday festivities with our families. I was able to report some important flaws in Marschak's model and to offer some constructive suggestions. One thing led to another. I was asked to join the commission, and in 1954 I was asked to become its research director, to succeed Koopmans as he had succeeded Marschak.

The offer was flattering, challenging, and tempting. But I was very happy at Yale, and Betty and I had come to like New Haven very much as a place to live and raise a family. It turned out that we could have our cake and eat it too. Koopmans was quite interested in relocating the commission, because of difficulties in attracting staff to Chicago at that time and problems in the relation between the commission and the university. He gave me not the slightest inkling of this interest until I had definitely declined the offer. The founder and financial angel of the commission, Alfred Cowles, was a Yale graduate; he hoped his creation could find permanent hospitality from his alma mater.

In 1955 the commission moved to Yale, renamed the Cowles Foundation for Research in Economics at Yale University. I became its research director after all. Cowles Foundation Discussion Paper 1 (1955) was a precursor of the Tobit analysis mentioned above. The coming of Cowles was an important factor in the rise of economics at Yale to front-rank stature. I broadened the scope of the foundation's research to include macroeconomics. I was particularly eager to make room for the interests and talents of a young Yale assistant professor, Arthur Okun, who was working on macroeconomic forecasting and policy analysis.

Developing Keynesian Macroeconomics; Synthesizing It with the Neoclassical Tradition

My main program of research and writing after the war continued my early interests in Keynes and macroeconomics. I sought to improve the theoretical foundations of macro models, to fit them into the main corpus of neoclassical economics, and to clarify the roles of monetary and fiscal policies. In this endeavor I shared the objectives of many other economists, notably Abba Lerner, Paul Samuelson, Franco Modigliani, Robert Solow, J. R. Hicks, and James Meade. A new mainstream, synthesizing the Keynesian revolution and the classical economics against which it was revolting, was in the making. I am proud that Paul Samuelson called me a "partner in [this] crime."

The building blocks of the Keynesian structure were four in number: the relation of wages and employment; the propensity to consume; liquidity preference and the demand for money; the inducement to invest. I have already referred to my work on the first. I turn now to the other three.

Keynes's "psychological law" of consumption and saving stated that saving would be an ever-larger proportion of income as per capita real incomes became greater. National income data between the two world wars appeared to confirm his law. Statistical equations, fit to those data, extrapolated to much higher incomes, foretold trouble after the Second

World War. Investment would have to be a much larger fraction of national income than ever before to absorb the high saving and avoid recession and unemployment. The extrapolation was wrong. Incomes rose as expected, but consumption was no smaller a proportion than before. This forecasting error triggered an agonizing reappraisal of the consumption function, with fruitful results.

My doctoral dissertation (1947) was on this subject. I thought Keynes's law should be interpreted to refer to the relation of lifetime consumption to lifetime income, not to a relation between those variables year by year. The same considerations implied that wealth, not just current income, determines consumption in the short run. As so often happens, this idea was in the air. Milton Friedman's permanent income theory and Franco Modigliani's life-cycle model were elegant explanations of saving behavior in this spirit. They showed how cyclical data could look "Keynesian" even though saving would be roughly proportional to income in the long run. I have written a number of papers on this subject over the years.

The episode is, I believe, an example of how economic knowledge advances when striking real-world events and issues pose puzzles we have to try to understand and resolve. The most important decisions a scholar makes are what problems to work on. Choosing them just by looking for gaps in the literature is often not very productive and at worst divorces the literature itself from problems that provide more important and productive lines of inquiry. The best economists have taken their subjects from the world around them.

The bulk of my work in the 1950s and 1960s was on the monetary side of macroeconomics. I had several objectives.

First, I wanted to establish a firm foundation for the sensitivity of money demand or money velocity to interest rates. Why was this important? The quantity theory of money, later called monetarism, asserted that there was no such sensitivity, that the velocity of money was constant except for random shocks and for slow, secular changes in public habits, banking institutions, and financial technology. The implication was that fiscal stimulus, such as government spending or tax reduction, could not affect aggregate spending on goods and services unless accompanied by money creation. The same implication applied to autonomous changes in private investment. In this sense Milton Friedman and other monetarists were saying not just that money matters, with which I agreed, but also that money is all that matters, with which I disagreed.

In an empirical paper in 1947 I let the data speak for themselves, loudly in favor of Keynes's liquidity preference curve. But I was not satisfied with Keynes's explanation of liquidity preference. He said people preferred liquid cash because they expected interest rates to rise to "normal" prosperity levels of the past, causing capital losses on holdings of bonds. As William Fellner, later to be my colleague at Yale, pointed out in a friendly debate with me in journal pages, Keynes could hardly call "equilibrium" a situation in which interest rates are persistently lower than investors' expectations of them. Fellner was espousing a principle of model building later called "rational expectations," and I agreed with him.

I found and offered two more tenable sources of the interest sensitivity of demand for money. One (1956) was based on an inventory theory of the management of transactions balances. As I learned too late, I had been mostly anticipated by William Baumol, but the model is commonly cited with both names. The second paper (1958) gave a new rationalization of Keynes's "speculative motive": simply, aversion to risk. People may prefer liquidity, and prefer it more the lower the interest rate on noncash assets, not because they expect capital losses on average but because they fear them more than they value the equally probable capital gains.

I had been working for some time on portfolio choices balancing such risks against expected returns, and the liquidity preference paper was an exposition and application of that work. Harry Markowitz had already set forth a similar model of portfolio choice, and our paths also converged geographically when he spent a year at Yale in 1955–56. My interest was in macroeconomic implications, his more in advising rational investors.

When my prize was announced in Stockholm in 1981, the first reports that reached this country mentioned portfolio theory. This caught the interest of the reporters who faced me at a hastily arranged press conference at Yale. They wanted to know what it was, so I did my best to explain it in lay language, after which they said "Oh no, please explain it in lay language." That's when I referred to the benefits of diversification: "You know, don't put all your eggs in one basket." And that is why headlines throughout the world said "Yale economist wins Nobel for 'Don't put all your eggs …,'" and why a friend of mine sent me a cartoon he had clipped, which followed that headline with a sketch of next year's winner in medicine explaining how his award was for "An apple a day keeps the doctor away."

The fact that one of the available assets in the model of my paper was riskless turned out to have interesting consequences. I felt somewhat uneasy and apologetic that I was pairing the safe asset with just one risky asset to represent everything else. This aggregation followed Keynes, who also used "*the* interest rate" to refer to the common yield on all non-money assets and debts. I proved that my results would apply even if any number of risky assets were available, each with different return and risk. The choice of a risky portfolio, the relative weights of the various risky assets within it, would be independent of the decision how much to put into risky assets relative to the safe asset, money. This "separation theorem" was the key to the capital asset pricing model developed by Lintner and Sharpe, beloved by finance teachers and students, and exploited by the investment managers and counselors who compute and report the "betas" of various securities.

The debate about fiscal and monetary policy, as related to the interest-sensitivity of demand for money, went on for a long time, too much of it a duel between Milton Friedman and me. In a Vermont ski line a young attendant checking season passes read mine and said in a French Canadian accent, "Tobeen, James Tobeen, not ze economiste! Not ze enemy of Professeur Friedman!" He was an economics student in Quebec; it made his day. He let me pass to the lift. This debate, I would say, ended for practical purposes when Friedman shifted ground, saying that no important issue of monetary policy or theory depended on interest sensitivity of money demand. The ground he shifted to was the basic issue between Keynes and the classics, the contention that the economy is always in a supply-constrained equilibrium wherein neither monetary nor fiscal policy can enhance real output.

Second, I proposed to put money into the theory of long-run growth. In the 1950s one phase of the synthesis of Keynesian and neoclassical economics was the development of a growth theory along neoclassical lines. Some, not all, Keynesians were ready to agree that in the long run employment is full, saving limits investment, and "supply creates its own demand." The short run was the Keynesian domain, where labor and capital may be underemployed, investment governs saving, and demand induces its own supply. Roy Harrod had started modern growth theory in 1939, followed by Evsey Domar in the 1940s and Trevor Swan, Robert Solow, Edmund Phelps, and many others in the 1950s and 1960s.

I was involved too. My 1955 piece, "A Dynamic Aggregative Model," may be my favorite; it was the most fun to write. It differed from the other growth literature by explicitly introducing monetary government debt as a store of value, a vehicle of saving alternative to real capital, and by generating a business cycle that interrupted the growth process. In three subsequent papers (1965, 1968, and 1985) I showed that the stock of capital in a growing economy is positively related to the rates of monetary growth and inflation.

Third, in a long series of papers I developed, together with William Brainard and other colleagues at Yale, a general model of asset markets and integrated it into a full macroeconomic model. In a sense we generalized Hicks's famous IS/LM formalization of Keynes by allowing for a richer menu of assets. As I already indicated, I had been uncomfortable with that unique "*the* interest rate" in Keynes and with the simple dichotomy of money versus everything else, usually described as money versus bonds. I thought nominal assets versus real capital was at least as important a way of splitting wealth, if it must be split in only two parts, and this is what I did in the growth models cited above.

Portfolio theory suggested that assets should be regarded as imperfect substitutes for each other, with their differences in expected yields reflecting their marginal risks. Our approach also suggested that there is no sharp dividing line between assets that are money and those that are not. The "Yale approach" to monetary and financial theory has been widely used in empirical flow-of-funds studies and in modeling international capital movements.

Our approach also explicitly recognizes the stock-flow dynamics of saving, investment, and asset accumulation, as in my 1981 Nobel lecture. These dynamics were explicitly ignored in Keynes, who defined the short run as a period in which the change in the stock of capital due to the flow of new investment is insignificant. Stock-flow dynamics are also ignored in IS/LM models. But flows do add to stocks. Investment builds the capital stock, government deficits enlarge the stocks of government bonds and possibly of money, trade surpluses increase the net assets of the nation vis-à-vis the rest of the world, and so on. Without these effects, macro stories about policies and other events are incomplete.

The bottom line of monetary policy is its effect on capital investment, in business plant and equipment, residences, inventories, and consumer durable goods. The effect is not well represented by the market interest rates usually cited, or by quantities of money or credit. Our approach to monetary economics and macroeconomics led us naturally to a different measure, closer to investment decisions. This has become known as "Tobin's q." It is the ratio of the market valuations of capital assets to their replacement costs, for example, the prices of existing houses relative to the costs of building comparable new ones. For corporate businesses, the market valuations are made in the securities markets. It is common sense that the incentive to make new capital investments is high when the securities giving title to their future earnings can be sold for more than the investments cost, i.e., when q exceeds one. We see the reverse in takeovers of companies whose qs are less than one; it is cheaper to buy their productive assets by acquiring their shares than to construct comparable facilities from scratch. That is why in our models q is the link from the central bank and the financial markets to the real economy.

Policy and Public Service

As must be clear from my narrative, I have always been intensely interested in economic policy. Much of my theoretical and empirical research has been devoted to analyzing and discerning the effects of monetary and fiscal policies. In the 1950s I began writing occasional articles on current economic issues for general readership, some of them in the *New Republic,* the *Yale Review, Challenge,* and the *New York Times.*

Some of my friends in Massachusetts were advising Senator Kennedy. They told him and his staff about me. In summer 1960 Ted Sorenson came to see me and arranged for the Kennedy campaign to employ me to write some memoranda and position papers on economic growth. Sorenson signed me up despite the fact that I had felt it necessary to tell him I favored Stevenson for the nomination. I didn't notice any effects of my memos during the campaign, but I was told that they were used by the Kennedy team at the party platform deliberations, mainly to oppose the exaggerated "spend to grow" views of Leon Keyserling and some union economists.

My message at the time was that we needed a tight budget, one that would yield a surplus at full employment, and a very easy monetary policy, one that would get interest rates low enough to channel the government's surplus into productive capital investment. The point was to have full employment, but by a mix of policies that promoted growth in the economy's capacity to produce. Incidentally, my message is similar today. After the 1960 election I served on a transition task force on the domestic economy chaired by Paul Samuelson. One day in early January 1961 I was summoned from lunch at the faculty club to take a phone call from the president-elect. He asked me to serve as a member of his

Council of Economic Advisers. JT: "I'm afraid you've got the wrong guy, Mr. President. I'm an ivory-tower economist." JFK: "That's the best kind. I'll be an ivory-tower president." JT: "That's the best kind." I took a day or two to talk to Betty and to my colleagues and then said Yes. I served for twenty months.

Walter Heller was the chairman of the council, and Kermit Gordon was the other member. We had a fantastic staff, including Art Okun, Bob Solow, Ken Arrow, and a younger generation whose names would also be recognized as leaders in our profession today. We were all congenial, intellectually and personally, and we functioned by consensus without hierarchy or bureaucracy. We were optimistic, confident that our economics could improve policy and do good in the world. It was the opportunity that had motivated me to embrace economics a quarter century before.

The January 1962 *Economic Report* is the manifesto of our economics, applied to the United States and world economic conditions of the day. The press called it "the new economics," but it was essentially the blend of Keynesian and neoclassical economics we had been developing and elaborating for the previous ten years. The report was a collective effort, written mainly by Heller, Gordon, Solow, Okun, and Tobin. It doesn't appear on my personal bibliography, but I am proud of it as a work of professional economics as well as a public document. The January 1982 *Report* is the comparable document of Reaganomics, likewise the effort of professional economists to articulate a radically new approach to federal economic policy. It is interesting to compare the two; we have nothing to fear.

The Kennedy council was effective and influential because the president and his immediate White House staff took academics seriously, took ideas seriously, took us seriously. JFK was innocent of economics on inauguration day. But he was an interested, curious, keen, and able student. He read what we wrote, listened to what we said, and learned a lot.

Our central macroeconomic objective was to lower unemployment, 7 percent in January 1961, to 4 percent, our tentative estimate of the inflation-safe unemployment rate. That goal was achieved by the end of 1965, with negligible increase in the rate of inflation and with a big increase in capital investment. The sweet success turned sour in the late 1960s, when contrary to the advice of his council and other Keynesian advisers President Johnson failed to raise taxes to pay for the escalating costs of the war in Vietnam. Critics looking back on the 1960s accuse the

Kennedy–Johnson economists of naive belief in a Phillips trade-off and of policies explicitly designed to purchase lower unemployment with higher inflation. The criticism is not justified. The council did not propose to push unemployment below what came to be known as the "natural rate." Moreover, beginning in 1961 the council and the administration adopted wage and price policies designed to achieve an inflation-free recovery—"guideposts for noninflationary price and wage behavior" were espoused in the report.

I returned to Yale in September 1962. I loved the job at the council, but I knew my principal vocation was university teaching and research. Fifteen-hour days and seven-day weeks were a hardship for me, my wife, and our four young children. I remained active as a consultant to the council, particularly on international monetary issues that had concerned me as a member. Moreover, I was now more visible outside my profession, so I wrote and spoke more frequently on issues and controversies of the day. But I knew that alumni of Washington often have difficulty getting back into mainline professional scholarship. I determined to accomplish that re-entry, and I believe I did.

Kennedy and Johnson added the war on poverty to their agenda. Walter Heller and the council were very much involved. I became quite interested in the economic disadvantages of blacks and in the inadequacies, inefficiencies, and perverse incentives—penalties for work and marriage—of federal and state welfare programs. I wrote major papers on these matters in 1965 and 1968. This was not macroeconomics, but one implication of the Keynesian-neoclassical synthesis was that welfare and redistributional policies could be, within broad limits, chosen independently of macroeconomic goals. Nothing in our view of the functioning of capitalist democracies says either that prosperity requires hard-hearted welfare policies and small governments or that it requires redistribution in favor of workers and the poor.

I favored a negative income tax. So did Milton Friedman—although his version seemed to me too small to fill much of the poverty gap, and he refused to join a national nonpartisan statement of economists favoring the approach. I helped to design a negative income tax plan for George McGovern in 1972. Unfortunately, he and his staff botched its presentation in the heat of the California primary; I am sure most people to this day think McGovern was advocating a kooky budget-breaking handout. After the election Nixon proposed a family assistance plan pretty much the same as the McGovern scheme he had ridiculed during the campaign.

I have lived long enough to see the revolution to which I was an eager recruit fifty years ago become in its turn a mainstream orthodoxy and then the target of counterrevolutionary attack. The tides of political opinion and professional fashion have turned against me. Many of my young colleagues in the profession are as enthusiastic exponents of the new classical macroeconomics as I and my contemporaries were crusaders against old classical macroeconomics in the 1930s. Many of the issues are the same, but the environment is quite different from the Great Depression. The contesting factions are better equipped—our profession has certainly improved its mathematical, analytical, and statistical tools. I do not despair over the present divisions of opinion in economics. Our subject has always thrived and advanced through controversy, and I expect a new synthesis will evolve, maybe even in my lifetime. I haven't abandoned the field of battle myself. I hope I learn from the new, but I still think and say that Keynesian ideas about how the economy works and what policies can make it work better are relevant today—not just as Keynes wrote them, of course, but as they have been modified, developed, and refined over the last half-century.

James Tobin

Awarded Nobel Prize in 1981. Lecture presented April 30, 1985.

Dates of Birth and Death

March 5, 1918; March 11, 2002

Academic Degrees

A.B., Harvard University, 1939
M.A., Harvard University, 1940
Ph.D., Harvard University, 1947

Academic Affiliations

Junior Fellow, Harvard University, 1946–50
Associate Professor of Economics, Yale University, 1950–55
Professor of Economics, Yale University, 1955–57
Sterling Professor of Economics, Yale University, 1957–88
Sterling Professor of Economics, Emeritus, Yale University, 1988–2002

Selected Books

The American Business Creed, 1956 (with S. E. Harris et al.)
National Economic Policy, 1966
Essays in Economics, Vols. 1–4, 1971–1982
The New Economics One Decade Older, 1974

Franco Modigliani

Ruminations on My Professional Life

It's been a lot of fun for me to prepare this talk because it has forced me to go over my history and pick up a number of things I had forgotten and see connections I did not see before. I was somewhat taken aback and overawed by the title, "My Evolution as an Economist." It sounded as if I had to start from my invertebrate state and then move up to higher states. I then suddenly realized or remembered a very important thing: economics is a very old profession. In fact I think it is the oldest profession in the world. I know this claim is disputed by others. There is a story, I think authentic, of an argument about this among an engineer, an economist, and a surgeon. The problem was that each claimed that his profession was the oldest. The surgeon spoke first and said, "Remember at the beginning when God took a rib out of Adam and made Eve? Who do you think did that? Obviously, a surgeon." The engineer, however, was undaunted by all this and said, "Just a moment. You remember that God made the world before that. He separated the land from the sea. Who do you think did that except an engineer?" "Just a moment," protested the economist, "Before God made the world, what was there? Chaos. Who do you think was responsible for that?"

So tonight I am going to tell you about my contribution to chaos. One thing I want to stress, because I want you to consider it as I move through my story, is the very important question regarding an award like the Nobel Prize: How much is deserved and how much is luck? After I received the award many people wrote to me asking for a prescription for getting a Nobel Prize. How many books do you need and how many hours do you work? I have always answered that you need many books and you must work many hours, but most important: manage to have lots of luck. I have had a lot of luck. And as you may have already gathered, perhaps the first piece of luck in my life was to marry my wife, Serena. It was luck in the sense that I was a fresh, brash kid at that time—very, very, young. It was hard to recognize what could come out of this, but she helped me come through. I am sure that she decided to prove that the brash kid she married really was a good investment, and I hope that she feels she has succeeded.

Let me now try to deal with the history of my development. I was born in Rome, Italy, in 1918 and spent my youth there under Fascism. My family consisted of my father, a leading Rome pediatrician; my mother, a dedicated volunteer social worker; and my older brother. I had a happy childhood protected by the love of my family, though I was supposedly very hardheaded. Otherwise there was nothing very notable in my early career. I was a middling student until I reached senior high school. I had the good fortune of attending one of Italy's outstanding high schools, a school in Rome that produced many popes, bishops, and cardinals. I didn't get to become one of them, but nonetheless the air was full of those great minds. I decided to try to skip the last year of high school and somewhat to my surprise succeeded, thus entering university at seventeen, two years ahead of normal schedule. But I did not know yet want I wanted to do. For awhile it was thought that I should study medicine because my father was a physician. Unfortunately he died when I was quite young, and there was an expectation in the family that I should follow in his footsteps. I went to the registration window to sign up for medicine, but then I closed my eyes and thought of blood! I got pale just thinking about blood and decided that under those conditions I had better keep away from medicine. So what to do then? I didn't have any other special interests, so I did what was fashionable at the time: I enrolled in the Faculty of Law, which at that time opened up many possible careers. The curriculum in law was really very easy, and I had a lot of time on my hands (there wasn't very much to do except when you were cramming for exams, and I didn't go to the lectures because they weren't particularly interesting). Casting about for something to do, I happened to get into some economic activities. I knew some German and was asked to translate from German into Italian some articles for one of the trade associations. Thus I began to be exposed to the economic problems that were in the German literature. At that time there was a lot about price controls.

There was then in Italy an essay competition among university students on various subjects. There was one in engineering, one in music, one in literature, and one in economics. The economic topic for that year was price controls because they had been imposed on Italy during the Ethiopian War (1935). I thought I was an expert, having translated at least twenty articles on price controls from German, and I decided to participate in the contest, albeit without high expectations. But to my great surprise I came out first. The commission told me that obviously I had some facility for economics. So I decided, why not? From then on I began to think of myself as a possible economist. That was around 1936, and at that time economics was one of the subjects in the Faculty of Law. What was taught in fact was the theory and institutions of the "corporate state" and bore little relation to modern economics. But on the good advice of some competent economists in Italy I began to study the economic literature. I studied Marshall and other classics, but could not get hold of Keynes. Although Keynes's *General Theory* already existed, I could not find it in Italian or even in English.

A year after I began my training in economics, we left Italy, as the political situation was deteriorating. The Fascist regime, under the pressure of its Nazi ally, passed a set of laws discriminating against Jews, making an academic career impossible. My then future father-in-law, Giulio Calabi, who had already experienced difficulties with the regime, decided to leave Italy immediately for France where he had many connections, especially with the great publishing house of Hachette. I was more than happy to take advantage of his offer to join the family. I tried to continue my study of economics in France. Again I was not very successful, because the French university was even worse than the Italian. People did go to class in large numbers but, as far as I could tell, their only purpose was to make noises of various kinds—very effectively so that you could not hear what was going on. Why they attended I still don't understand. I went to study in the library (the Bibliothèque St. Geneviève), and again made some progress with my studies. Then as the clouds were gathering in Europe, the Calabi family decided to come to the United States, more as tourists than as permanent residents. Serena and I were married in May 1939, after which I traveled to Italy to defend my thesis and thus complete my degree—just in time to depart for the United States in August 1939.

We arrived in September 1939, just as war broke out. So when we landed, we knew we were to be here for a long time. I then cast around for something to do. It was now a matter of finding a job in order to live, and I began to work selling Italian and other foreign books. But I also looked around to see what I could do to continue my study of economics. And here again I was lucky and obtained a scholarship at the

New School for Social Research, a great center for European scholars. There were many notable names in various disciplines, but a man who was particularly important to me was Jacob Marschak, recently arrived from England. Jacob Marschak was at once a great economist, a magnificent teacher, and an exceptional and warm human being. He took me in hand and persuaded me first of all that if I wanted to get anywhere as an economist, I had to study mathematics. I had had no training at all in math and in fact had a certain aversion to it. He persuaded me to carry out a certain amount of study of mathematics and statistics, which played a very important role as I tried to develop my own papers. The time was 1939. The *General Theory* of Keynes was the center of discussion, together with the work of Schumpeter on business cycles. We had seminars devoted to them and they were very exciting. Of course at that time we were coming out of the depression. Keynes gave you the feeling that the mysterious disease that produced the depression was something that could be understood and avoided in the future. So there was a lot of excitement associated with that study. In addition Marschak invited me to participate in a seminar that was held in New York, organized by Oskar Lange, the famous economist from Poland. The participants included, in addition to Lange and Marschak, such powerful economists as Tjalling Koopmans and Abraham Wald. It was a very exciting experience. Unfortunately in 1941 Marschak left the New School to go to the University of Chicago at the invitation of Oskar Lange, who was there permanently. But by that time I was well on my way, and furthermore, as Marschak left, another outstanding economist, Abba Lerner, came to the New School. I began to have some serious discussions with Abba Lerner, because although I respected him, I thought that he was oversimplifying the message of the *General Theory.* He accepted one aspect of the Keynesian theory that I think is not its essence, namely, the notion that rigid wages and a special feature of the demand for money—the so-called liquidity preference—could result in a "liquidity trap," where the economy is fundamentally an unstable system that will get buffeted by all shocks. There is no stable equilibrium to which it returns. I think Abba Lerner held very strongly to this view, and this led him to the idea that the only way to stabilize the economy is through fiscal policy. Running surpluses and deficits is the only way to compensate for shocks. I thought this was a much too simple view of Keynes. From my perspective this represented a limiting case of Keynes but not the normal run of things, and I began to work on the article that was to appear in 1944 under the title, "Liquidity Preference and the Theory of Interest and Money."

While I was working on the article, I began my first teaching job at the New Jersey College for Women, an institution within commuting distance of New York. I was able to get this offer because Pearl Harbor had been attacked and people were moving from colleges to Washington. As a result, an opening arose there for a term. I have fun these days telling our younger faculty what my teaching load was at that time: four courses per term, including two sections of economics, one section of statistics, and one section of economic history. On top of that I was teaching a course at the New School for Social Research. From the New Jersey College for Women I went to Bard College, which was then a part of Columbia University. It is there that I completed my 1944 article on liquidity preference, which was to attract a good deal of attention.

I had excellent students. Some of them are good economists and many have become personal friends with whom I still have contact. The companionship and friendship that often develops between professors and students is a characteristic of American higher education that is lacking in Italian universities, which are far more impersonal. Several of these students helped me improve my English (which was still a little rusty in 1942) and were helpful in editing my article.

It turned out that the referee for my 1944 article was Leonid Hurwicz, a very young economist with a great future who was to become a close friend when we were together at the University of Illinois. Its publication, while I was still relatively young, contributed greatly to my recognition as an economist and to my unexpected election to fellow of the Econometric Society in 1949. The main theme of the paper was that, except for the questionable assumption of absolute wage rigidity, the Keynesian system did allow in general for a self-restoring full employment equilibrium along classical lines. But there were some special circumstances under which this mechanism breaks down, and perhaps that is what happened in the Great Depression. These special circumstances should not have been regarded as the rule but as a limiting case. In particular the main stabilization device should be monetary policy, not fiscal policy. That was the theme of this paper.

My career at Bard College ended when I was called up for service in the armed forces. I had been left out for awhile because I had a pre–Pearl Harbor child—a very valuable item at that time! However, on the verge of my induction the draft board told me that they were able to find other nonfathers, and I was released. Not long afterward the war ended, and I was offered the opportunity of returning to the New School.

I was there in two capacities: as a researcher at the Institute of World Affairs and as a teacher of mathematical economics at the New School itself. My research project at the institute was to build, together with Hans Neisser, a large-scale (for the time) econometric model of the world economy showing the linkages between countries. At a time when the most powerful computational device was an electric calculator, this was a rather ambitious scheme. But at least we succeeded in putting together a structure that was later used as a guide and a source of ideas for similar projects.

The other thing that happened during this period was that I began to be very much concerned with the study of saving, which was to be a central theme throughout my life. Why was I concerned? Because there was an idea that had its origin in some of the Keynesian writings that people were saving too much. If people save too much, the consequence might be a serious depression. The Keynesian followers argued that saving depends on income and that the proportion of income saved grows with income: if you are richer you save a larger fraction of your income. Because income was expected to rise in the postwar period, there was the implication that the saving rate would get larger and larger, and there were great doubts as to whether there would be enough investment opportunities to absorb the saving.

I didn't believe that the saving rate would tend to grow and grow. It just didn't sound right to me. I thought that this was one of the fads of the time, and I began to work on this problem and pursue the idea that the saving rate has a cyclical characteristic but not a rising trend. My findings suggested that saving is determined more by a person's income relative to his accustomed level than by his absolute income in a given period. This idea happened to be pursued at the same time by James Duesenberry at Harvard. The resulting theory is now known as the Duesenberry–Modigliani hypothesis.

It was approximately at this time that I suddenly received an invitation from Harvard. At that time Harvard had the best economics department in the country—it was Harvard and then nothing and then nothing and then nothing, and then came Columbia and Chicago. So this invitation was not something that I could ignore, and I went to Harvard with some curiosity. I had a great day because the first thing that happened is that I was received by the head of the department who, although I did not know it at the time, had a reputation for not being very sympathetic to foreigners. He had been ordered by the faculty to offer me a job, so he did, but then he went on to say, "Now look, Modigliani, if you've got any sense, you will never accept this job, because you know we have people like James Duesenberry, Sidney Alexander, Richard Goodwin, and others—you will never make it. So why don't you go back to the New School and be a big fish in a small pond. Don't try to be a big fish in this pond." I had been uncertain about accepting the offer because it would have meant taking a cut in salary. Thus I was able to say, "Well fine, I think you have a very good idea," and so I said "No." After finishing my interview, I had meetings with various members of the faculty. I had lunch with Joseph Schumpeter and Gottfried Haberler, and they asked, "Well, how did it go?" and I told them. "Oh, you fool," they replied. "You should never listen to what Professor Burbank says. You should have accepted." But by that time I had made up my mind that if such a person was the head of the department, Harvard did not appeal to me. So I went back to the New School. Within a year I was offered the Political Economy Fellowship at the University of Chicago. This was a fairly prestigious and high-paying scholarship, something like $3,000 a year—a big salary at that time and enough to live on with the family. So I accepted the offer, took leave, and went there. But I had hardly arrived when I was approached by Howard Bowen, the dean of the College of Commerce at the University of Illinois, and asked to join the University of Illinois on a project entitled "Expectations and Business Fluctuations." The salary was excellent, and the university was prestigious and had some very good people. I accepted. Rejecting the Harvard offer turned out to be a blessing in disguise. I had a much faster career at Illinois and a much higher salary than my colleagues at Harvard. Also I had a chance to get to know the Middle West, which was very important for me, having been born in Europe.

The purpose of the expectations and business fluctuations project was to explain the role of expectations in business planning in order to answer the question: Can expectations independently be a source of instability in an economy? It was in the course of the project that I acquired some basic ideas that would play an important role in many of my later contributions. Let me mention them briefly. First was the idea that a lot of production scheduling in the firm was controlled by the notion of smoothing production in the face of seasonal fluctuations in sales. If you can produce at an even rate, you will have lower costs than if you fluctuate. If you try to hire and fire people or if you keep them idle and pay them overtime, it is more costly than producing evenly.

Production does not depend on current sales, it depends on the expectation for the current cycle. It will be seen in a moment why that is relevant to other things. Second, I found that this particular way of looking at production planning has some interesting implications for what expectations are worth forming and what information is needed to make decisions. An interesting implication is that, with few exceptions, the only information that is useful for production scheduling is that which pertains to the rest of this season, and you couldn't care less what's going to happen thereafter—within broad limits. Thus the whole notion of irrelevant expectations, that is, expectations not relevant for current behavior, was one of the interesting ideas that emerged from the project.

The third interesting idea developed from the study of actual business forecasts is that failure to adjust for seasonal factors can be a source of major forecasting errors. Yet many executives do not appear to really understand seasonal adjustments, falling back on the very inaccurate device of four quarter changes.

In addition to this research project I had other significant experiences while at Illinois. I ran into a brilliant and delightful young man by the name of Richard Brumberg, a first-year graduate student. He became a very close friend of the entire family. I had been asked by Kenneth Kurihara to write a paper for a book to be called *Post-Keynesian Economics,* and I invited Brumberg to work with me on the paper. We hadn't decided on a topic until we went to a conference on saving at the University of Minnesota and were both very unhappy with the papers given. On the trip back by car to the University of Illinois we hatched an idea that looked like a possible improvement: the hypothesis that came to be called the life cycle theory of saving.

While still at Illinois, I was invited to become an associate of the Cowles Commission, a Chicago-based organization connected with the Econometric Society. This connection put me in contact with another group of outstanding people that included Tjalling Koopmans, Jacob Marschak, Kenneth Arrow, Carl Christ, Herman Charnoff, and Herbert Simon.

The University of Illinois experience terminated with a dramatic fight in which essentially the McCarthy forces were trying to push out the dean, Howard Bowen, as well as the people he had brought in. He had attracted an excellent cast of people, but they were not from the "black earth" of Illinois. They came from the East Coast, they came from the West Coast, they were Keynesians—they had to be eliminated, particularly because they bothered the old guard who felt passé, inferior to this new group. So the old guard was able to orchestrate a very famous fight in which the main figure was a trustee, Red Grange; I think some of you have heard of this name. To me he was completely unknown, but everybody knew the great football player Red Grange (the Galloping Ghost), and Red Grange led the fight against Bowen. Bowen resigned as did most of the people who came with him. I still had to complete the project so I stayed on for a year, but I began to look around. When I received an invitation from the Carnegie Institute of Technology, now Carnegie Mellon, I wisely accepted and spent eight precious years there, from 1952 to 1960.

During my stay at Carnegie Mellon I matured into the economist I am today. How did that happen? Well, Carnegie at that time was a very exciting place. The key figure of course was Herbert Simon, a genius and a great colleague. But around him there were some other fine scholars like Charles Holt, Merton Miller, William Cooper, Richard Cyert, and James March—all outstanding people. We also had great students such as Jack Muth. He has become one of the heroes of the present time as the man who laid the foundations for the so-called rational expectations hypothesis, which is what young economists live by. All this provided an exciting atmosphere.

In this environment there were two kinds of activities. There were, first of all, important innovations in terms of teaching in a business school. Essentially Carnegie Mellon introduced the quantitative, discipline-oriented approach to business administration. And that was an exciting thing to be doing at that time. Second, there were research projects. For example, Simon, Holt, Muth, and I worked on a book about production scheduling, which again focused on the question of short-run decision making with respect to the scheduling of how much to produce, how many to hire, and how much to hold in inventories. In this book we developed a mathematical model embodying my idea about smoothing out seasonal fluctuations in sales. It has been influential in the production areas and has been used extensively in courses in production both here and abroad. This was a very good example of teamwork—that is, each of us was able to provide a new push when the others were at the end of their ropes.

The second important thing that happened is that together with Richard Brumberg I was able to complete a first contribution on the life cycle hypothesis that dealt with individual behavior and a second part that dealt with aggregate behavior. This hypothesis explained saving patterns in much the same way as I had earlier explained the production pattern of firms: People consume at a relatively constant rate determined by their lifetime earnings. Therefore when their income is highest, they save a great deal, but when it is low, such as during their youth and in their later retirement years, they actually "dissave." This is similar to Milton Friedman's permanent income hypothesis, but differs in that Friedman assumes an infinite time horizon for consumption and saving decisions whereas my hypothesis depends on life being finite and differentiated—dependency, maturity, retirement. In essence a person's lifetime pattern of wealth accumulation can be described as a hump. Wealth is low during one's youth but grows as one begins to earn. It reaches a peak during one's middle years before retirement and declines after retirement. There may be some bequest element. That is, we allowed for the fact that some portion of wealth may be bequeathed. Our estimates now suggest that maybe one-fifth of wealth is the result of bequest, but the remaining four-fifths—or something between 75 percent and 80 percent—is of this hump type.

Hump wealth has one important implication that Richard and I discovered to our great delight. When you aggregate, that is, when you look not at the individual family but at the economy as a whole, it turns out that the aggregate wealth of a country (the aggregate saving) can be different in different countries in which each individual behaves identically over his life cycle. That is, imagine that in every country each person over his life cycle has identical behavior. Yet one country can have no saving and another country can save a lot. Why? Because, if you think of the implication of hump wealth, you will see that the main determinant of national saving is not income—which should not affect the path of wealth relative to income—but growth; the faster the country grows, the higher the saving income. The less you grow, the less you save. If you don't grow at all, aggregate ratio saving is zero. This macro implication and a number of corollaries that follow from it are significant because they give an entirely different view of the saving process. People tend to say that the Japanese save a lot because they are thrifty and we save little because we aren't thrifty. If my model is correct, it says that's nonsense. We are equally thrifty. They are growing at 8 percent per year and we are growing at 3 percent per year, and that is why we normally save 12 percent and they save well over 20 percent of their income.

It turns out that there is a lot of evidence to support the life cycle hypothesis (or LCH) point of view. LCH does not imply that individual thriftiness is entirely immaterial. Rather it suggests that one can reduce the rate of saving to two elements: the shape of the path of wealth over life and how fast the economy grows. For a given path saving depends only on growth. However, the shape of the path has an influence. So it could be that the Japanese are inclined to postpone their consumption. If that were the case, they would have a bigger hump. Incidentally, there is some evidence that that is true. In Japan housing is enormously expensive, and there were until very recently very few facilities for the financing of housing—mortgages were very rare and extremely expensive. So people were forced to save a lot when they were young in order to be able to acquire a house. And that means they had to postpone higher consumption until after they had purchased a house.

There were several other contributions that were completed during this period at Carnegie Mellon. First, I took another crack at the working of the monetary mechanism in the economy, which I had handled in my 1944 article. I allowed for various developments that had happened in the meantime. This was 1963, and it represented a fairly definitive form of my view of how money works in the economy. In addition it was around 1957 that Merton Miller and I produced our two papers, the so-called Modigliani–Miller theorems, which have come to be known as Mo-Mi and Mi-Mo.

Mo-Mi is the proposition that the financial structure (debt-equity ratio) of a firm in a perfect capital market has no effect on its market valuation. This paper has since become quite well known, and it has been assigned to students in business and finance all over the world. And I regret that this is the case because students who read this paper usually come out hating me. They think it's a terrible paper, a very hard one to understand—and they are right. The reason is that this paper was never meant for students. The paper was meant to upset my colleagues in finance by arguing that the core issue that received most attention in corporation finance, namely finding out what exactly is the optimum capital structure, was not really an issue. It didn't make any difference. To be sure, it might make a difference if there were taxes. If so, you would have to approach the problem precisely in that way and ask, what is the effect of taxes and why do they make a difference?

Aside from the specific message about capital structure, the main methodological contribution—which I think is the reason the paper has become so important in the area of finance—was in changing the method of attack regarding the choice of financial structure and investment policy: The focus should be on the maximization of the market value of the firm debt plus equity rather than on the traditional, but not operational, maximization of profits. This contribution was much more general than the specific one about the fact that leverage doesn't count.

The second paper had to do with dividend policy. If you have a perfect capital market and no taxes, it makes no difference whether you pay a lot of dividends or very little; the market value of the firm would be unaffected. This once again went against the grain of the time. The profession spent a lot of time deciding whether you could fool the investors, seen as outsiders rather than owners of the firm, by giving them a little more of this or a little more of that. We essentially show that this is all irrelevant.

I produced two other articles at Carnegie Mellon. These were out of my mainstream, but have had considerable influence. One is an article written in 1958 while on leave at Harvard, on oligopoly theory, which developed a very simple way of understanding pricing behavior under conditions of oligopoly. The other one was even more unorthodox. It is called "The Forecastability of Social Events." Written with one of my colleagues, Emile Grunberg, the paper deals with the belief that economists can't forecast accurately because people respond to the forecasts and therefore behave differently, invalidating the forecast. This article said that accurate forecasts are perfectly possible even when agents react to them. When you make a forecast, you must simply take into account the effect of the forecast on behavior. Under some very general mathematical conditions (continuity) it can be shown that forecasting is, in principle, possible. The implied message to our colleagues was therefore: don't kid yourself, don't make excuses. If we can't forecast it's because of our ignorance, not because agents react.

An important aspect of my life at this time is that I reestablished relations with Italy. Until 1945 we had considered going back to Italy. But as we watched what was going on there, we decided that we had had enough and were going to become U.S. citizens and make this our home. For awhile I more or less cut off relations, but in the mid-50s I reestablished contact and began to be interested in issues of economic policy in Italy.

In 1955 I spent a year as a Fulbright lecturer at the Universities of Rome and Palermo. I had completely forgotten how profoundly different the Italian and the American systems of higher education were. The Italian system was a three-caste structure, with the few and mostly old full professors occupying the upper caste, close to God; a group of hopeful, sometimes servile assistants constituted the second layer; and the students were at the bottom of the heap. I will always remember an episode that occurred during my stay at the University of Rome when Professor Papi, then rector of the university and a symbol of the system, invited me to speak at his faculty seminar but introduced me (then thirty-eight) as a promising young star! I thanked him but remarked that in the United States I was regarded as a bit passé!

In 1960 we left Carnegie Mellon and went to Northwestern for just a year. After this year we moved permanently to MIT. Let me divide the MIT period into two parts: the period up to 1974—corresponding to the first oil crisis—and the period since.

The decade from 1960 to 1970 was what you might call the golden era of Keynesianism. It should be understood of course that when I speak of Keynesianism I speak of wise Keynesians. I speak of Solow and Samuelson and Tobin and Heller and others of their ilk. I don't speak of the many aberrations that always exist. In the mid-1960s I was asked by the Federal Reserve Board to build a model of the American economy that could be used for forecasting and policy analysis. That model was built in collaboration with Albert Ando along basically Keynesian lines, but our type of Keynesian lines in which money is very important. In fact we discovered that money was even more important than was thought because of the interaction between my consumption function and monetary policy. Because my consumption function shows that consumption depends on income and wealth, and because interest rates affect that wealth, here is one more channel through which monetary policy can have an effect on income. Furthermore we showed that in terms of our estimates this was faster than the traditional channel through investment, which involves considerable lags.

In terms of intellectual history I think it is important to acknowledge that there were two points on which we had to change our initial course. The first is that we started out with a model of the determinant of the price level that in the traditional Keynesian literature was referred to as the Phillips curve. This formulation allowed for the possibility of a long-run trade-off between inflation and unemployment. That mechanism was shown to be invalid by Ned Phelps and Milton Friedman, particularly in Friedman's presidential address to the American Economic Association during which he introduced the "vertical" Phillips curve. We readily accepted that, and by the late 1960s we had revised our model so that it included a vertical Phillips curve, for which we found plenty of support. The vertical Phillips curve essentially says that you cannot push unemployment below some critical level through inflation; if you try to have too much employment, you will get accelerating inflating, which will eventually have to be stopped by accepting a lot of unemployment.

As for the second change, when we started the model, inflation was not yet a problem. But by the late 1960s, however, it had become serious. We had to allow for various effects of inflation on the economy, beginning with such a simple thing as the concept of the real interest rate, the rate of interest adjusted for the effect of inflation. The model is still used at the Federal Reserve together with other devices.

The other contributions of that period included, first of all, a fair amount of work pursuing the implications of the life cycle model. One that has become very important of late relates to the economic effects of deficit financing, or more broadly, the public debt. Using the life cycle framework, one can show that these deficits or debts have an effect on the well-being of future generations because they displace productive capital. When the government borrows, it absorbs a certain amount of saving, reducing what's available for investment, or equivalently, for increasing the stock of capital. That is the fundamental mechanism by which a deficit is deleterious. It was recognized that the deficit need not displace investment dollar per dollar because of the fact that life, though finite, extends beyond the time of the deficit. People therefore should recognize that if the deficit is increased now, they will have to pay additional taxes over the rest of their lives, and that should be reflected in their current behavior by some increase in saving. But still much of the deficit should displace private investment.

Then there were several attempts at testing the life cycle model empirically. One of these attempts consisted of gathering evidence that the debt displaces private productive capital. Another one was a comparative study across countries testing whether differential saving behavior could be explained in terms of rates of growth and population structure. These were found to be the main determinants of saving, accounting for a great deal of the observed differences. Finally with my colleague Jacques Drèze there was an extension of the life cycle to a world of uncertainty, which has since given rise to a substantial body of literature, including the combination of life cycle with the theory of portfolio.

There is a third line of contributions (inspired by emerging economic problems), where I was led to pursue some current issues of economic policy. The major issue in the fifties and sixties, a golden period during which all the world was developing in a remarkable fashion, was the emerging stresses on the international payments system, a product of the Bretton Woods agreement. The problem revolved around the inadequate and unsatisfactory mechanisms for creating liquidity to finance world trade—basically through U.S. deficit on current and capital accounts. In a paper with Peter Kenen I suggested that the problem could be resolved through a mechanism for the creation of a new means for international payments called the Medium for International Transactions, which abbreviated into MIT. That was, I hope, a worthwhile contribution to the history of the international means of payment!

The suggestion was not followed, and the problem grew worse as the creation of liquidity by the United States got out of control. In 1971 a second suggestion was advanced, in collaboration with my former student Hossein Askari, to avoid the impending crisis. It involved ratifying the inconvertibility of the dollar but at the same time endowing the rest of the world with the power to control the U.S. deficit through unilateral control of exchange rates. Furthermore countries were to be given an option of protecting their dollar reserves through an exchange guarantee. But whatever its merits, the proposal came too late to prevent a run on the dollar. As the United States had neither the will nor the gold to convert its dollar liabilities into gold, the so-called Bretton Woods system came to an end.

It was also during this period that I agreed to write a regular front-page column for Italy's most prestigious newspaper, *Il Corriere della Sera,* a commitment that I fulfilled fairly faithfully for about five years beginning in late 1972. The most memorable episode in my journalistic career occurred in 1975. The Association of Manufacturers accepted the union's demands for a novel type of escalator clause, which gave for each one percentage increase in the cost of living the same number of liras (rather than the same percentage increase) to all workers, including white-collar workers. The agreement meant that higher-paid workers would not keep up with inflation, whereas lower-paid workers would achieve higher real wages. I warned my former compatriots of the dire consequences that contract would have for the country in terms of inflation, undermining incentive, etc., but I initially found little support. Even my fellow economists kept strangely silent. It was several years before the country, including the workers, understood the damage wrought by that form of indexation and nearly ten years until it was abandoned altogether.

This brings me to the last period: 1974 to date. The essay about which I am keenest in this period was my presidential address to the American Economic Association, of which I had become president in 1976. It was called "The Monetarist Controversy, or Should We Forsake Stabilization

Policies?" This was essentially a head-on collision with the monetarists, who had become very powerful for a variety of reasons. The theme of this essay is that the differences between monetarists and nonmonetarists are not about the working of the economy or the potency of monetary versus fiscal policy; they are instead basically philosophical and political. The monetarists do not want to give the government the power to use discretion because they believe that the government is incapable of using it well. Due to their stupidity or bad faith the monetary authority could not be trusted with any discretionary power in deciding on the appropriate expansion of the money supply. It must be left instead to a mechanical rule. You can trust a computer to compute 3 percent but not the chairman and the board of the Federal Reserve to change that number as circumstances dictate. My argument was to show that this was the only important difference. In addition I pointed to evidence that a fixed rule is not adequate to stabilize the economy, that there is room for stabilization. Finally I showed that in fact stabilization policy tended to work. That was the fundamental message. This issue has reemerged lately, and I'll come back to it briefly.

Other things that happened during this period were further extensions of the life cycle hypothesis. In particular, one interesting application was a study of the effect of transitory tax cuts. In our history we have had a few cases in which taxes were reduced or increased with the announcement that the original tax rates would be reinstated within a year or two. That's what we call a transitory tax cut. The life cycle hypothesis implies that such tax cuts are rather powerless to affect consumption. Since people know that the tax cut is only for a short time, the difference that it makes to their life resources is small. So if they are rational, their consumption will not change much. But if you make a tax change that is "permanent," then of course you will know that you are going to be poorer hereafter, and that will affect consumption. There is evidence, especially from the 1969 temporary tax increase, that in fact transitory tax changes are not very effective in terms of affecting consumption.

Finally there was a series of tests on the then-fashionable idea that the national debt makes no difference to the economy. This idea is associated with the name of Robert Barro, who happens to be one of my students. But despite this circumstance I completely disagree with his theory even though it can be viewed as an extension of the life cycle model. As I indicated before, the original life cycle model asserts the opposite. Mr. Barro's contrary result rests on the assumption of perfect rationality and infinite life. In this case if the government cuts your taxes, incurring a corresponding deficit, and you are rational, you would save the additional after-tax income because you would realize that otherwise you would consume more now at the expense of less consumption thereafter, when additional taxes would be levied to service and retire the debt. Numerous tests carried out for the United States, Italy, and a cross section of other countries all decisively reject the Barro hypothesis.

Another new approach is the rational expectations paradigm, whose foundation happens to rest on my earlier analysis of the forecastability of social events. That is, they have in common the notion that a warranted forecast must be based on all relevant information available for the economy and must take fully into account the effect of the expectation on the event forecasted. This approach has led to the conclusion that policy is altogether powerless in systematically affecting the real economy. The economy goes its own way no matter what you do. However, I happen to disagree wholly with their formulations, not in principle but in every application I have seen. In particular, the ineffectiveness of policy is derived from two highly questionable assumptions: (1) that the economy is unaffected by policy even in the shortest run, as long as agents believe it, and (2) that the agents believe it.

I reject both hypotheses, the first because of slow adjustments in the economy that can be offset by policy, and the second because in my view agents can be expected to use a variety of models, including extrapolation of past experience, and in any event few could be expected to believe that policy is instantly neutral, because it is not. Empirical evidence fully supports my rejection of monetarists' attempts to build their models on their assumptions. Indeed such models have produced much poorer forecasts than those obtained by models like the MPS.

I have tried to make a number of contributions to other current policy issues. I've done a certain amount of work on the effects of inflation. There are two schools here. One school thinks that inflation is catastrophic, and the other thinks that inflation makes no difference at all. Economists, for example, frequently take the position that money has no real effect on the economy and therefore that inflation has none. However, a great deal of work shows that inflation has a lot of effects, some of which are connected with the fact that agents (not unlike many economists!) do not understand the consequences of inflation. I've used that argument in particular to explain a phenomenon that is very puzzling. Why is it that in inflation the stock market typically goes down instead of rising in parallel with inflation? One would think it would rise because equities are a real asset. But, systematically, it goes down.

In the late 1970s the stock market was very low, and I wrote an article explaining the very low market in terms of irrational behavior generated by inflation. I argued that the public does not understand the difference between real and nominal interest rates and that in computing profits the interest rate component must be corrected for inflation. As a result, I said, if the stock market had been rationally valued, it would have been twice as high as it was. The stock market was then at approximately 800, and I predicted that it would double if and when inflation abated. Inflation did abate to 2 to 3 percent and the market did double. The problem was that it then trebled. Actually I had anticipated this possibility, relying on the experience of the World War I period culminating in 1929. Specifically I suggested that, in the process of returning to normal, there would be a lot of capital gain that would be misinterpreted as a maintainable addition to profits. As a result there would be a tendency for stock prices to be bid up beyond the level warranted by fundamentals. Well, I believe that is going on right now. The market is now overshooting. That is, when one takes into account the change in profits and the change in interest rates, one finds that the market is really overshooting rational valuation. Since the market can continue to behave irrationally, it may very well go even higher, but at some point the bubble may be expected to burst [as it finally did a few months later in October 1987].

As I contemplate my contributions, I find one unifying thread: a propensity to swim against the current by challenging the self-evident orthodoxies of the moment, be it that the classics are altogether outdated, or that the rich must save a larger fraction of their income than the poor, or that debt financing is cheaper because the interest rate on high-quality debt is lower than the return on equity.

I would love to be able to continue to play that role. But I don't want to think too much about where I am going. I just like to let things come and be ready to jump in where there is excitement.

Franco Modigliani

Awarded Nobel Prize in 1985. Lecture presented March 24, 1987.

Dates of Birth and Death

June 18, 1918; September 25, 2003

Academic Degrees

D (Jurisprudence) University of Rome, 1939
D (Social Science) New School for Social Research, 1944

Academic Affiliations

Instructor, Bard College, 1942–44
Assistant Professor of Economics, New School for Social Research, 1943–44, 1946–48
Associate Professor of Economics, University of Illinois, 1949–50
Professor of Economics, University of Illinois, 1950–52
Professor of Economics and Industrial Administration, Carnegie Institute of Technology, 1952–60
Professor of Economics, Northwestern University, 1960–62
Professor of Economics and Finance, Massachusetts Institute of Technology, 1962–70
Institute Professor, Massachusetts Institute of Technology, 1970–88
Institute Professor, Emeritus, Massachusetts Institute of Technology, 1988–2003

Selected Books

National Incomes and International Trade, 1953 (with H. Neisser)
Planning Production, Inventories and Work Forces, 1960 (with others)
The Collected Papers of Franco Modigliani, Vols. 1–5, 1980–1989

James M. Buchanan

Born-Again Economist

I have been tempted to expand my title to "Born-Again Economist, with a Prophet but No God." Both parts of this expanded title are descriptive. I was specifically asked to discuss my evolution as an economist, an assignment that I cannot fulfill. I am not a "natural economist" as some of my colleagues are, and I did not "evolve" into an economist.[1] Instead I sprang full blown upon intellectual conversion, after I "saw the light." I shall review this experience below, and I shall defend the implied definition and classification of who qualifies as an economist.

The second part of my expanded title is related to the first. It is my own play on the University of Chicago saying of the 1940s that "there is no god, but Frank Knight is his prophet." I was indeed converted by Frank Knight, but he almost single-mindedly conveyed the message that there exists no god whose pronouncements deserve elevation to the sacrosanct, whether god within or without the scientific academy. Everything, everyone, anywhere, anytime—all is open to challenge and criticism. There is a moral obligation to reach one's own conclusions, even if this sometimes means exposing the prophet whom you have elevated to intellectual guruship.

In an earlier autobiographical essay, "Better Than Plowing,"[2] I identified two persons who were dominant intellectual influences on my own methodology, selection of subject matter, attitude toward scholarship, positive analysis, and normative position. One of these, Knut Wicksell, influenced me exclusively through his ideas. I used the occasion of my Nobel Prize lecture to trace the relationship between Wicksell's precursory foundations and later developments in the theory of public choice, notably its constitutional economics component with which I have been most closely associated. By comparison and contrast this paper offers me the opportunity, even if indirectly, to explore more fully the influence of the second person identified, Frank H. Knight, an influence that was exerted both through his ideas and through a personal friendship that extended over a full quarter century.

The paper is organized as follows. In the following section I try as best I can to describe my state of mind, intellectually and emotionally, before I enrolled in the University of Chicago in 1946. Then I offer a retrospective description of my Chicago experience, with an emphasis on my exposure to the teachings of Frank Knight along with a subconscious conversion to a catallactic methodological perspective on the discipline. The next section briefly traces the catallactic roots of my contributions to public choice theory. After that I discuss the remembered events and persons who were important in giving me the self-confidence that was surely necessary for any career success. Frank Knight was important but by no means unique in this evolution (and in this respect the word "evolution" can be properly applied). I then discuss the influence of Knight's principle of the "relatively absolute absolute" upon my own stance, as moral philosopher, as constitutionalist, and as economic analyst. Finally, I defend my use of the title of my earlier autobiographical essay, "Better Than Plowing," which has been questioned by colleagues and critics. Here I try to examine the motivations that, consciously or unconsciously, may have driven me throughout the course of a long academic career. Why did I do what I did? It may be helpful to explore, even if briefly, this most subjective of questions.

Pre-Chicago: Standards without Coherence

From 1940 I called myself an "economist," as my military records will indicate. I did so because after graduating from Middle Tennessee State Teachers College in June 1940, I was awarded a graduate fellowship in economics at the University of Tennessee for the academic year 1940–41, and I earned a master's degree in 1941. By the academic counters, I took courses labeled "economics," and I made good grades. But as I have noted, however, I learned little or no economics in my preferred definition during that Knoxville year. I surveyed the workings and structures of the institutions of Roosevelt's New Deal; I came to understand central banking theory and policy; I learned something about taxation and budgeting processes; I learned a bit of elementary statistics, especially in practice. But neither in these courses nor in my prior undergraduate experience did I have proper exposure to the central principle of market organization. I remained blissfully ignorant of the coordinating properties of a decentralized market process, an ignorance that made me vulnerable to quasi-Marxist arguments and explanations about economic history and economic reality but also guaranteed that my mind was an open slate when I finally gained the exposure in question.

During the Knoxville year I did learn to appreciate the dedication of the research scholar though my association with Charles P. White, whose course in research methods was the intellectual high point. White instilled in me the moral standards of the research process. My experience with him, as both graduate student and research assistant, gave me something that seems so often absent in the training of the economists of the postwar decades, whose technology so often outdistances their norms for behavior.

By subject matter, by terminology, and with a bit of technique I left Knoxville as an "economist," but I lacked the coherence of vision of the economic process that I should now make the sine qua non of anyone who proposes to use this label. I have often wondered whether or not I was relatively alone in my ignorance, or whether something akin to my experience has been shared by others who purport to pass as professional economists without the foggiest notion of what they are about.

Chicago, 1946

I enrolled in the University of Chicago for the winter quarter, 1946. I had chosen the University of Chicago without much knowledge about its faculty in economics. I was influenced almost exclusively by an undergraduate teacher in political science, C. C. Sims, who had earned a doctorate at Chicago in the late 1930s. Sims impressed on me the intellectual ferment of the university, the importance of ideas, and the genuine life of the mind that was present at the institution. His near-idyllic sketch appealed to me, and I made the plunge into serious study for the first time in my life. In retrospect I could not have made a better selection. Sims was precisely on target in conveying the intellectual excitement of the University of Chicago, an excitement that remains, to this day, unmatched anywhere else in the world.

During the first quarter I took courses with Frank Knight, T. W. Schultz, and Simeon Leland. I was among the very first group of graduate students to return to the academy after discharge from military service during World War II. We swelled the ranks of the graduate classes at Chicago and elsewhere.

Within a few short weeks, perhaps by mid-February 1946, I had undergone a conversion in my understanding of how an economy operates. For the first time I was able to think in terms of the ordering principle of a market economy. The stylized model for the working of the competitive structure gave me the benchmark for constructive criticism of the economy to be observed. For the first time I was indeed an economist.

I attribute this conversion directly to Frank Knight's teachings, which perhaps raises more new questions than it answers. Knight was not a systematic instructor. More important, he remained ambiguous in his own interpretation of what economics is all about. He was never able to shed the allocating-maximizing paradigm, which tends to distract attention from the coordination paradigm that I have long deemed central to the discipline.[3] But Knight's economics was a curious amalgam of these partially conflicting visions. And for me the organizational emphasis was sufficient to relegate the allocative thrust to a place of secondary relevance. In this respect I was fortunate in my ignorance. Had I received "better" pre-Chicago training in economics, as widely interpreted, I would have scarcely been able to elevate the coordination principle to the central place it has occupied in my thinking throughout my research career. Like so many of my peers, aside from the few who were exposed early to Austrian theory, I might have remained basically an allocationist.

There are subtle but important differences between the allocationist-maximization and the catallactic-coordination paradigm in terms of the implications for normative evaluation of institutions. In particular the evaluation of the market order may depend critically on which of these partially conflicting paradigms remains dominant in one's stylized vision. To the allocationist the market is efficient *if it works*. His test of the market becomes the comparison with the abstract ideal defined in his logic. To the catallactist the market coordinates the separate activities of self-seeking persons *without the necessity of detailed political direction*. The test of the market is the comparison with its institutional alternative, politicized decision making.

There is of course no necessary implication of the differing paradigms for identifying the normative stance of practicing economists. Many modern economists remain firm supporters of the market order while at the same time remaining within the maximizing paradigm. I submit here, however, that there are relatively few economists whose vision is dominated by the catallactic perspective on market order who are predominantly critics of such an order. Once the relevant comparison becomes that between the workings of the market, however imperfect this may seem, and the workings of its political alternative, there must indeed be very strong offsetting sources of evaluation present.

The apparent digression of the preceding paragraphs is important for my narrative and for an understanding of how my conversion by Frank Knight influenced my research career after Chicago. Those of us who entered graduate school in the immediate postwar years were all socialists of one sort or another. Some of us were what I have elsewhere called "libertarian socialists," who placed a high residual value on individual liberty but simply did not understand the principle of market coordination. We were always libertarians first, socialists second. And we tended to be grossly naive in our thinking about political alternatives. To us, the idealized attractions of populist democracy seemed preferable to those of the establishment-controlled economy. It was this sort of young socialist in particular who was especially ready for immediate conversion upon exposure to teachings that transmitted the principle of market coordination.[4]

An understanding of this principle enabled us to concentrate our long-held anti-establishment evaluative norms on politics and governance and open up the prospect that economic interaction, at least in the limit, need not embody the exercise of man's power over man. By our libertarian standards, politics had always been deemed to fail. Now by these same standards market may, just may, not involve exploitation.

An important element in Knight's economics was his emphasis on the organizational structure of markets, and it was this emphasis that elevated the coordination principle to center stage despite his continued obeisance to economizing-maximizing. Once attention is drawn to a structure, to process, and away from resources, goods, and services, many of the technical trappings of orthodox economic theory fall away. Here Knight's approach became institutional, in the proper meaning of this term.

It is useful at this point to recall that Frank Knight's career shared a temporal dimensionality with the seminal American institutionalists Clarence Ayres, John R. Commons, and Thorstein Veblen. He treated their technical economics with derision, but he shared with them an interest in the structure of social and economic interaction. Knight did not extend his institutional inquiry much beyond the seminal work on human wants that exposed some of the shallow presuppositions of economic orthodoxy. He did not, save in a few passing references, examine the structure of politics, considered the only alternative to markets.

Public Choice and the Catallactic Paradigm

Public choice is the inclusive term that describes the extension of analysis to the political alternatives to markets. It seems highly unlikely that this extension could have been effectively made by economists who viewed the market merely as an allocative mechanism, quite independently of its political role in reducing the range and scope of politicized activity. I can of course speak here only of my own experience, but it seems doubtful if I could have even recognized the Wicksellian message had not Knight's preparatory teachings of the coordination principle paved the way.

The point may be illustrated by the related, but yet quite distinct, strands of modern inquiry summarized under the two rubrics "social choice" and "public choice." I have elsewhere identified the two central elements in public choice theory as (1) the conceptualization of politics as exchange, and (2) the model of *Homo economicus*.[5] The second of these elements is shared with social choice theory, which seeks to ground social choices on the values of utility-maximizing individuals. Where social choice theory and public choice theory differ—and dramatically— lies in the first element noted. Social choice theory does not conceptualize politics as complex exchange; rather politics is implicitly or explicitly modeled in the age-old conception that there must exist some unique and hence discoverable "best" result. This element in social choice theory, from Arrow on, stems directly for the allocative paradigm in orthodox economics, and the maximization of the social welfare function becomes little more than the extension of the standard efficiency calculus to the aggregative economy.

By contrast, the extension of the catallactic paradigm—the emphasis on the theory of exchange rather than allocation—to politics immediately calls attention to the institutional structure of political decision making. Without Frank Knight as teacher and as role model, would Knut Wicksell's great work have been discovered by the fledgling economist that I was in 1948? I have strong reasons for doubt on this score.

The Evolution of Confidence

When I reflect on my own experiences over a tolerably long academic career, I come back again and again to identifiable events and persons that built up or bolstered my confidence, that made me, always an outsider, feel potentially competent among my academic peers. The first such event came with the release of academic grade records at the end of my second year at Middle Tennessee State Teachers College in 1938. My name led all the rest. For the first time I realized that despite my rural origins, my day-student status, and my graduation from a tiny struggling high school, I could compete with the town students, the live-in students, and with all those whose earlier education was acknowledged to be superior to mine.

A second such event occurred in January 1942, when I finished a three-month stint as a midshipman and was commissioned an ensign in the United States Naval Reserve. Again, despite my Tennessee heritage and my mediocre academic experience at both Middle Tennessee and the University of Tennessee, I ranked sixth or seventh in a midshipman class of some six hundred college and university graduates from across the land. The Tennessee country boy could indeed hold his own.

After a successful, interesting, exciting, and easy four years on active military duty in the Pacific theater of war, which I spent for the most part on the staff of Admiral Nimitz at Pearl Harbor and at Guam, my confidence was once again put to the test when I entered graduate school at the University of Chicago in January 1946. Here the test was of a totally different dimension. I knew that I could compete successfully in terms of the ordinary criteria—academic grades, degrees, and honors. I do not recall ever entertaining the slightest doubt about my ability to finish doctoral requirements. What I did not know was whether I could go beyond these criteria and enter the narrowed ranks of producing scholars who could generate ideas worthy of the serious attention of their disciplinary peers.

At this point Frank H. Knight again enters my narrative. Had my Chicago exposure been limited to the likes of Jacob Viner and Milton Friedman, both of whom were also my teachers there, I doubt that I should have ever emerged from the familiarly large ranks of Ph.D.s with no or few publications. Jacob Viner, the classically erudite scholar whose self-appointed task in life seemed to be that of destroying confidence in students, and Milton Friedman, whose dominating intellectual brilliance in argument and analysis relegated the student to the role of fourth-best imitation—these were not the persons who encouraged students to believe that they too might eventually have ideas worthy of merit.

Frank Knight was dramatically different. In the classroom he came across as a man engaged always in a search for ideas. He puzzled over principles, from the commonsensical to the esoteric, and he stood continuously dismayed at the arrogance of those who spouted forth the learned wisdom. Knight gave those of us who bothered to listen the abiding notion that all is up for intellectual grabs, that much of what paraded as truth was highly questionable, and that the hallmark of a scholar was his courage in cutting through the intellectual haze. The willingness to deny all gods, to hold nothing sacrosanct—these were the qualities of mind and character that best describe Frank Knight. And gods, as I use the term here, include the authorities in one's own discipline as well as those who claim domain over other dimensions of truth. Those of us who were so often confused in so many things were bolstered by this Knightian stance before all gods. Only gradually, and much later, did we come to realize that in these qualities it was Frank Knight, not his peers, who attained the rank of genius.

As he was the first to acknowledge, Frank Knight was not a clever or brilliant thinker. He was an inveterate puzzler; but his thought process probed depths that the scholars about him could not realize even to exist. To Knight, things were never so simple as they seemed, and he remained at base tolerant in the extreme because he sensed the elements of truth in all principles.

There were many graduate students, both in my own cohort and before and after my time, who could not take in or relate to the Knightian stance before the gods. To these "outsiders" Knight seemed a bumbling and confused teacher, whose writings mirrored his thought and whose primary attribute appeared to be intellectual incoherence. To a few of us, what seemed confusion to others came across as profundity, actual or potential, and despite the chasm that we acknowledged to exist between his mind and ours, Knight left us with the awful realization that if we did not have the simple courage to work out our own answers, we were vulnerable to victimization by false gods.

My own understanding, appreciation, and admiration for Frank Knight were aided and abetted by the development, early on, of a close personal relationship. Some three or four weeks after enrollment in his course I visited Knight's jumbled office. What was expected to be a five-minute talk stretched over two hours, to be matched several times during my two and a half years at Chicago, and beyond. He took an interest in me because we shared several dimensions of experience. Both of us were country boys, reared in agricultural poverty, well aware of the basic drudgery of rural existence but also appreciative of the independence of a life on the land. Knight left his native Illinois in his teens for rudimentary college instruction in my home state of Tennessee, and he enrolled in graduate studies at the University of Tennessee where I too had first commenced graduate work. These common threads of experience established for me a relationship that I shared with no other professor. We shared other interests, including an appreciation of the gloomy poetry of Thomas Hardy and the fun of the clever off-color joke.

Of course I was a one-way beneficiary of this relationship. Knight was the advisor who told me not to waste my time taking formal courses in philosophy, who corrected my dissertation grammar in great detail, and who became the role model that has never been replaced or even slightly dislodged over a long academic career. In trying to assess my own development, I find it impossible to imagine what I might have been and become without exposure to Frank Knight.

Let me return to confidence, lest I digress too much. Both T. W. Schultz and Earl J. Hamilton deserve inclusion in this narrative account. Schultz encouraged students by his expressed willingness to locate potential merit in arguments that must have often approached the absurd. I was never a formal student of Earl Hamilton. I did not enroll in his economic history courses at Chicago. Nonetheless during my last year at Chicago, 1948, Hamilton sought me out and took a direct personal interest in my prospects. As with Knight, the sharing of common experience in rural poverty created a personal bond, supplemented in this case by a passion for baseball, reflected by trips to both Cubs and White Sox home games. Hamilton enjoyed giving advice to those he singled out for possible achievement, and with me two separate imperatives stand out in recall: the potential payoff to hard work and the value of mastery of foreign languages.

Perhaps Earl J. Hamilton's most important influence on my career came after 1948, during his tenure as editor of the *Journal of Political Economy*. First of all he forced me to follow up on his recommendation about language skills by sending me French, German, and Italian books for review. Second, he handled my early article submissions with tolerance, understanding, and encouragement rather than with brutal or carping rejections that might have proved fatal to further effort. Hamilton was indeed a tough editor, and every article that I finally published during his tenure was laboriously transformed and dramatically pared down through a process of multiple revisions and resubmissions. Without Hamilton as an editor who cared, my writing style would never have attained the economy it possesses, and my willingness to venture into subject matter beyond the boundaries of the orthodox might have been squelched early. With Earl J. Hamilton as editor, by the mid-1950s I had several solid papers on the record—a number sufficient to enable me to accept the occasional rejection slip with equanimity rather than despair.

I noted earlier how Friedman's analytic brilliance exerted a negating effect on those he instructed. An event occurred early in my post-Chicago years that tended to erase this negative influence by placing Milton Friedman too among the ranks of those who take intellectual tumbles. A relatively obscure scholar, Cecil G. Phipps, of the University of Florida, located and exposed a logical error in one of Friedman's papers,[6] an error that Friedman graciously acknowledged.[7] To this day I have never told Milton how this simple event contributed so massively to my self-confidence.

The Relatively Absolute Absolute

I have already discussed how Frank Knight's willingness to challenge all authority—intellectual, moral, or scientific—indirectly established confidence in those for whom he served as role model. Any account of such an influence would be seriously incomplete, and indeed erroneous, if the philosophical stance suggested is one of relativism-cum-nihilism against the claim of any and all authority. It is at precisely this point that Frank Knight directly taught me the philosophical principle that has served me so well over so many years and in so many applications. This principle is that of the *relatively absolute absolute,* which allows for a philosophical way station between the extremes of absolutism on the one hand and relativism on the other, both of which are to be rejected.

Acceptance of this principle necessarily requires that there exist a continuing tension between the forces that dictate adherence to and acceptance of authority and those very qualities that define freedom of thought and inquiry. Knight's expressed willingness to challenge all authority was embedded within a wisdom that also recognized the relevance of tradition in ideas, manners, and institutions. This wisdom dictates that for most purposes and most of the time prudent behavior consists of acting as if the authority that exists does indeed possess legitimacy. The principle of the relatively absolute absolute requires that we adhere to and accept the standards of established or conventional authority in our ordinary behavior, whether this be personal, scientific, or political, while at the same time and at still another (and "higher") level of consciousness we call all such standards into question, even to the extent of proposing change.

In relation to my own work this principle of the relatively absolute absolute is perhaps best exemplified in the critically important distinction between the post-constitutional and the constitutional levels of political interaction. More generally, the distinction is that between choosing among strategies of play in a game that is defined by a set of rules and choosing among alternative sets of rules. To the chooser of strategies under defined rules, the rules themselves are to be treated as relatively absolute absolutes, as constraints that are a part of the existential reality but at the same time may be subject to evaluation, modification, and change. In this extension and application of the Knightian principle to the political constitution—and particularly by way of analogy with the choices of strategies and rules of ordinary games—I was stimulated and encouraged by my colleague at the University of Virginia, Rutledge Vining, who had also been strongly influenced by the teachings of Frank Knight.

Why "Better Than Plowing"?

As noted, in 1986 I wrote an autobiographical essay called "Better Than Plowing," a title I borrowed directly from Frank Knight, who used it to describe his own attitude toward a career in the academy. To me the title seemed also descriptive, and it does, I think, convey my sense of comparative evaluation between "employment" in the academy and in the economy beyond. This title also suggests, even if somewhat vaguely, the sheer luck of those of us who served in the academy during the years of the baby-boom educational explosion, luck that was translated into rents of magnitudes beyond imaginable dreams.

To my surprise constructive critics have challenged the appropriateness of the "Better Than Plowing" title for my more general autobiographical essay. To these critics this title seems too casual, too much a throwaway phrase, too flippant a description of a research career that, objectively and externally considered, seems to have embodied central purpose or intent. This unexpected invitation to write a second autobiographical essay provides me with an opportunity to respond to these critics and at the same time to offer additional insights into my development as an economist.

The many books and papers that I have written and published between 1949 and 1987 make up an objective reality that is "there" for all to read and to interpret as they choose. These words and pages exist in some space analogous to the Popperian third world. There is a surprising coherence in this record that I can recognize as well or better than any interpretative critical biographer. As Robert Tollison and I have suggested in our analysis of autobiography,[8] the autobiographer possesses a record over and beyond that which is potentially available to any biographer. The person whose acts created the objective record lives with the subject record itself. And such a person, as autobiographer, would be immoral if he relied on the objective record to impute to his life's work a purpose-oriented coherence that had never emerged into consciousness.

I recognize of course that my own research-publication record may be interpreted as the output of a methodological and normative individualist whose underlying purpose has always been to further philosophical support for individual liberty. In subjective recall, however, this motivational thrust has never informed my conscious work effort. I have throughout my career and with only a few exceptions sought to clarify ambiguities and confusions and clear up neglected pockets of analysis in the received arguments of fellow economists, social scientists, and philosophers. To the extent that conscious motivation has entered these efforts, it has always been the sheer enjoyment of working out ideas, of creating the reality that is reflected finally in the finished manuscript. Proof of my normative disinterest lies in my failure to be interested in what happens once a manuscript is a finished draft—a failure that accounts for my sometimes inattention to choice of publisher, to promotional details, and to the potential for either earnings or influence.

I look on myself as being much closer in spirit to the artist who creates on canvas or stone than to the scientist who discovers only that which he accepts to exist independently of his actions. And I should reject, and categorically, any affinity with the preacher who writes or speaks for the express and only purpose of persuading others to accept his prechosen set of values.

In all of this, once again, Frank Knight has served as my role model. His famous criticism of Pigou's road case is exemplary.[9] By introducing property rights, Knight enabled others to see the whole Pigovian analysis in a new light. Something was indeed created in the process. I like to think that perhaps some of my own works on public debt, opportunity cost, earmarked taxes, clubs, ordinary politics, and constitutional rules may have effected comparable shifts in perspective. The fact that these efforts have been commonly characterized by a reductionist thrust embodying an individualist methodology is explained, very simply, by my inability to look at the world through other than an individualist window.

It is as if the artist who has only red paints produces pictures that are only red of hue. Such an artist does not choose to paint red pictures and then, instrumentally, purchase red paints. Instead the artist uses the instruments at hand to do what he can and must do, while enjoying himself immensely in the process. The fact that others are able to secure new insights with the aid of his creations and that this in turn provides artist with a bit of bread—this gratuitous result enables the artist, too, to entitle his autobiographical essay "Better Than Plowing."

Notes

1. James M. Buchanan, "The Qualities of a Natural Economist," in Charles. Rowley, ed., *Democracy and Public Choice* (New York: Blackwell, 1987), 9–19.

2. James M. Buchanan, "Better Than Plowing," *Banca Nazionale del Lavoro Quarterly Review* 159 (December 1986): 359–375.

3. For an extended discussion of Knight's ambiguity in this respect, see my paper, "The Economizing Element in Knight's Ethical Critique of Capitalist Order," *Ethics* 98 (October 1987): 61–75.

4. For a discussion of two kinds of socialism in this setting, see the title essay in my book, *Liberty, Market, and State: Political Economy in the 1980s* (New York: New York University Press, 1985).

5. James M. Buchanan, "The Public Choice Perspective," *Economia delle scelte publiche* 1 (January 1983): 7–15.

6. Cecil G. Phipps, "Friedman's 'Welfare' Effects," *Journal of Political Economy* LX (August 1952): 332–334.

7. Milton Friedman, "A Reply," *Journal of Political Economy* LX (August 1952): 334–336.

8. James M. Buchanan and Robert D. Tollison, "A Theory of Truth in Autobiography," *Kyklos* 39 (Fasc. 4, 1986): 507–517.

9. Frank H. Knight, "Fallacies in the Interpretation of Social Cost," *Quarterly Journal of Economics* XXXVIII (1924): 582–606. Reprinted in *The Ethics of Competition* (London: Allen and Unwin, 1935), 217–236.

James M. Buchanan
Awarded Nobel Prize in 1986. Lecture presented October 28, 1987.

Dates of Birth and Death
October 3, 1919; January 9, 2013

Academic Degrees
B.A., Middle Tennessee State College, 1940
M.S., University of Tennessee, 1941
Ph.D., University of Chicago, 1948

Academic Affiliations
Associate Professor, University of Tennessee, 1948–50
Professor, University of Tennessee, 1950–51
Professor, Department of Economics, Florida State University, 1954–56
Professor, James Wilson Department of Economics, University of Virginia, 1956–62
Paul G. McIntire Professor of Economics, University of Virginia, 1962–68
Professor of Economics, University of California, Los Angeles, 1968–69
University Distinguished Professor, Virginia Polytechnic Institute and State University, 1969–83
Holbert L. Harris University Professor, George Mason University, 1983–2007; Emeritus, 2007–13

Selected Books
Fiscal Theory and Political Economy, 1960
The Calculus of Consent, 1962 (with G. Tullock)
The Limits of Liberty, 1975
The Power to Tax, 1980 (with G. Brennan) *The Reason of Rules,* 1985 (with G. Brennan) *Liberty, Market, and State,* 1985
Economics: Between Predictive Science and Moral Philosophy, 1987
Explorations into Constitutional Economics, 1989
The Collected Works of James M. Buchanan, Vols. 1–20, 1999–2002

Robert M. Solow

To be honest, I should warn you that I am going to tell you as little about myself as I can get away with in a lecture about "My Evolution as an Economist." My reason is not that I have anything to hide. I wish I had more to hide; that would at least suggest an exciting life. My problem is that I think the "cult of personality" is slowly swamping our culture. You can see it at its most dangerous in presidential elections, where eyebrows seem to be more important than ideas. I tend to blame that on television, which is a better medium for eyebrows than for economic theory. But that sort of technological determinism won't quite do: it leaves us with the task of explaining the psychologization of almost everything, the success of pop books on character, the fact that seven out of ten nonfiction best sellers are biographies, the importance attached to the "personal relationship" between Mr. Reagan and Mrs. Thatcher. Something pretty deep is going on there. (I don't mean between Mr. Reagan and Mrs. Thatcher!) Fortunately, academic economists seem to have a big comparative disadvantage when it comes to personal interest. I wouldn't have anything to say to Barbara Walters even if she had anything to say to me.

Anyway, what I have called the cult of personality has to be a sign of cultural decay. ("Just lie back and tell us when you first had that feeling, Professor Solow.") I don't mean to twist and turn in order to avoid biographical details, but I would rather concentrate on social and intellectual currents of slightly broader significance.

Shortly after the death of John von Neumann some thirty-odd years ago Robert Strotz, who was then editor of *Econometrica,* asked me to write a memorial article about him. Von Neumann and Frank Ramsey must be the two noneconomists who have, in their spare moments, had the greatest influence on what professional economists actually do. (On the merits, Harold Hotelling certainly belongs in their class; but he is much closer to having been, or having become, a part-time professional economist.) I never wrote the article, but I did think about it for a while. A puzzle presented itself: How did von Neumann become interested in economics anyway? I asked a number of people who might have known, but none could give me a useful answer. Then I sent a note to Karl Menger (the grandson of the Menger who was a cofounder of the Austrian school of economics) because he had run a mathematical seminar in Vienna that was attended occasionally by von Neumann, Abraham Wald, and some economists. Menger gave me a wonderful answer to my question. He said that everyone in Austria-Hungary was interested in economics.

Well, I grew up in the 1930s—graduated from high school in January 1940, in fact. I can certainly say that everyone in Brooklyn in the 1930s was interested in economics. And not only in economics: intelligent high school students of my day were conscious not only of the Great Depression but also of the rise of Fascism and Nazism, events that were certainly not independent of the worldwide depression. It was an obvious fact of life to us that our society was malfunctioning politically and economically and that nobody really knew how to explain it or what to do about it.

This is important for the subject at hand. I think it throws some light on the current state and recent evolution of economics. I said that I graduated from high school in 1940. I was a couple of years younger than my classmates; but anyone who was eighteen in 1940 is sixty-six now. Soon there will be no more active economists who remember the 1930s clearly. The generation of economists that was moved to study economics by the feeling that we desperately needed to understand the depression will soon have retired. Most of today's younger and middle-aged macroeconomists think of "the business cycle" as a low-variance, moderately autocorrelated, stationary, stochastic process taking place around a generally satisfactory trend. That is an altogether different frame of mind from the one with which I grew up in the profession.

Now maybe they have the right idea. I don't want to sound like an old codger who goes around all the time bundled up in fear that the Blizzard of '88 may happen again tomorrow. The underlying intellectual problem is more complicated than that. I don't think for a minute that a major depression is a probabilistically frequent event. But I am not sure that it is useful to model it as a probabilistically rare event either. I rather doubt that the probabilistic way of thinking about major depressions sends the right signals—or receives them—in the first place. I think that a lot of my contemporaries regard the possibility of deep recession mainly as an indicator that there are mechanisms latent in an industrial capitalist economy that can cause it to stall for an uncomfortably long time away from any satisfactory equilibrium. The trigger may be a mixture of endogenous and exogenous events. One of the jobs of macroeconomics, perhaps its main job, is to understand what those mechanisms are and what defensive policies they call for. That is surely not the only way of sizing up or thinking about macroeconomics. But it strikes me as a mistake for contemporary macroeconomics to assume away any such possibility.

I arrived at Harvard College in September 1940. Economics A was one of my four freshman courses. I had no idea then of becoming an economist; I probably didn't know there was such a thing as a professional economist, or what one did. My recollection is that I had some notion of studying biology; I certainly took a two-semester course in biology that first year and got an A, but it was pretty clear that biology was not for me. So I opted for a sort of general social science major, and for the next year or two I took courses in sociology, anthropology, and psychology as well as economics.

Undergraduate students of economics at Harvard College in 1940–1942 did not learn any coherent way of thinking about the Depression from which the United States was just emerging. The fact that real GNP rose by 8 percent between 1939 and 1940 and another 18 percent between 1940 and 1941 and that the unemployment rate fell by 7.3 percentage points between 1939 and 1941 under the stimulus of war production, both for export and for use at home, might have offered some hint. (We didn't know what the real GNP was, you realize; the data came later. But industrial production, which was measured, rose by 15 and 18 percent in 1940 and 1941, respectively.) Our textbooks and courses offered us no sense of a systematic understanding of the dramatic events taking place all around us. The memoirs of political figures of the time make it clear that they had no clue either.

It wasn't all dull, of course. I heard Sumner Slichter and John Dunlop lecture about labor economics, and Paul Sweezy about Marxian economics, and I learned things from all of them that I still remember.

Two of the three books that really formed my generation of economists after the war had already been published: *The General Theory of Employment, Interest and Money* in 1936 and Hicks's *Value and Capital* in 1939. (The third, Samuelson's *Foundations of Economic Analysis,* appeared in 1947.) The galaxy of star graduate students of the time—Samuelson, Metzler, Musgrave, Tobin, Alexander, et al.—were no doubt clued in to these ideas that would come to dominate economics for a while. None of it percolated to undergraduates so soon. The ideas were too new and Harvard economics was too sclerotic at the time. The point is that I had no feeling that economic analysis could penetrate to the heart of what was going on in the world. I certainly hadn't made up my mind to major in economics or to become an economist. What I did instead was to volunteer for the army. It seemed more constructive than what I was doing.

Three years later I came back and, almost without thinking about it, signed up to finish my undergraduate degree as an economics major. The timing was such that I had to make a decision in a hurry. No doubt I acted as if I were maximizing an infinite discounted sum of one-period utilities, but you couldn't prove it by me. To me it felt as if I were saying to myself: "What the hell."

At that time, September 1945, Harvard still had an effective "tutorial system." Every junior and senior—I was still a junior—was assigned a member of the faculty as a "tutor" to be seen for an hour once a week. The tutor would assign things to read, occasionally ask the tutee to write a short paper, and then the two would discuss the week's work. My tutor was Wassily Leontief. Maybe it was just dumb luck. Maybe the powers that be took note of the fact that I had been an A student. Maybe it was just the opposite; maybe being tutored by a foreigner—and a theorist at that—was like being stuck in a ghetto. In any case it was a turning point for me. From Leontief I learned that economics was not a hodgepodge but a subject with a disciplined theoretical and empirical structure. Over the next few years he taught me the details of some of that structure. I would have to say that it was Leontief who turned me into an economist.

He did one other thing for me that will now seem quaint, but it is worth mentioning for just that reason. In those days you could do an undergraduate degree in economics at Harvard, and probably a Ph.D. as well, without knowing or using a bit of calculus. (Everyone had to read the text of *Value and Capital* [or at least part I] but not the mathematical appendix, elementary as that is by today's standards.) I had been a good math student in high school; it might have been my best subject. But it never occurred to me to do any more at the college level, certainly not in connection with economics. It was probably forbidden for Professor Leontief to recruit students to the study of mathematics and mathematical economic theory, nor did he do so. What he did do was to begin some of our weekly sessions by saying: "You should read thus and such an article ... but no, you can't. You don't know any mathematics. Well, try this one instead." I may be slow-witted, but I'm not *stupid*. I wanted to read the good stuff. So pretty soon I signed up for the calculus sequence and went on in mathematics until I had learned a little more than I needed to know for everyday work. That is probably less than any good graduate student with an interest in theory knows today. It is amazing that it was such a big deal in those days. People got hot under the collar about it.

What I did not learn from Professor Leontief—and in fact did not learn at all during the years 1945 to 1949 while finishing my undergraduate degree and taking courses and examinations for the Ph.D.— was macroeconomics. That is an anachronistic turn of phrase anyway. There were no courses in macroeconomics in the catalog. There were courses on "business cycles"; mine was taught by Gottfried Haberler, and a very good course it was. *Prosperity and Depression* sticks to the ribs. I recommend it to anyone. When I began to teach at MIT in 1950, one of the first economics courses I taught was called "Business Cycles." It first acquired the label "Macroeconomics" a decade later, I would guess.

By macroeconomics I mean the study of complete aggregative models of the economy. Back then it was almost a code word for Keynesian economics, what he called "the theory of output as a whole." Trivial historical accident was at work in shaping my education. My contemporaries, some of them, learned about macroeconomics from Alvin Hansen. The locus was the graduate course in money and banking that he taught jointly with John H. Williams. As luck would have it, I enrolled in "Money and Banking" right after the war, probably in 1945 or 1946. Hansen was on leave; the entire two-semester course was taught by Williams. Moreover, because of the flood of returning veterans the graduate and undergraduate versions of "Money and Banking" were combined. (We used to say that the only difference was that the undergraduates were graded to a higher standard.) So I was never called upon to take the specifically graduate-level course.

John Williams was a famous skeptic about Keynes, about macroeconomics, in fact about everything. Skepticism is a very good thing in an economist, and perhaps his lesson stuck with me. In the particular case of macroeconomic theory, however, I never really learned what it was I was supposed to be skeptical *of*. Caught up as I was in learning economic theory in the Leontief manner, I never had as much contact with Alvin

Hansen as I should have. I was never formally enrolled in the famous fiscal policy seminar, though I occasionally attended a session and my wife was a regular member.

There is a temptation to exaggerate this picture. I learned something about macroeconomics from slightly older and more advanced colleagues like John Duesenberry and Thomas Schelling. From Richard Goodwin, then an assistant professor, I learned not only the technique of building dynamic macroeconomic models but a whole attitude toward them that still strikes me as right. It emphasizes keeping them simple and focused, answering a simple question with a strong model. The art is in concentrating the subtlety in the right place.

And of course I could read. But graduate students then—and now?—had time to read only what they were expected to read. It is probably fair to say that I finished my coursework at Harvard in 1949 and passed my exam, still not having acquired what I thought economics was supposed to provide: a working understanding, not exactly of the business cycle but of the moving level of economic activity, its equilibrium or self-perpetuating properties, and its disequilibrium properties. It is hard to describe because the vocabulary that later came to seem suitable—that of Keynesian economics, not necessarily the "economics of Keynes"—is now unfashionable, and the vocabulary that is now fashionable seems designed to suppress the very curiosity that I am trying to describe.

I have gone on about this nevertheless because I think that the difference between the attitude I am reporting and the attitude that gives rise to today's "equilibrium business cycle theory" has to do with a sense of the precariousness of aggregate economic performance. It may be the experience of the 1930s and the dissolution of the 1930s in the Second World War that lies at the bottom of this difference in approach. But the difference is not simply to be dismissed as an anachronistic fear that 1932 might come around again. That is hardly the point. The point, to repeat my earlier remark, is rather the feeling that such extreme events suggest the existence of mechanisms that macroeconomic theory ought to be able to talk about.

Anyway, I had plenty to do. I spent all of 1949–50 and part of 1950–51, when I started teaching at MIT, producing a Ph.D. thesis that tried to model the dynamics of the size distribution of incomes, mostly wage and salary incomes, as the outcome of a random process into and out of employment with accompanying transitions from one wage level to another. It was entirely my own idea. There is a story behind that choice too.

The Harvard of my time taught statistics scandalously badly. I would hardly have known what I was missing if Sidney Alexander, filling in for a couple of weeks as lecturer in the graduate course in economic statistics, had not lifted the curtain and let the class peek at the real thing. Also, Frederick Mosteller arrived at Harvard in the Department of Social Relations and taught a one-semester introductory course in mathematical statistics and then took me in for a reading course. My recollection is that he taught me not so much technique as understanding. On his advice I grabbed the chance offered by a dissertation fellowship from the Social Science Research Council to work on my thesis while taking courses in mathematical statistics at Columbia University. So I learned the details of statistical theory from Abraham Wald (in his last year of teaching before his death in an airplane crash in India), Jacob Wolfowitz, and T. W. Anderson.

When I began teaching at MIT in September 1950 it was as an assistant professor of statistics in the Department of Economics and Social Science. In the glow of what I had learned from Mosteller and the Columbia department, I think I tended to spend my life working on probability models in economics. I already had a head start on my Ph.D. thesis. (It won the David A. Wells Prize at Harvard, good for five hundred 1951 dollars and publication in book form as soon as I submitted the manuscript. I never did so. The Harvard endowment is today several thousand dollars richer because I thought that the job could be better done but never found time to do it.) Anyone who gets his kicks out of making comprehensible models that are applicable to real life can hardly help noticing that the theory of probability rates pretty high on the scales of intrinsic interest and practical success. But that was not the way it worked out.

Along with statistics and econometrics courses, I taught, as I mentioned earlier, the graduate course on business cycles. Then of course I had to figure out for myself what it was that I wanted students to know. We often say among ourselves that the best way to learn a subject is to teach it. There is some truth in that, but one wants to be clear about what the kernel of truth is. You don't have to teach a subject to master its mechanical and technical details. Books will do quite nicely for that. The experience of teaching does, if you take it seriously, require you to figure out how to explain the subject at hand clearly; and that is already a higher level of understanding than the first. But there is a higher level yet. The second or third time you teach a course you may realize that you have a feeling for the topic's shape, its organizing principles, its message, its relation to the rest of economics and to real economic life. So it was; I began by teaching about business cycle theories—Pigou, Robertson, Haberler, Kalecki, Metzler, Hansen, Samuelson, Hicks, that sort of thing—and I ended up teaching macroeconomics (and growth). It would be satisfying to say that I educated myself. But that would be at most half true. My new colleagues at MIT—Paul Samuelson, of course, but also Robert Bishop and Cary Brown—had been part of the transitional generation. They had been among the first to feel the shock waves when J. M. Keynes invented macroeconomics. (Make no mistake: that is what he did. I have elsewhere quoted A. C. Pigou, who must have known, on this subject. "Nobody before [Keynes], so far as I know, had brought all the relevant factors, real and monetary at once, together in a single formal scheme, through which their interplay could be coherently investigated." That is exactly what I am talking about.)

Macroeconomics in that spirit is what I had been missing. I found it in the conversation of my colleagues in the MIT department and pretty quickly and easily made it part of my own mental furniture. Strangely enough, for an American, I was at that time more familiar with the writings of the Swedish economists than with Keynes or the immediate English Keynesians. Somewhere in graduate school I had read Lindahl, Myrdal, Ohlin, Lundberg, and most especially Wicksell. Those books are still on my shelves. It was probably Haberler who introduced me to the modern Stockholm school (and the GI Bill that paid for the books). Wicksell I found for myself, and he has always been a favorite for several reasons. The one that matters here is that he, among the great nineteenth-century economists, came closest to the spirit of macroeconomics. In *Interest and Prices* and again in the note on "Åkerman's problem" one gets the feeling that he is verging on Pigou's definition. If only Wicksell had been able to put the two together!

Elsewhere I have described how I came to work on the theory of economic growth in the 1950s, and I do not want to repeat that story now. What I did not sufficiently emphasize in my Nobel lecture—it became clear to me only in the course of thinking through what I have just been saying—is the extent to which involvement in growth theory can be seen as (and really was) an integral part of my education in macroeconomics. Harrod–Domar theory was addressed to serious issues about the path of a capitalist economy. I was led to modify the model just to make it yield a path that could more plausibly claim to look like what one actually saw in historical time series. But this is just part of the general macroeconomic problem of representing a complete, closed, aggregative model.

That my version of growth theory had capital-theoretic overtones was probably a residue from Wicksell.

The next evolutionary step was probably my stint at the Council of Economic Advisers during the Kennedy administration. Day-to-day economic policy had never been my specialty. I had been shocked to hear Paul Samuelson say at lunch one day that he thought the fundamental function of economic theory was to permit the writing of good financial journalism. I had to mature a little before I realized how close to true that was. But I was an onlooker during the campaign of 1960; no one asked me to serve on one of Kennedy's task forces or transition teams. So I was taken by surprise to get a late-night call from the three members of the council—Walter Heller, James Tobin, and Kermit Gordon—asking me to take leave and join the staff. The bait held out to me, the boy growth-theorist, was that I could be the council's ivory-tower economist and spend my time thinking about longer-term policy rather than the daily hurly-burly.

I believed it and I am sure they believed it. But it took me about two days in the old Executive Office Building to realize that all the action, and I mean intellectual action, was in meeting each day's excitement as it arose. It arose right away. The outgoing council had of course prepared the January 1961 *Economic Report*. The new council had to prepare a "mini-report" as the basis for its testimony before the Joint Economic Committee on March 6. Everyone pitched in of course, but the main authors of that statement were the three council members, Arthur Okun, and I (and Joseph Pechman, who was not on the staff but, as a longtime friend of Heller's, served as our old Washington hand). It was a six-week crash course in practical macroeconomics. I do not mean that phrase as a euphemism for sloppy macroeconomics. What I cherish about that experience was the conscious effort to use macroeconomic theory to interpret the world and, in a small way, to change it.

Tobin and I (alas, Gordon, Okun, and Heller are all dead) have just republished the 1961 statement and the January 1962 *Economic Report*, which was clearly intended as a kind of declaration of principle. (The volume also contains the January 1982 *Report*, introduced by the members of the first Reagan council. They can speak for themselves.) To many contemporary readers the 1962 *Report* will seem like a compendium of everything that was wrong with (Keynesian) macroeconomics before the "new classical" counterrevolution, a kind of "before" picture in a before-and-after advertisement. It goes without saying that neither Tobin nor I (nor Okun, if only he were still with us) would wish to write exactly the same things if we were writing the *Report* now, knowing what we have learned in the past quarter century. In fact it is not my purpose to defend the viewpoint of the *Report* even where I think it deserves defense. It is offered as a fair example of what people like me believed in 1961.

First of all—and perhaps here I am being defensive—there is no way we can be said to have neglected the supply side of the economy. There is a whole chapter on the importance of supply factors and supply-side incentives. We were, after all, the people who gave you the investment tax credit in the Revenue Act of 1962. How could the boy growth-theorist have neglected the supply side? What we did do was to give a reasoned argument that the U.S. economy was then, and had been for some time, operating with excess supply, involuntary unemployment, and underutilized capacity. We insisted on a sharp distinction between increases in real output that could be had just by stimulation of demand— what we called "closing the gap between actual and potential output"— and further increases in real output, which would require movement on the supply side. (It is worth remarking, especially now, that way back then Tobin and I were proposing that the right fiscal policy target was a federal budget surplus at full employment, maintained by monetary ease. Our goal was a higher rate of domestic investment and national saving, and we doubted that enough private saving was achievable. So much for the notion that "Keynesians" had some allergic fear of saving.)

A certain sort of contemporary economist would simply dismiss the very possibility of persistent excess aggregate supply. Is it not the hallmark of the well-trained economist to *know* that "markets clear"? Is there any coherent alternative? I have to admit that the 1962 *Economic Report* offers no sustained rebuttal of that view. It was, after all, written for the general public, not for other economists. So I have to reconstruct what we would have said had anybody put the question.

There are two possible answers. One is in a way Keynes's own: An economy can be in aggregative "equilibrium" with widespread involuntary unemployment and underutilized capacity. The equilibrium cannot be Walrasian, with all markets clearing, but it can be equilibrium all the same, in the relevant sense that there is no internal pressure for the situation to change. Keynes was not so precise, nor did he ever make good his claim to have demonstrated the theoretical soundness of this idea; but that is what he claimed. I think we would not have taken that line.

The alternative answer could have gone something like this. There are dozens of nitty-gritty reasons why nominally quoted prices and wages should be imperfectly flexible. A list of them would be just a list, not a theory. It hardly needs to be added that miscellaneous nominal rigidities imply that real quantities and relative prices will often be in the wrong place and perhaps moving in the wrong direction. In consequence the economy's approach to market-clearing equilibrium after any distur-bance may be intolerably slow and costly. Even if there were but One Equilibrium and It were Pareto-efficient, there would still be a large payoff to corrective policy, whether automatic or discretionary.

In the 1960s we would have taken that second line. It is the one that true believers have labeled "American Keynesianism," thus presumably classifying it with Wonder Bread and "Wheel of Fortune." Of course it had quintessential early expression in the famous articles by John Hicks and Franco Modigliani, not exactly backwoods Americans, but never mind that. The 1962 *Report* did not make such arguments, for the reason I have already stated, but I am sure that it is what was in Tobin's mind, and Okun's, and mine. The usual shorthand presumption was that the nominal wage is the sticky price; and that is enough to get the standard American-Keynesian results. But that was just a formality, an up-front way of establishing the model's credentials. If pressed, we would cheer-fully have produced a variety of rigidities and imperfections and noted that they only strengthened the case.

A few years later I wrote a paper with Joseph Stiglitz, then just out of graduate school, that formalized the view of the world I have just been ascribing to "the old folks." We took it for granted that nominal wages and prices both adjusted slowly to excess demand or supply. Thus neither market had to clear in the short run, and the "short-side prin-ciple" applied in both. We were able to show how such an economy might have quite perverse dynamics and might even get itself trapped in situations a little like unemployment equilibrium, though not quite. Our model was quite clearly a precursor of the Benassy—Drèze—Malinvaud "fixed-price temporary equilibrium" models that came to light five or ten years later (and have received less attention in the United States than they deserve). Our paper fell with a dull thud. This fate may have come about because we did not even discuss the "spillovers" from quantity-rationed markets to others that form much of the stuff of the French fixed-price models and give them their claim to be modeling "effective demand." We were not much interested in such microeconomic underpinnings; we were trying to show how a model economy could sometimes be demandlimited and sometimes supply-limited. Our intended goal was a contribution to the "neoclassical synthesis" or, more picturesquely, "Bastard Keynesianism."

The funny thing is that I now think that Keynes had the right instinct. It is a better move to look for alternative, non-Walrasian equilibrium concepts as a foundation for macroeconomic analysis of modern industrial capitalism. It is better partly because of the hold that equilibrium analysis has on economists; and more significantly it is better because it corresponds at least as well to our intuitions and observations of economic life. Keynes could not make good on his claim to have produced a consistent notion of "unemployment equilibrium" because he lacked the analytical tools to do the job. Those came into economics only much later.

Nowadays there is a body of macroeconomic theory that goes under the name "New Keynesian Economics" and pursues the task of showing how information symmetries, transactions costs, and similar facts of life can lead to the possibility of equilibria—self-sustaining situations—with "wrong" levels of employment and output. Usually, then, it can be shown that simple fiscal and monetary policies can improve the situation. (It is true, but hardly news, that inappropriate policies can make things worse. That is why baseball teams fire their managers.)

To my eye the New Keynesian Economics is a mixed bag. Its aims are right and its techniques are nice. But sometimes the particular facts of life it chooses to emphasize seem too farfetched or insignificant to bear the weight that is placed on them. It comes, maybe, from a kind of yearning for respectability and the well-founded belief that respectability comes from staying close to the traditional simplifying assumptions of economics. That is not wholly bad. It is certainly better than wholesale "new paradigm"-mongering. But there are times when common sense leads away from the tradition, and then I would choose common sense every time. If I am right that the main question in macroeconomics is why, after the inevitable real shocks, the economy can stay so far from full employment for so long, then transactions costs and information asymmetries seem too tangential to be the main answer.

In those days the Phillips curve was the particular way we coped with the idea of imperfectly flexible wages. Paul Samuelson and I wrote a paper in 1960 that may have coined the phrase "Phillips curve" and certainly helped to domesticate it in the United States. That is one of the things I would do differently now, but I want to say explicitly how.

About six months ago at a conference in Helsinki, Michael Parkin described that paper as "unfortunate." He didn't mean that it was unlucky in love; he meant that it had misled many people into the untrue belief that there was a stable trade-off between inflation and unemployment, along which policy could move and place the economy. I reacted defensively and pointed out that a careful reading of the paper would disclose that we had stated just about every qualification that one would now wish to attach to the Phillips curve idea. In particular we had remarked explicitly that any attempt to exploit the inflation-unemployment trade-off in policy terms, by buying low unemployment at the expense of permanently higher inflation, could easily have the effect of causing the Phillips curve to shift adversely, canceling the hoped-for gain. We even mentioned changing expectations as the route by which that could happen. It's true—we did.

After the conference Assar Lindbeck observed to me that I had dodged the issue. Yes, the formal qualifications were there; but the tone of the paper was certainly optimistic about the possibility of choosing, by standard policy means, a point on the Phillips curve. I had to admit the justice of that observation. The eclectic American Keynesians of the 1960s were not sufficiently alert to the force of inflationary expectations. They expected more from the Phillips curve than it could deliver in practice.

That raises the question: What do I believe now? What I do not believe is the notion of a reasonably stable "natural rate of unemployment." That idea asserts the existence of a knowable, at worst slowly changing, unemployment rate (or rate of utilization more broadly defined) with the crucial property that maintaining a lower unemployment rate entails ever-accelerating inflation and maintaining a higher unemployment rate entails eventually ever-accelerating deflation. There was a time when I think I was the only respectable(?) economist who rejected this so-called long-run vertical Phillips curve, but I am glad to see that I am now acquiring some allies. From the very beginning I found both the theoretical and empirical foundations of the natural rate hypothesis to be flimsy.

On the theoretical side, Milton Friedman had defined the "natural rate" as the unemployment rate "ground out by the Walrasian equations of general equilibrium." But surely not very many of those who accepted the natural rate hypothesis realized that it made sense only if they took Walrasian general equilibrium to be a valid description of the real everyday economy. Other theoretical foundations were just as farfetched. On the empirical side, econometric estimates of the natural rate were usually based on weak empirical relationships, any of which was susceptible to several interpretations. It is no great caricature to say that believers would assert, say, that the unemployment rate in Great Britain, some 9 to 10 percent, was below the natural rate. How do you know? Because inflation is accelerating. Why is inflation accelerating? Because unemployment is below the natural rate.

My preferred hypothesis is that there is no such thing as the natural rate, not in the sense of a well-defined number with the accelerationist property. Of course at any given time you can imagine puffing up aggregate demand so much that inflation accelerates. (Maybe, just maybe, you can imagine a level of demand so low that wages and prices fell faster and faster. I'd rather see than be one.) But what that critical level is depends on history, institutions, attitudes, and beliefs, including beliefs about the natural rate. If there are many equilibria for the economy, there are probably many possible "natural" rates.

You may have noticed that I have been very selective, even fragmentary, in telling you about my evolution as an economist. For instance, I have skipped completely over the famous Two-Cambridge controversy. That is because I regard that episode as a living counterexample to the proposition that where there is smoke there is fire. It was all smoke and no fire. If I were to tell you about it, I would soon drift into psychologizing, and that is the disease of which it purports to be the cure. You may also have noticed that I seem to have no intention of carrying the story much past the 1960s, except for the odd implicit comment about the course of recent economic research. That too is deliberate. It is hard to be cool about current ideas and controversies, and it is unfair to be hot about them.

That leaves me with the problem of getting off the stage in a dignified way, like the terrified pianist in *Beyond the Fringe,* who cannot seem to play the sort of notes that signify "The End." So I will just finish by telling you one or two things that I have learned about myself and about contemporary economics, more particularly things that I have learned or realized in the process of thinking about what to say in this lecture.

First of all, I have the feeling it is a mistake to think of economics as a Science, with a capital *S.* I also find it temperamentally uncongenial, and that may even be the source of my feeling. Theoretical physicists nowadays think they are on the verge of what they call, only partially self-mockingly, "The Theory of Everything." There is no Economic Theory of Everything, and attempts to construct one seem to merge toward a Theory of Nothing. If you think I am making a sly comment about some tendencies in contemporary macroeconomics, you are right.

That is perfectly consistent with a strong belief that economics should try very hard to be scientific with a small *s*. By that I mean only that we should think logically and respect fact. I will have more to say about "fact" in a minute.

I once heard Paul Streeten say that the world is divided into two kinds of people: those who think the world is divided into two kinds of people and those who do not. Economic theorists (and even some applied economists) seem to be divided into two classes of people, System Builders and Puzzle Solvers. What I have just been saying expresses a prejudice in favor of Puzzle Solvers. Puzzles are things that need explaining. They can arise from the pursuit of theory: paradoxes to be resolved, examples to be discovered (e.g., the optimal excise tax), questions in the form, "Is it possible that *X*?" Puzzles can just as well arise from observation: the cornhog cycle, the "constancy" of distributive shares, the regularities that led to Okun's law. The closest I ever came to system building in the theory of economic growth was actually an attempt to solve a puzzle: How to reconcile the intrinsic instability in Harrod–Domar theory with the failure of economic history to look that way? We can certainly afford some true system builders, and they are certainly highly decorative; my hunch is that the system is too complex and too embedded in the noneconomic ever to be built by our methods.

Now I want to say something about fact. The austere view is that "facts" are just time series of prices and quantities. The rest is hypothesis testing. I have seen a lot of those tests. They are almost never convincing, primarily because one senses that they have very low power against lots of alternatives. There are too many ways to explain a bunch of time series. And sure enough, the next issue of the journal will contain an article exhibiting quite different functional forms, slightly different models. My hunch is that we can make progress only by enlarging the class of eligible facts to include, say, the opinions and casual generalizations of experts and market participants, attitudinal surveys, institutional regularities, even our own judgments of plausibility. My preferred image is the vacuum cleaner, not the microscope.

I am not, repeat not, saying that common sense or the opinion of the "practical man" is always right. The theories held by practical men are very often wrong or empty. What I am saying is that the economist cannot dispense with keeping his or her eyes open, looking around, and forming judgments about what makes sense and what is simply farfetched. Those cannot be uncritical judgments, but judgments to be defended by appeal to observation and to logic.

Enough of the Dismal Science. A friend of mine once presented me with a Columbia University Economics Department T-shirt. It shows a helicopter-drop of money—a favorite abstraction of monetary theorists—falling on an island—the favorite abstraction of economists—and the slogan is "Not half as dismal as you think." With that thought, I leave you.

Robert M. Solow
Awarded Nobel Prize in 1987. Lecture presented October 13, 1988.

Date of Birth
August 23, 1924

Academic Degrees
B.A., Harvard College, 1947
M.A., Harvard University, 1949
Ph.D., Harvard University, 1951

Academic Affiliations
Assistant Professor of Statistics, Massachusetts Institute of Technology, 1950–54
Associate Professor of Statistics, Massachusetts Institute of Technology, 1954–58
Professor of Economics, Massachusetts Institute of Technology, 1958–73
Institute Professor, Massachusetts Institute of Technology, 1973–95
Institute Professor, Emeritus, Massachusetts Institute of Technology, 1995–present

Selected Books
Linear Programming and Economic Analysis, 1958, 1987 (with R. Dorfman and P. A. Samuelson)
Capital Theory and the Rate of Return, 1963
Growth Theory: An Exposition, 1970, 2000
A Critical Essay on Modern Macroeconomic Theory, 1995 (with F. Hahn)
Monopolistic Competition and Macroeconomic Theory, 1998

William F. Sharpe

Introduction

What an honor. What an opportunity. What a challenge. What a temptation.

To speak about oneself before a captive audience is a rare opportunity indeed. The possibilities for self-aggrandizement boggle the mind. Why not abandon all pretense of false modesty? At the very least, seize the chance to propagandize for causes held dear—academic, political, personal.

Had I not read the contributions of my predecessors I might have succumbed to these temptations. However, not one of the others did. And I shall try very hard to resist any siren songs to the contrary.

The Invitation

When invited to give this lecture, I happily accepted. Surely speaking about one's evolution as an economist would be both easy and pleasant. But afterwards I read the written versions of the previous lectures. Not surprisingly, I found that my colleagues had been eloquent, erudite, sagacious, humorous, and both deep and broad in their coverage. How to follow in such footsteps? I considered feigning illness. The possibility of employing a ghost writer crossed my mind. But ultimately, I did neither. Here, for better or worse, are my comments on the subject at hand.

The Prize

First, the prize and the citation.

The Royal Swedish Academy awarded the 1990 Prize in Economic Sciences in Memory of Alfred Nobel to Harry Markowitz, Merton Miller, and myself "for their pioneering work in the theory of financial economics." I wish to emphasize the latter, for with this award, the field of *Financial Economics* completed *its* evolution to achieve the status of a field in both *Economics* and *Finance*.

A field of inquiry is much more important than anyone who practices it. Hence I will precede the personal chronology with some remarks on my field.

Financial Economics

One defines a subject at one's peril. This is especially true if the subject is one's own. But let me try.

In his speech at the prize ceremony Professor Assar Lindbeck of the Royal Swedish Academy of Sciences focused on financial markets, and the use thereof, by firms. Certainly the characteristics of financial instruments and their proper uses are central. From a more theoretical viewpoint, one can focus on the nexus between the *present* and the *future*. A financial instrument typically represents a property right to receive future cash flows. Such cash flows will, of course, come in the future—hence the *economics of time* must be understood. In many cases the flows are uncertain, hence the need for an approach to the *economics of uncertainty*. In addition, cash flows in the far future may depend on actions taken (or not taken) in the near future. This gives rise to the need for a theory of the *economics of options* (broadly construed). Finally, one needs information to estimate likely future outcomes, hence the requirement for an understanding of the *economics of information*.

I define financial economics so that it embraces all four of these important, difficult, and fascinating aspects of economics. While some may dispute the attempted appropriation of so much territory in the name of a group of *nouveax-arrivistes*, I believe that I am not alone in regarding this as appropriate.

Financial economics can be found in both economics departments and in finance departments of business schools. It also pervades practice. In economics departments, *positive* aspects tend to be emphasized; in the finance departments and in practice, *normative* applications. Positive theory attempts to describe the world; normative to offer prescriptions for action. The dichotomy is, however, far from complete. Positive theories assume various types of stylized normative behavior, and normative theories require a *gestalt*, which is usually based on positive theory.

The central question for positive financial economics is *valuation*— what is the value today of a set of future prospective cash flows? The central question for normative financial economics is the appropriate *use* of financial instruments in a world in which values are set wholly or partially in accord with the principles of positive financial economics.

Finance

Business school finance departments often break their offerings into three categories. The study of *investments* deals primarily with the *purchase* of financial instruments by individuals, pension funds, and the like. *Corporate finance,* to a major extent, deals with the *issue* of financial instruments by corporations. The third category, *financial institutions,* concerns organizations for which both the purchase and issuance of financial instruments are key.

To oversimplify, one can think of three different prototypical balance sheets. For investments, visualize financial instruments on the left and the net worth (or utility) of an individual or organization on the right. For corporate finance, visualize bricks and mortar, turret lathes, and the like on the left and financial instruments on the right. For financial institutions, visualize financial instruments on both sides.

Some business schools now begin their finance curriculum with a core course in financial economics, followed by required and/or elective courses in these three major areas of application. I had a small hand in bringing the Stanford curriculum to a rough approximation of this model. However, such a structure is still relatively unusual. In most business schools, financial economics is simply part of the first course in each of the applied areas. But it is inevitably an important part.

It was not always thus. Let me engage in some self-plagiarism by quoting from the 1978 edition of my textbook, *Investments:*

In recent years the field of finance has truly undergone a revolution. Not too many years ago, investment textbooks were primarily devoted to … the mysteries of accounting, some of the details of the operations of major industries, and various rules of thumb for selecting "good" or "bad" securities. Institutional details … were presented, along with historical data, but the reader was provided with no framework for understanding such phenomena. A theory of the formation of prices in capital markets was lacking.[1]

Needless to say, I went on to suggest that such a theory was at hand and that the student who used my book could use it to illuminate the dark corners of finance. I was even bold enough to say that "... empirical analysis has shown that it [the theory] describes the behavior of major capital markets quite well." This view now appears to have been somewhat too optimistic. Again I quote, this time from the 1985 edition of the book:

Recent empirical work has cast some doubt on this comforting view of the world. Early statistical tests have been found to be relatively weak, suggesting that they may have been unable to identify important disparities between theory and reality. Moreover, systematic "anomalies" have been found, calling into question at least some aspects of the standard theories.[2]

This being said, however, theories of financial economics have not been discredited. Rather, they have become more comprehensive. In so doing they may have lost some of their simplicity and intuitiveness. But today only the foolhardy would venture into the world of finance without a solid understanding of financial economics. It is indeed here to stay.

Economics

Financial economics has had less impact on economics departments than on finance departments. Nonetheless, the synergy between the fields is great. And economists have had a profound influence on the development of financial economics. Again I beg indulgence for a quotation from my own writings. This from the Preface to a 1982 book entitled, *Financial Economics, Essays in Honor of Paul Cootner.*

In 1950 the intersection of the fields of finance and economics was small indeed. Academic work in finance relied more often on rules of thumb and anecdotal evidence than on theory and adequate empirical studies.

Economists showed only fleeting interest in financial institutions, speculation, and the host of other aspects of uncertainty that comprise much of the domain of the field of finance.

Three decades later the situation is radically different. There is now a rich body of theory relevant to problems in finance; and extensive empirical tests have been conducted to see how well the theoretical constructs accord with reality....

Many of those who helped bring about the changes in finance were trained as economists. They approached finance problems with the attitudes and the standard tools of the economist. When they found the paradigms of traditional economics inadequate for the subject at hand, they invented new approaches. But, throughout, their style was that of the economist. As a result, we now have a domain increasingly referred to as *financial economics.*[3]

Paul Cootner, a close friend and colleague who died at far too young an age, was (as I said at the time) one of the first and one of the best financial economists. But there were, of course, many others. And almost all of those in the vanguard of the field were trained as economists, including Harry Markowitz, Merton Miller, and myself. Interestingly, five of those who contributed articles in honor of Paul Cootner are now laureates in Economics, and four (Paul Samuelson, Bob Solow, George Stigler, and myself) were participants in this lecture series.

In pronouncing the name of this field one should thus put equal emphasis on both the first and the second words.

Professional Practice

I suspect that no other field taught in business schools has had such an impact on its associated profession as has financial economics. Professional investors routinely speak of expected values; standard deviations; correlations; R-squared, beta, delta, and gamma values; convexity; binomial processes, and the like. Concepts that seemed abstract if not abstruse only a decade or two ago are now part of the everyday life of large numbers of traders throughout the world.

Financial economics has also influenced financial institutions. It spawned the index fund—a strategy designed to replicate the performance of a segment of the overall market with great precision and low cost. It provided the impetus for the huge market in derivative securities such as traded options, index futures, index options, swaps, and so on. Each of these formerly exotic instruments provides an efficient way for individuals and institutions to better control risk while pursuing specific objectives. Financial economics provides the structure for both the valuation and efficient use of such instruments.

A phrase of which I am particularly fond is this: *practical theory.* Financial economics contains an incredibly rich set of examples of such theories, and Wall Street, LaSalle Street, and Main Street have been quick to adopt them.

For a fascinating view of how this came about I strongly recommend Peter Bernstein's recently published *Capital Ideas: The Improbable Origins of Modern Wall Street,*[4] which documents the influence of a number of people, including six past Nobel laureates, on investment practice.

Personal Evolution

I turn now to more personal reflections.

Whether one calls the development of financial economics a revolution (as I was wont to do in my youth) or evolution (in accordance with my charter here), it has been my great privilege to be both an observer of and a participant in the birth and maturation of this important field of inquiry. My own development was only a bit of a sideshow. But it may provide a better understanding of the larger canvas.

If there is a common thread in what follows it is the importance of luck. To be sure, good genes and hard work are necessary conditions for the attainment of this podium in this circumstance. But they are by no means sufficient. At many points in my decision tree, fortune decreed that I should take the branch on this path rather than another. To get here one must have the good luck to draw a great many favorable random numbers.

Undergraduate Work

My parents were both educators—my father a college president and my mother an elementary school principal. Due to disruptions caused by the Second World War, each had to return to graduate school in mid-life. More than most, I learned at an early age to appreciate the joys of learning.

After completing my secondary education in the (then) excellent public schools in California I enrolled at the University of California at Berkeley—intending to become the medical doctor that my mother wanted me to be. A lab course or two convinced me that such was not my me´ tier. I then transferred to UCLA, determined to major in business administration. In the first semester of my sophomore year I took required courses in accounting and microeconomics. The former was, in reality, bookkeeping—and mindless bookkeeping at that. I loathed it. But microeconomics had everything: rigor, relevance, structure, and logic. I found its allure irresistible. The next semester I changed my major to economics and never turned back.

Thus my first stroke of luck. I sometimes break out in a cold sweat thinking about what might have happened had I taken a modern accounting course and an institutional economics course.

I more or less supported myself while completing my education, through a succession of jobs including night work in a gas station, a swing shift posting transactions for a large company, grading papers for seven courses at once, various summer jobs, a teaching assistantship, and ultimately, a position as an economist.

As an undergraduate economics major I took an additional business course—one on investments. It was very traditional, very confusing, and very frustrating. Try as I might, I could find no unifying principle, no underlying structure. I was convinced that studying investments was not for me.

But again, luck was on my side. In my senior year I was able to work as a research assistant for J. Fred Weston, a professor in the business school and a major figure in the field of corporate finance. Fred introduced me to the early work in the then-nascent field of financial economics. I wasn't hooked yet, but I was certainly intrigued.

After graduation I interviewed for jobs in banking. Here my grades proved an impediment. The interviewer would typically look over my records, congratulate me, then ask why I hadn't considered graduate school. After a few such cases I tried grabbing the form, turning it over to the section on activities, offices held, fraternities, etc. then handing it back. Despite such attempts to show that I was a reasonably well-adjusted human being, nothing interesting came my way, and so I proceeded to a master's degree in economics at UCLA.

The Master's Degree

It was during this year that I irrevocably crossed the line to become an economist. Much of the credit (or blame) for this goes to Armen Alchian, who taught the graduate microeconomics sequence at UCLA. While personally gentle and traditional, Armen was (and is) clearly an eccentric economic theorist. He started the course by asserting that 95% of the material in economics journals was wrong or irrelevant—an assertion that I sometimes regard as not unduly pessimistic. He then proceeded to discuss the economics of the illegal market for buying babies. At one point he spent five of six lectures wrestling (somewhat unsuccessfully) with the meaning of *profit*. Indeed, most of his classes had the characteristics of a wrestling match. We witnessed a brilliant mind grappling (usually very successfully) with the most difficult concepts in economics in thoroughly creative and innovative ways. There could be no better training for a fledgling theorist and no higher standard. After two semesters with Armen Alchian, I was hooked. I wanted to be a microeconomist.

After obtaining the M.A., I fulfilled part of my ROTC obligation by serving as a Second Lieutenant in the Army Quartermaster Corps. I must admit that I rather enjoyed being outdoors much of the time and being (for once in my life) in reasonable physical condition.

The RAND Corporation

By indenturing myself to seven and a half years of reserve duty with two weeks of summer camp each year, I managed to limit my active duty to six months. Then through the good offices of Armen Alchian I was able to obtain a position at the RAND Corporation as a junior economist.

The RAND of 1956 was a truly unique organization. Funded almost entirely by the Air Force, it had contracted simply to do research that it considered worthwhile for its main client, along with a goodly dose of other work that would serve the public good. Employees were free to work any hours they chose, within wide limits. Office doors were open, intellectual discussions on the most wide-ranging topics were de rigueur, and everyone was expected to spend one day per week on research of strictly personal interest.

Those were heady days. Some of the key work in systems analysis, operations research, computer science, and applied economics was being done at RAND. One of our first computers was designed by John von Neumann. George Dantzig was working on linear programming. Some of the most illustrious academics served as consultants. Everyone was on a first-name basis. If ever there was a place for one interested in practical theory, the RAND Corporation in the 1950s was it.

Now, of course, the idea of working in a classified facility for the military establishment would prove an anathema for liberals (in the American political sense of the term), such as myself and most of the others at RAND. But those were simpler times. We truly believed that by improving the efficiency of the defense establishment we could help prevent war. There seemed to be no ambiguity and no moral dilemma.

At RAND I worked on problems involving optimization and trade-offs. We built many models, engaged in both data collection and empirical analysis, then brought all the pieces together using every bit of the then-available computer capacity at hand.

RAND pioneered in many aspects of computer science, leading me to become a "computer nerd" before the term came into common use. Time has in no way diminished my enthusiasm in this regard as my wife and my colleagues will attest.

Doctoral Work

Although RAND provided an extremely hospitable environment, I felt that ultimately I wanted to teach. Since personal economics precluded returning to full-time study, I thought my best choice would be to take the three education courses that, with my M.A. degree, would procure a credential for teaching in what were then termed junior colleges. I took only one of these—a night course on audio-visual education. It was, to be charitable, vacuous. The nadir came when the instructor showed a slide of a painstakingly constructed prize-winning bulletin board featuring the calendar for October. Another student pointed out that the bulletin board showed 30 days, not 31. The instructor was surprised but not embarrassed. While I would be the last to deny the importance of form, it seemed to me in this case it had totally triumphed over substance.

Rather than take the risk of having to endure another course of this caliber, I arranged to take the courses in the Economics Ph.D. program at UCLA while still working full-time at RAND. In addition to fields in microeconomics, monetary economics, economic history, and the development of economic thought, I managed to exploit a little-known provision in the department rules that allowed me to take a field in finance under Fred Weston. It was in this connection that I learned of the pioneering work of Harry Markowitz, which in large part began the development of financial economics.

After completing my courses and examinations, I set out to write what I hoped to be the definitive dissertation on transfer prices—the internal "shadow prices" that large firms sometimes use to provide incentives for divisions to operate efficiently. My interest in the subject had been piqued by some of the problems under investigation at RAND and by key work on the subject by Jack Hirshleifer, then at the University of Chicago. As it turned out, Jack moved to UCLA when I was approximately three months into the project. At Armen Alchian's suggestion, Jack read my work to date. To put it simply, he didn't consider it promising and strongly suggested that I find another topic.

To this day, I consider Jack one of my greatest benefactors.

Bent but not broken, I talked with Fred Weston. He suggested I talk with Harry Markowitz (who had recently joined RAND) about possible ideas for a dissertation. I did, and he suggested some. Armen Alchian was more than happy to have me work under Harry, even though Harry could not even appear as a member of my committee.

In 1952 Markowitz had shown that the investor's choice of a portfolio could be treated as a problem subject to mathematical and statistical formulation. Two key aspects of an investment strategy are its *expected return* and its *risk*. The former can be represented by the *mean* of a probability distribution of future return and the latter by the *variance* (or its square root, the *standard deviation*) of the distribution. An *efficient strategy* is one that provides the maximum expected return for given risk. Harry showed how to formulate the problem of finding all efficient strategies, given estimates of security expected returns, risks and correlations, and how to solve such problems using a quadratic programming algorithm that he had developed. His focus was strictly normative—he was concerned with the proper use of forecasts, not their properties.

My dissertation dealt with three related subjects. First, I explored the implications of a suggestion in Harry's 1958 book that one might characterize the "return-generating process" with what is today termed a *one-factor model*. In general, factor models identify one or more key influences, attempt to measure the sensitivity of each security to each of the specified factors, and assume that all other sources of risk are idiosyncratic—that is, unrelated across securities. In the dissertation I derived and experimented with computational schemes that would be efficient if only one such factor were posited. In later work I extended this to cover more realistic cases involving multiple factors.

Second, I worked with a practicing investment manager to attempt to apply the theory and the one-factor model using subjective judgments about future returns. This set of experiments was only partially successful. Curiously, the optimal portfolios kept producing large holdings of a relatively unknown company then called Haloid Xerox. Its price soon doubled several times over, perhaps justifying combining the manager's foresight with the discipline of the procedure. But I took from this experience the lesson that econometric methods are best suited to risk estimation, with judgment applied, if at all, to return estimation.

Third, and most important (as it has turned out), I asked the question that microeconomists are trained to ask. If everyone were to behave optimally (here, follow the prescriptions of Markowitz's portfolio theory), what prices will securities command once the capital market has reached *equilibrium*? To make the problem tractable I assumed that all investors made the same predictions and that returns were generated by the one-factor model. The conclusion was both startling and provocative. Security prices will adjust until there is a simple linear relationship between expected return and sensitivity to changes in the factor in question. Following the conventions of regression analysis, I used the symbol *beta* for the latter. Thus the result could be succinctly stated: securities with higher betas will have higher expected returns. Only the portion of risk due to the influence of the common factor will be rewarded in the long run. No compensation is needed nor available for the remainder (which I termed "nonsystematic risk"), since it can be reduced to a small amount by sensible diversification.

Thus was the capital asset pricing model born.

The University of Washington

Before completing my dissertation I had the opportunity to spend a day in Seattle. Uncharacteristically, the sun was shining and the waters were filled with sailboats. Since sailing was and is one of my passions, I applied for a position at the University of Washington. One was forthcoming, and I moved to Seattle.

At the time, the U.W. Business School was in the early stages of its transition from a traditional, nonrigorous, institutionally oriented program to the rigorous discipline-based academic school that it is now. This led to some frustrations but provided great opportunities. Teaching loads were heavy but those willing to try new courses were encouraged to do so. Continuing in the eclectic tradition of RAND, I taught courses in statistics, operations research, computer science and microeconomics, in addition to offerings in corporate finance and investments. It is certainly true that the best way to learn something is to attempt to teach it to others. At Washington I (at least) learned a great deal.

I also managed to complete a substantial amount of research. Most importantly, I derived the remaining essential elements of the capital asset pricing model in my first year there.

While the equilibrium results I had obtained in the dissertation were satisfying, they appeared to rely heavily on the strong assumption that only one factor was responsible for correlations among security returns. My instincts told me that it should be possible to generalize the model so that such an assumption would not be needed. After several false starts I found that in an efficient market of the type posited, the key relationship between expected returns and beta values would hold *no matter what the process generating security returns*. I proceeded to write the results, under the title "Capital Asset Prices: A Theory of Market Equilibrium under Conditions of Risk." Publication was delayed for over two years due to initial rejection by a referee and a change in the editorship of the *Journal of Finance*. In the meantime I presented my results and exchanged work with others in the rapidly developing field that we now call financial economics. One way or another we found each other and managed to convene at various conferences. The process of academic communication is somewhat mysterious, even to those who participate in it. But it is remarkably effective.

While at Washington but with funding from RAND, I combined two of my interests to produce a book called *The Economics of Computers*. I also took a year's leave to return to RAND to work on several non-military projects, including one investigating the possible use of time-varying fees to better allocate landing rights and air space at the three major New York airports.

Irvine

After several productive years at Washington I succumbed to an appeal to my entrepreneurial instincts and joined the School of Social Sciences at the University of California's new Irvine campus. The plan was to establish an economics department devoted primarily to the "economics of uncertainty." Unfortunately, life at a publicly supported campus in Orange County at the height of the antiwar movement was not one conducive to scholarly reflection. Everyone from the Chancellor on down had to be pressed into service to insure that the University remained free to investigate ideas of all kinds, be they from the left or the right.

While at Irvine I consulted with Merrill Lynch in New York, helping implement early practical applications of some of the concepts that I and others had developed. I also managed to complete another book, *Portfolio Theory and Capital Markets*, summarizing much of the work that had been done to date.

After a year it became clear to a number of us that our hopes to create innovative and high-quality new departments at Irvine would, at the very least, require a great deal of patience. Many found greener pastures, I among them.

Stanford

In 1970 I moved to my current home—the Stanford Graduate School of Business. At the time Stanford was already prominent in finance and eager to incorporate more of the recent economics-based work in both the curriculum and the research program. Accordingly, Alan Kraus, Bob Litzenberger, and I set up the first formal Ph.D. sequence in finance and taught it as a team. In the process, we began to see the outlines of what we now call financial economics. My knowledge of the area also grew phenomenally, thanks to Alan and Bob.

In the 1970s, the Stanford Business School was rushing to achieve the "balanced excellence" in both research and teaching that it had set as a goal. To build on a finance faculty that already included Alan Kraus, Bob Litzenberger, Alex Robicheck, Ezra Solomon, and Jim Van Horne, we hired Paul Cootner, John Cox, Sandy Grossman, and Myron Scholes. In the economics department, Joe Stiglitz was working in the area, and we were all using Ken Arrow's monumental contributions to the field. We also set up a joint seminar series with U.C.–Berkeley, which brought us into contact with the likes of Hayne Leland, Barr Rosenberg, and Mark Rubenstein. There could have been no better place for one with my interests.

At Stanford I taught finance and microeconomics at both the M.B.A. and Ph.D. level. Paul Cootner and I set up the Ph.D. sequence in microeconomics, from which I learned a great deal. However, I soon realized that I would rather concentrate my energy on financial economics, per se.

My biggest undertaking in these years was the writing of the previously quoted *Investments* textbook. It seemed to me that there was a need for a text in this area based solidly on financial economic theory. I postponed the project for two or three years since I realized that I would have to learn much about institutional details and industry practice if the book were to be sufficient for the purpose. Eventually I succumbed. The task proved to be formidable, but was a remarkable learning experience (to use a cliché).

In writing the text I found it necessary to not only document current theory but also to provide substantial amounts of new theory. The book thus became both the motivating force for my research and, in many cases, the venue for its publication.

Two examples of this stand out in my mind. One was an intuitive yet practical algorithm for solving a restricted class of portfolio optimization problems. Although simply a variant of a general class of approaches to nonlinear optimization, its rules can be stated in familiar economic terms such as utility maximization, choices based on marginal utilities, etc. The technique has proven quite useful and enjoys rather wide commercial application.

The second example concerned the valuation of options. The basis for the important Black—Scholes option valuation formula was, for me, hard to understand and virtually impossible to explain, since it was grounded in the difficult mathematics of continuous processes. Surely, I thought, there must be a discrete-time, discrete-state counterpart. Happily, there was. Moreover, numeric experiments showed that values obtained with the resultant *binomial process* converged quite rapidly to those of the continuous form as the number of discrete steps increased. I presented this approach in 1978 in my textbook. John Cox, Steve Ross, and Mark Rubenstein built on this foundation and showed that a wide variety of valuation problems could best be formulated in analogous ways. Such models, which we now realize to be special cases of the Arrow–Debreu state-preference paradigm, are also widely used by practitioners.

Wells Fargo

In the 1970s and 1980s I worked closely with an extremely innovative group at the Wells Fargo Bank in San Francisco to bring some of the lessons of financial economics to the world of money management. Under the leadership of Bill Fouse and Jim Vertin, Wells Fargo pioneered in the creation of index funds, passive portfolios tailored to meet investor objectives, estimation of beta values and expected returns using forecasts of future cash flows, estimation of risk, and more. Today Wells Fargo and Bill Fouse's Mellon Capital Management group manage over $125 billion using procedures based on financial economics.

Commerce

In 1986 I ventured more directly into the world of commerce. My wife, Kathy (who served as administrator), and I established a firm devoted to research and consulting on problems faced by the administrators of large, multiply managed pension, endowment and foundation funds. Our goals were to apply existing theory, develop new theory, and conduct empirical analyses to deal with issues associated with the *asset allocation* decision, taking into account the objectives of each fund. In all our work we assumed that markets were efficient—that is, we wished to help *tailor* a fund's investments to meet its needs, rather than try to "beat the market."

Working with a talented group of colleagues and a highly sophisticated and supportive group of clients, we accomplished much in this connection. Of the several new techniques that we developed, the one that we termed *style analysis* has proven particularly useful.

By far the largest part of the month-to-month variation of the return provided by, say, a mutual fund is attributable to the *types* of securities held, rather than the specific securities chosen within each type. For example, using a set of twelve *asset classes* to represent security types, we found that 80 to 90% of the variance in monthly returns for a typical U.S. mutual fund was due to "asset allocation." Given this, it is crucial that one be able to determine a fund's allocation across such major asset classes, which we termed its *style*.

Rather remarkably, we found that in many cases this can be accomplished quite well by comparing the monthly returns provided by the fund over past years with those that could have been obtained from index funds representing each of the major asset classes. The required procedure (quadratic programming) is simple in concept, although somewhat complex in practice.

Style analysis allows an external analyst to estimate a manager's exposures to key sectors of the market. The investor can thus align his or her holdings of funds much more efficiently than would be possible without this information. A fund's *performance* can also be separated into that due to its *style* and the remainder, which may be considered due to *selection*. This type of *performance attribution* makes possible far more precise answers to questions concerning market efficiency, the extent to which past performance can predict future performance, etc.

The firm's clients were not alone in welcoming this type of analysis. Our papers and lectures on the subject have been warmly received and several other firms are preparing to offer similar services. If imitation is the sincerest form of flattery, we have been well-flattered.

Further Research

Throughout my career I have tried to keep one foot in the academic world and one in the world of affairs. There is much to learn from each, and each needs the other. This is, of course, a difficult balancing act. At Sharpe Associates, I placed substantial emphasis on practice. After several years it seemed appropriate to stand back somewhat to allow more reflection, deeper research, and preparation of the proverbial book or two. Hence a decision to concentrate more on research and teaching.

It seems to me that my comparative advantage lies in the development, application and communication of *practical theory*. I expect to continue to focus on financial economics, with special attention to investment applications, with somewhat greater emphasis on the integration of existing ideas than the development of new ones (as befits one my age).

Conclusion

Academic practice dictates that one should end a paper or lecture with a set of conclusions. I shall not do so. This is due in part to a belief that I lack the necessary perspective and unbiasedness. I also fear that the result might sound too much like an obituary—which I hope would prove premature.

I will, however, say this. It has been exciting and satisfying almost beyond belief to have played a role, however small, in the evolution of a field of inquiry as important and lasting as that of financial economics. Happily, there is far more to come, so that many generations of financial economists can look forward to the same sorts of thrills that I have been fortunate to experience.

Notes

1. William F. Sharpe, *Investments* (Englewood Cliffs, NJ: Prentice-Hall, 1978).

2. William F. Sharpe, *Investments,* 3d ed. (Englewood Cliffs, NJ: Prentice-Hall, 1985).

3. William F. Sharpe and Cathryn M. Cootner, eds., *Financial Economics: Essays in Honor of Paul Cootner* (Englewood Cliffs, NJ: Prentice-Hall, 1982).

4. Peter L. Bernstein, *Capital Ideas: The Improbable Origins of Modern Wall Street* (New York: The Free Press, 1992).

William F. Sharpe
Awarded Nobel Prize in 1990. Lecture presented February 19, 1992.

Date of Birth
June 16, 1934

Academic Degrees
A.B., University of California, Los Angeles, 1955
M.A., University of California, Los Angeles, 1956
Ph.D., University of California, Los Angeles, 1961

Academic Affiliations
Assistant Professor, University of Washington, 1961–63
Associate Professor, University of Washington, 1963–67
Professor, University of Washington, 1967–68
Professor, University of California, Irvine, 1968–70
Professor, Stanford University, 1970–73
Timken Professor of Finance, Stanford University, 1973–89
Timken Professor Emeritus of Finance, Stanford University, 1989–92
Professor of Finance, Stanford University, 1993–99
Professor of Finance, Emeritus, Stanford University, 1999–present

Selected Books
Portfolio Theory and Capital Markets, 1970, 2000
Investments, 1978, 1999 (6th ed., with G. Alexander and J. Bailey)
Asset Allocation Tools, 1987
Fundamentals of Investments, 1989, 2001 (with G. Alexander and J. Bailey)

Douglass C. North

I knew where I was going from the day I decided to become an econo-mist. I set out to understand what made economies rich or poor because I viewed that objective as being the essential prerequisite to improving their performance. The search for the Holy Grail of the ultimate source of economic performance has taken me on a long and certainly unantici-pated journey, from Marxism to cognitive science, but it has been this persistent objective that has directed and shaped my scholarly career.

I was born in Cambridge, Massachusetts—not because my family had any connection with higher education, but because my father was a manager at the Metropolitan Life Insurance Company in a nearby town, and Cambridge was the nearest hospital in 1920. I was the youngest of three children, with a sister and a brother who were born before my father went off to Europe in World War I.

In the ensuing years we moved a number of times as a result of my father's business, first to Connecticut and then, when he became head of the Metropolitan's Canadian office, to Ottawa. Because my mother believed in education broadly construed, we traveled in Europe, and I went to school at the Lycée Jacquard in Lausanne, Switzerland, in 1929–30. I went to elementary school in Ottawa and then to a private second-ary school. When we moved back to the United States in 1933, I went to private schools in New York City and on Long Island and then com-pleted my high school education at The Choate School in Wallingford, Connecticut. While I was there I became deeply interested in photogra-phy, and indeed the most noteworthy event in my early life was winning first, third, fourth, and seventh prizes in an international photographic competition for college and high school students.

Our family life was certainly not intellectual. My father had not even completed high school when he started as an office boy working for the Metropolitan Life Insurance Company, and I am not sure that my mother completed high school. Nevertheless, she was an exciting person—intelligent, intellectually curious—and she played an important part in my intellectual development. My aunt and uncle were, and one of my aunts (Adelaide North) still is, a powerful influence. They introduced me to classical music and my aunt continues to be, to this day, a very special person in my life.

When it came time to go to college I had been accepted to Harvard when my father was offered the position of head of the Metropolitan Life Insurance Company office on the west coast, and we moved to San Francisco. Because I did not want to be that far from home, I decided to go instead to the University of California at Berkeley. While I was there my life was completely changed by my becoming a Marxist.

Marxism was attractive because it appeared to provide answers to the pressing questions of the time, including the Great Depression that we were in—answers missing from the pre-Keynesian economics that I was taught in 1939–40. I was opposed to World War II, and indeed on June 22, 1941, when Hitler invaded the Soviet Union, I suddenly found myself the lone supporter of peace since everybody else had, because of their communist beliefs, shifted over to become supporters of the war.

Because I was preoccupied with liberal student activities, my record at the University of California as an undergraduate was mediocre, to say the least. I had only slightly better than a "C" average, although I did have a triple major in political science, philosophy, and economics. I had hoped to go to law school, but the war started, and because of the strong feeling that I did not want to kill anybody, I joined the Merchant Marine when I graduated from Berkeley in May of 1942.

We had been to sea only a short time when the captain called me up on the bridge and asked me if I could learn to navigate: most of the officers had only rudimentary educations, and we were on our way from San Francisco to Australia. I became navigator and enjoyed it very much. We made repeated trips from San Francisco to Australia, and then to the forward positions in New Guinea and the Solomon Islands.

What the years at sea did give me were three years of continuous reading, and it was in the course of reading that I became convinced that I should become an economist. The last year of the war I taught celo-navigation at the Maritime Service Officers' School in Alameda, California; I took up photography again and had a difficult decision as to whether to become a photographer or go into economics. In the summer of 1941 I had worked with Dorothea Lange, head of the photographic division of the Farm Security Administration, traveling with and photographing migrants through the Central Valley of California. Dorothea tried to persuade me to become a photographer. Her husband, Paul Taylor, who was in the economics department at the University of California, tried to persuade me to become an economist. He won.

I went to graduate school at the University of California at Berkeley— the only graduate school that would take me with my poor undergraduate record. My objective as a graduate student was to find out what made economies work the way they did or fail to work. Economic history appeared to be the best field for that objective. I cannot say that I learned much formal economics as a graduate student in Berkeley. My most influential professors were all outside the mainstream of orthodox economics—Robert Brady; Leo Rogin, a very influential teacher of history of economic thought; and M. M. Knight (Frank Knight's brother), who certainly was agnostic, to say the least, about theory, but who had a wonderful knowledge of the facts and background in economic history. He became my mentor and my thesis advisor at Berkeley. But while I learned by rote most of the theory I was supposed to know, I did not acquire a real understanding of theory.

It was not until I got my first job, at the University of Washington in Seattle, and began playing chess with Don Gordon, a brilliant young theorist, that I learned economic theory. In the three years of playing chess every day from noon to two, I may have beaten Don at chess, but he taught me economics; more important, he taught me how to reason like an economist, and that skill is still perhaps the most important tool that I have acquired.

I had written my dissertation on the history of life insurance in the United States and had had a Social Science Research Council Fellowship to go to the east coast and do the spade work. That turned out to be a very productive year. I not only sat in on Robert Merton's seminars in sociology at Columbia but also became involved in the Entrepreneurial Center of Arthur Cole at Harvard. The result was that Joseph Schumpeter, who had been an intellectual source of the Entrepreneurial School, had a strong influence upon me. My early work and publications centered around expanding on the analysis of life insurance in my dissertation and its relationship to investment banking.

I next turned to developing an analytical framework to look at regional economic growth and this led to my first article in the *Journal of Political Economy*, entitled "Location Theory and Regional Economic Growth." That work eventually led me to developing a staple theory of economic growth.

I was very fortunate that, at a meeting of the Economic History Association, I came to know Solomon Fabricant, who was then director of research at the National Bureau of Economic Research; and in 1956–57 I was invited to spend the year at the Bureau as a research associate. That was an enormously important year in my life. I not only became acquainted with most of the leading economists who passed through the Bureau but also spent one day a week at Johns Hopkins University in Baltimore with Simon Kuznets, whose wise council had a lasting influence on me. During the year at the NBER I did the empirical work that led to my early major quantitative study of the balance of payments of the United States from 1790 to 1860.

I married for the first time in 1944. During my graduate training my wife taught school, providing our major source of support. We had three sons, Douglass, Christopher, and Malcolm, born between 1951 and 1957. After the boys were in school my wife became a successful politician in the Washington State legislature.

Between my year at the National Bureau and 1966–67, when I went off to Geneva as a Ford Faculty Fellow, I did my major work in American economic history, which led to my first book, *The Economic Growth of the United States from 1790 to 1860*. It was a straightforward analysis of how markets work in the context of an export staple model of growth.

By this time (1960) there was a substantial stirring among young economic historians to try to transform the field from its descriptive, institutional character to make it an analytical, quantitative discipline. The year that I was at the NBER, that organization and the Economic History Association had the first joint quantitative program on the growth of the American economy, a conference that was held at Williamstown, Massachusetts, in the late spring of 1957. It was at this meeting that I presented my paper on the balance of payments of the United States from 1790 to 1860. This meeting was really the beginning of the new economic history, but the new approach to economic history really coalesced when Jon Hughes and Lance Davis, two former students of mine who had become faculty members at Purdue, called the first conference of economic historians interested in trying to develop and apply economic theory and quantitative methods to history. The first meeting was held at Purdue in February of 1960. This conference was highly successful and became an annual affair. The participants were a mixture of economic historians, theorists, and econometricians. They were no-holds-barred meetings in which the speaker frequently got mauled, but we knew we were reshaping the field of economic history, and that was exciting. The reception that we received among economists was certainly enthusiastic. Economics departments very quickly became interested in having new economic historians, or, as we came to call ourselves, clio-metricians (Clio being the muse of history). Therefore, as I developed a graduate program jointly with my colleague, Morris David Morris, at the University of Washington we attracted some of the best students to do work in economic history, and during the 1960s and early 1970s the job market was very responsive, and our students were easily placed throughout the country.

In 1966–67 I decided that I should switch from American to European economic history, and therefore, when I received the above-mentioned grant to live in Geneva for a year, I decided to retool. Retooling turned out to change my scholarly life radically, since I quickly became convinced that the tools of neoclassical economic theory were not up to the task of explaining the kind of fundamental societal change that had characterized European economies from medieval times onward.

Neoclassical theory was concerned with the operation of markets and assumed the existence of the underlying conditions that were a prerequisite to the operation of markets. It had nothing to say about how markets evolved. Moreover it was a static theory, and we needed to have a theory that was dynamic and could explain the evolution of economies through time. We needed new tools, but they simply did not exist. It was in the long search for a framework that would provide new tools of analysis that my interest and concern with the new institutional economics evolved. As a graduate student I had read Thorstein Veblen and John R. Commons and been impressed by the insights they provided into the workings of economies, but they did not provide a theoretical framework. What we needed was a theoretical structure that we could use to explain and analyze economic history. The old institutional economics, because it failed to provide such a theoretical framework, never posed a serious alternative to neoclassical theory. Marxism was explicitly concerned with institutions, asked good questions, and had an explanation of long-run change, but there were too many flaws in the model. Making classes the unit of analysis and failing to incorporate population change as a key source of change were major shortcomings. The strengths of neoclassical theory were its uncompromising focus on scarcity and, hence, competition as the key to economics, its use of the individual as the unit of analysis, and the power of the economic way of reasoning. There had to be a way of melding the strengths of these diverse approaches into a theoretical structure. That is what I and others have set out to do in the new institutional economics.

Why focus on institutions? In a world of uncertainty they have been used by human beings in an attempt to structure human interaction. They are the rules of the game of a society and in consequence provide the framework of incentives that shape economic, political, and social organization. Institutions are composed of formal rules (laws, constitutions, rules), informal constraints (conventions, codes of conduct, norms of behavior), and the effectiveness of their enforcement. Enforcement is carried out by third parties (law enforcement, social ostracism), by second parties (retaliation), or by the first party (self-imposed codes of conduct). Institutions affect economic performance by determining, together with the technology employed, the transaction and transformation (production) costs that make up the total costs of production. Since there is an intimate connection between the institutions and technology employed, the efficiency of a market is directly shaped by the institutional framework.

My initial effort to incorporate institutions into historical economic analysis resulted in two books, one with Lance Davis, *Institutional Change and American Economic Growth,* published in 1971, and the other with Robert Thomas, *The Rise of the Western World: A New Economic History,* published in 1973. Both were early attempts to develop some tools of institutional analysis and apply them to economic history. In the study with Lance Davis on American economic growth we attempted to spell out the way new institutions and organizations evolved in the context of American economic growth. In the study of Europe we made the formation of property rights the key to economic performance and explored the contrasting way they evolved in the Netherlands and England on the one hand and France and Spain on the other.

Both studies were still predicated on the assumptions of neoclassical economic theory. But there were too many loose ends that did not make sense—such as the notion that institutions were efficient (however defined). Perhaps more serious, it was not possible to explain long-run poor economic performance in a neoclassical framework. So I began to explore what was wrong. Individual beliefs were obviously important to the choices people make, and only the extreme myopia of economists prevented them from understanding that ideas, ideologies, and prejudices mattered. Once you recognize that, you are forced to examine the rationality postulate critically. The long road toward a new analytical framework involved (1) developing a view of institutions that would account for why institutions produced results that in the long run did not manage to produce economic growth, as well as (2) developing a model of political economy in order to be able to explain the underlying source of institutions. Finally, one had to come to grips with why people had the ideologies and ideas that determined the choices they made.

It was Ronald Coase who provided a critical link which began to structure the evolving framework. In "The Nature of the Firm" Coase forced us to think about the cost of economic organization. But whereas Coase was concerned with the transaction costs that determined the existence of firms, I was concerned with the transaction costs that determined overall economic performance. George Stigler had once remarked to me that he thought the efficiency of economic organization had probably been as important as technological change in historical development. I was convinced that he was right. Transaction costs provided the wedge to examine the costs of economic organization. Coase's other critical contribution, "The Problem of Social Cost," provided the link to connect neoclassical theory to institutional analysis. The message of that essay was that when transaction costs were positive, institutions mattered and shaped the resultant market structure. I was fortunate in having several colleagues at the University of Washington who early on took Coase's work seriously. Steven Cheung, a student of Armen Alchian at UCLA, came to Seattle after a post-doctoral fellowship at Chicago where he became acquainted with Coase. Cheung made a number of important contributions to transaction cost theory—in particular his emphasis on the costs of measurement of the multiple dimensions of a good or service or of the performance of agents as a critical source of transaction costs (since imperfect measurement resulted in imperfectly specified property rights). Yoram Barzel continued work that Cheung began (after Cheung left to go to the University of Hong Kong). I have learned a great deal from both of them, and their influence is apparent in my next book.

In *Structure and Change in Economic History* (1981) I abandoned the notion that institutions were efficient and attempted to explain why "inefficient" rules would tend to exist and be perpetuated. In that study I began to explore the transaction costs underlying different forms of economic organization in history and also to explore the way ideologies altered free-riding to influence political and economic decision making. The theoretical chapters were followed by eight historical chapters that outlined a fundamental reinterpretation of economic history from the origins of agriculture in the eighth millennium B.C. to the twentieth century.

I was still dissatisfied with our understanding of the political process, and indeed searched for colleagues who were interested in developing political—economic models. Margaret Levi, a Marxist political scientist, and I had developed a political economy program but there was little interest in the subject among the faculty. This led me to leave the University of Washington in 1983 after 33 years and to move to Washington University in St. Louis, where there was an exciting group of young political scientists and economists who were attempting to develop new models of political economy. This proved to be a felicitous move. I created the Center in Political Economy, which continues to be a creative research center.

The central theoretical puzzle about politics was reflected in the diverse and conflicting perspectives that had evolved from the public choice theory that originated with Buchanan and Tullock's *The Calculus of Consent,* Mancur Olson's *The Logic of Collective Action,* and Anthony Downs's *An Economic Theory of Democracy*—three classics of the new public choice literature. Was the polity simply a leviathan to be contained as Buchanan and the Virginia school of public choice suggested? That perspective made the state little more than a giant theft machine. But how did that perspective square with the property rights argument that I had developed which made the political creation of secure and productive property rights the key to economic growth? The problem was hardly new. *The Federalist Papers* of Madison, Hamilton, and Jay were a brilliant exposition of many of the issues. In effect, you can't do with the state but you can't do without it. At a deeper level of analysis, Arrow's disturbing impossibility theorem had implications for the entire process of aggregating choices. In effect, one cannot achieve collectively rational choices by aggregating the individual choices of people with diverse values and preferences.

These issues are far from resolved and pose fundamental problems for polities and, therefore, for economic performance. In *Structure and Change* I had developed a neoclassical theory of the state which confronted the issue of why a ruler would ever produce inefficient property rights when efficient rights would increase aggregate income and hence the revenue of the ruler. In effect a competitive constraint (the threat of being replaced by competitors for the ruler) and a transaction cost constraint (efficient rules might have so much higher costs of tax collection that the ruler's revenue was decreased) were the sources of inefficient rules.

In "A Transaction Cost Theory of Politics" (*The Journal of Theoretical Politics* 1 [1991]), I developed a more general model of why political markets are inherently less efficient than economic markets; here I used the basic transaction cost framework I had developed to explore economic markets.

Transaction costs are the costs of measuring and enforcing agreements. In economic markets there are objective criteria (size, weight, color, etc.) to measure the physical dimensions of the goods and services exchanged and legal criteria to measure the property rights dimensions. Enforcement is carried out by the judicial system. Competition is a powerful force to reduce transaction costs but still economic markets are beset by high transaction costs. But political markets are far more prone to inefficiency. What is being exchanged are promises for votes; the voter has little incentive to be informed since the likelihood that his/her vote counts is infinitesimal; there is no comparable enforcement mechanism; and competition is very imperfect. The complexity of the issues (together with the lack of incentives of voters to be informed) leads to ideological stereotyping taking over. In effect the incentives for efficiency are diluted by the structure of political markets and the complexity of the issues.

The development of a political economic framework to explore long-run institutional change occupied me during all of the 1980s and led to the publication of *Institutions, Institutional Change, and Economic Performance* in 1990. In that study I explicitly attempted to evolve a theory of institutional change. The first step was to separate institutions from organizations. The former are the rules of the game but the latter are the players. That is, organizations are made up of groups of individuals with some objective function. They are firms, trade unions, cooperatives (economic organizations); political parties, legislatures, regulatory agencies (political organizations); churches, athletic associations, clubs (social organizations). Organizations and their entrepreneurs in the pursuit of their objectives (whether the firm maximizing profits or the political party trying to win an election, etc.) are the agent of change. The organizations themselves have come into existence because of the opportunities resulting from the incentives of the institutional framework. In the world of scarcity and competition that characterizes economies, they are in competition to survive. That competition will lead them to try to modify the institutional framework to improve their competitive position. The intensity of competition will determine the rate of change of institutions, but the direction of change will reflect the perceptions of the actors—the mental models that they possess that interpret the external environment for them.

I used this framework to examine the contrasting development of the Netherlands and Britain, where polities evolved that produced the property rights that underpin modern economic growth, and of Spain, where secular stagnation ensued from the polity.

In that book I began to puzzle seriously about the rationality postulate. It is clear that we need an explanation for why people make the choices they do; why ideologies such as communism or Muslim fundamentalism can shape the choices people make and direct the way economies evolve through long periods of time. One simply cannot get at ideologies without digging deeply into cognitive science in attempting to understand the way in which the mind acquires learning and makes choices. Since 1990 my research has been directed toward dealing with this issue.

Herbert Simon was the pioneer who attempted to persuade social scientists to examine the actor's subjective perception of the real world. Simon maintained that if both the knowledge and computational power of the decision maker are severely limited then we must distinguish the real world from the actor's perception if we are going to understand the choices that he/she makes. Moreover we must theorize about the reasoning processes that generated the actor's subjective representation. However Simon's emphasis was on bounded rationality—the limits on the computational power of the decision maker, whereas my concern with ideologies focused more on the information available to the actor and the imperfect feedback that the actor received as a result of the choices he/she made.

An understanding of how human learning occurs appears to be the most promising approach to the mental constructs that humans develop to explain and interpret the world around them. But the learning is not just a product of the experiences of the individual in his or her lifetime, it also includes the cumulative experiences of past generations embodied in culture. Collective learning, according to Hayek, consists of those experiences that have passed the slow test of time and are embodied in our language, institutions, technology, and ways of doing things. The accumulated stock of knowledge of past experiences is built into our learning and is the deep underlying source of path dependence—the powerful influence of the past on the present and future. Learning then is an incremental process filtered by the culture of a society that determines the perceived pay-offs, but there is no guarantee that the cumulative past experiences of a society will necessarily fit them to solve new problems. The learning process then appears to be a function of (1) the way in which a given belief system filters the information derived from experiences and (2) the different experiences confronting individuals and societies at different times.

This cognitive science/institutional approach to history offers the promise of making sense out of the economic past and the diverse performance of economies in the present. There is nothing automatic about evolving the conditions that will result in low-cost transacting in the impersonal markets that are essential to productive economies. Game theory characterizes the issue. Individuals usually will find it worthwhile cooperating with others in exchange when the play is repeated, when there is complete information about the other player's past performance, and when there are small numbers of players—in short the conditions that characterize small-scale societies with personalized exchange. Cooperation is difficult to sustain when the game is not repeated (or there is an end game), when information about the other players is lacking, and when there are large numbers of players—in short the conditions that characterize the interdependent world of impersonal exchange of modern productive economies. Creating the institutions that will alter the benefit-cost ratios in favor of cooperative solutions is the major issue of economic performance because it entails the creation of effective, that is productive, economic and political institutions. And given the inherent inefficiency of political markets and the key role that political institutions play in economic performance it is not surprising that economic performance through time has been less than satisfactory.

We still have a long way to go, but I believe that an understanding of how people make choices, under what conditions the rationality postulate is a useful tool, and how individuals make choices under conditions of uncertainty and ambiguity are fundamental issues that we must address in order to make further progress in the social sciences.

In 1972 I married again, to Elisabeth Case; she continues to be wife, companion, critic, and editor: a partner in the projects and programs that we undertake. It is as critic and editor that she has directly played an important part in my evolution as an economist. She has transformed my indifferent prose into good English, but more important, she has an unerring sense of when I have not thought out completely what I am trying to say and forces me to confront those ambiguities and confusions and clarify my thinking.

I would be remiss if I left the impression that my life has been totally occupied with scholarly research. My evolution as an economist has taken place within the larger context of a rich and varied life. True, economic research has been the fundamental focus of my life, but it has been intermingled with a variety of activities that have complemented that central preoccupation and enriched my life. I continue to be a photographer; I have enjoyed fishing and hunting with a close friend; and I have owned two ranches, first in northern California and then in the state of Washington. I learned to fly an airplane, and had my own airplane during the 1960s. I have always taken seriously good food and wine. In addition, music has continued to be an important part of my life.

My wife and I now live in the summers in northern Michigan in an environment that is wonderfully conducive to research, and where most of my work in the last fifteen years has been done. I work on research all morning. In the afternoons I hike with my dog, play tennis, or go swimming. In the evening, as we are only 16 miles from the Interlochen Music Camp, we listen to music as often as two or three nights a week. It is a wonderful place for that mixture of research and leisure which has made my life such a rich experience.

Note

The author would like to thank Alexandra Benham and Elisabeth Case for editing this essay.

Douglass C. North

Awarded Nobel Prize in 1993. Lecture presented October 25, 1994.

Date of Birth

November 5, 1920

Academic Degrees

B.A., University of California, Berkeley, 1942
Ph.D., University of California, Berkeley, 1952

Academic Affiliations

Acting Assistant Professor, University of Washington, 1950–51
Assistant Professor, University of Washington, Seattle, 1951–56
Associate Professor, University of Washington, Seattle, 1956–60
Visiting Associate Professor, Stanford University, 1958
Professor of Economics, University of Washington, 1960–83
Pitt Professor of American Institutions, Cambridge University, 1981–82
Henry R. Luce Professor of Law and Liberty and Professor of Economics and History, Washington University in St. Louis, 1983–96
Spencer T. Olin Professor of Arts and Sciences, Washington University, 1996–2012
Spencer T. Olin Emeritus Professor of Arts and Sciences, Washington University, 2012–present

Selected Books

The Economic Growth of the United States, 1790–1860, 1961
Growth and Welfare in the American Past: A New Economic History, 1966, 1983
Institutional Change and American Economic Growth, 1971 (with L. Davis)
The Rise of the Western World: A New Economic History, 1973 (with R. Thomas)
Structure and Change in Economic History, 1981
Institutions, Institutional Change, and Economic Performance, 1990

Myron S. Scholes

I was born in Timmins, Ontario, Canada on July 1, 1941. My only brother, David, was born five years later. My father was born in New York City but moved to Toronto as a young man to live with his older brother. After graduation as a dentist and after a start as a teacher at the Eastman Clinic in Rochester, New York, that was cut short by the Great Depression, my father ventured to Timmins, a relatively prosperous gold mining region in northern Ontario, to practice dentistry in 1930. This was targeted as a temporary move until the Depression ended. His temporary move, however, lasted for twenty-five years. My mother had a longer journey to arrive in Canada. As a result of the many purges in Russia, as a two-year-old she had fled with her parents to Canada around 1908 and settled in South Porcupine, a very small town six miles south of Timmins.

As a young woman, my mother and her uncle established a successful chain of small department stores in and around Timmins. At its height, they employed over 1,000 employees in approximately ten stores.

In 1941, the year I was born, her uncle left by train for Toronto, 500 miles to the south, to formalize the legal relations among my mother and her family and her uncle and his family. Unfortunately, her uncle died on the train trip before any of the agreements could be formalized. The death of her uncle resulted in a family dispute, my first exposure to agency and contracting problems. Although it was not an equitable distribution, her uncle's sons-in-law claimed all of the stores registered in his name as their own, forcing my mother out of a large fraction of the business. This episode always fascinated me. After turning over the stores that happened to be in her name to others on her side of the family who worked in the business, she devoted her efforts to raising me and subsequently my brother while running the rest of the family business on the side.

I was always very proud of my mother's business accomplishments. It was quite an achievement in those days for a woman to run an organization, let alone one in northern Canada. As you might imagine she was a powerful woman, a family leader, and insightful in subjects pertaining to business and in dealing with others.

My father was a scholar, an extremely intelligent man, who was well read in many diverse subjects. When I was young, he seemed to know everything. He was respected for his work; his personality was the exact opposite of that of my mother's. He was a quiet, gentle, but firm man. To my parents, education, learning, thinking, and discussing issues were of prime importance. And, given my love of participating and learning, I thrived in this environment.

As you might imagine, Timmins was a small town. There were about 25,000 people in Timmins, then and today. The temperature fell to 40 below zero at times in the winter. The summers were short, maybe lasting from late June to early September. The town and region were famous for mining gold and silver. The town produced great hockey players. In more recent years, Timmins has become famous because of Shania Twain, the country and western singer. She was born there as well. I think that I am the only Nobel Prize winner. I was once asked to appear on a television program with Shania, but I turned the opportunity down. I suspected that her economics was as good as my singing.

Because I was outstripping the school system in Timmins, my parents sought a greater challenge for us. At the age of ten, I moved with my family to Hamilton, Ontario, thirty miles outside of Toronto. Thankfully it was much warmer in Hamilton than Timmins, but it still wasn't Florida. I had opted for Florida, but my father could not receive a license there without significant payoffs or a lengthy return to school.

Although I was a good student, I didn't really realize it until my first year of high school, when I was forced to work on my own at home for three months because I was sick with pneumonia. I still ended the year near the top of my class, as I did throughout my high school years. I attended public schools in both Timmins and Hamilton. In Ontario, at that time, your first year of college was also your last year of high school (that is, grade 13). I was class representative throughout my high school years and valedictorian of the senior class. I enjoyed school but did not take it too seriously. I would spend a considerable amount of time playing poker or chess with my classmates. I was even the trainer for the high school football team. Although I enjoyed puzzles and financial issues, I did not have a life's plan.

The educational system was excellent. In high school, I completed subjects in algebra, trigonometry, geometry, and calculus, as well as physics, chemistry, and biology. I scored extremely high in physics and the university in Hamilton solicited me to enter their engineering program.

Soon after we arrived in Hamilton, my life changed dramatically. My mother developed cancer. She died five years later, a few days after my sixteenth birthday. Another shock, but of much less import, befell me. I developed keratoconus, a condition in which scar tissue developed on each of my corneas and impaired my eyesight. It became difficult for me to read for extended periods of time. Because of this, I learned to think abstractly and to conceptualize the solution to problems. Out of necessity, I became a good listener—a quality appreciated by subsequent associates and students. Luckily, at age twenty-six, a successful cornea transplant greatly improved my vision in my right eye. I have had a subsequent cornea transplant in my left eye as well.

Through my parents, especially my mother, I became interested in economics and, in particular, finance. As I mentioned, my mother loved business and discussed stocks, world events, and finance in general whenever there was an opportunity to do so. Before she died, she suggested that I consider joining her brother in his book-publishing and promotion business. During my teenage years, I was always treasurer of my various clubs; I traded extensively among my friends; I gambled to understand probabilities and risks. I invested in the stock market while in high school and university through accounts set up first by my mother and then by my father. I was fascinated with the determinants of the level of stock prices. I spent long hours reading reports and books to glean the secrets of successful investing, but, alas, to no avail. The Holy Grail still awaits me.

I did mention that I loved physics. I loved solving complex problems. So I was torn between physics and economics. During the summer after my senior year of high school, however, I realized why I would not become a physicist. While working for my uncle's firm, I designed a puzzle for a magazine sold to teenage girls. I worked on this puzzle for weeks to make it interesting but difficult. When I presented it to the board and editorial committee of the magazine, no one understood what I had done. I decided then and there that I really enjoyed working with people, being involved in activities that were direct and not too abstract, removed or singular. I came to realize that I loved creating with others and working on problems that had real-world applications. For me, the most rewarding activities have always been conceptualizing difficult problems and then immersing myself in the details to test my theories.

Because of my mother's death, I decided to remain in Hamilton and attend McMaster University, a school close to my home, for my undergraduate studies. At that time, there were approximately 2,000 students attending McMaster University. Although the McMaster University entrance committee thought that I would concentrate in physics or engineering, I decided instead to concentrate on economics and the liberal arts. McMaster does have one other Nobel Prize winner, a physicist. There, I worked as a reporter and advertising manager of the school paper and yearbook and was a referee for the intramural football league, although I can't remember why, for my eyesight was not particularly good.

McMaster turned out to be a fortuitous choice. Because it was such a small school, Professor McIver, a University of Chicago graduate in economics, worked closely with me in my studies. He directed me to read and understand the work of many classical economists, including the more contemporary teachings of Milton Friedman and George Stigler, two subsequent Nobel Prize winners in economics. I was impressed with their writings.

Upon graduation in 1962, I was deciding between entering law school or graduate school in economics. After considerable thought, I decided to follow my mother's wishes and join my uncle in his publishing business on the condition that I complete my studies in a graduate program. Because of my enjoyment of economics and my planned return to business, I decided on business school, not law school. Although my family wanted me to apply to other schools, such as Harvard, I wanted to go only to the University of Chicago, where Stigler and Friedman were teaching and conducting research.

I had learned an important lesson, maybe at McMaster University. Intuitively, I knew that if I wanted to grow and achieve my potential, I should learn and work with those who were the best and who could bring out the best in me. That strategy has become a cornerstone of my career. I have always tried to go where the best were located. My thought at the time was that this would enable me to "steal" knowledge from them, but I subsequently realized that I had to contribute to the interchange of ideas to enable me to learn from others.

Chicago was a marvelous school for me. I did not know what awaited me on my arrival. During my first year at Chicago, I met a few classmates, who would become life-long friends, and from whom I have learned and continue to learn a tremendous amount over the years. In particular, Michael Jensen and Richard Roll, both in the Ph.D. program in finance, who have become world-renowned scholars in their own right and should also be awarded the Nobel Prize, added immeasurably to my understanding of economics and finance. Marshall Blum and Joel Stern were significant contributors to my learning and growth. I credit Jack Gould, who later became Dean of the Graduate School of Business, for helping me clarify many of the finer points of economic reasoning.

The summer of 1963, my first summer at Chicago, changed the direction of my life forever. During the first year at Chicago I had worked on a project for my uncle. I evaluated the possibility of buying a children's book company called Golden Books. My recommendation to buy what was then a wonderful franchise but a mismanaged company, was turned down for other than economic reasons. Once again I understood agency problems. As a result, I decided not to return to my uncle's company.

For that first summer, although I had never programmed before nor knew what a computer was, I secured a junior computer-programming position at Chicago through the kindness of Dean Robert Graves. On telling him that I knew nothing about computers or programming, he said that I did not have to worry: I was the "number seven" programmer and I would learn to program over the course of the summer by interacting with the other programmers.

I was the only one who showed up in the office. During my first few days on the job, several professors asked for computer-programming assistance on their research projects. I was able to fend them off by arguing that the senior programmers would soon be on scene to assist them, as I was only the "number-seven" programmer. The other programmers, however, never did show up.

By the third day, I could no longer fend off the aggressive professors seeking programming assistance. On confronting Dean Graves, he informed me that I, a novice, was the only "programmer" left. He pointed me in the direction of the computer facility some six blocks from the school, and I was on my way. I spent the next four and one-half months falling in love with computers and with the researchers that I met that summer. I must have been one of the first computer nerds; I worked all hours of the day and night. Computers were far more primitive in 1963. We had to program in native languages. But by the end of that summer, I was becoming a computer wizard, a skill that I would continue to develop over many years. If Chicago had had a computer science school, or if computer science had been a more developed field, I might have been tempted to become a computer scientist instead of an economist. Programming allowed me to conceptualize solutions to problems and then apply the solutions to demonstrate the actual results.

Another powerful force, however, had taken hold of me that summer: the love of economics and economic research. I was mesmerized by how the professors who were my computer clients created and addressed their own research projects. This was empowering. They enjoyed the process; they were absorbed by discovery. From time to time I ventured to ask them to explain their research, and occasionally I made suggestions on how to improve the research design. Lester Telser and Peter Pashigian were two of my clients. Merton Miller and Eugene Fama, two energetic and creative financial economics professors were clients as well. Merton Miller was awarded the Nobel Prize in economics in 1990, and Eugene Fama certainly deserves the award as well. At times, they were quite frustrated when I provided them with research output that they did not seek, but I thought that they would find interesting. They became my mentors, shaping my understanding of finance. And, fortunately, both became lifelong friends.

Either because of my scholastic qualities or because he did not want to lose me as a programmer, Merton Miller suggested that I enter the Ph.D. program. I did, and I came to love economics and its young new branch, which has come to be called financial economics. Chicago provided me with a wonderful learning environment. Miller and Fama were blazing ahead in financial economics. Stigler was leading the way in a new field of economics called "information economics." Friedman was fighting on in the macroeconomic front, persuading us that Keynesian economics was based on false economic rigidities.

I became interested in relative asset prices and the degree to which arbitrage prevented economic agents from earning abnormal profits in security markets. My province became risk and return. I concentrated my economics research during 1965–78 on attempts to understand the trade-offs between risk and return in both frictionless and friction-filled economies. I made tremendous progress in this area.

My Ph.D. dissertation, for example, attempted to determine the shape of the demand curve for traded securities. Since, as I reasoned, risk and return characteristics were the features that distinguish one security from another, the extent of the market was far greater than that of the individual stock. It was new information that would cause a change in the price of the security, information that was signaled by the large sale by an informed investor. This was the first statement in finance of a rational expectations approach to understanding economic activity. That is, only new information could change the demand for securities, not whether an individual wanted to sell more or less of a particular security.

After formulating the theory, careful empirical tests provided evidence that the prices of securities change not because of a movement along a demand curve with increases in supply, but because of changes in the information set that affect valuations. Temporary supply/demand imbalances exist because of the time necessary for speculators to assess the importance of the new information, not the size of the sale itself. Even to this day, there is considerable confusion between attributing movement along a demand curve and changes in the positioning of the entire curve. For example, the effectiveness of "operation twist" during the 1960s, wherein the U.S. Treasury attempted to encourage long rates to fall in order to foster investment while retaining higher short-term rates, is only one of many examples along these lines.

In addition, I worked on measures of risk and the effect of differential risk on security returns in a paper with Merton Miller. I studied the relation between accounting and market-determined measures of risk in another paper with William Beaver and Paul Kettler.

After essentially finishing my Ph.D. dissertation in the fall of 1968, I became an assistant professor of finance at the Sloan School of Management at MIT. I had two job offers in 1968, one at MIT for $10,000 and one at the University of Texas at Austin for $17,500. I told MIT that $10,000 was too low a salary, and they increased it to $10,500. I went to MIT, but not for the pay. My professors wanted me to go to MIT for seasoning and to grow on my own. The next year, when MIT gave me a raise of only $250, I thought that I had failed as an MIT professor. But, the dean informed me that, on the contrary, the faculty was proud of my successes and that I had achieved one of the highest increases in salary that year. Given my scholarships at Chicago, I had made more per year after taxes as a graduate student at Chicago. I knew that MIT was going to be expensive. And again, relative, not absolute, pricing came to the fore.

Paul Cootner, Franco Modigliani, and Stewart Myers became my colleagues at the Sloan School. During my first year at Sloan I met Fischer Black, then a consultant working for Arthur D. Little in Cambridge. We hit it off immediately. We had many lengthy discussions about financial economics and research needs in the area. As a result of these discussions, we started to collaborate on many research projects. It was an extremely productive relationship for both of us. We would spend endless hours discussing financial economics, its models, how to test economic relations and the failings of economics to incorporate risk into economic models with sufficient prominence. In our minds, risk was a first-order consideration.

Although Paul Cootner unfortunately left the Sloan School in 1969, Robert Merton joined our group at that time. As you are aware, Robert Merton was my co-recipient of the Nobel Prize in 1997. Essentially, the senior faculty members in finance were not available to work with us; that is, Franco Modigliani was involved in large macro projects and Dan Holland was involved in macro tax policy, so the young assistant professors controlled the development of the financial economics teaching and research program at the Sloan school. We were on our own in both the research and teaching domains.

Stewart Myers greatly influenced my thinking in the area of corporate finance, and Franco Modigliani on macro and asset-pricing models. Robert Merton, Fischer Black, and I were interested in asset pricing and derivative pricing models. It was through many interactions that the three of us developed and extended the field of contingent-claims pricing. In my Nobel address I explained how we developed the Black–Scholes model and how Fischer Black and I used our understanding of risk, return, and arbitrage to define a new method to value risk and to price options. Although some have surmised a different approach, we developed the model from our economic intuition. We were confronted with an interesting economic problem, how to value options. We found the tools to solve it. We did not have a set of tools looking for a problem to address.

In 1973, soon after the Black–Scholes model was published, Texas Instruments (TI) marketed a calculator containing our formula. Traders on the options exchange such as the CBOE could use the calculator to calculate Black–Scholes model values given their inputs. I called TI and asked them whether they would provide us with royalties for using the model. They said no, the model was in the public domain. I asked if they would be willing to send me one of the calculators. They suggested that I buy one using my own nickel.

During my years at the Sloan school, I worked on testing the capital-asset pricing model with Fischer Black and Michael Jensen, and on developing the option-pricing technology with Fischer Black, while continuing to work with Merton Miller on several research projects. Fischer Black and I were interested in all aspects of finance but loved the capital-asset pricing model as a way to describe the trade-off between risk and return.

It gave us the insights to figure out how to value options. An option is the right but not the obligation to acquire or sell an asset. It is the value of flexibility. The more uncertain the view on future outcomes, the more valuable the option.

I learned a tremendous amount through many hours of discussion with Paul Samuelson, Robert Solow, and many others at the economics table in the faculty club at MIT. Although I knew that I would miss working on a day-to-day basis with Robert Merton, I returned permanently in 1973 to the Graduate School of Business at the University of Chicago after a visiting year. Although Robert and I are no longer at the same institution, we have remained life-long friends and continue to discuss economic problems.

Fischer Black took his first position in academics as a professor at the University of Chicago in 1972. I wanted to return to Chicago and, in particular, work with Fischer Black, Gene Fama, and Merton Miller. It was an important period in the life of the school, and I had the opportunity to interact with many interesting colleagues. Although Robert Merton was successful in luring Fischer back to Boston in 1974, I resisted taking the offer to return as well and remained at Chicago.

During my Chicago years, I started to work on the effects of taxation on asset prices and incentives. For example, I studied the effects of the taxation of dividends on the prices of securities in three papers, one with Fischer Black and two others with Merton Miller. Merton and I studied the interaction of incentives and taxes in executive compensation. Robert Hamada and I addressed capital structure issues with taxation, and George Constantinides and I studied the effects of taxes on the optimal liquidation of assets.

I became heavily involved with the Center for Research in Security Prices at the University of Chicago during the 1973–1980 time frame. As director of the center, I led the development of large research data files containing daily security prices and related information on all New York and American Stock Exchange securities from 1962 to 1985 (now updated by others through the present), and merged these data with monthly data files back to 1926. This effort added immeasurably to the research output of colleagues around the world conducting research in financial economics. I believe that great empirical work leads to additional theory and new theory leads, in turn, to new empirical testing. With this in mind, Joe Williams and I wrote a paper on the estimation of risk parameters employing nonsynchronous data, the so-called "Scholes–Williams betas."

In 1981, I visited Stanford University and became a permanent faculty member of the Stanford Business School and the Stanford Law School in 1983. I believe to this day that re-potting oneself keeps the intellectual juices flowing. Staying put just became too comfortable for me. Even to this day, I love traveling and discussing new ideas with associates around the world.

The period at Stanford was a time of significant learning for me. My close colleagues in the business school included William Sharpe, James Van Horne, and a host of up-and-coming younger professors, most notably Jeremy Bulow, Anat Admati, Paul Pfleiderer, and Michael Gibbons. My close colleagues in the law school included Ronald Gilson and Kenneth Scott. With Jeremy Bulow, I wrote several papers on pension planning.

Most important, I was fortunate to work with and become a close friend of Mark Wolfson. We wrote several articles together on investment banking and incentives. We developed a new theory of tax planning under uncertainty and information asymmetry. Many of our published articles on these topics were rewritten and incorporated into our book, *Taxes and Business Strategy: A Planning Approach*, which was published in 1992.

In 1990 my interests shifted back to the role of derivatives in facilitating the financial intermediation process. I became a special consultant to Salomon Brothers, Inc., and continued on as a managing director and co-head of its fixed-income-derivative sales and trading group, while still conducting research and teaching at Stanford University.

My life as an economist was shaped by attempting to conceptualize and test real-world problems. My first consulting relation occurred in 1968 when I consulted with the management science department of Wells Fargo Bank on the efficacy of their security analyst system. I wrote a report suggesting that they abandon active management entirely and concentrate their efforts on evaluating risk and return, and how to create portfolios that would provide alternative risk and return trade-offs.

John McQuown, head of the management science group at the bank, asked me to consult with them on such a project. Since Fischer Black wanted to leave Arthur D. Little at the time, he joined me on the project. We invented the concept of the *index fund*. Many of our research projects were funded under this research agenda. Although it took many years before index funds became mainstream, an entire industry was built on our efforts. John McQuown was correct in pushing this vision forward.

I enjoyed working with the Chicago Board Options market and with the clearing members to use the options-pricing technology to establish risk-management systems for the clearing-member firms. The clearing-member firms and the traders adopted the option-pricing technology to build the first quantitative-risk-management systems. They did so not because some regulator told them to do so for accounting or for some other purpose, but because they could offer more competitive prices on their products. Lowering their capital costs improved their competitive advantage; using models gave them an edge to set tighter spreads. The technology reduced transaction costs.

Absent a model, traders could neither price securities with embedded options with sufficient accuracy to compete against other traders with models, nor could they reduce the risks of their positions to employ their capital more efficiently at a low enough cost to compete with other traders. Although it is hard to prove, I do think that the success of the CBOE, the other exchanges, and the trillion dollar over-the-counter market in derivative products can be attributed to option-pricing models. Financial theory has spawned the development of an entirely new industry and changed how finance is practiced around the world. And, the risk-management technologies have become the backbone to risk-management systems now used in the banking community around the world.

In late 1993, I joined with several colleagues, many from the Salomon Brothers Group, to become a principal and co-founder of a firm called Long-Term Capital Management (LTCM). This experience has shaped my research interests in the last few years. In joining LTCM, I had hoped to further the application of financial technology to practice. My reason for joining Salomon Brothers and then LTCM was to achieve a deeper understanding of the evolution of financial institutions and markets and the forces shaping this evolution on a global basis. I felt that to achieve that deeper understanding, I needed to immerse myself in the markets. My research papers in the last few years have focused on the interaction and evolution of markets and financial institutions. I will return to that research program in a moment.

During 1997–1999 we have seen the movement of a financial crisis in the debt markets around the world. The Russian government default on their debt products in August of 1998 caused an increase in volatility and a flight to liquidity and to quality in markets around the world. The increase in volatility and the flight to liquidity around the world caused LTCM to experience an extraordinary reduction in its capital base in

August and then again in September of 1998. The August loss was attributable to the Russian crisis; the September loss was attributable to LTCM's own difficulties. The position sizes were too large and too concentrated to liquidate into a chaotic market. Correlations that had been low in the past became extremely high in all asset classes around the world as investors tried to reduce risks.

Some attribute this collapse to a failure of models, and, in particular, option-pricing models. In my opinion, this is false. First, option-pricing models were not used to determine the lion's share of LTCM's positions, and second, did not come into play in the risk-management system. The Salomon traders assumed that correlations would remain low enough to share capital among the positions. Instead, the correlations approached one as all positions lost money at the same time. The firm could not liquidate its illiquid positions into a chaotic market and its capital disappeared.

This reduction in capital culminated in a form of non-fault bankruptcy. A consortium of fourteen leading financial institutions, with outstanding claims against LTCM, infused new equity capital into the firm and took over its assets. The consortium hired the LTCM team to manage the portfolio under their direct supervision. The Federal Reserve coordinated this takeover. Although some called this a bailout, I have called it a coordinated liquidation to avoid the snails-pace processes of the bankruptcy courts, institutions that are not geared to handle a capital market crisis in an efficient manner.

The last few years have been terrific for me. I have been working on a book that models and explains why the prices of risk transfer and liquidity change in the market. I believe that understanding risk transfer and liquidity in modern financial markets in light of unanticipated changes in the opportunity set is an important and exciting research area. The book will be published by Princeton University Press.

Although I have not been teaching full time at Stanford, I have been giving lectures around the world to students, academics, and practitioners. This is enjoyable and lets me address much larger audiences efficiently. I will continue in this vein, for I enjoy it.

I have been working with former students and colleagues to build a hedge fund business, called Oak Hill Platinum Partners, an exciting and energizing enterprise. It allows us to marry theory with practice. As I stated earlier, I have always enjoyed the intersection of conceptualizing a problem with the testing and applying the results of the theory. Concepts to context and back to concepts is an important evolutionary process. Working with Chi-fu Huang, Ayman Hindy, T. S. Sung, and Lawrence Ng, my founding partners, has been rewarding, and we expect to build, work, learn, and develop new theories in the future.

Over the years, I have received honorary doctorates from three universities: University of Paris-Dauphine in 1989, McMaster University, my alma mater, in 1990, and Katholieke Universiteit Leuven in 1998.

I am fortunate to have two wonderful daughters, Anne and Sara, and a generous son-in-law—Anne's husband, Seth. All of them continue to add tremendous joy to my life. My fortunes have also risen immeasurably, for I have found Jan. She completes my life. We were married in chaotic times on October 4, 1998. But, together we create order out of disorder. We enjoy each other's company and insights and plan to do so for many years to come. Her two sons by a first marriage, Peter and Mike, have become part of the family.

Although I do not have time for many hobbies, I do enjoy skiing and golf, two sports that allow me to be outdoors in both winter and summer. We have a ski home in the mountains outside of Salt Lake City, Utah.

I ski the race course from time to time. To do so, it is necessary to sign a release form. On seeing my name the attendant asked whether I was the Scholes of the Black–Scholes model. I asked him how he knew about the model. He replied that he was a 1995 Ph.D. in economics from MIT. I did not realize that the program had gone that far downhill since we left.

We span many related and unrelated disciplines in the evolving field of financial economics. I remember the tale of a friend, who graduated with a Ph.D. in physics, when applying for a position at a renowned investment-banking firm in their quantitative finance group, he was asked what he was studying and working on in his current position. He responded, "Black Holes." On mishearing "Black–Scholes," the questioner responded that "he was hired."

Myron S. Scholes
Awarded Nobel Prize in 1997. Lecture presented April 7, 1999.

Date of Birth
July 1, 1941

Academic Degrees
B.A., McMaster University, 1962
M.B.A., University of Chicago, 1964
Ph.D., University of Chicago, 1969

Academic Affiliations
Assistant and Associate Professor of Finance, Sloan School of Management, MIT, 1968–73
Associate Professor, Graduate School of Business, University of Chicago, 1973–76
Director, Center for Research in Security Prices, University of Chicago, 1976–80
Professor, Graduate School of Business, University of Chicago, 1976–83
Frank E. Buck Professor of Finance, Graduate School of Business, Stanford University, 1983–96
Senior Research Fellow, Hoover Institution, Stanford University, 1985–96
Frank E. Buck Professor of Finance, Emeritus, Graduate School of Business, Stanford University, 1996–present

Selected Books
Taxes and Business Strategy: A Planning Approach, 1992, 2001 (with M. Wolfson)

Gary S. Becker

It is my pleasure to be here and to participate in the Nobel economists lecture series, a series that has had the great modern figures in economics speak, people such as Friedman, Samuelson, and Buchanan, among others. I'm supposed to talk about my evolution as an economist and the forces that influenced me. I will take that as my charge. Yet it is a difficult assignment. It is hard to assess the forces that have had a major influence on one's research. What I can do is to talk a bit about my development as an economist. I will emphasize the many instances where I was extremely lucky to come into contact with people—giants in the field—who had a great influence on me. I will also discuss instances where I started down research paths that at the time seemed to be rather natural and appropriate extensions of microeconomics; I was not fully aware that these would develop into more comprehensive, path-breaking, and often controversial contributions to economics and social science. Following very brief remarks about my days growing up, I will turn my attention to my student days at Princeton, where I first became serious about economics.

I was born in Pottsville, Pennsylvania, in 1930 but grew up in Brooklyn, New York, where our family moved when I was a young child. My father was a businessman and my mother was a housewife. My parents were very intelligent, I see in retrospect. I didn't always see that when I was growing up—they were not highly educated; neither one of them went beyond the eighth grade. My father, growing up in Montreal, Canada, left school because he was eager to make money, despite his mother's insistence that he remain in school. My mother's lack of schooling is not surprising since at that time most young girls were not expected to continue with their education. My parents did realize the value of a good education. They did not insist that we pursue higher education, although both my two sisters and my brother and I did so. We could tell growing up that there was an appreciation for education, in spite of the fact that there were not many books in our house and neither one of my parents read a great deal.

I was an excellent student, in general, at least to judge by grades, but up to the age of 16 I was not what I would call a serious student. I was more interested in sports than in academic subjects. I did the amount of work necessary to get good grades. I was not intellectually inclined in high school, at least initially. For some reason, I cannot precisely state what the forces were, but at about the age of sixteen my interests began to shift. I date them dramatically to when I voluntarily gave up on the high school handball team of which I was a member (I probably could have been the number one player), but instead chose to become a member of the math team. They met during the same period, and I had to choose one rather than the other. I went through a little bit of uncertainty, but finally chose the math team. I am glad I did so, because my subsequent academic interests were centered on mathematics and science.

What I liked about the math team was that we actually had competitions. This was in New York City, and there were competitions among schools in which we had to solve problems, two tough problems at a time, and solve them within an intense time frame, usually ten minutes to do both problems. And while there was a lot of pressure and tension, particularly when you did not know the answers, it was a fun and collegial process, with five members on each team. The math competitions had an important influence on me, first in seeing other students who were quite good, and second in proving to myself that our team could do well against Bronx Science and Stuyvesant and the other specialized high schools in science and mathematics.

My senior year in high school I became concerned about doing something for society. Here I was interested in math and science and then, all of a sudden, my interests began to shift as I became more socially conscious. Like most young people at the time, I considered myself a kind of a socialist and felt that I should move toward politics or history or some field where I could make more of a contribution to society. I had a really mixed view, continuing to be strongly interested in math, but no longer really wanting to become a mathematician.

A Princeton Undergraduate

I went to Princeton when I was seventeen and had this conflict going on—a strong interest in math but the desire to make a contribution to society. As freshmen we had to choose some electives and were required to take a course in the social sciences. And for some reason (I have no idea why) I chose to take the principles of economics. And for me this turned out to be a very good, or basically lucky, decision. As you will see, this was just one of several lucky decisions that came at various times. We used as our textbook an early edition of Paul Samuelson's *Economics: An Introductory Analysis*. It certainly has been one of the best-selling textbooks in economics, or in any other field. It is still in use. What I liked about this book was the rather brief section on microeconomics—how prices operate in a market system. It appealed to me because of its more mathematical discussion; basically microeconomics seemed to have a very compact mathematical foundation. Given my previous interest in math, microeconomics had a natural attractiveness for me, while at the same time it was dealing with social problems. I was less taken by Samuelson's extensive discussion of macroeconomics, which seemed to me to be rather vague and not fully satisfactory. I still feel that way about it, although there has been some real progress in that area.

I graduated from Princeton in three years, but during that period I read as many articles and books on economics as I could manage—probably the most influential being Stigler's *The Theory of Competitive Price*, as it was then called, and Hicks's *Value and Capital*. I remember reading Hicks one summer. When I saw one of my teachers in the fall and he asked what I was doing, I told him, "I read *Value and Capital* this summer, but I found it very hard." He said, "Don't worry about that, none of the faculty understand it either." So I felt they didn't understand it and I felt I didn't understand it either, but at least I was close to understanding it (or so I thought at the time). So that gave me a little confidence—maybe I could get someplace in economics.

The paper I wrote for my junior-year thesis (required at Princeton) was on classical monetary theory. I criticized some analysis of Leontief and others that had been in the literature and debated at the time. Several faculty members said that I was correct in my criticism, and I think, in retrospect, that I was correct. Eventually I collaborated with a teacher, William Baumol; we published the analysis from my junior thesis, plus other material, in the *American Economic Review* in 1952. The paper was titled "The Classical Monetary Theory: The Outcome of the Discussion." My senior thesis was also published in the *American Economic Review* during 1952, in a paper titled "A Note on Multi-Country Trade."

So I was doing well in economics. During my senior year at Princeton, however, I was losing interest in economics and began to think that I should go into something else. Economics seemed excessively formal to me. I'm sure that cannot be true of anything you have been reading as students nowadays, but then that is how it seemed to me. Economics appeared incapable of helping me understand the issues in which I had an interest: inequality, class, race, prestige, and similar issues that were important for society. A sociology professor at Princeton suggested I look at Talcott Parsons's *Structure of Social Action.* Parsons, then the dominant figure in American sociology, started his career as an economist and believed that social theory included economics as a special case. I tried to read this book, but it contained an enormous quantity of jargon that did not lead anywhere, or at least anywhere that I could follow. I concluded that sociology was too hard, and returned, somewhat reluctantly, to economics. I remained unhappy—unhappy by what seemed to me a disconnect between what economists would talk about in textbooks and elsewhere and what I wanted to talk about.

I decided nevertheless to go on for a doctorate in economics. Adlai Stevenson once defined a graduate student as someone who didn't know when the party was over. Well, I wanted to continue in this party atmosphere, so I went for a doctorate. Most of the faculty wanted me to stay at Princeton, although I had already taken many graduate courses at Princeton; I felt, and some of my teachers agreed, that it would be better if I went someplace else. I was choosing between Harvard and Chicago and, for a variety of reasons, I decided to go to Chicago.

Chicago: The Early Years

From a professional point of view, the decision to go to Chicago was probably the most important decision I ever made. The atmosphere at Chicago was enormously stimulating. Original work was going on in many different areas and by many economists there, most notably Milton Friedman. The Cowles Commission (which subsequently left) was very active in mathematical economics and econometrics.

Milton Friedman became the greatest influence on my development as an economist. Attending his graduate course in price theory was just exciting, and I would eagerly wait for that course to come twice a week. Some people would even ask my friends, "How can he be so excited about attending class?" A lot of the classes were boring, but that is nothing new for students. Friedman's class was different. Here I saw economics as a tool and not simply as a game played by clever academics, which is what had worried me most about economics. In Friedman's hands, economics was a powerful tool to understand a whole host of problems—in the class Friedman dealt with things such as birthrates, insurance and lotteries, personal and business responses to taxes, how labor markets functioned, and the effect of having unionized versus non-unionized markets. And, on and on, economics was used to understand business practices of all types. "Let's see," Friedman would have asked, "how can we understand what Microsoft is doing?" (had Microsoft existed at that time).

It was a great course that showed me what I thought was not possible. You can do economics and do it in a rigorous way and nevertheless talk about important problems. So my indebtedness to Milton Friedman, one of the greatest economists of the twentieth century, is unlimited.

There were other people in Chicago who were doing important, original work: Ted Schultz in human capital, Gregg Lewis in labor economics, Aaron Director in law and economics, L. J. Savage in statistics and probability. It was a wonderful intellectual environment, and as I developed within that environment, I no longer had this feeling that economics couldn't do it. Indeed I developed the Chicago chip-on-the-shoulder attitude that economics could unlock the mysteries of the real world. Right or wrong, it was a great feeling to have. Here I was being given this powerful tool and a belief that the mysteries of the social world could be unlocked if we applied this tool in some creative fashion. I began to believe this as a graduate student. I still believe that it is true.

I stayed at Chicago for six years, the first three as a graduate student. During the second year I was looking for a thesis topic and had already done some research on an economic approach to political democracy. My paper on this topic was almost published in the *Journal of Political Economy,* but one of my teachers, Frank Knight, was the referee, and he did not like it. I have kept his comments to this day. Knight was a great economist, but he looked at democracy with what I would characterize as a normative point of view. He defined democracy as government by discussion. I wanted to employ an approach to democracy that looked upon it as an institutional system operating in a particular way, for good or bad, which you could analyze using economic analysis. The approach I took in this paper was a very early work in what we now call public choice theory. The editor wanted to publish it in the *JPE,* but was persuaded not to by the referee. It eventually got published in 1956, in a shorter, toned-down version in the first issue of the *Journal of Law and Economics.*

I thought of developing this topic more broadly as one of my possible thesis subjects. But, finally, I hit on something in which I became more interested—an economic approach to the issue of discrimination against minorities, whether religious minorities, racial minorities, gender, or anything else. It was a topic that I had been interested in, of course, but never thought about systematically until I began to think in response to a question put to me by Friedman and Ted Schultz—how might we analyze the fact that there is discrimination in the economy? It occurred to me at the time, but again I am not sure exactly how, that we can associate with each person a taste for discrimination. This taste or prejudice would be measured based on how much income an employer is willing to forfeit in order to avoid hiring somebody who he didn't like from a group that he didn't like; or how much an employee is willing to forfeit to avoid working with a member of a group that he didn't like; or how much a consumer will pay to avoid a product that is served by or produced by a group that he didn't like. So my approach to discrimination was to look at the willingness to pay, or forfeit income, in order to exercise a prejudice. This is still the only right way that I can tell to look at discrimination in mortgage lending, searches for drugs in cars, and other issues that are of great contemporary interest right now. Once you took this approach, then you had to think about how to link the observed discrimination that we see in the marketplace to these personal preferences or prejudices.

To make the link between market discrimination (that is, market outcomes) and personal preferences for discrimination required that I provide a model and analysis. My Ph.D. thesis showed how the degree of market discrimination depended not only on the discriminatory preferences of employers, employees, and consumers but also on the degree of competition in product markets, production technologies, and many other economic variables.

As I was working on my dissertation, I was fortunate to get encouragement from my faculty advisors, but some members of the faculty were highly dubious whether this was an appropriate subject. Their attitude was: "What's a good economist doing working on discrimination?" They could not talk me out of this topic, however, so they insisted instead that a distinguished sociologist at Chicago, Everett Hughes, become a member of my thesis committee, just to make sure that I did not go off the deep end. I do not think Hughes was much interested in what I was doing. The nice part was that he did not object to anything I was doing either. I would go to see him once every nine months and he would say "okay" and that was it. That satisfied the faculty who were dubious whether this was a worthwhile project.

Prior to entering the academic job market, I went to Harvard to present some of my work and also to MIT to discuss this work with some people. I remember talking to a younger faculty member at MIT (a subsequent Nobel Prize winner who gave one of your lectures); he asked me what I was working on and I said "racial discrimination." He said, "I thought you were a neoclassical economist?" I said, "I *am* a neoclassical economist, but isn't this part of neoclassical economics?" But I could not convince him that discrimination was a legitimate subject for economists to work on.

And this was the general experience I had with my dissertation research on discrimination. Eventually a revised version was submitted to the University of Chicago Press. The Press received very negative reviews on my manuscript when it was sent out to readers. The editor did not want to publish it. The economics department finally "bribed" the press. You see, Chicago believes in the market system. So the department said we would put up part of the cost and would share any profits on the book. The press agreed to publish my book, but only because of that bribe.

It gave me great pleasure that about ten years after the press published *The Economics of Discrimination,* the then editor of the press (who was also editor when my book came out) wrote an article, published in the *American Economic Review,* in which he admitted that my book was attracting sizeable interest. It was not selling a lot—but it was creating a great deal of interest.

The negative reaction to my work on discrimination, coupled with Frank Knight's hostility toward my article on democracy, made it clear to me that using economic analysis to discuss social and political issues was not going to be welcomed with open arms by most economists. I initially had expected economists to applaud attempts to widen the scope of their field. I was surprised that the main hostility toward my work, at least as it was explicitly stated, came from economists, not non-economists. I began to realize that my original view was naive. All disciplines have a strong and probably justified degree of intellectual conservatism. You do not give up ideas and concepts you have held for a long time without a fight. It is necessary to fight to get new ideas accepted.

Even after I became aware of the extent of the hostility, I remained confident that the contribution of the economic approach to broader problems would eventually be recognized. This confidence in what I was doing helped me persist against sometimes considerable and vicious opposition. There were two reasons why I remained confident. First, it just seemed to me obvious that economics could contribute to these areas. Economics was not the whole story, it was not the final word on discrimination, but how could economists justify that prior to my book on discrimination, with two or three exceptions, there was virtually no work by economists on a topic as enormously important as discrimination in the marketplace? I mean, it's incredible! So it seemed obvious to me that there was a role here.

That was one factor. As important as this was, I do not think that this would have been sufficient to enable me to persist against continuing hostility. The other factor was that I was fortunate to have intellectually powerful people on my side. I gained strength from the support of senior economists I greatly respected. Support came from my teachers, like Milton Friedman and Gregg Lewis, George Stigler—who soon effectively became my teacher—and other friends I had met along the way such as Armen Alchian and Jack Hirshleifer.

In short, this was a period in which my research and intellectual discourse encountered an enormous amount of opposition. There was little demand to hire me from the major institutions. After three years as a graduate student, I accepted an assistant professorship at Chicago. And these six years, looking back on it now, were perhaps the most important and most exciting of my career. I formed the foundation of what I was going to do later on. And I was learning at a rapid rate as I absorbed so many new things that were coming from people at Chicago and from others who came through Chicago. Four of my teachers went on to win the Nobel Prize: Milton Friedman; Friedrich Hayek, who was then on the Committee for Social Thought (I attended his seminars); Tjalling Koopmans; and Ted Schultz. And in addition to that, the Chicago intellectual vitality had many others, some mentioned here, who did not win the Nobel Prize but have done very important work that has been continually recognized.

Chicago wanted me to continue there after my three-year term was up, but I wanted to leave, even though Chicago offered me more money and a good chance of getting tenure. I felt it was more important for me to leave the nest and go out on my own. I had protection at Chicago with the likes of Friedman, Schultz, and Lewis, among others, and that was great, but I wanted to see if I could make it on my own. I said in effect, "I appreciate the offer, but I really don't want to stay at Chicago." So I looked around, went on the job market, and as a lot of other students have experienced, I did not find a overwhelming demand for my services. Major universities, like Harvard, MIT, Berkeley, and Yale showed no interest in me and did not interview me at any of the meetings. This was probably because I was a Chicago graduate and Chicago at that time was an "outlaw" department in the profession. Its students were treated as suspect by representatives of most of the major institutions. It is not that extreme now.

I had only two interviews, with Johns Hopkins and Columbia. Hopkins decided not to make me an offer. So I considered all my choices and decided to choose among them and went to Columbia, which I was happy to do. I also was offered a position at the National Bureau of Economic Research, which was then in New York City, so I could combine the two. I spent a dozen highly productive years at both institutions.

Columbia and the National Bureau of Economic Research

I started my work on human capital at Columbia and the National Bureau of Economic Research. When I came to the bureau, the then director, Solomon Fabricant, asked me what I would like to work on. From my work on discrimination, I had seen that there were enormous gaps in earnings between workers with different levels of education, among both blacks and whites. I knew the work Ted Schultz had been doing on human capital, which I found to be of considerable interest. So I told Fabricant that I would like to do a study on the rates of return to education and training. This would be a new departure for the bureau, but he said, "I will see what I can do." He got a small grant for me to work on education and earnings, which I began in 1957.

I soon realized that much more was needed in the human capital field than to calculate rates of return. There were no foundations for the theory of investment in human capital. My study was intended to be empirical, but I set about trying to sketch out a small set of foundations to give the work theoretical content. As I was sketching out some basic theory, I had no vision at all of what this would lead to. Once again, here is an example of the role of luck. As I delved into the theory and tried to develop a basic foundation for human capital investment, it looked to me that the theory could explain the way earnings rise with age (a concave age-earnings profile), the effect of education on the distribution of earnings, externalities of human capital, and many other issues that continue to this day to be discussed and debated. I was amazed and then greatly excited when I began to realize that this framework could integrate scores of observations and regularities in individual earnings, occupational differences in earnings, and employment.

In 1959, I made the first public presentation of some of my results at a session of the annual meetings of the American Economic Association. I presented a short paper that compared rates of return to schooling and returns on physical capital in the United States. And the discussants, to my amazement, were absolutely outraged. Once again, I continued to be surprised by what I should have anticipated. What was it that so outraged my discussants? In retrospect it seems silly. They were outraged that I was treating education as an economic activity, believing that this assumption somehow denigrated the cultural or non-economic aspects of education. I replied with some fervor and bluntness to my critics. It was one of the more heated sessions of the meeting. I was taken aback, but truth be told, I did not lose any confidence about what I was doing because their comments seemed so silly to me. I could not really believe that senior economists—I was 29 years old at the time—were making such dumb comments on my paper.

I continued working on the economics of human capital and in 1962 published an article on it. It was in fact well received. Then, in 1964, I published a book called *Human Capital: A Theoretical and Empirical Analysis, with Special Reference to Education*. The long subtitle is now forgotten—it is now called *Human Capital*. Actually, I debated a long time before I used the title *Human Capital* because I had been aware that people said that if you call it "capital" you are treating human beings as if they had no soul. Some people would make fun of it and call it "human cattle," suggesting that one is not treating humans as individuals. I knew that, and could have weaseled a little and called it "human resources," a phrase that was becoming common at the time. I decided to take the bull by the horns and title the book *Human Capital*, although it had this long subtitle to protect myself a little.

By the time I finished this research, I was indeed convinced that human capital was a crucial concept to understanding economic and social issues in many areas of life. Still, and this I will also confess, I was not prepared for the magnitude of its impact. Eventually, it would be referred to endlessly, and by that language—human capital—not only in academic writing but by politicians of both parties, journalists, even in ecclesiastical encyclicals. After a while some of the people who had resisted using this term began to think, "Well, look, if we call everything human capital and say we are investing in people, this can provide a good rationale for obtaining public monies." I remember the superintendent of the Chicago school system at that time, Benjamin Willis, inviting me to deliver an address to a meeting of superintendents. He told me, "I don't know why people dislike that word; it can be a great tool for us superintendents to get more money." So I think that this partly explains its success. Everything is now called human capital, including some things that should not be so called.

The more fundamental reason why the term human capital has been so successful and has continued to grow rather than shrink in importance is that it integrates into one basically simple concept a lot of actions and behavior that affect the individual and economy. In essence, human capital analysis puts individuals at the center of attention in an economy, not machinery, plant and equipment, or other inanimate objects. It is people who move an economy, people who determine whether an economy is rich or poor; human capital is a major aspect of the productivity and well-being of people. And it is investment in human capital, by acquiring skills from one's parents, through going to school, or through training and knowledge in the workplace, that helps determine a person's and an economy's stock of human capital wealth. I think this explanation is the fundamental reason why the term human capital has proven appealing and durable. It integrates diverse aspects of human behavior, pushing people to the center of the economic stage, so to speak.

At the same time that I was doing research on human capital, I was also working on the economics of the family and the demand for children. I began this work by asking what determines how many children that families have. I gave my first paper on this topic in the late 1950s, around the same time that I presented my early work on education. At a conference on the economic analysis on fertility, I drew an analogy between the demand for children by parents and their demand for durable consumer goods. I used that language in my paper. Well, you can imagine the reaction from my audience—as soon as I used this language everyone started laughing. Well, not everyone. This was a mixed audience of economists and non-economists. One economist who was the discussant on my paper, a youngish economist at Harvard, was very negative about it, stating that this approach could not explain much about the demand for children. I had learned over time to expect a negative reaction from the audience. But, once again, I was a little surprised by just how much hostility (and this was verbally expressed in public comments) my work aroused among some eminent economists. And yet again, this was an instance in which I feel indebted to Milton Friedman.

Friedman had been a participant at the conference and was attending my session. He got up and vigorously defended my paper during the discussion period. I felt, well, there are these fools on the one side criticizing me, but I have people like Friedman defending me. And that is all I needed. I had enormous respect for Friedman—I still do—so I thought, "Now look, if Friedman is defending my work, there must be something to what I am doing."

Another subject I was working on at this time was the theory of the allocation of time. As I worked on the economics of education, it soon became apparent, not only to me but to Schultz and others working in this area, that the major costs of going to school were generally the earnings students give up by not working full time. Even at private colleges and universities, where the tuition is high, the major cost is generally foregone earnings, or the opportunity cost of one's time. This seemed to me to be important, but apart from labor-leisure choice analysis used to understand labor supply, there was little formal role for the value of time or the allocation of time in microeconomic analysis. Once again, as I was working on one subject, I was led by the logic of the analysis into a different, albeit related, subject.

So I began at that time to try to generate a systematic analysis of time use. I eventually published an article called "The Theory of the Allocation of Time," (*Economic Journal*, 1965), which treated each household like a small-scale factory or enterprise that used time and goods to produce various commodities that they could not buy directly, like children, good health, a good meal, and things of that kind. Unlike the work on discrimination, human capital, and fertility, my work on time allocation was less controversial and more quickly and readily accepted within the economics profession.

As evident from the previous discussion, my time in New York was highly productive. At Columbia, Jacob Mincer and I jointly conducted a labor economics workshop that gained a large following among a new generation of labor economists. I greatly benefited from my colleagues at Columbia and the bureau; in addition to Mincer these included Victor Fuchs, Robert Willis, Finis Welch, and Sherwin Rosen. I had a remarkable group of students at Columbia, too numerous to mention here, that have gone on to make major contributions in the fields of human capital and labor economics, health, crime, and law and economics. So I was quite happy professionally at Columbia. I did not consider many other offers, partly because I did not get many. It made life easy.

In 1968 and 1969, student rebellions hit American universities. And there were few schools that were harder hit than Columbia. I was very disturbed by this, not so much by what the students were doing, but by the faculty's weakness and eventual unwillingness to stand up to disruptive and, in my opinion, intolerant student tactics. I was especially disappointed by the attitude of senior members of my department (not all, but most). They seemed to me to be weak and vacillating at a time when I thought there existed clear-cut and simple steps that could be taken to protect the intellectual integrity of the university.

I began to think of leaving Columbia at that time. The future to me looked dim, having lost a lot of confidence in my colleagues. I began to look around. I received an inquiry from the economics department at Harvard through an old friend of mine from undergraduate days, Otto Eckstein, who was a professor at Harvard. And he said: "Would I be interested in coming to Harvard? It would be a good change for me." I said I was interested, but then somebody else called me back and said Harvard had unanimously voted to give me a one-year visiting offer. On the spot I said, "I am not interested." To be unanimously voted a one-year visiting offer did not seem to me to be a display of great interest. Eckstein had been talking of my becoming a permanent member. It seemed obvious to me that a permanent offer had run into difficulty among some members of the department. So I turned the offer down. For years Chicago was the only major institution interested in me, and they again renewed their offer for me to come back. I told them, "I will come back for a one-year visit." I did what Harvard had asked me to do, but I knew that Chicago wanted me to stay for good.

Return to Chicago

Upon my return to Chicago, I found it to be at least as stimulating as when I was a graduate student. Friedman was still there in his prime, Stigler was doing very important work in industrial organization and political economy. They had Black, Fama, Miller, and Scholes working out rigorous approaches to finance and the evaluation of options. Coase, Posner, Landes, Demsetz, and others were doing law and economics, building on the pioneering work of Aaron Director. My work on the economics of crime fit in well with their interests. We had Bob Fogel doing path-breaking work in economic history—slavery at first and then other topics. It was a magical place!

During my year there, following a lot of soul searching (because I did like my setup in New York), I decided to stay in Chicago and accepted an offer there. I thought that a permanent return to Chicago would help renew my energies, and it did. I developed a very close friendship with George Stigler, who became my best friend and collaborator on a number of projects. I learned a great deal from George over the years. Unfortunately he died in his prime. Although he was 80 at the time, his mind was still very active.

While I was at Chicago, I decided to continue my work on the family. I remember sitting in a hotel room in New York and thinking about the question of marriage—who marries whom? Now why I started thinking about this at that time, I do not know. True, my first wife had died and I was unmarried at the time, so perhaps that had something to do with it. As I thought about the question of who marries whom, it seemed to me that there is something we might think of as a marriage market. Not a market à la Li'l Abner on Sadie Hawkins Day, if any of you remember Al Capp's comic strip *Li'l Abner*. It's not literally a market with explicit buying and selling, but you can think of the matching of partners as operating like a market—people make their choices, they date, and so on. I worked out some rules that would determine who would marry whom, threw in a couple of "theorems," and submitted a paper to the *Journal of Political Economy*. The same distinguished economist that could not accept my discrimination work ended up as a referee (George Stigler was the editor and told me this). This referee hated the paper, saying, "What is Becker doing wasting his time working on these questions?" Stigler disagreed. He told me that he liked the paper, to take account of the referee comments as best I could, and that they would publish the article, which they did. I then submitted a paper a couple of years later on the economics of divorce. Another very good economist wrote back and said they should not accept this paper. And Stigler again overrode the referee recommendation and, following revision, published my paper. Each of the papers turned out to have a good market, leading to a considerable body of subsequent research.

At about that time I decided that I should try to weave all this together into a book on the economics of the family. The book was to combine and integrate the topics of fertility, divorce, marriage, investment in children, and the evolution of the family over time. I even dealt with some nonhuman species. I worked very hard on this book for four or five years. I would wake up in the middle of the night, many nights, and work on it. It was very intense and, finally, in 1981, I published *A*

Treatise on the Family. I was exhausted by that time, and it took me roughly two years to regain my mental energy. A comprehensive treatment of the family is inherently such a difficult problem, with so much history, so many cultures, and the like. I found it very difficult. And to this day the book remains controversial. When the Nobel Prize committee awarded me the prize in 1992, their news release stated, "Gary Becker's analysis has often been controversial and hence, at the outset, met with scepticism and even distrust." Nowhere has this characterization been truer than with my work on the family.

Time does not permit me to discuss much of my work in recent years. But I would be remiss if I did not mention my rewarding collaboration with Kevin M. Murphy, a former student and now a brilliant young colleague at Chicago. Building on earlier work on preferences and addiction in a paper I wrote with Stigler ("De Gustibus Non Est Disputandum," *American Economic Review* [1977]) and a Chicago dissertation by Laurence Iannaccone, Murphy and I have written several articles on "rational addiction," among other topics.

Writing for a Popular Audience

Throughout my career, I had worked on topics closely related to public policy—education, crime, the family, discrimination, addiction, and politics, for example—yet I remained aloof from debates over public policy. I had never given advice to any political figures. Prior to 1985, I had never written one single word in the popular media, not a word, be it a newspaper, magazine, or the like. By 1985 I was 55, so I had gone through roughly 35 years of doing economic research, and not one single popular work. Nowadays, some economists hit 30 and begin writing op-ed pieces. I always felt it was a good division of labor on my part to concentrate on my research.

You can imagine then that it was a great surprise to me when in 1985 I received a telephone call from someone at *Business Week*, a magazine I had criticized a couple of years earlier because they misquoted me on something. Their representative said, "Would you be willing to write a regular column for the magazine—a one-page column every four weeks?" My initial reaction was to reject their proposal. But what I said was, "It is not something I have done, it would take me away from my research, but I will think it over and give you an answer." The response back was, "Oh good, I thought maybe you would turn us down on the spot."

So I went back and told my wife, Guity, and she said, "You should do it." She prevailed on me to try it for a while. She argued that the columns would help spread my ideas and might even have a small influence on public policy. And if I did not like doing it, I could always stop. Guity also promised that she would read my early drafts and provide comments. I am happy to say that she gave me good advice. And I might add at this point that I have been very fortunate for almost thirty years to be getting excellent advice and encouragement from her, both professional and personal. She has had an enormous influence on me.

So I got back to *Business Week* and said, "Okay, I am willing to write a column on a trial basis." They said, "Don't worry, we are looking upon it as a trial as well." And the contract sent to me stated that "either party can terminate the agreement with one month's notice." In academia we are used to tenure; there was no tenure here.

It was hard for me to learn how to write a popular column. The hardest part about writing is writing something short. I think it was Oscar Wilde who wrote to someone saying that he was sorry his letter was so long, but he did not have time to make it short. Writing short requires far more effort than writing long. I had to write roughly 800 words—one *Business Week* page comprising a certain number of *Business Week* lines—and to write in simple and nontechnical language.

And it was hard. But again, I was lucky. I do not know why they asked me, to tell the truth, but the experience has been great for me. It has taught me how to express economic ideas in a simple and nontechnical way. I will make the assertion that every single important economic idea can be stated simply. To develop an idea, you may have to use some apparatus to do it in a systematic way, of course, but you can state the essence of any idea simply. At least I have never heard one that could not be stated simply. And when people say that an idea is too complicated to state simply, it usually means they do not know how to state it simply, sometimes because they do not fully understand it.

Writing for a popular audience, I have addressed a wide range of topics. My interests in economics are broad and my column has resulted in my interests becoming even broader. I have written about baseball, the unfairness of the NCAA in not allowing student athletes to be paid, marriage contracts and religion, immigration, education, and the policies of different presidents or political candidates. Once again, this was one of several lucky events that ended up having a positive and important effect on me.

The Prize

The final thing I will discuss is the Nobel Prize. When I entered economics there was no Nobel Prize in economics; it is a recent award, having begun in 1969. There were two prizes awarded by the American Economic Association, the John Bates Clark medal for economists under the age of 40 (I was honored to receive this award in 1967) and the Francis Walker Prize for senior economists. The AEA abolished the latter once the Nobel Prize began.

By 1980 I began to be mentioned as a serious candidate for the Nobel Prize. I realized then that there were many older, highly deserving economists in the Nobel queue, mainly because the prize had not existed for very long. I realized that if I were ever to get the prize, and this was not assured, it would have to come later.

By the latter part of the 1980s, however, I felt pressure mounting on me because my name was so often mentioned as a leading candidate. A betting pool organized by some American economists had me listed as their favorite (i.e., the lowest odds person) for three or four years running before I got the prize. And so individuals and reporters had begun asking me with some regularity "When will you get the prize?" or, once the prize was announced each year, "Why didn't you get it this year?" Of course this bothered me.

I admit that I wanted to be awarded the prize, and for several reasons. Clearly the prestige and financial rewards were important. But there was another reason as well. I had a lot of students and others who had been pursuing research along the lines indicated by my work, often working outside the more narrow range of traditional economics topics. These economists were often given a tough time in the profession, and several had difficulty getting good jobs. One of my top students years ago, who worked on religion, generated almost no job market interest. Now he is considered a preeminent economist working in religion, perhaps the preeminent person in any field doing research on religion. But he had a difficult time getting a job. People would ask, "Religion, what kind of topic is that for an economist?" I wanted myself and others to get the validation that the Nobel Prize would provide—that the economic approach to human behavior is acceptable work and that we are doing real economics. Yet in 1992, my work continued to be controversial, especially in Western Europe, and I began to wonder whether I would ever receive the prize.

I thought there was no chance I would receive the prize in 1992. Economists from Chicago were among the three winners in 1990, and another Chicagoan, Ronald Coase, won in 1991. I concluded that the committee would never choose three Chicagoans in a row. In the fall of 1992, I had a terrible flu with a very high fever. Doctors wanted to put me in the hospital, but my wife resisted that move. For both these reasons, the last thing on my mind was the Nobel Prize. I had no idea when the announcement was coming. I had not been into school for a week and was in bed at 5:30 on the morning of October 13, sleeping soundly for the first night in about a week. My wife, who had been up grading papers, answered the phone when it rang that morning, worried that it might interfere with my sleep. She was a bit nasty, she said to me later, but the caller said this was an important phone call for Professor Becker. My wife did not think it was the Nobel Prize, at least not for me. She went and woke me up and I kept saying, "I want to sleep, I haven't slept so well for a long time." "No, it's a call from Sweden," she said, and that was the magic word. A call from Sweden! I did not know that the prize was announced. But when I heard "a call from Sweden," I figured, "well, maybe" and picked up the phone. My wife subsequently said that she was sitting there as I was saying, "yes, yes" with no expression on my face, and she figured that they had called for my input on somebody else who was being considered. Finally, she hears me say "Thank you very much; tell the committee what a great honor it is that you have conferred on me." This of course was the call telling me I had been awarded the prize. The first thing Guity did was to let out a yell and the first thing I said was "I'm glad that monkey is off my back." We called our four children and then we took the phone off the receiver to have breakfast in some peace. Before 6:30 or so, the reporters, the *New York Times*, the university people, and so on, had found us.

So the long years of fighting attacks were largely over, although the official Nobel announcement called my work controversial. Still, they awarded me the prize. I did not realize at the time that there were some protests in Sweden about my getting the prize. Some Swedish feminist groups in particular complained about my receiving the award, charging that my work on the family was anti-feminist (I do not believe it is) and they had discussions about whether to picket my Nobel lecture. Perhaps that helped publicize the lecture—the hall was packed. People were standing all over the place, but they caused no disruptions, everything went very smoothly, and it was a great week.

The prize recognized my research in four broad areas: investments in human capital; behavior of the family (or household), including distribution of work and allocation of time in the family; crime and punishment; and discrimination in the markets for labor and goods. In private I was told that some members of the committee did not want to award me the prize. But because in the last couple of years I had been nominated the most often by the economists asked to identify potential recipients, the committee felt they had to give me the prize. Well, better than not. And so, it was a great week and a great period of recognition.

Some people have studied Nobel laureates and discovered that they did a whole lot less work after receiving the prize than before. I was aware of that work, done by several sociologists, and there is no doubt that there are many demands on your time as a result of getting the prize. I resolved to continue to do research and not change my life drastically. Since I have received the prize I have published three books. Two of the three books include new research; the other published book, *The Economics of Life,* is a collection of my *Business Week* columns. I hope that in my case the iron law of the negative effect of the Nobel Prize on productivity has been overcome.

To the best of my ability, I have tried to assess the factors that were most important in facilitating whatever accomplishments I have had. I have to give many thanks to my parents; my wife, Guity; my children; my sisters; my brother; and certainly my teachers and colleagues. A series of lucky events over my life have put me into contact with enormously outstanding people and led me down paths whose rewards I could not have anticipated. I'm not suggesting that the Nobel Prize, or whatever is one's accomplishments in life, is simply a matter of luck. I am suggesting that success requires a number of fortuitous events to occur, many of which one cannot readily imagine, plan for, or determine. I suspect that there are a lot of equally able people out there, and it is only those who are particularly lucky or fortunate who end up receiving a Nobel Prize or some other noteworthy accomplishment. I have been fortunate.

Gary S. Becker
Awarded Nobel Prize in 1992. Lecture presented April 13, 2000.

Dates of Birth and Death
December 2, 1930; May 3, 2014

Academic Degrees
B.A., Princeton University, 1951
M.A., University of Chicago, 1953
Ph.D., University of Chicago, 1955

Academic Affiliations
Assistant Professor of Economics, University of Chicago, 1954–57
Assistant Professor of Economics, Columbia University, 1957–58
Associate Professor of Economics, Columbia University, 1958–60
Professor of Economics, Columbia University, 1960–68
Arthur Lehman Professor of Economics, Columbia University, 1968–69
Ford Foundation Visiting Professor of Economics, University of Chicago, 1969–70
University Professor of Economics, University of Chicago, 1970–83
University Professor of Economics and Sociology, University of Chicago, 1983–2014
Senior Research Fellow, Hoover Institute (Stanford), 1990–2014

Selected Books
The Economics of Discrimination, 1957, 1971
Human Capital: A Theoretical and Empirical Analysis, with Special Reference to Education, 1964, 1993
The Economic Approach to Human Behavior, 1976
A Treatise on the Family, 1981, 1991
Accounting for Tastes, 1996
The Economics of Life, 1997 (with Guity Nashat Becker)
Social Economics: Market Behavior in a Social Environment, 2000 (with K. Murphy)

Robert E. Lucas, Jr.

1

Jane Templeton graduated in Seattle's Roosevelt High School's first class, in 1927. The Templetons lived right across 68th Street, in a house built the same year as the new high school. Jane enrolled as an art student at the University of Washington, hoping to become a fashion artist. But the art courses at the university were trivial—"tie-dyeing," she later dismissed them—and unrelated to the world she wanted to enter. She got the idea to study in New York, and she and two girlfriends planned to rent an apartment and spend a year there. In 1930, when she was 20, Jane took the two-day trip to Chicago on the Northern Pacific and spent a few days visiting with her aunts Ruth and Mary. Then she was on to New York, beginning to enjoy the image she found she had back east, as a girl from the western edge of the country.

But the New York art school was a disappointment too: maybe schools were not where you learned design and the skills of a commercial artist. She picked up some work freelancing, looked around for a job, and—amazingly, in 1930—found one. She became the girl Friday for a fashion artist with the single name Leonard—lay-o-nard—a recent immigrant from Austria, as far ahead of his American counterparts (I imagine) as were the physicists and psychiatrists who were also emigrating from central Europe around that time. He liked to talk to Jane about every aspect of the business: she was smart, talented, eager to learn, and fun to be around. Jane knew this was the real thing, and there were no more thoughts of school. But she was homesick and never considered staying longer than the year she and her friends had planned. She returned to Seattle, and on the strength of the portfolio put together from her work for Leonard, got a job drawing newspaper ads for Best's Apparel.

All this and much more my brothers and sister and I learned from stories about our mother's New York adventure. We saw some of it first-hand during the war, when she resumed work to supplement our father's earnings in the Seattle shipyards. She would take the three of us, at ages 6, 4, and 3, all of us struggling to keep up with her clicking heels, on the half-mile walk to the bus and then on the long bus ride downtown, to the McDougal's store. There we would sit still while she handed over her drawings from last week, discussed her assignments for the week to come, and put the articles to be advertised into a shopping bag. On the return home, we received praise—if earned—for our successful venture into the world of adult work. At home, she took out a dress, shoes, and a belt from the shopping bag. She hung the dress up on a hanger near the drawing board, in the living room of the shabby house we rented during the war, and put the accessories in front of her, at the top of the board. She set out her paints—pure white, glossy black, elegant grays—and her tiny brushes, and as I watched there came into being on paper a confident and attractive woman, stylishly dressed in what I had seen as nothing more than an ordinary dress, limp on the hanger.

2

My own train trip east took place in September 1955, when I entered the University of Chicago as a scholarship student. Like my parents, I had graduated from Roosevelt High School, but I did not want to follow most of my classmates to the University of Washington. My mother chose to view my first year at Chicago as a temporary stay, as her year in New York had been. I may have seen it this way myself at first: my letters home made references to a possible transfer to the University of Washington, to study engineering. If so, it was not for long. I was homesick, for sure, and had doubts about my ability to succeed, but when my first quarter transcript showed a couple of A's— not just in calculus, where I could coast on my high school training, but in Humanities I, where everything was new—I knew I was at Chicago to stay.

This humanities course and several others I took over the next three years were part of the glorious Hutchins fourteen-year-long general-education courses that not long before had entitled a student to a Bachelor of Philosophy degree. By the time I got to Chicago, the Hutchins curriculum had been partially abandoned, and supplemented with enough conventional college courses to entitle you to a regular, four-year B.A. or

B.S. in some specific field. But it was the Hutchins "great books" courses that were the real excitement for me, and except perhaps for the science majors, for most of us. It was these courses that gave us the sense of getting a distinctive education, of entering into a new world of culture and ideas, of becoming a new person.

Early in my first year, we were assigned to write a page or two on Brahms's *Variations on a Theme by Haydn*. A group of us checked out the LP from the library and sat around a dorm room, playing it over and over. My musical experience then consisted of Christmas carols and the top 40. What was the connection between Haydn's theme and all this music that Brahms claimed were variations? What could one *write* on such a topic? I'm sure I would not enjoy re-reading whatever it was that I handed in, but I can still hear Brahms's music in my head. I learned to listen to serious music with pleasure and was grateful for what Allan Bloom much later described as this improvement in my ability to care for my soul.

The only science course I took in college was Natural Sciences II—a biology course. We read a modern anatomy text and also selections from Darwin, Mendel, and others. I remember struggling over an incomprehensible paper on embryology by Spemann and Mangold and one by another German author called "The Continuity of the Germ Plasm" that had mysterious overtones.

But there was nothing spooky about Mendel's genetic theories. They were clear and made some kind of sense (though there was nothing molecular in our Nat Sci II readings); you could work out predictions that would surprise you, and these predictions matched interesting facts. We did a classroom experiment with fruit flies, focused on eyes, and pooled the results. Our assignment was to write up the results in a lab report and compare them to predictions from a Mendelian model. I had not enjoyed the lab work, but I liked writing the report and spent the better part of my weekend on it. It was the first time I can recall ever working out the predictions of a scientific theory from its basic principles and testing these predictions against experimental evidence.

On Sunday evening, my friend Mike Schilder returned to the dorm from a weekend that had clearly not been occupied with fruit flies. The report was due Monday, and he asked to copy mine. I agreed, in part just to get some reaction to a report that I was very pleased with. Mike came back in half an hour, and told me: "This is a good report, but you forgot about crossing over." "Crossing over" was a term introduced to us to describe a discrepancy between Mendelian theory and certain observations. No doubt there is some underlying biology behind it, but for us it was presented as just a fudge-factor, a label for our ignorance. I was entranced with Mendel's clean logic and did not want to see it cluttered up with seemingly arbitrary fudge-factors. "Crossing over is b—— s——," I told Mike.

In fact, though, there was a big discrepancy between the Mendelian prediction without crossing over and the proportions we observed in our classroom data, too big to pass over without comment. My report included a long section on experimental error, describing the chaotic scene that generated the data and arguing that errors could have been large enough to reconcile theory and fact. I handed it in as written. Mike, on the other hand, took my report as it stood, except that he replaced my experimental error section with a discussion of crossing over. His report came back with an A. Mine got a C-, with the instructor's comment: "This is a good report, but you forgot about crossing over."

I don't think there is anyone who knows me or my work as a mature scientist who would not recognize me in this story. The construction of theoretical models is our way to bring order to the way we think about the world, but the process necessarily involves ignoring some evidence or alternative theories—setting them aside. That can be hard to do—facts are facts—and sometimes my unconscious mind carries out the abstraction for me: I simply fail to *see* some of the data or some alternative theory. This failing can be costly and embarrassing to me, but I don't think it has any effect on the advance of knowledge. Others will see the blind spot (as Mike did with crossing over), keep what is good, and correct what is not.

3

The reality addressed by natural science always seemed to me someone else's province. In public school science was an unending and not very well organized list of things other people had discovered long ago. In college, I learned something about the process of scientific discovery, but what little I learned did not attract me as a career possibility. Introductory physics and chemistry were huge courses, designed to weed out pretenders, which I feared I would soon be discovered to be. More important, I think, was a sense that these areas were in good hands, that they would progress in pretty much the same way with my participation or without it.

What I liked thinking about were politics and social issues. My parents had become politically aware in the 1930s, and politics were always the leading topic of discussion in our house. My letters home, from undergraduate days through middle age, were full of politics and social commentary. I had read widely on these matters, and with this background, I got advanced placement in social science. It was not until my second year at Chicago that I could take Social Sciences III and the History of Western Civilization. I had never worked so hard or with as much enthusiasm as I did in these two courses.

When the time came to specialize, I wanted to prolong this excitement. By my second year I was fully socialized to Chicago's pristine intellectualism, and occupational considerations played no role in this decision. Since everything interesting seemed to begin with the Greeks, I majored in history, specializing in the history of ancient Greece and Rome and the European Middle Ages. I was drawn to the idea that economic forces were centrally important, but somehow never took an economics course. The general education courses from the Hutchins era paid no attention to economics. When I mentioned an interest in economics to my instructor in Social Sciences III, he suggested Heilbroner's *The Worldly Philosophers* and Galbraith's *American Capitalism*, books written for people who dislike economics and want their prejudice entertainingly humored. Neither book gives any clue to what economics is or what economists do.

I won a Woodrow Wilson Fellowship for graduate study in history, and was admitted at the University of California at Berkeley. The trip west was my honeymoon: Rita Cohen and I were married in New York in the summer of 1959. My weakness in languages—a classical historian needs five—discouraged me from pursuing my interests in ancient and medieval history. I took an English history seminar course—tweedy students imitating every mannerism of their tweedy professor—and courses in economic history from Carlo Cipolla and David Landes. For Landes, I wrote a bibliographical paper on nineteenth-century British business cycles—a topic I chose from Landes's list because it looked like the most theoretical, and so it was. I could see that without a better economics background I would always be on the fringe of a topic like this. I wanted to transfer into economics, but even with Landes's support the Berkeley economics department was not encouraging.

Rita and I were also homesick for Chicago. I talked the Social Sciences Division at Chicago into accepting me back as a graduate student. I talked the Woodrow Wilson Foundation into transferring my fellowship to Chicago. With the help of my brother Pete, who passed through Berkeley on his way to the Rose Bowl in Pasadena, we loaded a rented trailer and headed back to Chicago.

4

By the summer of 1960 my young wife was pregnant, I had lost my Woodrow Wilson Fellowship, and I had spent the better part of the year making up for the fact that I had had no economics as an undergraduate. But I had found a field that I loved and was good at, and I could hardly wait to start the regular first year graduate program with Milton Friedman and the rest of Chicago's faculty.

At the end of spring quarter, I had looked in the back of Kenneth Boulding's textbook and read Boulding's description of Paul Samuelson's *Foundations of Economic Analysis* as "the most important book in economics since the war." I had a summer to prepare for the beginning of graduate work in earnest, and there was no point in wasting the time on the second most important book. I got a copy from the library and all that summer, during lunch and coffee breaks from my research assistant job, I worked through Samuelson's first four chapters. When I got home each night, I wrote out what I had learned that day, line by line. It is impossible to invest this much in a single book unless you trust it, and though no one at Chicago had confirmed Boulding's recommendation for me, I immediately sensed that Samuelson was dealing with essential material in a way that was congenial to me.

Of course, I knew that Samuelson was regarded as a leading—perhaps *the* leading—economist in the world. I also knew that as an undergraduate at Chicago, he had taken Jacob Viner's graduate course along with Milton Friedman and George Stigler. In the preface, Samuelson says the book had "been conceived and written primarily in 1937," which is to say it was the product of Samuelson's early years of graduate school, at Harvard, when he was about the age I was then, in 1960. With this as background, the book's broad sweep and supremely confident tone was exhilarating. He patronizes the feared Viner: "As Professor Viner has pointed out with great insight ...," crediting Viner with understanding a mathematical point that Samuelson has just shown on the preceding page. He disagrees with Alfred Marshall—then the god of Chicago economics: "I have come to feel that Marshall's dictum that 'it seems doubtful whether anyone spends his time well in reading lengthy translations of economic doctrines into mathematics, that have not been made by himself' should be exactly reversed." He goes out of his way to quarrel with *our* feared teacher, Milton Friedman, by disagreeing with a point in Friedman's 1935 article on elasticities, and this after dismissing the whole idea of elasticities as unimportant "except possibly as mental exercises for beginning students!" Here is a graduate student in his 20s, reorganizing all of economics in four or five chapters, right before your eyes, and let Marshall, Hicks, Friedman, and everyone else get out of the way!

I could see that some of this style was just youthful brashness, and I imagine there are passages that Samuelson would say differently now. But what a waste it would have been if he had waited until his views had matured! The book would have lost the excitement of discovery that carries the reader forward and the patient instructions to the student on how economics is *done* that only an author who has only recently learned something for himself can provide effectively. Samuelson was the Julia Child of economics, somehow teaching you the basics and giving you the feeling of becoming an insider in a complex culture all at the same time. I loved the *Foundations*. Like so many others in my cohort, I internalized its view that if I couldn't formulate a problem in economic theory mathematically, I didn't know what I was doing. I came to the position that mathematical analysis is not one of many ways of doing economic theory: it is the only way. Economic theory *is* mathematical analysis. Everything else is just pictures and talk.

5

Before the various University of Chicago libraries were consolidated in Regenstein Library, economics Ph.D. students studied in the business and economics library, on the top floor of what is now Stuart Hall. The room had been designed as the law library, and its Gothic arches and leaded glass windows lent a welcome seriousness to our efforts to gain some intellectual control over the vastness of economic knowledge. In this room, Neil Wallace set an issue of the *Review of Economics and Statistics* on the table in front of me: "Look at this." The issue contained a symposium on monetary policy, including the papers that had been presented along with commentary by assigned discussants. Neil had opened it to the opening paragraphs of Milton Friedman's comments on a paper by the Harvard economist Seymour Harris. I read the introduction, in which Friedman criticized Harris for mixing "prediction and prescription so thoroughly that it is difficult to tell when he is recording what is going to be done and when recommending what should be done." Section II then began,

The role of the economist in discussions of public policy seems to me to prescribe what should be done in the light of what can be done, politics aside, and not to predict what is "politically feasible" and then to recommend it. Accordingly, I shall not attempt a detailed criticism of Harris' comment.[1]

What excited me about this passage—and what I knew had excited Neil—was the confidence of Friedman's dismissal of Harris in this public, face-to-face interchange, and his own focus on what he saw as the economics of monetary policy without regard for how popular he or his analysis would be with his listeners. This focus and fearlessness was what we admired in Friedman's class: he was a moral example to us, just as Frank Knight had been for him and George Stigler.

Friedman rarely lectured. His class discussions were often structured as debates, with student opinions or newspaper quotes serving to introduce a problem and some loosely stated opinions about it. Then Friedman would lead us into a clear statement of the problem, considering alternative formulations as thoroughly as anyone in the class wanted to. Once formulated, the problem was quickly analyzed—usually diagrammatically—on the board. So we learned how to formulate a model, to think about and decide which features of a problem we could safely abstract from and which we needed to put at the center of the analysis. Here "model" is my term: it was not a term that Friedman liked or used. I think that for him talking about modeling would have detracted from the substantive seriousness of the inquiry we were engaged in, would divert us away from the attempt to discover "what can be done" into merely a mathematical exercise.

The quality of discussions in Friedman's classes was unique in my experience. He did not call on students by name, as I recall, permitting me and many other classmates to experience the intensity of engaging Friedman directly only vicariously. It was not dismissal that I feared—no graduate student would have been dismissed the way Harris had been—but the exposure of my confusion next to Friedman's quickness and clarity. He would engage a particular student in a dialogue, and once engaged no escape but assent was possible. Exit lines like "Well, I'll have to think about it" were no use: "Let's think about it now," Friedman would say. Friedman did not want to win the debate by convincing the rest of the class he was right, using the student as a foil—any experienced teacher can do that. He wanted the student he was engaged with to join him in thinking the problem through to the end, to be not merely exhausted but truly convinced. Of course, this meant that Friedman was completely exposed, too.

Students at Chicago, then as now, formed into study groups to prepare for the Core Exam that tested for knowledge of the entire first year curriculum. The Core questions were like the questions Friedman used in class: loose, notation-free statements of some economic question. Our job was to formulate the question sharply, focusing on essentials, and then answer it. Neil and I were in a study group of four or five, and we enforced the rule that everyone should prepare in advance. I still have the typed notes I prepared for these meetings. Looking at them again after all these years, I find little that I would change. The economics I learned from Friedman and Samuelson is a unified and manageable body of knowledge. It can be learned in a few months, and anyone who has mastered it can think about any problem in economics. I passed the Core Exam in winter quarter, 1961, less than a year after I had completed my first, remedial, undergraduate economics course.

6

My doctoral thesis was concerned with estimating the degree of capital-labor substitution in U.S. manufacturing. It was a part of a larger project that Arnold Harberger organized, involving many students, to calibrate a general equilibrium model he was using for tax analysis. The question involved capital, so a dynamic theory would seem to be called for, but I based my econometric work on a static marginal productivity condition that did not require either measuring capital or studying its determinants. These may have been econometric virtues, but they only postponed my entry into economic dynamics. I couldn't wait to finish my thesis and get on to something more interesting and ambitious.

The example I wanted to follow was the work of Dale Jorgenson, who was visiting at Chicago during my last year there. His study of the investment decision of the firm mixed theory, econometrics, and careful measurement in a way that I much admired (and still do). The modeling of firm and industry dynamics was at the top my agenda in 1963, when I became an assistant professor at the Graduate School of Industrial Administration (GSIA), the business school at Carnegie Tech.

Jorgenson had derived a formula for a firm's long-run capital-output ratio, but the theory did not explain why the adjustment to such a long-run target should be slow, as it appeared to be in the data. I modified the model by adding a penalty for rapid change—an adjustment cost—and used the calculus of variations to derive both the long-run target and the gradual approach to it from a single set of assumptions. I sent the paper to Dale, who directed me to an earlier paper by Eisner and Strotz that contained everything I had done. This was a setback, but somehow a stimulating one. I worked out a theory of firm-determined technological change, using the same variational methods. I generalized the Eisner—Strotz theory to many capital goods. It seemed there were enough unsolved problems in firm dynamics to support a lot of theorists.

Dick Schramm's GSIA thesis showed how to make a multiple capital good model operational econometrically. His model involved a lagged adjustment of price expectations to movements in actual prices. I remember a seminar presentation of Schramm's at which Jack Muth asked Dick why he had not assumed rational expectations. Of course, we all knew and admired Jack's paper "Rational Expectations and the Theory of Price Movements," but none of us knew how to exploit this idea econometrically. At that time, I thought of rational expectations as an elegant rationalization of the kind of lagged adjustment of expectations that Schramm assumed in his thesis, not as an alternate model. This was a half-truth that kept me from seeing the force of Jack's objections.

Schramm's thesis dealt with decisions of competitive firms, taking prices and expected future prices as given. So did the Eisner and Strotz paper, and my extensions of their work. Since these theories did not treat the determinants of prices, there was no internal inconsistency in the nonrational expectations they assumed. Serious inconsistency did emerge, though, when I made an entire Marshallian industry the unit of analysis, instead of the individual firm. In my "Adjustment Costs and the Theory of Supply," I took the industry demand function as a given, and solved for the time path of prices along with the paths of production and capital stock. I postulated "myopic" expectations—price expectations formed by simply extrapolating the current price into the future—and then deduced from this and other assumptions an equilibrium price path that was not constant but rather grew or declined in a predictable way. In such a model, you could *see* the profit opportunities that firms were passing up. Why couldn't they see these opportunities too? But if they did, the model couldn't be the right way to describe their behavior. Now I could go back to Muth's 1961 paper and see that this inconsistency was exactly his argument: In his words, "the marginal revenue product of economics" should be zero, or close to it. If your theory reveals profit opportunities, you have the wrong theory.

The context in which I came to this understanding was deterministic, so the assumption of rational expectations reduces to perfect foresight, using a terminology that I take from Buz Brock. Calculating a perfect foresight equilibrium for an industry, say, sounds as though it should involve solving a fixed point problem in a space of price paths: the actual path implies a forecast path, which in turn implies an actual path. This sounds hard, and it can be. But under competitive conditions, one can show that an industry over time will operate so as to maximize a discounted, consumer surplus integral—a problem that is mathematically no harder than the present value maximizing problem faced by a single firm. Who, exactly, is solving this planning problem? Adam Smith's "invisible hand," of course, not any actual person: but the mathematics of planning problems turned out to be just the right equipment needed to understand the decentralized interactions of a large number of producers. One can calculate equilibrium quantities over time using this fact and then read the equilibrium prices off the demand curve. I saw this in a particular context just by comparing the Euler necessary conditions for the equilibrium problem to those from the consumer surplus maximization problem. In fact, it is a consequence of one of the classic theorems of welfare economics.

In my first years at GSIA I worked furiously to pick up the mathematics of optimization over time—calculus of variations, the maximum principle of Pontryagin, Bellman's dynamic programming—and of the differential equations systems these optimization problems produced. I worked on applications of these methods to problems in economics and operations research. Theoretically minded economists of my cohort were doing the same thing all over the world. I was studying the dynamics of investment at the firm and industry level, as were many others. Still others were studying optimal growth of an economy, optimal accumulation of human capital, optimal advertising and R and D investment, and so on.

In 1966 I was invited to a workshop on economic dynamics, conducted in Chicago by Hirofumi Uzawa, that involved some of the best people in this group of younger theorists. Uzawa was a charismatic figure, an enormous influence on theoretically minded students, who had moved to Chicago from Stanford just after I had left. The seminars ran all day, through dinner, and into the evening. Discussions were noisy and intense, but friendly and constructive: I remember people going to the blackboard in the middle of a talk, to show how a speaker's argument had gone wrong and to try to help fix it.

Dave Cass spoke about work that he and Menahem Yaari were doing, trying to understand the logic of a model of an economy with an infinity of overlapping generations that Samuelson had published in 1958. This paper had not been on reading lists of mine, but I was immediately attracted by its simplicity and the role it had for money. This was the first model I had seen in which paper money had a useful role to perform and had a command over goods in equilibrium. This was exciting, and the following fall I began to use this setup in my graduate courses in macroeconomics.

The paper I had written for the Uzawa conference was never finished: I couldn't establish the mathematical result that was to be the paper's centerpiece. I proposed to Ed Prescott, a friend of mine from his student days at GSIA who was then on the faculty at Penn, that we work together on it. Even with Ed's help, the original problem proved intractable, but we found ourselves thinking together about the behavior of firms in a competitive industry that is subject to unpredictable demand shocks. Ed had used dynamic programming methods in his thesis, and introduced me to a paper by David Blackwell that worked out the underlying mathematics in a useful and beautiful way. We applied these methods to the problem of maximizing expected, discounted consumers' surplus in the industry. The solution takes the form of a Markov process or stochastic difference equation describing the evolution of capacity and production in response to recurring shocks to demand. Buz Brock and Leonard Mirman were thinking about optimal growth in similar terms at about the same time.

But then how can the solution to this maximum problem be related to a competitive equilibrium in which firms have rational expectations? Part of the answer lay in reformulating the rational expectations hypothesis in a way that did not require the linearity Muth had assumed in his analysis. The other part of the answer came from applying the competitive general equilibrium theory of Arrow, Debreu, and McKenzie, theory developed in the 1950s and gradually being extended to ever more general mathematical contexts. The potential of this body of theory for more applied work was, at that time, unrecognized. Prescott and I saw that it would be helpful to us, and plunged into a self-taught crash course. Putting the pieces together, we wrote "Investment under Uncertainty."

In 1963, I had thought of a competitive industry in terms of firms solving short- and long-run, deterministic profit-maximization problems, under the (false) belief that current prices would maintain their current values forever, and with the passage from one to the other and all the effects of unpredictable shocks tacked on as afterthoughts. Five years later, I thought of the same economics in terms of firms maximizing expected discounted present value, with rational expectations about the probability distributions of future prices, and with stochastic shocks and adjustment costs both fully integrated into the theory. From an objective point of view, this transformation can be viewed as a product of decades of research by many economists. From my subjective viewpoint, it was the most rapid, radical change of view I have ever experienced as an economist.

7

In those early years at GSIA, my closest friend was Leonard Rapping, a Chicago Ph.D. about two years ahead of me. As Leonard said in a 1982 interview,

I expect that we talked once or twice every day from '63 to '68. We talked about everything: about economics, about politics, about business school problems, just about everything. We would have coffee from about three until five. We were the two people who would always be at the afternoon coffee hours. Everyone else would be back at their offices.[2]

Maybe it was inevitable that we would do joint research, but it was surprising that this should turn out to be research in macroeconomics—a field in which neither of us had even taken a prelim. We got there by the back door, through labor economics: at Chicago, we had both studied with Gregg Lewis.

At that time, many people were regressing changes in nominal wages on the unemployment rate, a statistical relation known as a Phillips curve, interpreting the negative coefficient of unemployment as describing a trade-off: lower unemployment means higher wage inflation. People had just begun to consider what kind of economics might underlie this statistical connection. Leonard and I started discussing supply and demand models of joint wage and employment determination, and tried these out in the classroom. We decided to formulate and test such a model more carefully. To get an aggregate time series of decent length, back then, one needed to go back to 1929, so our project turned into an attempt to understand wage and employment behavior through the Depression and war years.

Like everyone else, we thought that the ultimate source of employment fluctuations in both these periods came mainly from the demand side: fluctuations in spending on goods and services. But all the evidence we knew about indicated that labor supply was very inelastic. How could we get large employment swings out of demand shifts in such a setting? We used a device based on the old Keynesian idea of "money illusion": people in booms (like World War II) are willing to supply a lot of labor temporarily at the high money wage rates available then, without realizing that when they spend these dollars it will be at higher prices. Symmetrically, people in depressions temporarily pass up jobs at low money wages, not realizing that these low wages will buy a lot more goods than they would have two years earlier. This was the idea we used to reconcile an elastic short-run supply of labor with an inelastic long-run supply. I thought of my parents, both working throughout the war and saving most of what they made to build up a down payment for the house they bought when the war was over.

In our model, wages and employment levels were always in a kind of temporary equilibrium, and this equilibrium had the property that inflation would stimulate employment. What about *un*employment? We added a labor force participation equation that, combined with the rest of the model, gave us a Phillips curve.

Leonard and I did a careful job of working through the decision problems of households and firms in a world subject to these "illusions," and another careful job putting together a set of compatible time series. The econometric work came out well, and the ambitions of the project began to dawn on us. "Bob, we're going to be famous!" Leonard would say. It frightened me, and I managed to be out of town on the day that Leonard presented the paper to our colleagues at a GSIA seminar. We were both right. Albert Rees refereed the paper at the *JPE*: his outraged reaction was later published as a comment. But why outrage? Another economist, we heard, called the paper "fascist economics." Fascist! For writing down a labor supply curve and taking it seriously!

Before our paper was finished, Milton Friedman had used his presidential address to the American Economic Association to argue that in the long run, the unemployment rate would be independent of the inflation rate: there would be no Phillips-like trade-off between inflation and unemployment. Friedman's argument was theoretical, but his premises all seemed to Leonard and me to hold for our model. Yet our model *did* imply a long-run trade-off. Later, we came to see that this difference was due to our use of adaptive, rather than rational, expectations, but at the time we simply accepted it as an unresolved puzzle.

Edmund Phelps had been trying to use an equilibrium framework to think about unemployment and wage determination at about the same time, and he had reached the same theoretical conclusion that Friedman had. While making the rounds of the seminar circuit he had run across others engaged in the same kind of investigation he and Rapping and I were engaged in. He assembled these papers in a 1970 book, *Microeconomic Foundations of Employment and Inflation Theory*, now universally known simply as the "Phelps volume." This was the kind of fame that Leonard and I had dreamed of, and the book and the conference Ned organized around it gave us the first experience either of us had had of being at the forefront of an important research area.

In an early draft of the introduction to the volume, Phelps had written that "... perhaps Lucas and Rapping are 180 degrees to the truth," by which he meant that perhaps we should have emphasized income effects in our theory of employment fluctuations rather than the substitution effects we did emphasize. On a social occasion soon after the conference—when Leonard and I were still high—we joked about this remark. This shocked Elayne Rapping. She said, "All you two care about is being cited by a well-known economist, about being famous. It doesn't matter to you whether you are right or 180 degrees off." Elayne's remark stung, and she was certainly right that the source of our good mood that evening was the boost the conference had given to our ambitions. The desires for fame and truth are not inconsistent, though, and in fact we were laughing because we were so sure that Phelps's criticism could be dealt with. But this was not the occasion to try to explain income and substitution effects to Elayne, and anyway we knew that she was as pleased with our success as we were.

Not long after this occasion, Leonard and Elayne were swept up in the opposition to the war in Vietnam and moved far to the left, politically. Leonard lost interest in the kind of economics we had done together. When the *JPE* published Rees's comment on our paper, both of us signed the reply, but I had written it alone. Our friendship had been based on conversations that ranged much more broadly than our joint work, and we tried to maintain them, but without success. Soon after, Leonard moved to the University of Massachusetts, which was then becoming a center for radical economics.

8

By the end of the '60s, I was leading two lives as an economist. With Rapping, I was an empirical macroeconomist, estimating Phillips curves and aggregate labor supply functions. Working with Prescott, I had immersed myself in the mathematics of dynamic programming and general equilibrium theory and was applying these methods to construct tractable, genuinely dynamic models. In my graduate teaching, I was putting these elements together, using the overlapping generations models that I had learned about from Cass, to build models of monetary economies that would, I hoped, be helpful in addressing questions of macroeconomic policy.

At the Phelps volume conference, Ned Phelps had pushed one such question to the front of my thinking: if Rapping and I were right that monetary shocks affected people's willingness to supply labor by "fooling" them about their future options, then we needed to explain why everyone gets fooled in the same direction. Why isn't the worker who is over-optimistic about his job prospects offset by another who is too pessimistic? Phelps outlined an answer to this question in his essay in the volume, based on the idea that workers at any one location are short on information about what is happening elsewhere. When a worker sees a wage change, he thinks it is specific to his own market, not realizing that the same thing might be happening everywhere. I thought I could capture this effect with the kind of overlapping generations models I was using in class. I tried out one version in 1968. Further work led to "Expectations and the Neutrality of Money," submitted to the *American Economic Review* in 1970 and finally published in the *Journal of Economic Theory* in 1972.

The paper contained a careful and explicit construction of a theoretical example of an economy in which the motives, opportunities, and information of every economic actor was unambiguously spelled out. Expectations were rational. In this setting, as in Friedman's AEA address, there was no long-run trade-off between employment and inflation. Yet the model also implied the kind of correlations between employment and inflation that were then widely interpreted as hard evidence that such trade-offs did exist. I felt I understood for the first time both why

Friedman and Phelps were right in arguing there was no long-run trade-off between unemployment and inflation and why econometric tests continued to reject this "natural rate" view.

Working out this example took me to the limit of my technical skills and beyond: it was not easy reading, nor had it been easy writing. It built closely on Rapping's and my view of the labor supply decision as well as on the formulation of rational expectations that Prescott and I had developed working on "Investment under Uncertainty." It is easy for me to see the influences of Phelps, Rapping, Prescott, and Cass in this paper, but the combination was new and striking: no one else was doing macroeconomics this way in 1970. The paper made my reputation.

9

My family and I spent the summer of 1970 in Seattle, driving our underpowered Plymouth Valiant into the headwind for days to get there. I had an office at the University of Washington. My ambition for the summer was to write a paper on Phillips curves for a conference to be held that fall at the Federal Reserve Board. I had been invited, I assumed, as a spokesman for the Friedman-Phelps position that there was no long run trade-off between unemployment and inflation. My plan was to translate what I had learned from writing "Expectations and the Neutrality of Money" into linear examples that would make it clear to a much wider readership why the standard tests for "long-run" effects—tests of the sort Rapping and I and dozens of others had used—were not informative about the Friedman–Phelps hypothesis. This paper became "Econometric Testing of the Natural Rate Hypothesis."

The stay in Seattle was a pleasure—I enjoyed being close to my Seattle family—but by the summer's end, I found I missed the more intense atmosphere of GSIA and was eager to get back to Pittsburgh. On my first day at the office Marty Geisel handed me a working paper by Tom Sargent, saying only, "I think you will be interested in this." Sargent's paper involved exactly the logic of the paper I had just completed (which of course Tom hadn't seen), applied to Irving Fisher's predicted relation between expected inflation and interest rates. Rational expectations connected expected inflation, which we cannot observe, to actual inflation rates, which we can, in just the right way to give Fisher's idea content. Sargent had based a test of Fisher's theory on this observation—the first econometric application of Muth's idea.

I gave my paper in Washington in the fall. It was the first time that many in attendance had heard of rational expectations. James Tobin gave it a generous review when he summed up the proceedings of the conference: it was clear that I had made my point. When my session ended, an economist of about my age whose work on Phillips curves I knew and respected came up to the podium and told me, "You just explained why everything I've done in the last few years is worthless." This shocked me: I was viewing myself as an underdog in the conference setting and was not prepared to assume this very different role. I protested, "Oh no, that wasn't what I said at all." He insisted, "Yes it was. It was exactly what you said. And you were right." I had not experienced anything like this before.

As Sargent's test of the Fisher hypothesis showed, the idea that rational expectations implied restrictions across equations was not special to Phillips curves. When Allan Meltzer and Karl Brunner asked me to give a paper on empirical Phillips curves for the first meeting of the Carnegie–Rochester Conference Series, I decided to try to illustrate this fact with a variety of econometric applications. The resulting paper, "Econometric Policy Evaluation: A Critique," explained in detail how rational expectations undermines the then-conventional uses of econometric models in simulating the effects of policy changes. This "Lucas critique," as it came to be known, is probably the most influential paper I have written.

My critical writing on the Keynesian macroeconometric models of the day showed that simulations of these models could not be expected to give accurate answers about the effects of changes in economic policy. Parallel work by Sargent, and Sargent and Neil Wallace, showed the same thing. These demonstrations effectively ended the role of these models in policy debates and eliminated the main intellectual basis for monetary and fiscal fine-tuning of the economy. We were certainly not the first economists who were skeptical of Keynesian econometric models—the whole monetarist tradition of Milton Friedman, Allan Meltzer, and Karl Brunner anticipated our conclusions—but Sargent and Wallace and I were critics from *within*. We were committed to the use of explicit models to evaluate policy changes; we knew the work we were criticizing in detail, and we could articulate the reasons for our skepticism in a way that those we criticized could see the arguments and respond usefully to them. Macroeconomic debate had changed course.

10

Not long after "Investment under Uncertainty" was finished, Ed Prescott returned to GSIA as a faculty member. I was working on monetary theory, a topic that Ed had never been much interested in. I was also thinking about unemployment, using a theoretical setting in which workers are distributed over a large number of distinct markets, and these markets are subject to persistent shocks to demand. If your market is hit with a bad shock, wages are likely to be low for a while. You are tempted to leave, to set out for brighter prospects elsewhere, but this will entail a spell of unemployment. The risks must be balanced and how this balancing comes out depends on what everyone else is doing. After some weeks of work, I felt I was very close to having a successful mathematical model of this situation, a theory of what Milton Friedman had called the "natural rate of unemployment."

But the pieces would not fall into place. I believed that my formulation had the economics of these interactions just right and that the problem was that I didn't know and couldn't invent the mathematics to work out the implications of the theory. Once again, I asked Ed to collaborate, and after I had taken him through the model, he agreed. This was late on a Friday afternoon, so we stopped working and went downstairs to the faculty—student TGIF.

After the party, walking home by myself through the Schenley Park golf course, thoughts of regret came over me. I had formulated, on my own, a great theoretical problem and had carried the analysis of that problem close to completion. Now I had shown the problem to Ed, who would surely see a quick resolution of the mathematical issues that I had been stuck on. He could write the paper by himself and since I had shown him no actual results, claim credit for himself. He might not even thank me for "helpful discussion" in his opening footnote! As soon as I got home I took out my typewriter and, in a kind of paranoid frenzy that lasted through the weekend, I wrote a draft of the entire paper: Introduction, Theorem 1, Theorem 2, and so on, right through to the end.

On Monday I felt foolish as soon as I saw Ed, but I handed him the draft anyway. Of course we soon discovered that most of the results stated in the draft were false and that we had no idea how to prove the theorems that were possibly true. How could it have been otherwise? If I had really known how to finish the paper I wouldn't have asked Ed to work with me! So we began work in earnest.

Some days, perhaps weeks, later I arrived at the office around 9 and found a note from Ed in my mailbox. The full text was as follows:

Bob,

This is the way labor markets work:

$$v(s, y, \lambda) = \max\{\lambda, R(s, y) + \min[\lambda, \beta \int v(s', y, \lambda) f(s', s)ds']\}.$$

Ed

Of course since our project was well underway, we had agreed on notation: s stood for the state of product demand at a particular location, y stood for the number of workers who were already at that location, $R(s, y)$ was the marginal product of labor implied by these two numbers, and $v(s, y)$ stood for the present value of earnings that one of these workers could obtain if he made his decision whether to stay at this location or leave optimally. Other features of the equation were as novel to me as they are (I imagine) to you.

The normal response to such a note, I suppose, would have been to go upstairs to Ed's office and ask for some kind of explanation. But theoretical economists are not normal, and we do not ask for words that "explain" what equations mean. We ask for equations that explain what words mean. Ed had provided an equation that claimed to explain how labor markets work. It was my job to understand it and to decide whether I agreed with this claim. This took me a while, but I saw that Ed had replaced an assumption of mine that workers who leave any one location hit on a new location at random—maybe a worse location than the one they had left—with the alternative assumption that searching workers were fully informed about options elsewhere and bee-lined for the best destination. Mathematically, this meant that a single parameter—Ed's λ—stood for two different things: the present value of earnings that all searching workers would have to expect in order to leave a location and the present value that a particular location would need to offer to receive new arrivals.

Mathematically, Ed's equation was a very familiar, comfortable object for me to analyze: once I convinced myself that it described some sensible economics, it took a few minutes to see that its properties could be established by standard methods and that these properties were interesting and reasonable. By lunchtime, I could see that I was to be a coauthor of a very sharp paper, unlike anything anyone had seen before, a paper with a potential for helping us to think about important events.

If I had to pick a single day to represent what I like about a life of research, it would be this one. Ed's note captures exactly why I think we value mathematical modeling: it is a method to help us get to new levels of understanding the ways things work. No one could have written Ed's equation down at the beginning of an inquiry into the nature of unemployment: it is too far from earlier ways of thinking to be grasped in one step. The new understanding that this equation represents could be gained only through a trial-and-error process, involving formulating and analyzing explicit models. It is this struggle to capture behavior in tractable models that leads us deeper into the economics of market interactions and forms the progressive element in economic thought.

11

In October, 1978—leaf season—the Federal Reserve Bank of Boston sponsored a conference at the Bald Peak Colony Club in New Hampshire. Ed Prescott and I rented a car at Logan Airport and drove up together. Night fell before we reached the conference center and we got lost on country roads. We stopped for directions at a crossroads store, but after a few minutes of laconic "Nope, yep" New England conversation we realized that the two old men in the store were amusing themselves at our expense, conveying no information. We left in disgust and anger. The incident heightened my sense of entering foreign territory.

On the drive, neither Ed nor I discussed the papers we were to give at the conference. Ed had been reading Simon Kuznets's work and treated me to a review of Kuznets's main findings. I was grateful for the chance to learn something from this central figure in research on economic growth without actually having to read him. We talked about the kinds of theoretical models that might fit the regularities that Kuznets had documented. What better and more productive way to deal with anxieties about how one's work will be received than looking beyond to the next project?

When the conference began, the next day, it became clear that this was not the occasion for such anxieties. The attenders included representatives of the Keynesian establishment—including Paul Samuelson himself—and some "new classical" rebels. In my memory, the conference was a kind of triumph of the new classical views. My own paper was a reprise of Milton Friedman's 1948 paper, "A Monetary and Fiscal Framework for Economic Stability," emphasizing the support that recent research provided for Friedman's positions, with no pretense of new findings. I viewed it as my day to stand up and be counted as a Chicago economist. I later wrote to my parents:

The influence my work has had was astonishing to me. I was very nervous about my presentation, which was extremely negative on what most of this group is up to, yet people were lining up in the question period to take their turn to say how right I am.

The question period I referred to was chaotic, and I remember people calling for me to denounce work by John Taylor and Stan Fischer that, like some of my own work, attempted to account for real effects of monetary instability. I also preferred my approach, but I understood that this preference was not really defensible empirically. I said that on the basis of the evidence available now, I did not see how it was possible to distinguish between my views and Taylor's. Looking back on the occasion, an exciting one for me, I am pleased and a little surprised that I managed such a level-headed reply.

Though I did not see it at the time, the Bald Peak conference also marked the beginning of the end of my attempts to account for the business cycle in terms of monetary shocks. At that conference, Ed Prescott presented a model of his and Finn Kydland's that was a kind of mixture of Brock and Mirman's model of growth subject to stochastic technology shocks and my model of monetary shocks. When Ed presented his results, everyone could see they were important but the paper was so novel and complicated that no one could see exactly what they were. Later on, as they gained more experience through numerical simulations of their Bald Peak model, Kydland and Prescott found that the monetary shocks were just not pulling their weight: by removing all monetary aspects of the theory, they obtained a far simpler and more comprehensible structure that fit postwar U.S. time series data just as well as the original version. Besides introducing an important substantive refocusing of business cycle research, Kydland and Prescott introduced a new style of comparing theory to evidence that has had an enormous, beneficial effect on empirical work in the field.

12

By the time of the Bald Peak conference, I had moved from Carnegie Mellon to the University of Chicago. I was just over forty years old. The work that was later recognized by the Swedish Academy of Sciences was done. I had arrived at a research style that has continued over the years to lead me into new ways of seeing things.

In the more than twenty years since, I have continued to devote virtually all of my time to teaching and research. I have written on many subjects and participated in collaborations with Andy Atkeson, Esteban Rossi-Hansberg, and, especially, with Nancy Stokey, that have been as interesting and fruitful for me as those with Leonard Rapping and Ed Prescott. Perhaps at some later occasion I will review these years, too: I have enjoyed them, produced some work I am proud of, and accumulated enough memories for many more memoirs.

Notes

1. Reprinted in Milton Friedman, *Essays in Positive Economics* (Chicago: University of Chicago Press, 1953).

2. Arjo Klamer, *Conversations with Economists* (Savage, MD: Rowman and Littlefield, 1983), 223.

Robert E. Lucas, Jr.
Awarded Nobel Prize in 1995. Lecture presented April 5, 2001.

Date of Birth
September 15, 1937

Academic Degrees
B.A., University of Chicago, 1959
Ph.D., University of Chicago, 1964

Academic Affiliations
Lecturer, Department of Economics, University of Chicago, 1962–63
Assistant Professor of Economics, Carnegie Institute of Technology, 1963–67
Associate Professor of Economics, Carnegie Mellon University, 1967–70
Professor of Economics, Carnegie Mellon University, 1970–74
Ford Foundation Visiting Research Professor of Economics, University of Chicago, 1974–75
Professor of Economics, University of Chicago, 1975–80
Visiting Professor of Economics, Northwestern, 1981–82
John Dewey Distinguished Service Professor of Economics, University of Chicago, 1980–present

Selected Books
Studies in Business-Cycle Theory, 1981
Models of Business Cycles, 1987
Recursive Methods in Economic Dynamics, 1989 (with N. Stokey and E. Prescott)
Lectures on Economic Growth, 2002

James J. Heckman

I write this essay with some trepidation. Most of the essays in this series are retrospectives rather than progress reports of scholars in mid-career. I am not ready to announce my retirement. I won the Nobel Prize at a relatively early age (56) and hope that I have many more years of active research ahead of me. I welcome the Nobel Prize as an award that opens doors for further growth and learning. So I write this essay in the spirit that past is prologue. I describe my evolution as an economist to this point (March 2003) and my current vision of how my future research will unfold.

My evolution as an economist was not direct. I drifted among academic fields before I settled on economics. Even after I decided to become an economist, I drifted among subfields of the discipline. Eventually I became a labor economist with a strong interest in empirical research, public policy, and the methodology of doing empirical research. If this essay meanders, so did my life.

I proceed in the following way. I present a few remarks on my early background that help to explain some of the motivations and choices throughout my career and how I came to address the problems I have worked on.

I then discuss my interactions with colleagues and students at two key environments: the place where I started as a professional economist, Columbia and the New York NBER in the early 1970s, and the place where I have spent the greatest amount of time: the University of Chicago from the mid '70s to the present. The practice of economics is a social activity greatly affected by the environment in which one works. Feedback, stimulation, and encouragement are central to this activity. I have been lucky to have had many brilliant and stimulating colleagues and students who have helped shape my approach to economics.

Early Influences

I was born in Chicago in 1944 near the University of Chicago, although neither parent was employed by it. Both of my parents were high school graduates. My father was a middle manager for the Armour meat-packing company, and my mother was a housewife. Both parents came from families with modest means. My father's high school degree was delayed several years by his having to drop out of school to work full-time on his father's farm to support his family. My father's post–high school training was limited to a semester at the University of Oklahoma in the fall of 1929, an unpropitious time to start college, and night school training in accounting and management in the Executive Degree Program at the University of Chicago in the 1940s. Both my sister (who is four years older) and I received strong encouragement from our parents to get the college degrees that they lacked. There were books around our home, and my mother took us on frequent trips to museums, cultural events, and historical sites. The first institution of higher learning I ever saw was the University of Chicago, and my father always spoke with admiration about it. Thus began my relationship with an institution that has had a profound influence on my life.

My father fell victim to company politics and suffered various demotions and lateral transfers throughout his career. These transfers gave me a chance to visit many new places with very different social and cultural traditions. These involuntary transfers and demotions were a deep source of anxiety for my father. He urged me at an early age to enter a profession where I could develop an independent reputation and avoid the politics of the bureaucracy of middle managers that he had experienced. I took his message to heart and decided early on to enter a profession where I could make my own mark and be independent of the good will of any superior and where I would never have to be a company man.

My family on both sides is of southern origin. There is a Heckman family farmstead and gravesite in southwestern Virginia that survives to this day. The Heckmans of Virginia were an Old Baptist (Dunkard) family that migrated to North America in the 1740s from Germany to escape religious persecution. The family tradition was anchored in a strong form of fundamentalist Protestant Christianity in which I was raised. My father's father was a farmer-preacher. My mother's family also traces back to Virginia and had strong fundamentalist roots.

As a young child, I fervently embraced the faith of my parents and by age eight, I was a child minister giving sermons on Sunday evenings introduced by a motto taken from the New Testament, "A little child shall lead them." It was expected that when I became an adult, I would be a minister. The church in Western Springs, Illinois, where I preached, was the only pastorate held by the evangelist Billy Graham when he was a student at Wheaton College. After he started his famous crusades, he would occasionally visit his former church. As a child, I met him on several occasions, and he encouraged my calling.

My deep religious belief led me to read and study the Bible very closely. I committed vast passages of it to memory. I interacted with ministers to further my knowledge and even wrote a few tracts that were mimeographed and circulated. I attended religious camps and revival meetings and read with interest about the work of missionaries in exotic environments.

By my early teenage years, while living in Denver, Colorado, I began having doubts. The fundamentalist creed I was raised in and espoused took the Bible very literally. But I began to notice inconsistencies in the Bible, and as I read more broadly in science and philosophy, I came to question the literal interpretations of creation and other aspects of the fundamentalist Christianity with which I was raised. Matters came to a head in a high school term paper I wrote on the parallels between Zoroastrianism (which predated Christianity) and Christian teaching. I began to recognize the eclectic nature of Christian theology. A Zoroastrian origin for Christian traditions was not a welcome idea in the church I attended, nor was any departure from a strict and literal reading of scripture.

These intellectual doubts caused me at age fifteen to break with fundamentalist Christianity and abandon my plan to become a minister. This was not an easy decision for me because at the time my life was in the church and my parents had hopes for me to become a great evangelist. I respected the sincerity of the beliefs held by my family and by members of my congregation, but I no longer shared them. My doubts were later reinforced by the virulent anti-Catholic rhetoric produced by many fundamentalist churches in the 1960 campaign of John F. Kennedy. The intolerance, bigotry and unwillingness of most of the elders in my church to discuss ideas left me deeply dissatisfied. I found that I was unable to accept authority qua authority, a trait that has characterized me ever since. At the same time, my break with the church isolated me from my family and friends. I learned to go it alone without much support at an early age. Having a deep faith and then abandoning it because of intellectual doubt was a wrenching experience. At the same time, I learned early to live off my own intellectual and emotional resources. My ability to go it alone, without the approval of others, has been a major asset to my career. I learned to stick to my guns irrespective of what others around me thought.

During this period, I applied and was encouraged to attend college at the University of Chicago in a special program for bored but high-achieving high school students. I was tempted to go to escape the awkward situation in which I found myself. However, family finances were poor and my parents thought me too young.

At about the same time I broke with fundamentalist Christianity and was considering enrolling at Chicago, a whole new world of ideas opened up to me thanks to the accidental introduction of Frank Oppenheimer into my life. Frank Oppenheimer was the brother of J. Robert Oppenheimer, the famous physicist and head of the Manhattan Project. Frank was an accomplished experimental physicist in his own right who had worked at Los Alamos during World War II and at the University of Minnesota afterward. Much later he gained fame for developing the Exploratorium—a major science teaching museum in San Francisco that has been emulated around the world. Frank Oppenheimer had been a member of the Communist Party, which raised questions about his brother's loyalty. It led to Frank's dismissal from the University of Minnesota during the height of the McCarthy era.

It was my good luck that the local superintendent of schools in Jefferson County, Colorado, invited Frank Oppenheimer to teach physics to a countywide class of selected students after he had spent five or so years ranching in rural Colorado. The offer of enrollment in his class convinced me to stay in high school to learn from him. That class and my exposure to him were truly life-transforming experiences. He was the first truly brilliant mind I had ever encountered. He introduced me to the life of the mind. Our class read everything he told us to read in science and other subjects. We rushed out to read the books and articles he casually mentioned while he conducted physics experiments with us. We learned to love the late quartets of Beethoven at his house, and we discussed the philosophy of science into the night. In the second year of his course, he introduced us to leading scientists such as George Gamow and Stanislaw Ulam, who came into our high school classroom to discuss cutting-edge science.

Oppenheimer transmitted a love of physics in his classroom evident today to any visitor to the Exploratorium. He showed us how theory explained facts. In a lab book I still own, I derived all the basic laws of

Newtonian mechanics and tested them on a set of beautiful experiments designed in the post—Sputnik era to promote science literacy among American youth. The objective nature of physics and the ability of the laws of physics to predict empirical regularities was a splendid alternative to a religion and authority I no longer accepted. I became an enthusiastic protoscientist, amazed and gratified that theory worked so well in practice. The theory was beautiful. But it was the confirmation of theory, and the insistence that any physical law worthy of that name should conform to and predict physical reality, that were so pleasing. I remember a classroom discussion with Oppenheimer on Eugene Wigner's then recently written article, "The Unreasonable Effectiveness of Mathematics in Physical Science." The profound simplicity of the physical world and the ability of mathematics to predict it overwhelmed me. If I had any religion at that time, it was Deism. I was impressed by God the watchmaker. In my senior year in high school, I had decided to study physics at Cornell at the urging of Frank Oppenheimer. The possibilities of science seemed limitless.

But even then, I was interested in other things. My father's demotions and transfers took my family on a tour through the Border South and the West: St. Louis, Lexington (Kentucky), and Oklahoma City, ending up in Denver, Colorado, where I withdrew from organized religion and met Oppenheimer. In the first three towns, I saw firsthand the last vestiges of the Jim Crow system of racial discrimination. Its protocols and intrinsically demeaning effects on all participants fascinated me. Coming from Chicago, I had heard of racism (especially after the lynching of Emmett Till in 1955), but I had never witnessed it. My parents, while southern in origin, never uttered racist remarks. The Jim Crow system of social regulation intrigued me, and I became an avid follower of the activities of the civil rights movement that dismantled it through social activism. The late '50s and early '60s were times of great social change, and the politics of the era captivated me. When I was not doing science, I was reading history, philosophy, and politics. In the late 1950s, *Life* magazine, then a popular weekly, ran a series on the national purpose written by many distinguished Americans. I read every essay in the series and debated the contents of these essays with teachers and fellow students.

So despite my love of science, I also had a deep fascination with politics, social science, and history. In deciding where to go to college, Cornell or Stanford looked like good bets because they had strengths in history and social science, not just physics and mathematics. As fate would have it, I applied and got fellowship support from both schools. However, I also won a Boettcher Foundation scholarship. Boettcher scholarships were very generous. This gave me financial independence at an early age and allowed a graceful exit from an estranged relationship with my parents, thereby giving me independence at seventeen—something I valued greatly. The only stipulation for receiving the fellowship was that I had to attend a college in Colorado. That did not seem like a severe limitation at the time. I debated between the University of Colorado (where Oppenheimer had been hired in my senior year) and Colorado College, which by many accounts was the best school in the state.

College Days: A Drift to Economics

My choice of Colorado College was more eventful then I could have forecasted. After a few semesters, I found the physics there disappointing and gravitated toward math and just about everything else. The liberal arts environment let me try my hand at many things: anthropology, philosophy, English literature, political science, and economics. I edited the student paper, protested civil rights abuses, fought anti-Semitism, and anti-black restrictive policies by fraternities and took a trip through the segregated South with my Nigerian roommate, which led to some hair-raising encounters in Birmingham, Alabama, and Hattiesburg, Mississippi, which we wrote about in student newspapers. I also interacted with the organizers of the Freedom School, a libertarian organization near Colorado College where I learned about Friedrich Hayek, Frédéric Bastiat, Ayn Rand, and Milton Friedman. In my junior year, I took a readings class in economic growth from Ray Werner. It was my first serious introduction to economics. We read Ricardo, Smith, and Arthur Lewis, a future Nobel laureate and previous speaker in this series. The professor also loaned me his copy of Paul Samuelson's *Foundations of Economic Analysis* (which I still own) to read as an extra bonus.

Samuelson's *Foundations* had a major impact on me. It demonstrated to me that economics could be as rigorous and empirically relevant as physics. The theorem–proof format of the book appealed to my mathematical side. At the same time, it showed that economics had empirical content through the theory of revealed preference. I saw a counterpart in social science to the hard science I had first experienced in Oppenheimer's classroom.

Lewis's *Theory of Economic Growth* appealed to my liberal arts training. It synthesized economics, politics, history, and sociology into what appeared to me at the time to be a convincing theory of economic development. I could not put the book down. I read and reread it. Smith and Ricardo were also exciting, even if their language was more arcane. My junior year readings class led me to decide on economics as a career. It did not hurt that at the time the influence of economists was on the rise in the society at large, thanks to the apparent success of the 1962 Kennedy tax cut. Economics was perceived to be a science. It showed society how to control the business cycle. I entered the field in the era of "fine tuning," where the possibilities of prediction and control of the economy seemed endless. I could have my science and my social science too. The apparent scientific success of economics in controlling the macro economy led to the establishment of a Nobel Prize for the field in the late 1960s.

I graduated from college as a math major because I had taken so many math courses during my drift through college. However, I had decided to become an academic economist, studying economic development. The academic life, as I perceived it, being led by professors at Colorado College, was a life of the mind with interplay across fields. It seemed to me (and my parents) almost idyllic to be paid to discuss and research ideas. Tenure and publication would provide me with the autonomy and personal independence I craved. My first choice of graduate school was Princeton, which had Arthur Lewis plus a strong tradition in demography, which I saw as a handmaiden to development. It also had a strong tradition in mathematics. I also applied to Chicago at the urging of Ray Werner. I knew little about Chicago except that I had heard that Milton Friedman was good. I was familiar with some of his popular essays. I had also read his methodology of positive economics and enthusiastically supported his approach to testing theory with evidence. Swayed by his essay, a generous scholarship, and the urging of my undergraduate advisor, I chose Chicago. From childhood, I had respected the school. It didn't hurt that my wife could easily get a job teaching high school in a nearby suburb.

Graduate School

When I arrived at Chicago in 1965, I was overwhelmed by the large classes, impersonal atmosphere, the threats to physical safety in Hyde Park at that time and the race riots that plagued the city. Living near an encampment of National Guard troops during a race riot was an unforgettable experience. Despite my exposure to a few classics, my training in economics was weak compared to that of most of my fellow students, although my math skills were superior. As formal proofs were not encouraged in the program at that time, my math skills gave me no advantage whatsoever and may have handicapped me: I was always looking for formal statements of verbal and graphical propositions that I found vague and confusing. I took all of Milton Friedman's first-year classes and found them fascinating, albeit sometimes difficult to follow. He taught first-year students in monetary theory about natural rate theory before that term was widely known or used and before he made that term famous in his presidential address to the American Economics Association. To my amazement, I got high marks in his classes, and he was personally friendly to me. I also found Harry Johnson's classes on income distribution and capital theory interesting. He taught me two sector general equilibrium models and introduced me to Gary Becker's work on human capital, albeit in a cursory way. He also gave stimulating lectures on general topics in economics, which I admired greatly. He was surprisingly generous with his time.

I discussed my still-burning interest in the field of economic development with Harry Johnson, and to my surprise, he was very negative about the offerings at Chicago in development, and suggested that I go to Princeton to study with his friend and former Manchester colleague Arthur Lewis. In retrospect I think Johnson underrated the fundamental work of Chicagoans Ted Schultz and D. Gale Johnson on agriculture in development. However, at that time, I was not interested in agriculture and failed to appreciate its important role in development. I admired Lewis's book and its bold vision of the development process.

After consulting with Harry Johnson and with labor economist Albert Rees, who was then on his way from Chicago to Princeton, I decided to transfer to Princeton. The bucolic environment, small classes, and private tutorials at Princeton were much more to my liking and were more suited to my liberal arts background.

I also did not like the impersonality of Chicago or the cult of Friedman that characterized the graduate program at that time. Although I greatly valued my interactions with Friedman and found him brilliant, open, and stimulating, I did not like the uncritical, almost religious devotion to his ideas by many of my fellow students. The followers were much worse than the master and created a subculture imbued with a religious zeal reminiscent of the zeal of the groups I had recently rejected.

I also appreciated the wide array of courses in applied mathematics available at the time at Princeton. I concentrated on development and demography, and offered these as my principal fields. Lewis was friendly to me and encouraged my interest in development. Ansley Coale's courses in mathematical demography were fascinating to me although he was personally hostile to economics. My interactions with the Colombian polymath Alvaro Lopez at the office of Population Research were highly stimulating. I took a range of courses in probability theory, statistics, and game theory from first-rate people such as Willy Feller, John Tukey, and Albert Tucker. Courses in mathematical economics by Harold Kuhn were comprehensive and clear.

I immersed myself in development economics, finding Lewis to be brilliant and insightful but somewhat old fashioned even in his field as it was then being practiced. He was an intuitive economist at a time when development was becoming more formal. In addition, his theory was more speculative than I had imagined. Ironically, I discovered Schultz's work in Lewis's course, and I began to realize the importance of agriculture in development. I realized that Lewis's book, which had been a main motivation for me to enter economics, had serious limitations as an empirical description of the development process.

The new breed of development economists at Princeton treated the field as a branch of nonlinear and integer programming. While technically interesting, their vision of the field seemed sterile to me. I lost patience with results like "if you know the dual prices, you can solve the primal problem" because they begged the question of where the dual prices came from. For a while, demography intrigued me, and I came dangerously close to writing a Ph.D. thesis on the role of complex roots on the rate of convergence of populations governed by the classical Lotka integral equation of population. I came to my senses and realized that I would leave economics for good if I chose to work on that topic. So I began drifting again.

In retrospect, drifting was not so bad. It enabled me to acquire a large array of skills in economics and applied math, most of which proved useful. I have applied most of the skills I learned.

In my third year, I took a tutorial in labor economics from Al Rees. Rees was a hard-nosed, no-nonsense empirical economist with deep interest in public policy who was a direct descendant in a long lineage of first-rate Chicago empirical economists such as Paul Douglas, Henry Schultz, and H. Gregg Lewis. People sometimes forget that Chicago has a strong empirical tradition and think of the Chicago School as a body of scholars who embrace particular ideas about free markets. In fact, a central feature of the Chicago approach has been that it values careful empirical analysis and generally demands empirical justification for policy proposals.

Rees knew his price theory, but he rooted his research in data and encouraged students to take data very seriously. His vision of economics, like that of many Chicago economists of his generation, was that it is only of value if it is practically useful. He was an honest, open, friendly person who encouraged curiosity and imposed high standards on those around him. He had been helpful to me in making my decision to transfer to Princeton.

Rees introduced me to the exciting new field of neoclassical labor economics being pioneered by Gary Becker and Jacob Mincer at Columbia. Johnson's lectures at Chicago had briefly exposed me to some of this work, and I found it fascinating. Rees drew out the empirical implications of this work much more than Johnson had done. The economics of this new field was simple but the theory was empirically powerful. I read every article I could find by Becker, Mincer, and their students. Reading Jacob Mincer's famous article on the labor supply of married women for the first time was an exciting experience. Simple price theory applied to aggregate data reconciled a number of conflicting pieces of empirical evidence and explained how wage growth and household production could explain a major social phenomenon. The work combined basic economics with simple econometrics.

At about the same time, Al Rees also introduced me to the vast array of microdata sets on the labor market and the household that began to be produced on a wide scale in the 1960s. These data sets were a byproduct of the Kennedy–Johnson era. They were developed to evaluate its numerous programs, to monitor social life, and to assess the efficacy of alternative policies. At that time Rees was working on the first major social experiment to determine the impact of negative income taxes on labor supply. At his request, I even helped enroll some of the first participants in the experiment. The topic of the disincentive effects of welfare and taxation on labor supply attracted a lot of interest at that time, given the expanding size of the welfare state. Rees drew my attention to this debate. The empirical work on these topics largely ignored economics and used "simple" empirical methods that produced estimates difficult for me to interpret either as economic parameters or as answers to interesting policy counterfactuals.

I have closely followed the social experiment movement ever since those days. I am impressed by the blind enthusiasm the term "experiment" evokes and by the serious limitations of social experiments. The more carefully one looks at the product of social experiments, the less enthusiastic one can be about them. Human beings are purposeful in a way seed corn and laboratory rats are not. Economic policy design requires that analysts know more than the dose-response relationships produced by experiments. Years later I wrote on social experiments. What impressed me then was how little had been learned from the first wave of social experiments and how powerful and evocative the term "experiment" is to both popular and professional minds. The failed negative income tax experiments did little to prevent an uncritical embrace of social experimentation in the 1980s and 1990s.

Rees introduced me to theories rich in empirical content and to data on which it was possible to test them. During my tutorial with him, I decided to become a labor economist. There were many research opportunities to be exploited, and the possibilities for generalizing the theory seemed limitless. My goal was to make labor economics a rigorous branch of empirical science.

Although I greatly admired Mincer's article on female labor supply, I felt it did not go far enough in using the newly available data to test the theory of family labor supply. I saw an opportunity to apply the rigorous price theory of Samuelson's *Foundations* to the newly available cross section and panel data. My thesis developed a life-cycle model of family labor supply with wage growth induced by learning by doing. It was the first systematic test of the family theory of labor supply and the first model of labor supply with learning by doing as a determinant of wage growth.

My goals were to integrate labor supply with human capital theory and to test the theory of family labor supply using both aggregate and microdata. I was happy to be able to combine rigorous economic theory with microdata. I felt that the Becker–Mincer research program was wide open with lots of opportunities for theoretical and empirical work.

I shared my enthusiasm for this general research program with Orley Ashenfelter, who was two years ahead of me in the graduate program and who took a job at Princeton in my final year of residence there. Ashenfelter's enthusiasm for economics, data and life was infectious. We would discuss topics into the night. We shared a common vision about applying economic theory to empirical work in labor economics. We wrote several papers estimating Slutsky income and substitution effects in labor supply. He also acquainted me with Becker's *Economics of Discrimination* and shared with me his research ideas on explaining the time series of racial wage and employment patterns. Ashenfelter was the first to notice the improvement in black economic status after the passage of the 1964 Civil Rights Act. Yet his evidence, based as it was on aggregate data, was far from convincing. We discussed the economics of Jim Crow. I found these discussions to be very stimulating, given my personal observations of the Jim Crow South. They shaped some of my later research on government policy and racial wage differentials.

Together we wrote the first papers on the impact of a major federal government affirmative-action program on black employment. From this work, I learned the important lesson that racial employment and occupational advances in the 1960s were greatest in the South, a point I would build on and amplify in my later work.

My early interests were not at all motivated by econometric questions. Indeed my initial reaction to econometrics was negative. Princeton had a project on time series (spectral analysis) started by John von Neumann and continued by Oskar Morgenstern. Distinguished scholars such as Clive Granger and Michio Hatanaka were still around, although the project was winding down during my graduate student days. My experience with the new methods was not satisfactory. Although overtly nonparametric, choices of "windows" (or, in modern jargon, "bandwidths") and the like affected empirical conclusions in the short macro time series to which the new methods were applied. Most econometrics seemed very mechanical to me, and I had no interest in the big macro models of the day. I did not even take the econometrics field exam for the Ph.D.

The only work in econometrics that appealed to me was Richard Quandt's work on discrete choice and travel demand, which opened up an entire field that was enhanced and made fully rigorous by my co-laureate Daniel McFadden. I read Quandt's work with interest. Only after I left Princeton did I come to realize its relevance for my work on labor supply. I read a lot of statistics, however, because in my thesis research I faced an apparently unending array of new problems in using microdata that were not treated in any econometrics textbooks. I discussed many of these problems with the eminent statistician John Tukey, although his format was daunting. He would assemble a gallery of statistics graduate students to listen to our exchanges. Although I often disagreed with Tukey, I found his ideas interesting and helpful. I spent hours poring over statistics journals and books at Princeton's Fine Hall to get some guidance on the empirical questions I faced in my daily work. I got little guidance from econometrics books except for the masterful textbook by Arthur Goldberger. Even Goldberger treated the topics I needed for my thesis in a cursory way.

Columbia University

I was hired at Columbia in 1970 as a labor economist and was excited by the opportunity to work firsthand with Gary Becker and Jacob Mincer. Becker left Columbia for Chicago shortly after I accepted the Columbia offer, so we were never colleagues there. My three years at Columbia were a major learning experience. At that time, the senior faculty was first rate and open minded. Daily lunches would produce intense discussions on wide ranging topics. I learned about capital theory, marginal cost pricing, Marxist economics, optimal control theory, and the economics of characteristics from my colleagues.

I faithfully attended the legendary Labor Workshop at Columbia. This workshop was founded by Gary Becker and Jacob Mincer and was the forum where so many important ideas in labor economics in the 1960s were first presented. Even though Becker had left, feelings about him were intense. Indeed, the first time I attended the workshop, I arrived late and sat down in an open chair at the head of the seminar table, just to the left of the speaker. When I sat down in that chair, I was told to take another chair. The one I had occupied was permanently reserved for Gary Becker even though he was now at Chicago.

Even without Becker, the workshop was remarkable. Mincer was an austere, often blunt, figure who demanded clarity and precision from all speakers. I learned something new from every seminar and learned even more from being the third reader on the dissertations of Becker–Mincer students, many of whom went on to become leading labor economists. The rules of the seminar were clear—simple price theory, simple econometrics, simple empirical work. Becker visited Columbia for several thesis defenses. I found interactions with him stimulating and informative.

In my second year at Columbia, I was invited to join the NBER in New York; the bureau supported my research. Victor Fuchs was the guiding organizational force who generously supported young scholars such as myself, although he was more than a little wary of my technical interests. There was an active labor group comprised of Jacob Mincer, Finis Welch, Bob Willis, Jim Smith, and a host of distinguished visitors who made the place an exciting venue.

The younger people in the group all attended the Labor Workshop at Columbia, but there were separate informal workshops at the NBER and intellectual free-for-alls that were profoundly stimulating. NBER was a complement to the more austere environment of the Labor Workshop—

a place to relax with ideas in an informal setting. Discussions were intense. One workshop I participated in started at 1:30 p.m. and concluded at midnight.

Finis Welch was the intellectual leader of the group of young economists at NBER. Gifted with a deep economic intuition and a powerful sense of the data, he made provocative suggestions on my work and that of many others. He was the ideal leader for a young research group of empirical economists. Active, engaged, and encouraging, he taught me a lot and offered both intellectual and financial support.

My most intense interactions at NBER were with Robert Willis. By separate routes, we had independently discovered the importance of accounting for heterogeneity across people in understanding patterns found in microeconomic data. Working together and apart, we later developed panel data models for fertility, earnings, and labor force dynamics. Anyone who looks at microdata cannot help but be impressed by heterogeneity among agents. R. G. D. Allen and Arthur Bowley had already documented this phenomenon in the analyses of budget data in the 1930s, but the new flood of microdata, and especially panel data, forced this point home.

The econometrics of the time, developed as it was for representative agent models, ignored individual heterogeneity, although there were dissenting voices such as those of Marc Nerlove, Arnold Zellner, and Zvi Griliches. The whole approach to heterogeneity and unobservables in econometrics in this period was typified in a famous 1960 paper by Hendrik Houthakker on addilog utility functions. Turning to the data, after developing his model, he wrote,

I adorn the equation with an error term.

That phrase pretty much summarized the dichotomy between the model and the sources of error typical of the econometrics of the day. In my work on labor supply, I had become aware of the importance of accounting for unobservables in developing econometric estimators of economic parameters. The sources of error and the way unobservables entered agent decisions mattered greatly. Yet they were barely discussed in any econometrics text.

An Accidental Econometrician

At the end of my first year at Columbia, the chair of the department, Kelvin Lancaster, approached me to teach graduate econometrics because the resident econometrician was leaving and no one else in the department knew anything about econometrics. I took this as an occasion to teach myself Henri Theil's then-new *Principles of Econometrics*. His was a breakthrough book that introduced basic asymptotic theory into econometrics. Teaching this course enabled me to break into graduate teaching.

I was lucky to be given this challenge because it forced me once and for all to confront the existing literature in econometrics to see if it was helpful for the problems I was working on. I deepened my understanding of the available tools but found that they did not solve my problems. In the course of my work on labor supply, I had encountered a whole host of empirical problems that seemed rather mundane but which, on reflection, had no easy answers.

The prototypical problem was the missing wage problem. In my thesis I faced the recurring problem of having missing wages for about half the women whose labor supply I was seeking to determine. Moreover the missing wages were associated with women not working (zero hours of work).

Three problems were conjoined: (1) What values to assign the missing wages? (2) What labor supply function(s) described the work–no work decision and the hours-of-work decision for workers? Could the various dimensions of labor supply be reconciled in a common framework? (3) How could heterogeneity and measurement error be accounted for in a common framework?

These problems were very much in the air. Mincer's seminal article on female labor supply answered question (2) under strong implicit assumptions that time was intertemporally perfectly substitutable. Notes by H. Gregg Lewis and Yoram Ben-Porath treated the work—no work decision as a corner solution for each period. Mincer, my Columbia senior colleague, strongly rejected this approach.

Some relevant econometrics was around, too. James Tobin's "Tobit" model (the term was coined by Goldberger) showed how to estimate models with truncated dependent variables, but surprisingly, in light of his eminence as an economic theorist, he offered no *economic* interpretation of his statistical model. In a paper written in 1972 and published in 1974, I wrote down an econometric model that addressed all three questions. I used the reservation wage ("virtual price" or "shadow wage") derived from consumer preferences to unify the different dimensions of labor supply in a common economic framework. I specified the unobservables in market wage and reservation wages to generate a consistently specified labor supply function. Using this setup I could interpret all previous approaches to the estimation of different types of labor supply functions as special cases of this model. I was able to show which empirical specifications estimated economically interpretable parameters (Hicks–Slutsky income and substitution effects), which ones did not, and how they approximated the desired parameters. I was fortunate that Reuben Gronau, who was visiting the NBER and working on related issues, let me try out my models at his blackboard. He made many constructive comments at that crucial time in my thinking. I followed up this work with a life cycle version also published in 1974 in which I explicitly outlined a method for estimating preference heterogeneity in the marginal rate of substitution between goods and leisure. I developed a framework for estimating the effect of taxes on labor supply and for measuring exact welfare gains and losses from taxation and public policy.

These two papers let me answer nagging questions that had bothered me since I had begun to work on labor supply. I viewed them as contributions to labor economics and to the economics of shadow prices and rationing. I could now consistently account for the error specification of my empirical models and do Samuelson-like revealed preference on real data. The asymptotic theory needed to justify the model was not to be found in Theil or in the published literature. Fortunately, Takeshi Amemiya of Stanford had just written a fundamental paper on the asymptotics of nonlinear models, which I could adapt to my framework. Work on "limited dependent variables" was in its infancy in econometrics, and work on general models with joint discrete-continuous random variables was unknown in econometrics before I wrote the paper. I became aware of the work of McFadden on discrete choice only after completing this work. In fact it was not until a 1974 conference at Berkeley organized by McFadden that I became aware of the emerging wide-scale interest in discrete choice and limited dependent variables models. McFadden proved to be a steady source of stimulation and support after that conference. I organized a follow-up conference in Chicago in 1975 and collected the papers from the two conferences into a special issue of the now-defunct *Annals of Economic and Social Measurement*. That publication established the new field of discrete choice and limited dependent variables.

The framework I developed in these early papers has proven to be useful to many economists. Indeed it has become common coin. It has been used to estimate the demand price for new goods (read "virtual price" in place of "virtual" or "shadow" wage), the purchase of durables and the effects of taxes and other social programs on labor supply, among other applications. It also provided a rigorous framework for analyzing causal effects of policies.

While still working at Columbia, I began to develop a general framework for organizing discrete, continuous, and joint discrete-continuous variables in a common framework. I realized that my method for using economic theory to produce counterfactual missing wages was more generally applicable. In early 1973, I wrote a paper called "Dummy Endogenous Variables" that spelled out a general framework for modeling interrelated discrete and continuous choice models. It handled the simultaneous probit, Tobit, and other frameworks, and it unified many strands of the literature using the notion of an "index function" (a term I coined) representing latent variables (like shadow prices). I also developed a simple estimator for these models that has subsequently been widely used (the "inverse Mills ratio" method).

I circulated unpublished versions of this paper and discussed it freely with students and colleagues. While I received considerable credit for this work, and various versions of it were published in good places, I was slow in getting it to print. Some of this work did not appear until as late as 1979.

Leaving Columbia

I developed my latent variable framework and an entire agenda based on it during three crucial years in New York. I found my colleagues at Columbia and NBER very stimulating. At the same time, my work was very "econometric" in the context of the Labor Workshop and violated its implicit rules of play, which emphasized simple ideas and often ruled out considerations of simultaneity or reverse causality in explaining data.

Columbia had many diverse groups in economics. There was a strong Marxist or radical economics group that had grown up in the wake of the 1968 riots. A steady stream of Marxist scholars came through, and Luigi Pasenetti was a frequent visitor. For me the high point of this activity came when Joan Robinson visited for a month, wearing a North Korean commissar's uniform. I had high hopes for her visit because I had admired her early work. I moderated a debate between her and Abba

Lerner on the impossibility of capitalism based on the inability to form simple aggregates of capital. I found her position absurd. She was unwilling to listen to any objection. I found the entire reswitching debate sterile on both sides and was amazed that it had attracted the attention of good minds.

As a junior faculty member, I was asked to be on the dissertation committees of Becker–Mincer students as well as on the dissertation committees of Marxists. Two dissertations impressed me with the difficulties of resolving conflicts between these warring factions. Two students ran the same wage regression. Both found that mother's education raised wages. The Marxist interpreted this as showing the power of networks and family influence to affect the child's placement in the labor market. The human capital student claimed that this evidence showed that mothers invested in child human capital. Although I was inclined to take the latter view, I was more than willing to grant that a simple regression could not settle the matter. When I asked each student to read the work of the other, and to present more cogent identification arguments to discriminate between these interpretations, I got angry phone calls from their chairs.

Human capital theory for me is too elastic and inclusive. In many forms, it verges on tautology. Too many models of the pricing of labor services and the production of skills can explain the same least-squares wage equation. Sharper models are needed that use additional information. At Columbia, I began a line of work that continues to this day that goes behind the celebrated Mincer wage equation to explain investment, labor supply, and wage growth using explicit models of optimization based on a common set of technology and preference parameters. The optimal control theory and nonlinear econometric methods used to formulate and estimate these models were not welcome by either faction at Columbia.

In early 1973, I was pleased to be invited to speak at Chicago in Becker's workshop and to discover that Chicago was proposing to make me a job offer as a labor economist and as an econometrician. Both Gary Becker and Marc Nerlove were very supportive of my work, and I respected both greatly. When the offer came, I accepted it. The main group at the New York NBER was moving to Palo Alto so that important source of stimulation was leaving. I felt that Chicago was a bigger stage, with a higher level of intellectual activity. I had flirted with Chicago all my life. I had tried it once but was not ready for it at that time. I now felt ready and was eager to learn from it.

Chicago in the 1970s

The Department of Economics that I joined in 1973 was a cauldron of intellectual activity. The pantheon of economists in residence was impressive. In the department I joined, there were at least five future Nobel laureates in economics (Lucas arrived two years later), and the business school and law school had at least two more. Unquestionably, Milton Friedman was the dominant mind, but there was a wide range of talent in the environment. Chicago at that time emphasized price theory. If anything, it was weak in formal mathematical modeling. However, even that gap was being closed by William A. Brock and José Scheinkman.

The entire department seemed to embrace Friedman's methodology of positive economics. Indeed, carved onto the facade of the social science building (1929) was Lord Kelvin's motto:

When you cannot measure, your knowledge is meager and unsatisfactory. (Lord Kelvin, 1889)

This motto seemed to embody the ethos of the department. No theory was worthwhile unless it survived a reality check. A rigorous empirical test was preferred. In that department, it didn't take a theory to beat another theory; it took a fact. Having a "clean" model was never enough; it had to explain real-world phenomena. The contingent of empirical economists in residence was strong. At that time, Becker conducted empirical tests of his theories. Ted Schultz and D. Gale Johnson promoted empirical studies in agriculture and development. H. Gregg Lewis was a renowned taskmaster in labor economics who in the words of Zvi Griliches (who preceded me at Chicago and left before I came) "kept everybody empirically honest."

The workshop system was the heart of Chicago in the 1970s. Founded by D. Gale Johnson, it was perfected by Milton Friedman. There were as many as three workshops a day. People came to these workshops having read the speaker's paper, and discussions were intense. A high premium was placed on verbal quickness, and some workshops, most notably George Stigler's, seemed to delight in humiliating speakers with verbal insults. I remember one day when my former Columbia colleague Ned Phelps came to Stigler's workshop to present a paper on the then-taboo subject of altruism in economics. The response was a torrent of invective that went on for one and a half hours. The image that came to my mind during that workshop was that of Russian Prime Minister Nikita Khrushchev pounding his shoe on the table at the U.N. in 1960.

Friedman's workshop set a very high standard. All participants read the paper being presented in advance of the seminar, and discussions were of the form "any questions on line two of paragraph three?" He was very quick and intimidating. I later learned that students presenting papers would deliberately put errors in their papers so that they could answer questions motivated by them quickly and thus appear to be very intelligent. Becker's workshop was less exacting, but it allowed one to learn Becker's views. Whereas Friedman explored a paper using the author's framework, Becker would force the speaker to recast his paper into a Beckerian framework.

In my early years, I immersed myself in this system, going to as many as two workshops per day. It was a marvelous learning experience that would be supplemented by pre-workshop lunches and post-workshop dinners. Another form of learning was reading scores of Ph.D. theses, a practice suggested to me by Harry Johnson.

These workshops had a collective mind. One person would make a suggestion that would spark another suggestion that would make the discussion vastly better than any one person could conduct. I have presented many workshops at Chicago. Knowing that a paper will be closely and publicly scrutinized induces the author to sharpen his argument. After all, one of the credos of Chicago is that a person is "only as good as his latest paper." So one's local reputation is at stake when one gives a paper. The workshop inevitably leads to improvements in the paper if only because it forces the author to recast his thoughts to respond to the perspectives of others. I have learned that grudging acceptance of a paper at Chicago means that the paper will be a hit everywhere else.

The intellectual honesty fostered by the workshop system makes Chicago an impersonal environment compared to many other academic economic environments that more closely resemble country clubs. Chicago is not a place for the faint-hearted or the weak. It can be very demanding on even the best people. At the same time, it fosters excellence in many dimensions, albeit at the cost of some personal stress. The Chicago system de-emphasizes networking and cronyism and emphasizes intellectual honesty and candor.

The Chicago department that I joined believed in the power of simple economic models to explain the economy and the power of incentives in motivating behavior. At that time, the dominant Keynesian view did not recognize incentives and the Chicago position was quite distinctive. It is fair to say that in the past thirty years the Chicago view has prevailed.

Chicago also had an aversion to the technocratic vision of economic policy making then favored by many leading schools. Rather than endorsing the concept that a brilliant elite should make policy for the masses, Chicago believed in the innate common sense of the common man if an argument were presented clearly. There was the belief that anything really important could be conveyed in a simple, effective manner. Friedman's steady stream of clearly written *Newsweek* policy columns was the best demonstration of this approach to public policy. People should be educated to make informed choices, not managed by technocrats who know more than they do.

In retrospect, the array of first-rate work done at Chicago in the early 1970s was astounding. George Stigler was busy developing the political economy of regulation. Robert Fogel was completing his work on slavery. Becker was developing models of marriage, divorce, social interactions, and parental altruism. Ted Schultz, in his 70s, was vigorously working on development and agriculture. D. Gale Johnson was active in serious policy analysis of world agriculture, despite undertaking heavy administrative burdens at the university and in the community at large. William Brock and José Scheinkman were extending the formal theory of economic growth. Harry Johnson had become ill and was much less in evidence than I had hoped. Nonetheless his influence on students in trade and development was felt. H. Gregg Lewis, who was slow to publish, was engaged in constructing market equilibrium evaluations of the impact of unionism and regulation on the economy. Arnold Harberger was actively engaged in developing cost–benefit analysis and in introducing market reforms into the Chilean economy. In the business school, Arnold Zellner and Hans Theil, while often in conflict, were producing volumes of interesting econometric research (Marc Nerlove left before I arrived, and Zvi Griliches was long gone). Myron Scholes, Fischer Black, Gene Fama, and Merton Miller were making pathbreaking advances in finance.

The vitality of the entire enterprise invigorated me. Ideas were abundant, and new discoveries were being made every day. I could test out my ideas on colleagues all of the time, and this made research rewarding and easy to do. Exchange benefited everyone.

I do not want to suggest that Chicago was nirvana. The Chicago School had brilliant minds, and engaging with them was often exhilarating. Yet even brilliant minds have their weaknesses. A great weakness of many bright people is their frequent inability to distinguish between agreement with their personal views and genuine intelligence and creativity. A second-tier group of people at Chicago, selected more for their agreeability than their creativity or originality, left much to be desired. Often rabidly political, they were careless with data and careless with theory. However, they concurred with the masters and were valued as disciples or co-religionists to spread the truth. They were the downside of the place.

George Stigler once wrote that economics was a conservative field because it emphasized the cost of social policy. Yet, there is nothing intrinsic in economic thinking that should lead one to ignore the benefits of public policy either. No serious empirical economist who looks at the facts can be conservative all of the time. There was a conservative undercurrent that tended to shade empirical evidence and analysis among the believers who invariably found all government interventions harmful. However, among most of the intellectual leaders, politics played no role in day-to-day economic analysis or discussions.

Dynamics, Counterfactuals, Selection Bias, and Missing Data

Chicago in the 1970s was an ideal environment for me to conduct research. One-on-one interactions and seminars improved my thinking on any project I undertook. I had developed an agenda in my first three years at Columbia, and I expanded on it and generalized it in my early years at Chicago.

Although I have had many brilliant colleagues, and I have benefited greatly from them, it is to the students of Chicago that I owe my greatest debt. Top students at Chicago are brilliant and hard working. Early on in their careers, they get caught up in the intensity of the place. They are deeply curious and willing to learn. Interacting with them on their work has taught me a lot. For years I have run a kind of apprenticeship system in which students do empirical work, applied econometrics, and theory under my close supervision. Students participating in this system have been very helpful sounding boards for my ideas over the years, and many have been coauthors on papers on which they have been full partners. I am proud that many first rate Chicago students now prominent in the profession coauthored their first publications with me. They were and are a major stimulus to my own work. They helped me extend the research program I had brought with me from Columbia.

Stepping back from the particular details of the labor supply problem I had been working on, I realized in the mid-1970s that I had developed a new framework for addressing the problem of missing data when the data were missing nonrandomly. Statisticians who had previously addressed the problem of missing data assumed that they were missing at random, but the economics of the problem suggested that in many contexts (e.g., the wages of women) data were missing in a selective way. Using the economics of the problem joined with distributional assumptions provided a general answer to this problem. This work attracted a lot of attention when it was published. One reason for its success was that I developed a simple estimator that was easily applied to many problems. I also developed a general framework that unified a variety of scattered special cases. I developed a class of simple, easily applied estimators based on what is now known as the "control function" principle (the term was coined in my papers with Richard Robb). The initial reception of these models by economists and statisticians was very enthusiastic. Only much later would the statisticians develop "parallel" analyses of selectively missing data, based on these ideas, and ignore the earlier work by economists.

I applied these models to areas outside of labor supply to show their generality. Building on a paper by my Columbia and Chicago colleague Bill Landes on the economics of fair employment laws, I analyzed the effect of accounting for the endogeneity of laws in estimating the impacts of legislation. Happily, Landes's results held up. I also examined the effect of selectively greater withdrawal of black males from the work force on the growth in black (relative to white) wage rates. Accounting for drop-outs greatly reduces the measured wage gains of blacks. The process of selective withdrawal has, if anything, accelerated since I did this work, and recent analyses (for example, by Amitabh Chandra) demonstrate the even greater relevance of this issue.

At about this time H. Gregg Lewis, one of the pioneers of modern labor economics, asked me to teach his graduate course on labor demand. This was a daunting task: his class was legendary; he was in residence; and I was required to teach his classic 1963 book, *Unionism and Relative Wage Rates*. That book is not a model of clarity, but its first chapter introduced me to the problem of constructing and measuring counterfactual states. I locked myself in my apartment for about two weeks as I tried to make sense of the book. The effort was worth it. Most people read the later chapters, where Lewis reanalyzed earlier empirical studies of unionism conducted under his guidance. This is a valuable exercise. However, the first chapter was the most interesting to me because in it he considered the definition of various unionism "effects" in a market equilibrium setting. It also became clear to me while reading his work that my framework could be used to address the problem of constructing and estimating counterfactuals (e.g., what would a union member have earned if he or she were a nonunion member), and in fact I addressed this problem with George Neumann in a paper written in 1976. Any good answer to this problem should also take into account the extent of unionism because it affected the pricing of labor services, but we did not take the required step in our paper.

With a long gestation period (twenty-five years), Lewis's book influenced my work with Lance Lochner and Christopher Taber on the general equilibrium evaluation of social programs. The immediate effect the book had on my research was that it led me to think about the issue of defining and estimating policy counterfactuals, albeit initially in a partial equilibrium setting. This led to my work on evaluating educational reforms and job training programs.

I continued my research, begun in New York, on the dynamics of the life cycle. I developed and estimated dynamic models of human capital accumulation and labor supply. I formulated a dynamic panel version of the latent variable index models that I had developed for cross sectional data. I applied these models to the dynamics of female labor supply to address the implicit assumption of perfect substitution of time over time in the Mincer model. His model implied a Bernoulli process (a random flipping of a coin each period where the odds were determined by lifetime wages and income). My framework nested the Bernoulli assumption as part of a more general stochastic process. Empirical work with Robert Willis and later work on my own demonstrated the untenability of the assumption and the importance of accounting for temporally persistent unobservables in explaining labor force dynamics. Willis applied this framework to the analysis of earnings dynamics in an important paper with Lee Lillard.

The empirical evidence on persistent heterogeneity in earnings, labor supply, and fertility forced me to confront the difficult problem of accounting for unobservables in nonlinear frameworks. A dynamic extension of my earlier cross section model developed such a framework but the economics was implicit. More explicit economic models were developed in the early 1980s with first-rate graduate students Tom MaCurdy and Chris Flinn, who went on to distinguished academic careers. In this work, we integrated economic models and panel data, accounting for heterogeneity. Everywhere we looked, we found heterogeneity, and those who followed us have found the same. It is a feature of employment and unemployment durations, labor force participation, preferences toward leisure (as I discovered in my 1974 papers), and in many other areas of economic life.

My work on labor force and earnings dynamics attracted considerable attention. I was invited to a 1977 SSRC conference on longitudinal data methods in the social sciences and became aware of a vast body of very good work in mathematical sociology on longitudinal methods. I met James Coleman, an eminent sociologist, who I knew socially but not professionally, and Burt Singer, a polymath applied mathematician.

In an effort to understand the literature in sociology, I taught a joint course on panel data analysis with Coleman and learned a lot from it. I also developed a life-long intellectual and personal relationship with him, frequently attending the mathematical sociology workshop. I also began to collaborate with Burt Singer, who taught me a lot of new mathematics and statistics. We wrote a series of papers on heterogeneity and dynamic sampling plans.

At this point in my career (in the late 1970s and early 1980s), I had multiple lines of research going simultaneously. I was deeply engrossed in the mathematics and statistics of heterogeneity. I was also engaged in building structural dynamic models and estimating them on data.

With the usual gestation period, the methods I had developed began to be applied by many scholars to a wide array of problems. The practitioners wanted simple methods to solve hard problems. This led to universal application of normal distributions in settings where normality was not appropriate. It led to some bizarre empirical estimates: union wage "effects" of 350%; labor supply estimates by Jerry Hausman where consumption was an inferior good, and so forth. In a 1986 book, far below the quality of his earlier book, H. Gregg Lewis (then at Duke) denounced the application of selection methods to the study of unionism, because "they didn't work." What he really meant is that they did not produce numbers that accorded with his priors, which were based on least-squares estimates.

There were many responses to the perceived sensitivity of selection estimators to normality. Some tried more general non-normal distributions that nested the normal model. Many began to reject the approach entirely. My own approach was to develop a nonparametric approach that was more robust.

Burt Singer and I were working together on unobservables in duration models. We developed an identification strategy and estimator for the distribution of unobservables that has wide applicability outside of duration analysis. We showed that we could identify the parametric portion of models while being robust with respect to distributions of unobservables. The method is widely applied, but it is not directly tied to the original selection framework.

In 1980, I developed a simple nonparametric alternative to the parametric normal selection estimator based on polynomials in the probability of selection, but surprisingly, at that time, it attracted little attention. In subsequent work in 1985 and 1986 with Richard Robb and in 1990 with Bo Honore, I developed a systematic investigation of semiparametric identification in economic selection models. This work has had a lot of influence, and in work with Pedro Carneiro and Lars Hansen published in 2003, I have extended the basic setup to a variety of dynamic and cross-sectional settings, recently completing work on the identification of distributions of counterfactuals under much more general conditions. In related work with Ed Vytlacil, we developed robust, easily applied, nonparametric instrumental variable approaches to the selection models. This work built on my 1998 *Econometrica* paper with Hideko Ichimura, Jeff Smith, and Petra Todd.

This area continues to be a research frontier as I write. But the original concerns of the applied economists have not been fully met. Nonparametric identification analyses are important. They determine whether or not *in principle* it is possible to identify key parameters without imposing arbitrary distributional assumptions. We now know that selection models (and closely related auction models) are nonparametrically identified under very general conditions.

Estimation is another matter. High dimensional nonparametric estimation is not feasible in the sample sizes available to most economists. Choices of "auxiliary" parameters (smoothing parameters, penalty functions, and bandwidths) matter greatly. This is a lesson learned forty years ago in spectral analysis that is being relearned in the applications of nonparametric econometrics today. With the sample sizes available to most economists, general nonparametric methods for models with many explanation variables are often not useful, except for very low dimensional models.

The Conditional Nature of Causal Knowledge

In the mid-1980s, in the course of my research with Richard Robb on the nonparametric identification of selection models and causal models, I was invited to an interdisciplinary conference on inference from self-selected samples. Robb and I presented a paper before an audience that consisted largely of statisticians. Our discussant was none other than John Tukey, the distinguished statistician with whom I had interacted in graduate school.

Robb and I welcomed the opportunity to present our work before a distinguished group of statisticians. We discussed the fundamental identification problem that arises from self-selection when evaluating the impact of "treatment" on outcomes. How can one separate true treatment effects from preexisting differences among treatment and comparison group members? We used as an example the evaluation of job training programs, but our message was more general. We presented the fundamental causal model that economists have been using since the work of Trygve Haavelmo in the 1940s, and we showed how alternative assumptions about agent program participation rules, outcome equations, distributions of unobservables and access to different types of data solved the problem of causal inference.

We were stunned by the overwhelming negative reaction to our paper and especially to our main point about the conditional nature of causal knowledge. We made what we thought was the obvious point that in the absence of an idealized experiment, answers to causal questions required assumptions. We sought to identify the minimal assumptions and trade-offs among these assumptions. We demonstrated the value of making implicit assumptions explicit. We showed the value of economic models of choice in selecting a particular set of identifying assumptions. We were not happy with this intrinsic ambiguity in causal models, but we felt it was necessary to be intellectually honest about it. In later work, I have developed this theme in a number of contexts.

The response to our paper took many forms. Some statisticians with proprietary interests wanted to claim that explicit models of counterfactuals were not first developed in econometrics, although the recent influential work by Judea Pearl recognizes the priority of econometrics in developing casual models. Others sought to deny the problem entirely. Tukey wrote a condescending review of our paper, which we rebutted. As a result of this episode, I realized the great value of the economic approach to causal modeling. Economists have theories that produce the set of admissible counterfactuals. The statisticians have only vague appeals to "closest worlds" without any precise definition of what "close" means. Economists can use economic theory to settle which particular selection of treatment model is appropriate. Statisticians typically assumed random assignment or random assignment conditional on observables, i.e., the method of matching.

One of the many estimators Robb and I discussed was the standard method of instrumental variables. This was rejected at that occasion as being useless, but was later "invented" and popularized in statistics by one of the statisticians present.

The conditional nature of causal knowledge was disturbing to this group, and to many others. I learned the hard way that most people deny this basic point and prefer to gloss over it with implicit assumptions. "Let sleeping dogs lie" is a more popular approach to solving identification problems. Making people aware of the difficulty of reaching simple conclusions from analyses of widely used samples and estimators is not a popular activity.

At its very heart, any causal conclusion rests on maintained assumptions. My quest for an objective economics was thwarted by my understanding of the identification problem. Econometrics and statistics could only go so far. However, there was more information that could be used, but it was not in the form of precise probability distributions or selection rules.

Toward a More General Approach to Identification

While I was working on the econometric aspects of the identification problem in general treatment and selection models, I was also engaged in investigating the sources of the economic progress of black Americans. My interest in the status of black Americans began in my early years in the border South and later trips to Alabama and Mississippi. A trip to the same locations after passage of the 1964 Civil Rights Act revealed how dramatically the Jim Crow system had been dismantled. Using aggregate time series data, Ashenfelter had demonstrated that the post–1964 Civil Rights Act era showed greater progress than before. The data were fragile. An update of his study by Freeman showed stronger effects. However, that study was still highly aggregated.

Ashenfelter and I had analyzed firm level panel data on the progress of blacks, 1966–1970. We established that government contractors covered by an affirmative action program were more likely to integrate and to upgrade their black work force. The most dramatic effects were in the South.

All of this suggested that government policy had improved the status of black Americans. This view ran counter to the prevailing Chicago view that it was improvements in basic economic forces: (1) schooling, (2) schooling quality, and (3) migration that promoted black economic progress and not some law. My work with Richard Butler showed that a substantial part of the wage growth of blacks was illusory and was due to selective withdrawal of low-wage black labor from the work force, which induced apparent wage growth in the aggregate that was not experienced by anyone. This work was well received at Chicago and elsewhere, and its empirical importance in accounting for aggregate distributions is now well established. But this work did not foreclose other explanations for black economic progress.

Around 1978, I became aware of a unique data set from South Carolina collected to enforce a 1915 law forbidding employment of blacks as operatives in textile mills, then the largest industrial employers in the state. The data were annual observations by county for about 60 years. Casual inspection of the data revealed a huge breakthrough in black employment in the post-1964 era when textile companies were targeted by government affirmative action policies.

There were numerous competing explanations: (1) tight labor markets in the 1960s due to the Vietnam War, (2) entry of higher wage nontextile industry into the state, (3) tough foreign competition from abroad that made discrimination more costly, and (4) improvements in the educational quality of the black population. I was convinced that these competing explanations were more plausible than the government activity hypothesis. Indeed, such a conclusion was congenial with the Chicago view that government policy is ineffective or harmful. For more than 10 years, and with three graduate students, I tried to establish this case. But, after employing a variety of methods, and drawing on context and historical accounts as well as various statistical adjustments, I was forced to admit that there is no plausible alternative explanation for the breakthrough in black economic progress other than government pressure. Using all of the data, including the contextual evidence, I crafted a powerful case for the effectiveness of law in the 1960s and early 1970s. Laws directed against southern discrimination had their greatest effect in the South. John Donohue and I synthesized this evidence, and a variety of supporting pieces in a 1991 article. We showed that the law worked with minimal enforcement precisely because it allowed employers to break informal community norms and respond to competition by hiring black workers.

This work is widely cited by scholars of discrimination and civil rights. It is ignored, to this day, by many conservative economists who cling to the "basic economic forces" interpretation of the evidence, despite the fact that many of the "basic economic forces" were caused by government policy and that the rapid response of firms in hiring black labor once informal sanctions were broken demonstrates the power of self-interest in markets.

The larger lesson I took from this research was that one had to use all of the available information to analyze causal questions. The available information does not necessarily come in the form of sampling distributions from government surveys or bounds on the ranges of random variables. Knowing the problem being studied and its context, which in this case meant reading the relevant history and newspapers, reading court and legislative records, using the relevant theory, and looking at all of the available data, were essential in reaching any causal conclusion. There is no algorithm to crank out convincing evidence, although econometrics textbooks are often written as if there were. This lesson forever impressed on me the limitations of standard econometrics, the even greater limitations of the universal context-free nostrums for finding causal relationships offered up by statisticians, and the need to understand the relevant economic models and contextual information in establishing causal relationships.

Chicago after the 1970s

In this essay, I dwell on Chicago in the 1970s because that department was so distinguished and had the greatest impact on my intellectual development. Chicago renews itself. First-rate people attract other first-rate people to work with them. The Chicago department is a living demonstration of this maxim. I have learned greatly from the successors to the Chicago School I encountered in 1973 and hope to learn much more from them. Their intensity, curiosity, creativity, and intellectual honesty stimulate me and keep me honest and down to earth.

Among all of the arrivals after 1980, Lars Hansen, more than anyone else, best embodies the virtues of the place. I have learned much from him, as has the rest of the profession. I am grateful for incisive discussions with him on a wide array of topics in economics.

My Approach to Economics

Economics is useful only if it helps to explain the economy and solve practical problems. It produces wise policy advice when it is anchored in data and potentially dangerous advice when it is not. If rigorous empirical testing were required of economic models, many fewer papers would be written, the subject would become boring to many current practitioners, and the scientific reputation of the field would rise. There would be fewer fads and more lasting contributions. The criterion of success would be to understand phenomena rather than to maximize citation indices. In the words of John Maynard Keynes,

If economists could manage to get themselves thought of as humble, competent people, on a level with dentists, that would be splendid! (Keynes, 1931)[1]

This vision of economics does not sanction an atheoretical, purely empirical field. Solutions to practical problems and interpretations of real phenomena require formal models to define questions and produce answers to them. Tool building is an essential activity. Adam Smith built new tools when he described the British economy of his day; so did David Ricardo and Alfred Marshall. Much of the creative and lasting work in economics of the past century was research that fashioned new models to explain real phenomena. Economic and social reality is complex. Digesting and understanding it is a major source of new ideas in economics and econometrics.

An alternative approach to economics is to build "clean" models that improve upon earlier models but that do not make contact with any phenomena. In place of testability and empirical content, in this approach, models are evaluated by their cleverness, by the power of the methods used and their distance between assumptions and conclusions in developing the theory. This is an internally motivated vision of economics as a branch of applied mathematics. But mathematics and science are not the same thing, although mathematics is essential to the execution of good economic science.

My work on labor supply, schooling, affirmative action, labor force dynamics, evaluating job training programs, the sources of improvement in black economic status, on the pricing of labor services and the formation of skills over the life cycle, and more recently, my studies of regulation and deregulation in Europe and Latin America have all had a very practical focus. Yet at the same time, they have led to new theory and new econometrics that are required to address these problems adequately. These questions, carefully addressed, pose formidable challenges to standard theory and econometrics. Good answers to these questions require good theory and econometrics. It is unfortunate that many economists now equate public policy analysis with careless once-over-lightly analysis suitable for journalism but not for science. Careful public policy analysis requires good science.

Anchoring my own research in serious empirical analysis has protected me from the fads that plague the profession and has given me the autonomy and independence I have always craved, albeit at the cost of sometimes appearing to be stodgy. There will always be a market for good answers to important social questions. This is my way of following my father's advice of being independent and developing an independent reputation and my way of avoiding appeals to authority in any form—whether mathematical or divine—that motivated my early break with organized religion.

Notes

I wish to thank Pedro Carneiro, Barry Hirsch, Derek Neal, Greg Orlowski and Lynne Pettler Heckman for helpful comments on this essay. References to the papers mentioned in this lecture, as well as to my other research are available at my website: http://jenni.uchicago.edu.

1. John Maynard Keynes, *Essays in Persuasion* (1931), in *The Collected Writings of John Maynard Keynes*, Vol. 9 (London: Macmillan, 1972), 332.

James J. Heckman
Awarded Nobel Prize in 2000. Lecture presented March 19, 2003.

Date of Birth
April 19, 1944

Academic Degrees
B.A., Colorado College, 1965
M.A., Princeton University, 1968
Ph.D., Princeton University, 1971

Academic Affiliations
Instructor, Assistant Professor of Economics, Columbia University, 1970–72
Associate Professor of Economics, Columbia University, 1972–74
Associate Professor of Economics, University of Chicago, 1974–77
Professor of Economics, University of Chicago, 1977–84
Irving Fisher Visiting Professor of Economics, Yale University, 1984
Henry Schultz Professor of Economics, University of Chicago, 1985–94
A. Whitney Griswold Professor of Economics, Yale University, 1988–90 (on leave from Chicago)
Henry Schultz Distinguished Service Professor of Economics, University of Chicago, 1994–present

Selected Books
Longitudinal Analysis of Labor Market Data, 1985 (ed. with B. Singer)
Handbook of Econometrics, Vol. 5, 2001 (ed. with E. Leamer)
Inequality in America: What Role for Human Capital Policies?, 2003 (with A. Krueger)
Law and Employment: Lessons from Latin America and the Caribbean, 2004 (with C. Pagés)

Vernon L. Smith

Limestone is something you get interested in and something you learn to like. And then you become part of it. You know every move to make: just how to mark it off, drill it, load it, shoot it and then you see a real straight break, and you feel good.

—McClure Stilley, Chase County Kansas quarry man, as quoted in W. Least Heat-Moon, *PrairyErth*, 1991

One cannot take advantage of his fellowman and come out ahead. It just cannot be done.

—Quintin Lomax, 1947

Prison guard: "Don't you know that you can't change the world by carrying that sign."
Lone picketer, protesting capital punishment: "I'm not trying to change the world. I am just trying to keep the world from changing me."

—Dialogue in movie, *The Hoodlum Priest*, 1961

You Can Go Home Again[1]

I want to begin by letting you walk through a part of my childhood home as it would have appeared that day in 1927 when I was born.

Walking west through the front door you enter the living room. You see my mother's old, but always-tuned, solid walnut upright piano on your left, facing north in the southeast corner. When you sit on the piano bench there is a window on your left, bathing the piano and sheet music with daylight, even on one of those rare cloudy days in Kansas—a condition that has already attracted the attention of the great entrepreneurs who would make Wichita the center of the light airplane industry.

Lifting the hinged lid on the piano bench you find it stuffed with Bach, Beethoven, Stephen Foster, and Hoagie Carmichael sheet music, along with the complete scores of *Cavaleria Rusticana* and *HMS Pinafore*, to name only a few of my favorites in that treasure chest. Decades later, when I write my memoir, I will still have a cardboard box full of those musical scores. If I pull out three of those yellowing old scores and read lines like, "I am the builder, come walk with me," "I am the very model of a modern major general," or "when the deep purple falls over sleepy garden walls," the memory of that piano bench will be fresh, sharp, and black.

To your right on the north wall of the living room you see an open ceramic grated gas fireplace, a mantel, and glass-enclosed bookcases containing my father's set of rust red Harvard Classics. My father had an eighth-grade education, and has always needed to work long hours for a living. He aspired to read more, but actually read little that was not related to earning his bread and butter. For me, however, these books will come to symbolize the immensity of that which is knowable, and I will keep them all my life. One of the classics, volume 17, will become severely worn and frayed, with a shredded, loose, dangling binding from being read over and over again by me—Grimm, Andersen, and Aesop tales.

In my early childhood years I will think of libraries as infinite extensions of my father's bookcase; libraries surely contain all that is known, and I will aspire to go to college because that is where one learns all that is known, which is everything. Nothing is unknowable; you had only to seek it in a book or some source somewhere. I will know so little and be hungry to know, but I will gradually learn that the action—all the learning and understanding—will be in the pursuit, not in the consummation of knowledge, and that the questions always grow faster than the answers. Every answer sprouts multiple questions so that knowledge becomes an unending quest, but therein lays its charming challenge. I will learn that any three-year-old can force you to the outermost limits of your knowledge on any topic by asking "Why?" three times in response to each of your answers. It is a sobering observation that every child passes through a short "repeat-why" stage, pressing to identify the limits of what is known, before learning to stop asking, and arbitrarily to accept living with less—a state that I will find troubling again and again throughout my life.

I will learn to read early and well, and Harvard Classics volume 17 will become one of my two childhood treasures. The other will be Tal: His Marvelous Adventures with Noom-Zor-Noom *(1929, 1937, 2001) by Paul Fenimore Cooper, whose great-grandfather was James Fenimore*

Cooper, novelist of the American wilderness. I will read Tal to all my children, and my copy will come to have no binding left to dangle, so thoroughly will it be consumed, loved, and enjoyed. My oldest daughter, Deborah, will name her son Tal (Taliesin). Sixty years after first reading Tal I will conceive of the idea of having the book reprinted at my own expense, believing that no one else would have such an interest. I will procrastinate and be pleasantly surprised to discover a third edition inspired by the author's nephew, Henry S. F. Cooper, Jr., appearing in 2001, with an introduction bearing testimony to its loyal and dedicated readership. I will have no idea that I was far from alone in loving that book. Fantasy is important to the child. Dreams are fashioned of fantasy, and out of dreams come the desire for adventure, for learning, and ultimately the realization that learning is about learning to learn, and is a self-teaching process. In dreams and fantasy nothing is unattainable, and this is a model for seeking, overcoming, and coming to know, but most important a model for life.

To the left of the fireplace is an open light oak staircase, which you ascend facing west, that immediately circles left up to a landing with a balcony overlooking the living room. Two or three years later, if it is 7:00 p.m., you might see my father standing in the living room, facing the balcony, singing an Irish ballad for me just after I have retired to my bed upstairs. There are no upstairs bathrooms, and the closets are very small, closely matching our clothes, toy, and "things" budget. Toys, I will learn to design and make, much as my father learned to design and make machine tools.

If it is a hot summer day, the "evaporative cooler" may be set up and running in the middle of the kitchen floor, or behind you in the dining or living room. The evaporative cooler consists of an ancient oscillating fan with a line strung between two chairs in front of it for hanging wet tea towels. The fan air evaporates the water from the towels and cools the room. This is an effective air cooler in the 1930s' climate of Kansas with single-digit humidity, but the towels require resoaking often, so quickly do they dry out. You cannot help but notice from the faded colors and printing on all our tea towels that they have been made from old, worn, and empty twenty-five-pound cotton flour bags by removing the stitches. I will discover that we were poor and governed by the maxim "Waste not, want not."

Straight west of the back door behind the clothesline is a chicken yard. You may wonder why there is a large chopping block behind the garage with a big ax stuck into it. That is for dispatching one of the chickens for a regular Sunday or a special dinner.

Before Me

We hadn't received any more orders. Down the track we went, approaching Vaughan, which is twelve miles from Canton. Vaughan was at the lower end of a double S curve. The north switch was just about the middle of the first S, and as we roared down on it we saw two big red lights ... it was a train not in the clear. I could see the lights, but Mr. Casey couldn't because there was a deep curve to the fireman's side. I yelled to Mr. Casey, "look out! We're gonna hit something!" "Jump Sim!" he shouted, and these were his last words. I heard him kick the seat out from under him and apply the brakes ... I swung down ... and hit the dirt. When I came to ... Mr. Casey was dead. Our engine had ploughed through the caboose of the freight, and ... a car of shelled corn and a car of hay. When Casey's body was found in the wreckage, an iron bolt was driven through his neck, and a bale of hay rested on his chest.[2]

Grover Bougher, my mother's first husband and father of her two oldest children, was a fireman on the Santa Fe Railroad. For those not brought up on railroad lore, a fireman puts on, not out, engine fires; he makes and stokes the locomotive's boiler fire by shoveling coal and maintaining the locomotive's steam pressure. A fireman was commonly a locomotive engineer apprentice; you served time in the cab mastering the engine's operations and learning from the engineer, who is essentially the captain of his train. This subordinate role is clearly indicated in the exchange recorded above with the famous Casey Jones, "Mr. Casey," as his fireman, Sim Web, called him. At some point, after getting added experience in the cab as an engineer by working the extra board, if you were proved fit for the task and were of a mind to continue, then you were promoted to engineer. An engineer lived by the maxim "Get her there and make time or come to the office and get your time."

I have a letter Grover wrote to his brother, George, a private in the American Expeditionary Force serving in France, dated October 3, 1918. Two days later Grover was killed instantly in a train wreck when his passenger train engine and its cars were diverted by a manual cutover switch that had been inadvertently left open on to the sidetrack, colliding with a waiting freight engine. A similar type of incident is what killed Casey Jones in the wreck of the Cannonball in 1906.

The letter was returned to Newton, postmarked the following April and forwarded to Wichita, where my mother had moved, with a notation by the command post office that George had been killed eight months earlier, before Grover had written to him, on September 17, 1918, fighting the war in France. Thus, neither brother knew of the other's death. When Grover was killed, my grandfather-to-be, Aseal Lomax (1874–1945), had been laid up for some period with a badly injured leg caused by a railroad accident. He was an engineer on the Missouri Pacific Railroad, and was injured on a straight track accident, not an S curve as in the spectacular Cannonball wreck, when one of the rods on the great drive wheels bolted loose from the drive wheel and flailed up through the cab's wood flooring. Grandpa Lomax and his fireman both "hit the dirt" from each side of the cab, enabling them to escape the likelihood of death. On a straight open track the train will come to a stop without assistance by the engineer, and you can be heroic not a bit from the inside of a demolished cab. He often said that years later his leg still contained splinters that had erupted from the floor of the engine cab.

Enter My Father

Unemployment occurs when large numbers of people can't find work.
—Calvin Coolidge

Fortune smiled for us all when my father, Vernon Chessman Smith (1890–1954), a machinist who had apprenticed in Cleveland, Ohio, met my mother, Lulu Belle Bougher (Lomax) (1896–1957), in Wichita and was delighted to find a warm and caring woman already with a family. They were married on August 16, 1921. Her diary entry for August 16, 1944, states, in beautifully simple language, "Our 23rd wedding; thought of it Monday—forgot it today. Vern (my father's spoken name) remembered today. A wonderful 23 years. I love him." I will say more of my parents, and what kind of people they were, but this closet diary entry, a private and unadorned personal message, says almost everything there is to say.

I well remember our car, a 1927 Oldsmobile four-door sedan. I opened the rear door one day to hop in and stepped smack in the middle of a chocolate cake positioned on the floor to keep it from sliding off the seat. My mother had put it there to deliver to Don Eaton's first restaurant next door to Lloyd's Barber Shop near the northeast corner· of Meridian and Douglas. Don was a restaurateur known to my family for many years. Throughout the 1930s my mother home-baked desserts that Don bought for his restaurant—angel food cake, chocolate devil's food cake, and Boston cream pie were the most common—for twenty-five cents each. Don sold the cut pieces to his customers for five cents each as a home-baked special. My mother also baked cakes for other restaurants, but Don was her largest and most loyal customer, who raved about her baking skills and spread the word to the other restaurant owners.

A very memorable event for me was the privilege of eating one ice cream cone per week. I bought it from the ice cream truck—later known as "the Good Humor man," but I have no memory of that designation then. Every Thursday I was given a nickel to buy an ice cream cone, and I remember sitting on the curb in the street listening, watching, and waiting anxiously, well in advance of this savored experience.

My father's study of voice led to the development of a considerable repertoire of songs. There was a period, probably age two to four, when at bedtime he would sing me a song. I remember being ushered upstairs to my bedroom at 7:00 p.m. After being "tucked into bed" by mom, he would stand below the balcony downstairs in the living room and sing—often it was an Irish ballad. I learned the music and the words to many of these songs, such as the one by Carruth, below, and I know fragments of them still, as in *Mother Machree*.

There's a spot in my heart which no colleen may own.
There's a depth in my soul never sounded or known.
There's a place in my memory, my life that you fill.
No other can take it, no one ever will.
Sure I love the dear silver that shines in your hair,
and the brow that's all furrowed and wrinkled with care.
I kiss the dear fingers so toil worn for me.
Oh, God bless you and keep you, mother Machree.
Every sorrow or care in the dear days gone by,
was made bright by the light of the smile in your eye.
Like a candle that's set in a window at night,
your fond love has cheered me, and guided me right.
Sure I love the dear silver that shines in your hair,
and the brow that's all furrowed and wrinkled with care.
I kiss the dear fingers so toil worn for me.
Oh, God bless you and keep you, mother Machree.

Anticipating my father's tenor voice put me in a mood to sleep in spite of my great resistance to going to bed. I remember wanting to go to bed much later than "bedtime," because it always interrupted something I had going. I think this set the stage for me to feel irritation when I am in deep mentalese and someone succeeds in diverting my involuntary attention. But it was one of those fixed rules that my mother enforced.

It was always publicly claimed that children need the sleep, but in later years, mom revealed that it was simply a matter that "parents have to live too."

Then in 1932, my father was laid off for lack of enough work and became one of many who fitted Cal Coolidge's definition of "unemployment." The three of us moved to the farm located near Milan (pronounced "mile-n," in them there parts, not "mil-awn"), Kansas. The farm had been purchased earlier with the insurance money my mother had received from the Santa Fe Railroad after Grover's death.

From City Lights to Star Lights

A haze on the far horizon,
The infinite tender sky,
The ripe, rich tint of the cornfields,
And the wild geese sailing high—
And all over upland and lowland
The charm of the golden rod—
Some of us call it Autumn
And others call it God.
Like tides on a crescent sea-beach,
When the moon is new and thin,
Into our hearts high yearnings
Come welling and surging in—
Come from the mystic ocean,
Whose rim no foot has trod,—
Some of us call it Longing,
And others call it God.
A picket frozen on duty,
A mother starved for her brood,
Socrates drinking the hemlock,
And Jesus on the rood;
And millions who humble and nameless,
The straight hard pathway plod,—
Some call it Consecration,
And others call it God.
—William Herbert Carruth, "Each in His Own Tongue"[3]

The farm brought new dimensions of hard work and hard times for my parents, but also survival for two years when there was no acceptable alternative. Farming was not yet hydrolyzed, electrolyzed, or mechanized. Neither was our house, which had no indoor drinking water, electricity, central heating, or toilet facilities.

With no electricity on the farm, indoor lighting depended on the use of what *everyone* called "coal oil" lamps, which they were not.

It was a couple of decades later before I would learn that it was not coal oil at all, as my parents and grandparents always called it, but kerosene that we burned in those lamps. Still later I would learn that coal oil derives from a process invented about 1830 by a Canadian chemist to extract oil from coal. The coal oil industry thrived in competition with more expensive whale oil for lamps (and for "medicinal" purposes, used for god knows what) until crude oil was discovered in Titusville, Pennsylvania, in 1859, and yielded kerosene, a far cheaper source of lamp oil that rapidly wiped out the coal oil industry. If only presidents, congressmen, the Department of Energy, and political environmentalists like Paul Ehrlich could understand that when the price is right, there is no problem extracting clean-burning fuel from coal, shale (the early settlers learned from the Indians how to heat western shale rock to "sweat" lamp oil out of the rock—a far cheaper source than hauling in whale oil by wagon from the coast), the sun, wind, or fuel cells. Also, there will be no permanent shortages of energy over the next two hundred years any more than there has been in the last two hundred years because demand will respond to price change, inducing substitution and innovations to economize on the higher-cost scarce materials. As we learn from the clarity of Julian Simon's scholarship, the long-term historical trend has been down, punctuated by temporary upward spikes in inflation-adjusted resource prices, as economizing technologies allow more to be extracted with less.

In place of indoor flush toilets we had the outhouse or "privy"— sweltering hot in the summer, then icy cold in the winter with the Kansas wind howling through the cracks. For indoor winter nights, there was of course a crock or pot in each bedroom with a lid so that you did not have to suffer the outdoor wind and cold at 3:00 a.m. in the morning. But without heat in the bedroom you had no bloody desire to use that pot either. I can tell you for sure that at age six, I had no difficulty learning to hold off until wake-up time in the morning. Toilet training started early and was learned well on those farms.

For me, however, if not for my parents, the farm yielded trivial memories of personal inconvenience for the simple reason that there existed no alternative known to me. This was life, and you were here to make the most and best of it without bellyaching. I always seemed to minimize any discomfort from most things that were less than the best. That farm was a great place and time to be a kid looking for adventure. For me it was not "hardship"; it was more like high-class "camping out."

My really significant memories were vividly those of adventure, and learning about chickens, milk cows, hogs, gardens, wheat and cafricorn (it looked like small white BB shots and you could pop it), rabbit hunting, priming well pumps, Coleman lanterns, and nights with stars clean bright down to the unobstructed horizon—a phenomenon that can only be experienced, not imagined—in a great expanse of tender sky, like being in the open sea. And, oh yes, that marvelously tender sky was punctuated and contrastingly defined by Kansas lightning storms that had for aeons assured a treeless landscape, by wind storms, dust storms, and incredible "gully washer" rainstorms. At night in a lightning storm you could read newspaper print during the bright bolts, if you could afford to buy a newspaper.

From my mother I learned about cooking on a woodstove on the Kansas prairie, where there is precious little wood—cottonwoods lined the few streams; the pastures and grain fields were barren of trees. We supplemented by burning dried corncobs and—euphemistically—dried sunbaked "cow chips." One of my jobs was to collect the chips. The early settlers had burned "Buffalo" [(sic) B. bison] chips, as had the Indians before them. Decades later I learned that the first Americans, who crossed to Alaska on the Bering Strait land bridge stretching from Siberia, burned Mammoth chips, the only source of fuel on the dry windswept plains of northern Siberia across into Alaska, and I felt intimately and warmly bonded to those ancient peoples of thirteen to fourteen thousand years ago whose ancestors settled the entire continent by eleven to twelve thousand years ago.

We had an outdoor storm cellar where we took refuge if we thought tornadoes were in the air. There was no tornado watch, no broadcasts or warnings, but you could just feel the tension of them in the air. You could sometimes see them to the west and south as they snaked down from a squall line with bright light and clear sky beyond the line, and black boiling clouds overhead and behind. Normally, it seemed that tornadoes always snaked back up to disappear into the squall line of clouds. I never saw one that came to earth, except in the Judy Garland movie. When tornadoes were in the feel of the air, you were up against the one thing that was really, really scary. You could see it on the faces of the adults who let on that everything would be OK, and it always was OK in those two years that we lived there. If you want to get a sense of it and you just happen to be passing through Topeka, Kansas, go to the capitol building and enter the main-floor rotunda. There you will find the magnificent Thomas Hart Benton mural circling the room, depicting the essence of Kansas and its history. In one scene, you will see the tiny insignificant figures of a farm family rushing from their house to the storm cellar. Behind them is this immense, towering cone snaking down into a twister from a sky of black clouds above.

In autumn 1932, at age five, I took my place in the first grade along-side more seasoned farm children for primary education in the classic rural one-room schoolhouse. A neighbor, Mr. Hemberger, part of a German community, had the distinction of being able to speak, read, and write English, knew arithmetic, and therefore was deemed fully equipped to be our grade-school teacher. A wise decision, I think, although my mother was always a bit irritated when he used the word "ain't," a completely grammatical contraction of which English has many; mom was something of a language maven, as Steve Pinker would say. Each morning my teacher/neighbor faced rows of old-fashioned desks with lids that could be raised to take out your books, notes, and paper, always stored in your desk. "Homework" was farmwork, as you never were asked to take home any schoolwork described by that term; otherwise what the hell was the classroom for if education could not be fully and completely accomplished there. A quarter century later when my own children were in public school, I found myself naturally resistant to the concept of homework in the first grade.

The first row on Mr. Hemberger's right as he faced the class, where I sat, was grade one, the second row grade two, and so on for all the grades. I sat in the front of row one because I could not see the black-board—no one knew yet, and it would be two years before anyone knew, that I was severely myopic, and nothing written on that blackboard had any meaning for me. After some first-row recitation every morning, and left with an assignment, I had the opportunity to listen in on the second- and third-grade recitation lessons—the grades seated closest to me.

As I later became aware, this classroom implemented the original "progressive system" in which you were part of a single seamless community consisting of all elementary grades. At the end of grade one, Mr. Hemberger gave me a note to take home to my mother stating unceremoniously that "Vernon can read the second-grade reader and therefore next year he will be in the third grade." There were of course only three subjects—reading, writing, and arithmetic. Reading seemed to be the litmus test; if you were less strong in arithmetic or writing, the next year you could participate along with those in the row on your left before

Mr. Hemberger got to your row. The whole purpose of this management style was to move each person along at her own pace of accomplishment, get her through school and into farmwork, where she could be useful. I understand that the earliest achievement tests showed high performance in Kansas and Nebraska because of these rural schools. It's no wonder to me that Kansas bred the Eisenhowers, William Allen Whites, Beeches, Garveys, and so on, by the hundreds, maybe thousands.

City Lights Again

In 1934, my father returned to the Bridgeport Machine Company for alternate week half-time work and subsequently full-time work. This was fortuitous, as we lost "ownership" of the farm to the mortgage bank, with which we had always shared ownership, unable to meet payments on the loan. We would have had to move back to Wichita, whether dad had employment or not. We would also have lost our home in Wichita, but my parents recognized this possibility and earlier had temporarily deeded the asset in the name of Grandpa Lomax to protect it from being added to the default obligation; so the issue never arose—probably some kind of horrible criminal offense.

We were returning from the farm world of personal exchange through the trading of favors to a world of impersonal exchange through markets. More, but far from all, of our needs would be met from store-bought goods, and that world would gradually be emerging, reinvigorated, from the Great Depression.

Taking inventory, my parents now had nothing left of the original Santa Fe life insurance asset. Of course, losing the farm just confirmed my mother's political commitment to socialism, but my father, certainly disappointed, seemed to take it in stride. At some point in the 1930s I remember that dad refused to apply for public employment in the WPA [Works Progress Administration]. Grandpa Lomax always said that WPA meant "we piddle around," and that IWW meant "I won't work" instead of the International Workers of the World. This was coming from the railroad engineer who admired "Gene" Debs, but had even greater admiration for a strong work ethic. Similarly, dad considered "working" for the WPA to be very demeaning—a point of contention with my mother, who thought he was being completely unreasonable. Yet in spite of all the socialist rhetoric, she had the same ingrained work ethic. As I think back, there seemed to be contradictions all over the place, but they were not evident to any of the principals at the time. My mother was as fiercely independent and productivity oriented as she was collectivist minded, but had not a clue that collectivism completely destroys the freedom needed to nourish the former. That requires far more understanding of the nature of humans and the social mind, and what they can accomplish through the extended order of markets than an otherwise sensible person like my mother could muster.

Wichita and farm life were separated by location, by intellectual and economic activity. The city had homegrown a surprising breadth of prominent business life. Beech, Stearman, and Cessna Aircraft, the Coleman Lantern Company, Dold meatpacking, and the Fred Koch, Jack Vickers, and other petroleum companies provided tangible initial evidence of the machinery of markets, specialization, and globalization. Bold independent actions by Coleman, Cessna, Beech, Koch, Garvey, and many others instilled a midwestern sense of freedom and entrepreneurship. When Walter Beech died, his wife, Olive Ann Beech, cofounder of their company, took over the management of Beech Aircraft to become one of the truly great early women executives. She built it into an internationally successful manufacturer of light planes, and continued to be active on the board well into her eighties. A parallel story can be told of Olive Garvey, the matriarch of the Garvey family who built the largest grain storage facility in the world.

In 1920, my mother cast her first vote for Eugene Victor Debs, the socialist candidate for president who was campaigning from jail, where he had been sentenced as a result of his opposition to World War I. Bertrand Russell once said that there had been only two wars worth fighting: the American Revolution and World War II. He was surely right about World War I: we won the war, but then lost the peace in a fit of retribution that set the stage for the rise of Hitler and World War II, which we had to fight to stop the beast. Russell did not live to see the Vietnam War that Eisenhower avoided. Russell's favorite war (and mine) has always been the American Revolution. Our ancestors were doing God's work when they threw the redcoats out of this land. Going after the Tories in Canada was a little headstrong, but the War of 1812 might well have been another good one for the arrogant Americans to win.

When I entered the voting booth for the first time in 1948, at age twenty-one, I repeated my mother's history of 1920, and cheerfully voted socialist, for Norman Thomas. I doubt that I have voted for anyone since who approached Thomas's incredible integrity and compassion for humanity. Remarkably, I still have a warm memory of that experience, although intellectually, of course, command-and-control systems do not and cannot work, and demonstrably cannot manage the economy. They perpetuate poverty, destroy freedom, subordinate the individual to a mindless bureaucracy of doublespeak, and in their worst incarnations, brutalize their most imaginative and independent citizens, all the time claiming otherwise. An understanding of why I could feel warmly toward that first voting experience would go a long way to explaining why in the name of freedom, fairness, and justice we realize less and less of all three; why, even when liberalization efforts break through the political process—for example, the worldwide privatization and decentralization movement of the 1980s—the pendulum also swings back and gradually undermines wealth-creating as well as poverty-reducing reforms.

The answer, I think, based in ongoing behavioral research with my colleagues, is found in an inherent tension between the individual's experience in social exchange and the requirements of freedom in the external order of impersonal exchange through markets. As I have written in my research, you can make the case that the collectivist individual impulse is nourished by the human perceptions and understanding that comes experientially from what the economic historian and Nobel laureate Doug North calls "personal exchange." Personal exchange is what was prominent on the farm, and takes the form of trading favors and barter in close-knit communities based on trust, trustworthiness, and reputations for being a reliable social exchanger. In this more intimate environment, our individual experience is that good comes from reciprocity—doing good and receiving good in return—being cooperative, and a good neighbor. At the level of the family, extended family, and our social groupings, our direct experience is that you produce good by intentional acts of doing good.

In impersonal market exchange through prices, we do not see that it involves the same reciprocal benefits for buyer and seller that characterize personal exchange. Neither do we see that specialization—or task subdivision—derives from and is supported by markets. We do not experience the fact that millions of people, with differing cultures, languages, skills, and resources, cooperate through long networks of interdependence connected by prices. If the price of gasoline increases, we see that the oil companies get more money and we get less, and that is not "fair." What we do not see is that some remote disruption of a source of supply has caused the price increase, and that this sets in motion an adjustment *process providing incentives for supplies going elsewhere to be rediverted to us—or one of dozens of other causes and effects.*

Consequently, we readily come to believe that markets perform badly, and by better planning and intervention we can make them work better— for us—but such a myopic policy has unintended consequences, making us worse off, and these consequences are invisible to our experience. Emotionally, we easily and warmly relate to programs of redistribution and control in political economy that can unintentionally do far more harm than good. Any human good that is claimed will flow from some interventionist scheme seems to ring true, but the creeping and accumulating harm it causes in limiting the growth of wealth and welfare is not plainly visible to our experience.

New Zealanders are a caring and egalitarian people—I have experienced it—but this leads so easily to policies in which they unintentionally shoot themselves in the foot. The New Zealand economy came out of World War II with the third-highest per capita income in the world—tied with Switzerland—and then piddled away this accomplishment, unable and unwilling to compete in growing world markets. A small country competing in world markets cannot afford the wastes of socialism; a large country can afford it only for as long as it has the resources to sustain the waste.

The crux of the socialist disease and its unintended destruction of community were captured for me in 1978, in a taxicab trip from the Wellington airport to my hotel. The driver was friendly, and I asked him, "Tell me about your country." He replied, "It's really wonderful. I don't like paying half my small income in taxes, but we receive so much that is free: health benefits, prescriptions, free education through college and advanced graduate study. I am just a cab driver, but my son is going to be a medical doctor. He has finished his medical degree and internship, and will begin practicing next year." In recognition of his obvious pride, I said, "How wonderful. You have every right to be proud. Is he going to practice in Wellington?" He replied, "Oh no, he's going to Australia. You can't make any money here." The New Zealand economic crisis hit about two years later.

In 1940, my father lost his job permanently when the independent entrepreneur owner of Bridgeport, A. A. Bushaw, closed his factory rather than cede control of his oil field equipment factory to President Franklin Roosevelt's defense industry production. (Bushaw's Bridgeport plant was taken over by another company and of course used for defense, then war production; markets are not sympathetic to waste, unless someone is willing to pay for their preferences.) My father changed employment to the Coleman Lantern Company for less than a year. Then on October 24, 1940, he hired on at Stearman Aircraft, on the east side of town; it had been purchased by Boeing in 1938, the year that Hitler marched into Poland. I remember the larger-than-normal headlines in the *Wichita Beacon* proclaiming Hitler's unopposed invasion.

Sixty-six years later Boeing has come full circle. As of April 2004, the company is looking for a buyer of its Kansas and Oklahoma production facilities.

Wichita became the national, then international, center for light plane manufacturing. Why? I always heard that it was because Kansas had more clear flying days than any of the other state candidates. This industry and the stock market in the 1920s were part of a classic bubble with many new products in great demand. In 1929, Wichita had some fifteen different airplane manufacturers: Travel Air, Stearman, Cessna, United, Laird, Swift, Lark, Knoll, Bradley, Yunkers, Wichita, Watkins, Mooney, Sullivan, and Buckley.[4] A decade later, the surviving company names would be Beech, Cessna, and Stearman (Boeing). Three companies rose as a phoenix from the bankruptcies and consolidations of the many beginners early in the century that were financed by over-exuberant investors. Clyde Cessna, Walter Beech, and Lloyd Stearman had been essential to the entrepreneurial survival process. Incredible long-term value was created from those risky experiments in new technology, technology management, and determining who should be the surviving managers out of the fifteen original upstarts. Every bubble and crash, fueled by a wave of innovation and new products, from steamships, railroads, and mass retailing in the nineteenth century to the computer, communication, and Internet revolution of the 1990s, writes a similar story.

After my stellar first-grade academic achievements, I continued to perform well in the city elementary schools. My school performance, however, deteriorated beginning in the eighth grade and all through high school. I found high school very uninspiring—"girls," as they were known as in them there days, were far and away more interesting—but I always expected to go to college. My inspiration was just temporarily diverted, as is common with teenagers. I vividly recall that my mother helped me with my English homework when we were learning to diagram sentences in the tenth grade. I also recall her complaints about the deterioration in the quality of the public schools, circa 1941–1942. She had learned to diagram sentences in the eighth grade. It was not evident to me why one should learn it in any grade, but what did I know? I never got the point of diagramming, nor did I ever understand what language was all about, until fifty-odd years later, when I had the great pleasure of reading Steve Pinker's *The Language Instinct* (1994).

College Years: From Friends U to Harvard U

Great teachers are valuable not only for what they teach but more so for the pattern they put on one's life.
—Personal letter from Dr. Arthur E. Hertzler, 1945

Our sole directly related family "intellectual" was my mother's uncle, Sullivan Lomax, who according to family lore that I have verified, was left "crippled" by a leg injury as a child in a farm accident.

He was handicapped for life. Being ill suited for anything "useful" like arduous farmwork, he was passed around among various relatives who could ill afford to keep him, but somehow, according to family records, "he got a fairly good education, and taught district schools in Kansas." Naturally, this gives me an image of a Mr. Hemberger, but more specialized and educated as a teacher. In 1905, he "entered Kansas University and graduated in the law in 1907. He took up practice in Cherryvale [Kansas]."

My mother and indeed all of us were proud of Sullivan, our family intellectual. Consequently, neither I nor my parents had any idea how to go about choosing a college. So I went to the city library, found a book on choosing a college, and learned among other things that the "best" college in the United States was Caltech. Being naive and impetuous, I decided that I should prepare myself to enter Caltech as, without further preparation, my C average in high school would not even qualify me to take the entrance exam. A small, very serious Quaker college, Friends University, was located near my home in West Wichita. I enrolled in physics, chemistry, calculus, astronomy, and literature courses for one year, earned top grades, and at eighteen sat for the entrance exams for Caltech in spring 1945.

My attitude at Friends University was 180 degrees opposite to what I had nurtured in high school. I was a very serious and highly motivated student. I knew what I wanted. I was there to make up for my high school shortcomings and to enter Caltech.

Returning to my preparations for entering Caltech, there was only one hurdle: the entrance exam embracing physics, chemistry, and mathematics. This exam was a unique creation of the Caltech faculty, and the entry decision was famously dependent on how well you performed on that examination and not on prior grades. The exam consisted of problems: How fast is a snowball thrown against a wall if the snowball melts on impact? Let's see now, if the mass of the snowball is m, and its velocity, v, then its kinetic energy is $(1/2)mv^2$. Since it takes C (was it 528?) calories of heat energy to convert each gram of snowball (ice) into water, you had only to equate the meltdown energy with the kinetic energy and solve for v with suitable account taken of the units of measurement. The exam went to the heart of basic principles, and although a working knowledge of mathematics was essential, it required no special mathematical virtuosity.

I passed, took the Santa Fe's California Limited (the Chief and Super Chief were out of our ticket class) passenger train west out of Newton through La Junta, Colorado; Tucumcari, Clovis, Gallop, and Albuquerque, New Mexico; Winslow, Flagstaff, and Kingman, Arizona; then Barstow, California, arriving in Los Angeles in September 1945. It was "all the way, on the Santa Fe" as the concessionaire would announce in each car as he went through with peanuts, gum, candy, pop, and cigarettes. This route would become familiar in the next four years, whether I was traveling by train or driving on the parallel famous Route 66. Forty-six years later, curious about the bar in Wellington, New Zealand, named Route 66, I walked in, and asked the small coterie of customers and service persons clustered in the rear, "Anyone here who knows where Route 66 is?" The friendly reply, "Where is it, Yank?"

Caltech was a meat grinder like I could never have imagined. The first thing to which one has to adapt is the fact that no matter how high people might sample in the right tail of the distribution of intelligence or whatever it is that measures college performance, that sample is still normally distributed in performing on the materials in the Caltech curriculum. The second thing you learn, if you were reared with my naive background, is the incredible arrogance that develops in conjunction with the acquisition of what you ultimately come to realize is a really very, very small bit of knowledge compared with our vast human ignorance. My new awareness was captured years later in the story I heard about the difference between Harvard and Caltech: "at Harvard they believe they are the best in the world; at Caltech they know they are the best in the world."

I studied night, day, and weekends, and survived hundreds of problems, but what a joy it was to take freshman chemistry from the inspiring Linus Pauling, who would be given standing ovations occasionally at the end of class (Bohnenblust, the differential geometer who we called "Bony," would also receive such ovations in freshman calculus); hear physics lectures by J. Robert Oppenheimer on his frequent visits to Caltech; attend a visiting lecture by Bertrand Russell; and regularly see von Karman, Anderson, Zwicky, Tolman, Millikan, and other legendary figures of that time on campus. I discovered that one kind of great teacher is the kind that simply thinks out loud, in commonsensical terms of basic principles, and you easily can read his thought processes.

I was majoring in physics, but switched to electrical engineering (EE), which was then in the same division (of mathematics, physics, and electrical engineering), as a senior. In this way, I did not have to take the dreaded "Smyth's course." It was rumored that Carl Anderson, awarded the Nobel Prize in physics for discovering the positron, had flunked Smyth's course. The course was required for physics majors, but not EE majors, so I received my B.S. (in EE) on schedule in 1949, unmoved by those for whom it was a big ego trip to take Smyth and pass it. But it was Anderson whose contribution people came to know, not the egocentric smart alecks. I'm sure glad I learned that lesson early enough to save my soul in the here and now, and therefore in the future.

I relished the unbending rigor of mathematics, physics, and engineering, but then, as a senior, I took an economics course and found it very intriguing—you could actually learn something about the economic principles underlying the claims of socialism, capitalism, and other such "isms"? Little did I know, but I was intrigued. Curious about professional economics, I went to the Caltech library, stumbled on Paul Samuelson's *Foundations of Economic Analysis*, and later that year, Ludwig von Mises's *Human Action*. From the former, it was clear that economics could be done like physics, but from the latter there seemed to be much in the way of reasoning that was not like physics. I also subscribed to the *Quarterly Journal of Economics*, and one of the first issues had a paper by Hollis Chenery on engineering production functions. So economics was also like engineering. I had not a hint then as to how much those first impressions would be changed in my thinking over the decades to follow. But in 1962, my book *Investment and Production* would have a chapter on engineering production functions. Later, since I taught it as part of the graduate theory course at Purdue, the graduate students would call it "enginomics."

From Caltech I returned to Kansas, took an M.A. in economics, then went to Harvard for a Ph.D., and on to Purdue and a career in the study of markets. I was not a likely person to develop a career in the study of markets. I had to overcome two severe handicaps: my mother was a socialist, and I had a Harvard education.

In closing I have learned a few maxims along the way that I like to share with students when possible. Here are three:

First, it's not what you know that counts; it's what you can do with what you know. Education, science, and the performance of the economy are all about the utilization of knowledge.

Second, by far the most important thing to learn is to learn how to learn.

Third, if you are not learning, then you are not teaching.

Notes

1. This essay is based on an edited excerpt from *Discovery: A Memoir* (Bloomington, IN: AuthorHouse, 2008).

2. Quoted in Alan Lomax, *The Folks Songs of North America* (New York: Doubleday, 1960), 554. Reported by Sim Webb, fireman for Casey Jones—crack passenger engineer at age twenty-six for the Cannonball Express—on the spectacular wreck of the Cannonball on April 30, 1906. The great Negro ("black" nowadays) folk poet and roundhouse worker Wallace Saunders began composing the ballad of Casey Jones as he wiped Casey's blood off of No. 382.

3. This excerpt excludes the first verse; see http://www.poetry-archive.com/c/each_in_his_own_tongue.html.

4. *Wichita Century: A Pictorial History of Wichita, Kansas, 1870–1970* (Wichita: McCormick-Armstrong, 1969), 145–148.

Vernon L. Smith
Awarded Nobel Prize in 2002. Lecture presented April 14, 2004.

Date of Birth
January 1, 1927

Academic Degrees
B.S., Caltech, 1949
M.A., University of Kansas, 1952
Ph.D., Harvard University, 1955

Academic Affiliations
Assistant Professor, Krannert School of Management, Purdue University, 1955–58
Associate Professor, Krannert School of Management, Purdue University, 1958–61
Professor, Krannert Outstanding Professorship, Purdue University, 1961–67
Professor, Brown University, 1967–68
Professor, University of Massachusetts, 1968–75
Professor, University of Arizona, 1975–98
Regents' Professor of Economics, University of Arizona, 1998–2001
Professor of Economics and Law, George Mason University, 2001–08
Visiting Rasmuson Chair in Economics, University of Alaska, 2003–present
Professor of Economics and Law and George L. Argyros Chair in Finance and Economics, Economic Science Institute, Chapman University, 2008–present.

Selected Books
Economics: An Analytical Approach, 1958, 1962 (with R. Davidson and J. Wiley)
Investment and Production: A Study in the Theory of a Capital-Using Enterprise, 1961
Economics of Natural and Environmental Resources, 1977 (ed.)
Research in Experimental Economics, Vols. 1–3, 1979, 1982, 1985 (ed.)
Experimental Economics, 1990 (ed.)
Papers in Experimental Economics (collected works), 1991
Experiments in Decision, Organization, and Exchange, 1993 (ed. with R. Day)
Bargaining and Market Behavior: Essays in Experimental Economics (collected works), 2000
Law and Economics of Irrational Behavior, 2005 (ed. with F. Parisi)
Discovery: A Memoir, 2008
Handbook of Experimental Economics Results, Vol. 1, 2008 (ed. with C. Plott)
Rationality in Economics: Constructivist and Ecological Forms, 2008

Edward C. Prescott

But do let me say something: Thanks so much for being a great adviser. You have always made economics exciting, exciting, exciting. And whatever strange little ideas I've had, whatever direction my research has gone, you have always been incredibly supportive (while at the same time challenging my ideas to improve them).

—James Schmitz, congratulatory message, October 11, 2004

The Joy of Being a Teacher-Researcher

I was asked to lecture on my development as an economist, and this is what I will do. Before doing this, however, I will introspect a little on the related question of why I turned out to be successful as a teacher-researcher. I hyphenate teacher and researcher because in my case these two activities are joint activities, and cannot be separated. I love the enthusiasm of former students for economic research and teaching, as shown in the above quotation. In this essay, I will be discussing several collaborations with past teachers and students. I have a great debt to my students, from whom I have learned so much, and I think they have learned from me. At the end of this essay, I list the students whose dissertation I signed or played a major role in thesis supervision. I dedicate this essay to these special people.

Virtually all my research is joint research, and when I say "joint," I mean with one other equal collaborator. Both collaborators contribute to all phases of the research, and both are senior authors on the resulting paper or papers. These collaborations typically originate in discussions that give rise to an economic problem that warrants analysis. My style is to get things done in the morning and wander the halls talking to people in the afternoon. In these talks a good research problem sometimes arises. Even when it doesn't, I often learn something that enhances my stock of useful economic knowledge. I emphasize that discovery of a problem is a joint activity, and assigning credit for discovering a good research problem is impossible.

A little about my personality, which is related to why I gravitated to economics, is as follows. Throughout my life I liked figuring out puzzles, and making complex things simple and orderly. I get joy out of understanding why something is true, and I am not content to just know that it is true. As an example, I played a fair amount of bridge in high school. I remember when my partner, Joseph Dodge, stated the principle of restricted choice for finessing. I just had to either disprove the principle or understand why it was true. In the process of figuring out why the principle is true, I rediscovered Bayes's theorem for the case where the probabilities are rational numbers, as they are in bridge. Understanding the theory underlying the principle of restricted choice put my mind at ease.

Another feature of my personality is that I am a skeptic; I have to be convinced. I remember many arguments with my father, who was also a skeptic. This personality trait has served me well, because often what is generally accepted economic knowledge should not be. When working on a problem with someone, I have intense concentration, and solving the problem becomes important to me. In these joint efforts, it does not matter who has the insight that leads to the solution to each of the many subproblems that come up along the way to solving the problem. What matters is that the problem gets solved.

I am a bit of a dreamer, and in high school I wanted to be a rocket scientist. It was the Sputnik era, so the fact that I dreamed of being a rocket scientist is not surprising. This dream led me to major in physics my first three years at Swarthmore College, a small liberal arts college eleven miles southwest of Philadelphia. A number of lucky events led me to becoming an economist. One stroke of luck occurred in my junior year at Swarthmore. That year I had two all-day honors laboratories—one in physical chemistry, and one, I believe, in electricity and magnetism. I did not like the all-day laboratories, and this led me to drop out of the physics honors program and major in mathematics. Another lucky event was that I took a course in the engineering department in my senior year. The course was taught by an enthusiastic, supportive professor named Sam Carpenter. This course influenced me to go to graduate school in operations research—a discipline that brought mathematical modeling into management. This was then a new and exciting field. I attended Case Institute of Technology for graduate studies.

At Case I learned recursive methods, which proved so useful when made applicable to economics. On a methodology note, a statement made by Russell L. Ackoff, then the head of the operations program at Case and one of the fathers of operations research, sticks in my head to this day and continues to influence my approach to research. He said that there is no theory without measurement, and no measurement without theory. He went on to say that a science progresses through the back-and-forth between theory and measurement.

I was lucky that experimental physics was not to my liking and that I took the engineering course that led me to Case, where I learned a set of tools that proved to be invaluable in helping to make macroeconomics part of economics. At Case I decided to go on for a Ph.D., and my choice set was Case and the Graduate School of Industrial Administration (GSIA) at the Carnegie Institute of Technology. The program at GSIA was multidisciplinary, not interdisciplinary. My program was economics, statistics, and industrial administration. The latter field included accounting, finance, and marketing, which in large part are subfields of economics. I am not sure why I chose GSIA, but I was lucky I did. Otherwise, I would not have become an economist.

My Development as an Economist as a Student at GSIA

Michael Christopher Lovell, Teacher and Collaborator
When I arrived at GSIA, the dean was Dick Cyert. He had the policy of matching, in an informal way, an incoming Ph.D. student with a faculty member. I was matched with Mike Lovell, another stroke of luck. Mike helped me so much to gain confidence in my ability to do research. We wrote two joint papers, one in the old business cycles tradition of Samuelson's multiplier-accelerator model, but with money. The primary contribution of the paper was to make a point in a debate that was then ongoing in macroeconomics. But we innovated methodologically in that paper in assuming rational expectations for the targeted capital stock, which was an argument of the investment equation in the model we developed and used. We determined the operating characteristics of the model for various monetary and fiscal policy rules. This model was not a dynamic general equilibrium model and therefore not in the tradition of what has become macroeconomics (or for that matter, what virtually all of aggregate economics has become).

The other paper was a statistics paper in which we analyzed least squares estimators with linear inequality constraints. It turns out that

proving the obvious—the constrained estimator is better than the unconstrained estimator—was very difficult. Indeed, in the process of trying,
we proved that the obvious was not true in general by coming up with
a counterexample. We did prove that under weak conditions, the restricted
least squares estimator was better than the unconstrained estimator. We
conjectured but did not prove that the result holds under more general
conditions. I must admit that not being able to prove the conjecture has
bothered me for over forty years. Sometimes when I'm on an airplane
and I have some time to waste, I come back to this problem. This says
something about my personality, I guess.

The skills I learned from Mike Lovell have contributed to my success
as a teacher, and I owe a big debt to him for what I learned. Unlike
factors determined by the genes, the skill in helping students develop into
teacher-researchers has been transmitted to my students and to students
of their students. Key is helping students to believe in themselves and be
honest with themselves.

An important event in my development as an economist was meeting
Janet (Jan) Simpson in Pittsburgh in 1964. She became my wife a year
later. She has always had a nonconformist streak and did not expect me
to make much money. She was more interested in having a family and a
career than in having high consumption levels. She raised three children,
got a Ph.D. in industrial psychology after the children were all in school,
and then had a successful career working for an industrial psychology
consulting firm.

I was lucky that she is adventuresome. In 1974, I obtained support
from the Guggenheim Foundation and the National Science Foundation
for a year's leave. I was advised to take this opportunity to visit MIT,
which was a very attractive possibility, but at Jan's urging decided to visit
the Norwegian School of Business and Economics (NHH), where Finn
Kydland was then a faculty member. Going with three young children
aged seven, five, and one to a city with no English-speaking school was
quite an adventure. Nobody in the family spoke Norwegian when we
arrived, although by the time we left my oldest son was fluent, my daughter understood it but wouldn't speak it, and my wife could communicate
a little.

It was a crazy career decision, but that year at the NHH working with
Finn proved to be a productive one. Finn and I wrote our paper "Rules
Rather Than Discretion and the Time Inconsistency of Optimal Plans,"
one of the two papers for which we were awarded our Nobel Prize. I
guess being away from the mainstream has some advantages. We were

relatively free to think differently and go our own way. It turned out that visiting Norway was not a career sacrifice as I, and my colleagues, thought would be the case.

Robert E. Lucas, Jr., Teacher and Collaborator
Robert (Bob) E. Lucas, Jr., and I arrived at GSIA in fall 1963, he as a new assistant professor and I as a Ph.D. student. I was fortunate to take two of Bob's courses at GSIA. The first was econometrics, where I learned some of the principles of using the statistics discipline to draw scientific inference in economics. The second was a capital theory course, where I learned some invaluable economic theory. Many of the things he said with respect to methodology I learned to appreciate only later.

There were many methodological discussions at GSIA. Herbert Simon, who was awarded a Nobel Prize in 1977, would argue that firms face mathematical problems that are unsolvable and therefore the assumption of profit maximization in economics should be abandoned. Herb was right about firms facing combinatorial problems that are unsolvable. Bob accepted this fact, and went on to argue that the way to proceed is to treat firms *as if* they maximized and, for that matter, to treat all decision makers in economic models *as if* they consistently maximized. This led to the then-radical view that assuming maximizing behavior is the way to proceed even when agents are faced with dynamic problems and there is uncertainty. I learned from Bob that we have to build our economic intuition from the study of model economies that we can analyze.

Bob was on my dissertation committee, but it was the great statistician Morris DeGroot and my adviser Mike Lovell who provided me with constructive criticism when writing my dissertation. My dissertation was primarily a contribution to statistical decision theory and not to economics. After my defense Bob asked in a nice way, "Why are you doing that?" I knew that he knew that what I was doing was the logical thing to do if one accepted the assumptions underlying the then-dominant macroeconometric model framework, and I was sure that he thought my research was innovative and well done. Consequently, I was puzzled by his question. Collaborating with him on the paper "Investment under Uncertainty" a few years later, I came to understand what he was saying with that question.

The history of our collaboration is as follows. Edmund (Ned) Phelps, who was at the University of Pennsylvania when I was, identified a number of papers concerned with laying the micro (which now means neoclassical) foundations for macroeconomics and put together the book

Microeconomic Foundations of Employment and Inflation Theory. Ned brought the authors of these papers to a meeting at Penn, where the authors presented their papers and were subject to the constructive criticism of the other contributors.

I was not an author and so did not participate, but I did go to the reception after their long day. At that reception, I talked with Bob Lucas about an interesting problem. We thought that we could solve it, and we decided to submit our idea to the North American Summer Meeting of the Econometric Society. Submission meant writing up and sending in an abstract for a paper. The paper was accepted for presentation. The problem turned out not to be straightforward, and as a fallback Bob proposed extending his 1967 "Theory of Supply" paper to uncertain environments in order to develop an investment equation. The paper did much more than extend his paper to uncertain environments. The concept of recursive competitive equilibrium, a tool needed to apply the dynamic economic theory to modeling aggregate phenomena, is developed there. Equilibria are Markov processes with stationary transition probabilities, and the behavior of model time series can be compared with the behavior of the time series of the economy being studied.

With this collaboration, I understood the comment he made after I defended my dissertation. He was telling me to use dynamic economic theory to model aggregate phenomena. With this collaboration I became a Bob Lucas student and an economist. To return to the theme of this lecture, Bob Lucas is the most important person in my development as an economist. Having been at the right place at the right time was another stroke of luck.

The principle guiding my research is the importance of theory interacting with measurement. I came to the conclusion that there was no hope for the approach being used in macroeconomics of empirically searching for the policy invariant laws of motion of the economy. I had read the Lucas critique. Something else was needed. Given this, I stopped teaching what was then called macroeconomics and began using dynamic equilibrium models to study aggregate economics as practiced by Bob Lucas.

I disagreed with Bob on one point: the importance of the national accounts, behind which there is a lot of theory. These accounts are based on a recursive capital theoretic framework for technology, which is the framework used in capital theory, which in turn is the theoretical framework used in aggregate economics. I made the big switch from organizing empirical knowledge around equations to organizing empirical knowledge around preferences and technology, or in layman's terms, around the ability and willingness of people to substitute. Supply and demand in general equilibrium theory have no empirical counterparts, and are used only to establish the existence of equilibrium. I love the title of Tom Sargent's paper "Beyond Supply and Demand." Tom was my valued colleague for one year at Penn and five years at the University of Minnesota.

I came to think in Bob's economic language, and we came to very quickly agree where we disagreed. By this I mean we agreed on each other's logic, while differences in conclusions were a matter of different assumptions. Differences in assumptions are something to be resolved by better measurement.

After I returned to GSIA in 1971 as a faculty member, Bob and I became colleagues. We had an additional collaboration, "Equilibrium Search and Unemployment," a paper he loves as evidenced by his lecture in this series. We had a number of jointly supervised students who had highly creative dissertations that exploited the methodology of using common knowledge dynamic competitive equilibrium models. With common knowledge, information differs across people in the model economy, but everyone knows the probability structure of the world. These analyses also assume that people maximize expected utility. Our student Jean-Pierre Danthine, for example, used this methodology to develop a model with the prices of securities revealing information about the information set of others.

I remember Bob holding court at coffee times at 10:30 a.m. and 3:00 p.m. The topic of discussion was economics and more generally social science. They were serious discussions.

My Development as an Economist at the University of Pennsylvania

My first academic position was at Penn, where I began my shift from statistician to economist. A group of exceptional young economists there contributed to my transformation. I also interacted with a number of talented students there. One of those students, in particular, influenced my development as an economist.

Thomas F. Cooley

The one student at Penn with whom I subsequently collaborated is Tom Cooley. As a graduate student, he engaged in the life of the 1960s to the fullest. The senior faculty knew he was talented, but had doubts that he would bother to complete the program, given his lifestyle as a student. We became friends, and over a beer would talk about some of the practices and problems of economic forecasting. He was supported by WEFA, Larry Klein's forecasting center at Penn, as was I during the summer. At the end of his program, to the surprise of the faculty, Tom put his mind to research and wrote an outstanding dissertation, with little guidance and in a very short time. I learned later that the senior faculty gave me credit for Tom's dramatic turnaround, which I did not really deserve. We subsequently wrote a series of papers in which we built on the ideas that arose in our discussions.

Tom went on to have a highly successful career as an econometrician and then shifted to the new macroeconomics nearly fifteen years after receiving his Ph.D. He has contributed in an important way to macroeconomics. Beginning in 2002 he became the dean of NYU Stern School, where he has been highly successful. Tom keeps amazing me with his accomplishments. We developed some new empirical tools in the hope of saving macroeconomics as then practiced. The fact that these tools were not of much use in macroeconomic forecasting, despite their mathematical elegance, led me to the Lucas dynamic economic theory approach to macroeconomics.

My Years at GSIA as a Carnegie Mellon Faculty

Finn Kydland

After returning to GSIA in fall 1971 as a faculty member, I met Finn Kydland, a truly great stroke of luck. He had completed his qualifying examinations and was writing a dissertation. He was not in the best of positions because his mentor, Sten Thore, with whom he had come to GSIA, had gone back to Norway. Both Finn and I were out of the operations research tradition. We knew recursive methods and could use the computer to solve maximization problems. I gave Finn feedback on the third essay of his dissertation dealing with a dominant firm problem. I remember so distinctly when he made a claim to which I said, "That can't be right." In the most confident way, Finn said, "I don't make mistakes," and he doesn't. He has to be certain of something before he will make a statement.

The year before he returned in fall 1973 to NHH, we began working on the use of recursive methods to evaluate policy rules. I joined him in Norway a year later. The lifestyle at NHH was then very different from what it is at other academic places I have been. Lunches were tea and a piece of goat cheese on a piece of bread. In the late afternoon, there were only three people in the building: Finn, me, and the woman who waxed the floors. That woman was annoyed by us getting in the way of her doing her job. Everyone else was home working on their house. A common sight in the Bergen area was a cement mixer in the front yard, along with a pile of stones and a half-built stone wall. They called the area along the fjord, just a little way from NHH, Porridge Hill, because most of the disposable income of the people living there was going to making mortgage payments. There was very little left to spend on food, which was very expensive.

The first half of that year at NHH, I did a lot of thinking about economics, but did not get much done. Then it dawned on Finn and me that the fact that the time consistent policy rules we had been computing are not optimal was an important finding. In the spring, we sat down and showed how bad outcomes could be if there is discretion, and best action is chosen in the current situation given the state of the economy. We wrote the first draft of the paper "Rules versus Discretion: The Time Inconsistency of Optimal Plans," an extended version of which appeared in 1977.

This was not the last of our major collaborations. Finn visited GSIA in 1977–78 after visiting Minnesota the previous year. We became more interested in a positive theory of business cycle fluctuations than in a theory of policy. We started interacting theory with observation, but were not that successful in that endeavor because we were beginning modeling at the linear-quadratic economy level.

Academic year 1978–79 was my turn to be on leave. I had presented our not-very-successful paper at Northwestern that year and received some criticism. Back at GSIA for the summer, Finn and I had extended discussions about what to do differently. We decided to investigate if beginning with the neoclassical growth model as the starting point would be more fruitful. We had to extend that model to include the labor-leisure decision, because business cycles were fluctuations largely accounted for by fluctuations in the labor input. Starting out with the extended neoclassical growth model turned out to be incredibly fruitful.

This exploration was carried out in summer 1979 at GSIA. Finn and I worked away with the programming in the basement of GSIA, and developed a new methodology that has proven so useful. We found that if people are highly willing to intertemporally substitute market time or, in more popular jargon, "make hay while the sun shines," and if productivity shocks are persistent and of a certain magnitude, business cycles of the nature observed are a prediction of the extended neoclassical growth model. I used the tools of statistics to estimate the parameters of the process governing the productivity shock. I found that the process was highly persistent and that the shocks were of the magnitude that gave rise to fluctuations of the magnitude observed.

Whether people were as willing in the aggregate to reallocate their work effort over time as needed for the neoclassical growth model to predict business cycles was the open question. Finn and I knew we could get a good fit to the aggregate observation by choosing a high value for the parameter governing this willingness. The needed number was far larger than the one that economists had estimated using panel observations for continuously employed, full-time, prime-age males. A fact for this population was that when compensation per hour worked went up, market hours increased little. This conflict between individual and aggregate behavior was subsequently resolved, and I will come back to this point when I discuss another student with whom I only recently collaborated.

Rajnish Mehra, student and subsequent collaborator

Another student at GSIA with whom I have had subsequent fruitful collaborations is Rajnish Mehra. He is the antithesis of Finn. In each of our three collaborations, he initiated the project and stuck my name on the paper at an early stage. Each of these papers addressed a good problem, but the early papers had flaws and required a sizable effort before we had something worth reporting to the profession.

Our "Equity Premium Puzzle" paper, written in 1979 and appearing in 1985, was important in my development as an economist. There we used theory to determine how much of the historical difference in the average return on the stock market and virtually risk-free short-term debt is a premium for bearing nondiversifiable aggregate risk. Our finding was that nondiversifiable risk accounted for only a small part of the difference in historical average returns.

The reason this paper was important in my development as an economist was that it led me to stop thinking in terms of finding the model to *fit* some data set to simply using theory and measurement to make quantitative statements. Given that the big difference in these average returns was not a premium for bearing aggregate risk, Raj and I concluded that it had to be for something else. Recently, important progress has been made on finding what other features of reality account for most of the difference in average returns.

We had problems getting the paper published and had given up trying. Robert King and Charlie Plosser came into my office at the Minneapolis Federal Reserve Bank and encouraged the submission of the paper to the *Journal of Monetary Economics*, which we did. This was another stroke of luck. The paper turned out to foster a considerable body of very interesting research.

Other Collaborators at GSIA

When I returned from Norway in 1975, there was a new young assistant professor on the faculty: Robert M. Townsend. Having been a Neil Wallace student at Minnesota, he was careful in his use of language. He opened my eyes when he told me the way to deal with problems with private information was to add incentive constraints to other constraints that determined whether or not an allocation is feasible. Subsequently, we wrote a couple of papers in which we extended the theory of valuation equilibrium to environments with private information. It was a matter of finding a commodity vector with the needed properties—easier said than done. With this commodity vector, households' problem is to maximize utility given prices of the commodities subject to their consumption and budget constraints, and firms' problem is to maximize value given prices and technology constraints. In addition, all markets must clear.

My Years at Minnesota

In late fall 1979, to my joy, I received an offer from the University of Minnesota, which was then the best place in macroeconomics and a great match for me, given its abundance of smart, adventuresome students who were well trained in economic theory. I have Tom Sargent to thank for engineering this appointment, along with Walter Heller, who provided some crucial support. This was another stroke of luck.

One student whose dissertation I signed as adviser, but met only briefly a couple of times, was Richard Rogerson. He resolved the puzzle of why aggregate observations were saying people are highly willing to substitute work hours over time, whereas panel studies of individual behavior were saying they were not. The version of Rogerson's dissertation that I approved had two essays. He presented a short third essay at his defense. He had observed that most variation in aggregate hours worked is accounted for by fluctuations in the number working in a given week and not in the number of hours worked per week per full-time worker. This led him to introduce a labor indivisibility where people either work or don't work in a given week. He found that the model explained both the micro and macro observations.

Gary Hansen, another of my students with whom in subsequent years I had fruitful collaborations, took the Rogerson labor indivisibility and introduced it into the neoclassical growth model. He found that predicted business cycle fluctuations were even bigger than those observed. His paper was beautifully written, and had all the noncrucial elements stripped from the business cycle model that Finn and I developed. His paper immediately got great attention. This was another stroke of luck.

A few years later Andreas Hornstein, another student and valued collaborator, developed a model that endogenized this labor indivisibility. Very recently, Rogerson, his student Wallenius, and I came up with another endogenization, which I think will better interact with measurement, including differences in workweek lengths across occupations. Much remains to be done to ascertain whether my expectations will be realized.

Stephen Parente

At Minnesota I did not teach macroeconomics. I taught a valuation equilibrium and recursive methods course in the macro theory sequence. I taught the students the language of economic theory, not how to use it. You have to know the vocabulary and grammar of a language before you can use it productively. I also taught an industrial organization course where a variety of economic questions were addressed.

In the 1980s, growth and development returned to center stage in economics. I had read Paul Romer's economic development paper and Bob Lucas's mechanics of economic development paper on endogenizing growth, and wanted to develop some aggregate models with explicit micro foundations. Some students became very interested in this topic and requested that Minnesota again have a field exam in this area. I shifted my teaching to that area to fill a need, as Minnesota had enough good people willing and able to teach industrial organization.

At that time, everyone was emphasizing the importance of the savings rate and the accumulation of factors of production, including not only physical productive assets but also human capital. Stephen Parente, in a highly original dissertation, took another approach that focused on the role of barriers to efficient production. Countries were poor because they were good at setting up barriers to efficient production. He developed a dynamic micro-based general equilibrium model where barriers were key in determining living standards. After he wrote his dissertation, we began to talk about how to modify his model so that it could be quantified in the hopes of replicating the success of the extended neoclassical growth models in the study of business cycles. This turned out to be a ten-year collaboration that resulted in our book *Barriers to Riches*.

More Ambitious Exercise

In our business cycle research, Finn and I focused on the business cycle facts, which were a set of statistical properties of the economic time series. Along with Gary Hansen and Tom Cooley, I addressed the question, Did technology shocks cause the 1990–1991 recession? The answer is yes, but the behavior of these shocks in that period implied a recovery much sooner than occurred. The fact that there is a deviation from theory is evidence that macroeconomics has become a hard science like the natural sciences had become many years before. No longer was macroeconomics an exercise in storytelling with many explanations of every observation. Incidentally, this deviation from theory has been resolved with the inclusion of tax rates, which were increased in the early 1990s, but the importance of taxes for business cycles was only later evaluated and measured.

At the Minneapolis Fed in 1999, Hal Cole and Lee Ohanian broke a taboo and used the neoclassical growth model to study the Great Depression. Motivated by the study, and the very strong support and encouragement of Arthur Rolnick, director of research, Tim Kehoe and I organized a conference at the Minneapolis Fed on great depressions of the twentieth century. All contributors used the neoclassical growth model to study a great depression. My paper was written with Fumio Hayashi, and it examined Japan's lost decade of growth between 1992 and 2002.

In that paper, we didn't know what expectations of future productivity and tax shocks to impute to the model people. We simply imputed the model people with perfect foresight, hoping the findings would be robust to the expectation assumption. As found out later, our hopes were realized. We found that this lost decade of growth, which greatly depressed output per working-age person, was due to a lack of productivity growth. (Why productivity growth was absent is less well understood.)

We found that great depressions in output per working-age person corrected for trend occurred in a number of countries in the last thirty years of the twentieth century. I was surprised that Japan, New Zealand,

and Switzerland had experienced great depressions in this period, and not so surprised that a number of Latin American economies had as well.

The Federal Reserve Bank of Minneapolis

Ellen R. McGrattan

Ellen McGrattan addressed the expectations for robustness conjecture and found that our conjecture stood up. She generated equilibrium realizations of a dynamic stochastic neoclassical growth model. She introduced an economist who incorrectly uses the perfect foresight to study the artificial economy. She then compared what that economist would conclude with what an economist who knew the correct expectation assumption would conclude. For all practical purposes, the conclusions are the same.

The Value of the Stock Market

In 1999, it was again time to fill the Federal Reserve Bank of Minneapolis *Quarterly Review*. More important, Gary Stern, president of the Minneapolis Bank, wanted to know more about stock market valuation and whether there was something the Fed should be doing. My motivation was not just intellectual curiosity; I was worried about the stock market because that is where all my retirement savings were. I didn't know what I should do and didn't think anybody else knew either. There was no scientific basis for saying the market was overvalued or undervalued. The *Quarterly Review* issue had two articles: one written by Ravi Jaganathan and Ellen McGrattan taking the traditional finance approach, and the other written by Ellen McGrattan and me.

Ellen and I took an approach different from the one standard in finance. The standard approach exploits the equilibrium relation that equity values are equal to the present value of dividends. We exploited the equilibrium relation that the value of corporate debt plus equity is equal to the value of its productive assets. With our approach, all the variables used to derive the prediction of the fundamental value of the stock market were current-period national account variables. We innovated in developing a way to deal with unmeasured productive assets using corporate accounting profits. The value of the Coca-Cola brand name is large, as are the value of Microsoft know-how and the value of drug companies' patents. Our initial finding was that at the end of 1999, the value of the stock market was as predicted by theory. The stock market peaked in March 2000 at a level 15 percent above what it was at the end of 1999, so relative to theory the market was overvalued in March 2000.

We presented this paper in a bag lunch seminar at the Minneapolis Fed. These seminars get a bit wild. Tim Kehoe attacked the findings by pointing out that our theory predicts that the value of the stock market should have been twice as high as it actually was in the 1960s. Tim's point was well taken. Ellen and I asked each other, What could account for this huge deviation from theory in the 1960s? We spent a week working on the problem. Then Ellen came running into my office with a big grin on her face. She said it was taxes. We, of course, had corporate income taxes and taxes on corporate property in the first version of the neoclassical growth model that we were using. But we had omitted taxes on distributions to owners. Consequently, our estimate of the fundamental value of corporations is a good one only when the tax rate on distributions to households is near zero. At the end of 1999, tax-deferred accounts included pension fund reserves, IRAs, 401(k)s, and the like; taken together they held the majority of corporate equity. Because of these accounts, the tax rate in 1999 was low, and introducing taxes on distributions (dividends plus part of buybacks) would have decreased the predicted value of the stock market by only about 5 percent. This was not the case in the 1960s, however, when the tax rate on distributions was closer to 50 percent than to 5 percent. With this correction to our model, the value of the stock market in the 1960s is very close to, rather than far lower than, that predicted by the model.

Our paper was rejected by an American journal so we sent it to a British journal, the *Review of Economic Studies*. The editor wanted to see the analysis done for the British economy, which we did. This was a stroke of luck. The United Kingdom had even bigger movements in the value of its stock market relative to GDP than did the United States—a factor of 3 for the United Kingdom versus a factor of 2.5 for the United States. The theory predicted the behavior of the British stock market even better than it predicted the behavior of the U.S. stock market. On this one we owe a debt to the editor for requiring us to use our analysis for the United Kingdom.

Another question that arose at some Minneapolis Fed policy briefings in the late 1990s was why people were working so much. It was not productivity if GDP is used as the measure of output. It was not low tax rates or reforms in labor market policies. We didn't want to rely on some contagious virus that led people to work more than normal. More seriously, the neoclassical growth model with exogenous population, productivity, and taxes worked well for the U.S. economy up to the 1990s. In the 1990s, observations were greatly at variance with this theory.

People were working more than theory predicted, and accounting profits were not increasing as they did in other booms. We introduced a technology that absent nonneutral technology change, gives the same predictions as the basic neoclassical model. But we permitted nonneutral technology change, which was a reasonable thing to do given the high-tech boom. Many observers said the importance of investment in developing new products and markets for these products was abnormally large. The national accounts do not report this type of investment, and as a result there was an abnormally large amount of this unreported investment in the 1990s. We determined the total factor productivity parameters from both activities, and computed the equilibrium path of the economy taking as exogenous the paths of these total factor productivity parameters, population, and tax rates. Predicted and actual behavior of the economy matched beautifully. Further theory predicted the abnormally high average capital gains for the period. Theory works. We were a little late in answering Gary Stern's question about the stock market, but it was answered. Likewise, we were a little late in answering another important question that arose in policy briefings in the late 1990s: Why are Americans working so much?

More on Labor Supply
Teaching was influential in my development as an economist. For political reasons, I never taught the methodology I discuss in this essay at the graduate level. But in the late 1990s, I began teaching it at the undergraduate level. This teaching is time-consuming and challenging. I wanted the students to use the neoclassical growth model to address a question. I had them calibrate the model to the growth facts and use the model to run business cycle experiments. They verified that business cycles were generated by the model if, and only if, people have a high willingness to intertemporally substitute leisure. For the value of this parameter that generated business cycles, I had them evaluate the model using a consumption tax versus an income tax to finance sizable transfer payments to households. The students said there was something wrong with the program, because they could find no income tax rate that would finance the transfer. When I saw this, I knew it was important. The Laffer curve was something of consequence and not an intellectual curiosity, as I had assumed.

This led me to do cross-country analyses using the theory. The finding was that cross-country differences in tax rates account for much of the huge differences in market hours per working-age person. These international observations are well designed to estimate the key parameter because predictions depend on tax rate differences, and these tax rate differences are larger. The marginal effective tax rate includes all factors in the budget constraint that affect the relative price of consumption and leisure. We now know why Europeans work so little in the market sector relative to residents of other advanced industrial countries. Their tax rates are much higher.

The Wise Guy in My Undergraduate Class

There was a wise guy in my undergraduate course—at least he thought he was one. He kept asking why we use one technology for the Malthusian era and another for the modern growth era. I recognized that he was smart and was asking an important question that was not addressed, at least in the quantitative dynamic equilibrium theory I espouse. At the time, I didn't have an answer and mumbled something about elasticity of substitution. I discussed the problem with a number of colleagues. Gary Hansen, who was visiting the Minneapolis Fed, was one of these colleagues. After extended discussion, I think it was he who had the idea of having two technologies, both of which get better over time. At some point in time, a transition begins from using the traditional land-intensive technology to the neoclassical growth technology. The transition occurs when the neoclassical technology progresses to the point where it is profitable to operate it at the Malthusian wage and rental price of capital. Undergraduates who are smart and not programmed to think one way are valuable inputs into the research process.

Conclusion

In this essay, I reviewed my development as an economist. I see my and Finn's key contribution as developing a methodology for the study of dynamic economic phenomena. Using this methodology, so many people have contributed so much to advancing our economic understanding. This is the golden age of economics with numerous advancements being made using these tools and extensions of these tools. A rich class of important problems remain that can be addressed using our existing tools of analysis. Another important development is that the data sets available have become richer and have made it possible to address questions quantitatively. I cannot underestimate the importance of measurement in drawing scientific inference.

A number of other valued collaborators were instrumental in my continual development as an economist. They include John H. Boyd and Harold Cole at the Federal Reserve Bank of Minneapolis, and Ayse Imrohoroglu, Javier Díaz-Giménez, Hugo Hopenhayn, and Victor Rios-Rull, who were my advisees at Minnesota. A list of all those for whom I was a dissertation adviser or co-adviser, or played a significant advisory role, is at the end of this essay.

Edward C. Prescott

Awarded Nobel Prize in 2004. Lecture presented April 10, 2006.

Date of Birth

December 26, 1940

Academic Degrees

B.A., Swarthmore College, 1962
M.S., Case Western Reserve University, 1963
Ph.D., Carnegie Mellon University, 1967

Academic Affiliations

Assistant Professor of Economics, University of Pennsylvania, 1967–71

Assistant Professor of Economics, Graduate School of Industrial Administration, Carnegie Mellon University, 1971–72

Associate Professor of Economics, Graduate School of Industrial Administration, Carnegie Mellon University, 1972–75

Visiting Professor of Economics, Norwegian School of Business and Economics, 1974–75

Professor of Economics, Graduate School of Industrial Administration, Carnegie Mellon University, 1975–80

Professor of Economics, University of Minnesota, 1980–98

Senior Adviser, Research Department, Federal Reserve Bank of Minneapolis, 1980–2003

Professor of Economics, University of Chicago, 1998–99

Professor of Economics, University of Minnesota, 1999–2003

Senior Monetary Adviser, Research Department, Federal Reserve Bank of Minneapolis, 2003–present

W. P. Carey Chair and Professor of Economics, Arizona State University, 2003–present

Selected Books

Contractual Arrangements for Intertemporal Trade, 1985 (ed. with N. Wallace)

Recursive Methods in Economic Dynamics, 1989 (with N. L. Stokey and R. E. Lucas, Jr.)

Barriers to Riches, 2000 (with S. L. Parente)

Great Depressions of the Twentieth Century, 2007 (ed. with T. J. Kehoe)

Ph.D. Dissertation Committees Chaired or Co-supervised by Edward C. Prescott (listed chronologically by university)

University of Pennsylvania

Thomas F. Cooley

(continued)

(continued)

Carnegie Mellon University
  Finn E. Kydland
  Leon Courville
  Costas Azariadis
  Marie-Therese Flaherty
  Robert Crawford
  Jean-Pierre Danthine
  Thore H. Johnsen
  Ralph LaVar Huntzinger
  Rajnish Mehra
  Barbara Judith Spencer
  Charles A. Holt, Jr.
  Edward J. Green
  Chandra Kanodia
  Marinus Bouwman
  V. V. Chari

University of Chicago
  Jay R. Ritter

Northwestern University
  Pipat Pithyachariyakul
  Yong J. Yoon

University of Minnesota
  Yoon Yoon
  Shinichi Watanabe
  Richard D. Rogerson
  Ian Robert Milne Bain
  Yuet-Chang Joseph Lin
  George Lo
  Rodolfo E. Manuelli
  James Andrew Schmitz, Jr.
  Michael James Meurer
  Gary D. Hansen
  Ann Guenther
  Ayse Okten Imrohoroglu
  Bruce Carlton Horning
  Gerhard Glomm
  John Lester Rodgers
  Scott David Hakala
  Hugo Andres Hopenhayn
  Maria Eugenia Muniagurria
  Yuojin Eugene Yun
  Beverly Lapham

(continued)

Stephen Parente
John C. Proctor
Jose-Victor Rios-Rull
Javier Díaz-Giménez
Andreas Hornstein
Mark Richard Huggett
Allen Charles Head
Ricardo Raineri
Fernando Enrique Alvarez
Marcelo Luis Veracierto
Terry Jay Fitzgerald
Antonia Diaz
Andres Erosa
Raphael Bergoeing
Ricardo de Oliveira Cavalcanti
Elizabeth Miriam Caucutt
Arilton Carlos Campanharo Teixeira
Ronald Alan Edwards
Dirk Krueger
Tianshu Chu
Daria Zakharova
Jessica Delores Tjornhom
Pedro Gabriel Correia Sérvulode Amaral
Igor Livshits
Sami Alpanda
Evridiki Ioannis Tsounta
Alexander Ueberfeldt
Simona Cociuba

Thomas C. Schelling

In reflecting on this autobiography I have two impressions. They will appear, but I want to acknowledge these in advance and alert the reader.

One is that I have been blessed with all kinds of advantages and opportunities. I grew up immune to the depression of the 1930s. (My father was a naval officer.) I had great school teachers at San Diego High School, especially Miss Olson, who spent two years teaching me to write a five-paragraph essay and so on, in college and graduate school, and in my first professional job, and my second and third. Everything good that might have happened to me did. I had splendid colleagues everywhere I went. Most of what I accomplished intellectually depended on opportunities. And the opportunities came.

The second, related impression is that nearly everything I've done was stimulated by opportunities I didn't seek but came to me, and many things I've done, including some of the things I'm most satisfied with, I did at the suggestion of somebody else or as a result of some unsolicited invitation.

For example, I was invited—I've never known why, or who suggested me—to join a committee of the National Academy of Sciences on "Substance Abuse and Habitual Behavior," on which I was surrounded by experts in heroin, alcohol, marijuana, nicotine, eating disorders, and various self-destructive habits. It was believed that every committee needed an economist, in case economics became pertinent. Economics never became salient, but I became, over a period of five years and fifty days of meetings, a wonderfully educated amateur. It was doctrine among the experts that nobody could cope with addictions without professional help. I thought there were things people might do to help themselves, and said so, and was challenged to put something on paper. My earlier work on "commitment"—about which more later—led me to some tactics that seemed likely to be at least occasionally helpful. What I wrote got published, as "The Intimate Contest for Self-Command," and led to six or seven more publications over a decade or so. I called it "self-command" (and even coined the phrase "egonomics") to separate it from "self-control," which usually meant something else. Somebody somewhere is responsible for my ever having got into the subject.

Again, I happened to run into Kenneth Boulding outside the Yale Cooperative Store in New Haven one afternoon. Ken had been the referee for an article I'd submitted to the *American Economic Review*—actually, the best article I ever wrote—and he'd been so enthusiastic that the editor printed it verbatim (except for asking me to eliminate the term "threatee," for one who is threatened). I told Ken that there was one topic I'd wanted to include in the article that I couldn't get a grip on, and I tried to express what it was. I couldn't be explicit or else I'd have been able to deal with it in the article. Boulding said something to me—I've never been able to reconstruct what it was—that clicked in my brain and revealed what it was I was trying to formulate. Just one sentence on a sidewalk in New Haven and I had the grasp I needed. His suggestion—actually it wasn't a suggestion, just a hint of some kind—led me to the idea of a "focal point," and the concept of tacit bargaining and its influence on explicit bargaining.

I mention here an experience in my development of the focal point idea. I spent summer 1940 driving from San Diego to New Hampshire and back with two college friends. Somewhere I stopped so one of the other two could buy some crackers and peanut butter. A policeman made me move on; I tried to go around the block but was frustrated by one-way streets, and when I got back to where I'd let him out, he wasn't there. (Not seeing me, he had gone looking.) I went around again, and there he was. As we drove on, eating crackers and peanut butter, one of us said, "You know that could happen. Suppose we got separated in a strange city. How would we find each other?" There were no cell phones in those days. "Let's make a plan." Then somebody said, "No, let's think about it and see if we can arrive, separately, on a solution." So instead of making a plan, we all three contemplated how we'd get together if, in some yet-unnamed city, we were separated and needed to concert on a meeting place.

After supper—we were sitting out around a campfire—we compared solutions. We had all gone to the same place. We had all reasoned the same. There was one adventitious clue, or otherwise we had simply reasoned that if there was some "obvious" meeting place in a yet-unnamed city, it had to be something that every city had, that every city had just one of—a place that could be reached by public transportation, and a place that any policeman could locate for us. That reduced the alternatives to very few, but still a few. We each recalled that we had arranged to look for mail in a few cities. It was unlikely that the city in which we lost each other was one in which we'd promised to look for mail, but the one location in some city that was unique to us was the general delivery window of the main post office. Every city had a main post office, and every main post office had a general delivery window where one could show up and ask if there was anything for Schelling. The person at the window would thumb through a pile of letters, and say either "no" or "Here's something for Schelling."

That experience was still vivid when I needed a focal point to concert expectations.

I left the University of California at Berkeley in the middle of my junior year to go to Chile. I wanted a year abroad but there was a war in Europe, and a Chilean housemate sold me on Chile. After Pearl Harbor, I was "frozen" in my job at the U.S. embassy for two years—actually exciting years, mostly as a personal assistant to the FBI agent who arrived to set up a counterespionage office. I developed stomach pains; the ambassador returned my passport; the navy got me onto a ship to the States; my former roommate, now a medical student, put me in touch with an internist who diagnosed a duodenal ulcer; and I learned that neither the army nor the navy would touch me. I was Section Eight of the draft code: psychoneurotic and likely to hemorrhage under stress.

I re-enrolled at Berkeley and majored in economics. There were few men on campus; it was 1943, the draft age had been lowered to eighteen, and except for a naval officers' program, few healthy men were enrolled. Few women did economics, so economics classes, in the largest university in the world, were small, sometimes intimate. It was an excellent faculty, mostly no longer remembered, but William Fellner held a graduate theory seminar that was conducted so modestly, so inquiringly, so invitingly, that I was charmed, intrigued, and persuaded I wanted to be an academic economist.

With an A.B. in economics and about a year's graduate study, I decided to go to Washington, DC, where I got an introduction to the Fiscal Division of the U.S. Bureau of the Budget. Arthur Smithies, an Australian on leave from the University of Michigan, interviewed me. First he showed me a section of that year's budget that for the first time had "national economic accounts," what later became a standard piece of fiscal analysis but was an innovation in spring 1944. Because I recognized it, I incurred his immediate interest.

Second, he somewhat apologetically asked me whether I'd be willing to add a column of figures; he said he always asked a candidate to do that. I said "sure," and he showed me a table in the budget. Confident, I added the numbers and handed him my results. He studied my total and pointed out that several of the numbers I'd added had little footnotes affixed. Some said "negative, subtract," and others said "subtotal." I had added all the negatives and subtotals. I was deflated, knowing I'd flunked the test. But Smithies smiled, said it was a good lesson, and hired me. (For a while I wasn't sure whether he was so impressed with me that a little faux pas didn't make any difference, or instead there were so few people available with any economics training that he had to make do with somebody who couldn't be responsible with numbers.) Later we were colleagues at Harvard.

We were the division of the bureau that became the prototype for the Council of Economic Advisers, and one of my responsibilities was to keep track of what was going on at the Treasury, Federal Reserve, Commerce, and various wartime agencies in preparing for the postwar economy. The Employment Act of 1946, which established the Council of Economic Advisers, was being discussed on Capitol Hill, and I spent many days at Senate and House committees, and had a wonderful course in executive-congressional relations.

I chose Harvard for graduate study and had so many influential contacts in Washington that I was able to become a full-time teaching assistant and resident tutor at Kirkland House—free room and board, and a decent salary. I already knew a lot of economics, but teaching the elementary economics course taught me a lot more. I attracted the attention of the faculty, and in my second year was asked by Alvin Hansen, Gottfried Haberler, and Edward Chamberlin to be their teaching assistants. It was a lot of work, but again I learned a lot by having to be interrogated by graduate students.

As a resident tutor at Kirkland House I was available for helping economics students. One senior asked me for help with some national income analysis, and I spent an hour showing him how a little algebra could solve his problems. He was so impressed that he thought I ought to make it available. I began to put together a brief essay showing how a little first-year high school algebra could make short shrift of problems like the one he'd brought me. The little essay grew and grew, and two years later, having worked nights and weekends in Copenhagen and Paris, I finished my little essay. It was published in 1951 by McGraw-Hill as *National Income Behavior: An Introduction to Algebraic Analysis.*

It was a good job, had lots in it that was original, and was accepted by Harvard for my Ph.D. The book had a brief successful life; for some years after the war, graduate students needed the help my book could give them. After that, they all knew more than enough mathematics and could do without my book.

In 1948, I passed my oral exams and the economics department nominated me for a junior fellowship with the Harvard Society of Fellows—a three-year fellowship with a good stipend. The prestige was considerable. I was all set when I got a phone call from Sidney Alexander, an instructor at MIT with whom I was acquainted, who said he was in Washington with the new Marshall Plan. He had an opportunity to go to Paris but needed a replacement. Would I come spend the summer in Washington with the Marshall Plan, which had commenced in April of that year, 1948. (You will notice how a phone call from an acquaintance changed my life forever.)

I said yes; my wife and I spent the summer in Washington; my boss was named program officer for the Marshall Plan in Copenhagen and asked me to join him; I said yes. After a year I was ready to resume my junior fellowship at Harvard, but was invited to join the central European office of the Marshall Plan in Paris. Paris sounded good, the work sounded interesting, and I resigned my junior fellowship. (Another opportunity out of the blue!)

My main responsibility in Paris, where I spent September 1949 to December 1950, was helping to devise and negotiate the European Payments Union (EPU). All trade between Marshall Plan countries was bilaterally negotiated, with a constraint to balance payments bilaterally; all had strict exchange controls. The EPU was to be a clearinghouse where each participating country would need only to balance its total intra-European receipts and outlays. It was evident that the EPU would need a substantial endowment, and the United States had proposed to allot some $300 million of the total Marshall Plan annual appropriation for an EPU endowment. The response was negative; the governments preferred the $300 million in direct aid. Negotiation got nowhere until Congress was persuaded, in its appropriation for 1951–1952, to set aside $300 million that could be used only for the establishment of a payments union. All, or almost all, went smoothly after that, and I had observed commitment as a negotiating tactic.

Ambassador W. Averell Harriman, who headed the Paris office, left in summer 1950 to become White House foreign policy adviser to President Truman, and took my boss, Lincoln Gordon, with him. By November the EPU was locked up, and Gordon arranged for me to join the Harriman office in the White House. We sailed first-class on the *Isle de France*, and I was back in the building I'd always known as "Old State"—it is now the Old Executive Office Building at 17th and Pennsylvania, the loveliest building in Washington. In 1945–1946 I'd been on the fourth floor, looking over the White House; now I was on the second floor, looking over the White House again. (My career had reached its pinnacle at the end of 1950, when I had a personally assigned parking space on West Executive Avenue, the short guarded street between Old State and the White House.)

The European Recovery Program, as the Marshall Plan was called, became the Mutual Security Program in spring 1951; Harriman became the director of mutual security, I became the officer in charge of European program affairs, and essentially we were the budget bureau for foreign aid. I'll give three examples of what I, and a very small staff of mine, did.

The U.S. Army proposed, for the fiscal year, $1.6 billion of equipment and ammunition for NATO troops. The breakdown was $1.3 billion for equipment and $300 million for ammunition. I chaired the budget review, and challenged the breakdown between ammunition and equipment. The declared objective was to make NATO able to conduct military operations in the event of war for thirty days. My staff and I argued that ammunition stocks were so meager that much of the new equipment couldn't be used. The army people said they'd re-examine the recommendation, and came back still proposing $1.6 billion, but this time with $1.3 billion for ammunition and $300 million for equipment. (The army had been interested in disposing of some of its old equipment and replenishing it with new.)

For fiscal 1952–1953, the proposal from the aid agency was for $15 million for the Netherlands. We didn't see that the Dutch needed any such small amount and proposed cutting the aid to zero. The U.S. ambassador argued that it would be an embarrassment to the Dutch government to be the first nation to be cut off from the program, and the small amount was a token of a continued relationship. We suggested that he use his ambassadorial skills to persuade the Dutch that they had achieved such success that they could be the first to forego further aid from the

United States. He did, and they did, and we saved $15 million and made the Dutch happy.

Under the new Mutual Security Act, "economic aid" had become "defense support," emphasizing the role of NATO. Congress was reluctant to appropriate enough defense support money to meet the NATO nations' requirements for dollar imports. We invented a concept known as "offshore procurement," the use of "military-aid" money to procure equipment and supplies in Europe for delivery to European NATO allies. Thus, some NATO countries exported military equipment to the United States in exchange for dollars, with the equipment going to other NATO countries, and the dollars available for imports. It was determined that France would need at least an extra billion dollars to meet its dollar import requirements. Congress showed no willingness to appropriate such funds for the French, but Congress was enthusiastic about the French military effort in Indochina. The solution was to procure, with military-aid money, more than a billion dollars' worth of supplies from French sources for the French military effort in Indochina. This was a kind of subterfuge, providing dollar "export" earnings to the French central bank. I never knew whether Congress was hoodwinked or was simply complicit in taking advantage of the public's gullibility over Indochina.

With the election of Dwight Eisenhower, Harriman was replaced by Harold Stassen in January 1953. (Stassen had been a youthful governor of Minnesota, nominator of Wendell Wilkie at the Republican National Convention in 1940, and the naval officer who led the navy contingent that rescued the POWs interned by the Japanese in the Philippines.) By that summer I was ready to leave, had an invitation from the Yale economics department, and told Stassen of my decision. He approved, saying that if I wanted a career in government, I should establish a firm base outside so that whenever, or if ever, I wanted to resign in protest, I'd have a secure profession to repair to.

At Yale I was surrounded by a distinguished faculty. William Fellner, whom I've mentioned, was there; James Tobin, whom I'd known in graduate school at Harvard; Robert Triffin, with whom I'd worked in Paris on the EPU; Tjalling Koopmans and Jacob Marschak, who moved to Yale from Chicago with the Cowles Foundation; and of course distinguished scholars in political science, psychology, and other social sciences. One of my first graduate students was Ned Phelps, who received the Nobel Prize the year after I did.

At Yale I taught international economics and embarked on a textbook. It was finished in 1958, just as I left Yale. I tried to make it a "modern" textbook, treating foreign aid, strategic trade controls, international cost sharing, national security trade controls, economic integration (as appeared to be imminent in Europe), international investment, and even protectionism (of which the international was only one dimension) as needing theoretical analysis on a par with traditional trade theory. I hoped to broaden the subject from traditional trade theory. I also hoped to make some money. I accomplished neither.

The Yale years produced what I believe were the main contributions that appealed to the Nobel selection committee. I had decided, on leaving government, to make "bargaining theory"—as I called it, for want of a better term—my primary theoretical interest, thinking my years in international negotiation had given me insight. I spent two years producing a manuscript of some 250 pages, mainly developing the idea of commitment as applied to threats, promises, and negotiation. It occurred to me that an article in a major journal would reach more readers than a book; I decided to see whether I could compress the 250 pages into something article length.

I spent the better part of three months trying to convert pages into paragraphs, paragraphs into sentences, and finding simple examples that illustrated complex ideas, and in the end had a manuscript that as far as I could tell, had sacrificed nothing in the compression to what was eventually about thirty printed pages. I called it "An Essay on Bargaining," and it appeared in the June 1956 *American Economic Review*.

Ever since then I've had, as a motto for writing, an observation of Antoine de Saint-Exupéry from *Wind, Sand, and Stars*. He was an early French aviator who pioneered airlines in North Africa, Chile, and Argentina. It was the design of aircraft that led him to the generalization, "In anything at all, perfection is finally achieved not when there is nothing more to add, but when nothing more can be taken away." When I write I try to honor that maxim. (Even in this essay.)

I later enlarged on that essay in London in 1958; I'll come to that later. What I did next was the article on focal points that was triggered by that conversation with Boulding. It was my only foray into "experimental" research. I decided to test whether people can actually concert their intentions by some process of logic or imagination, by recognizing a need for clues or hints or some process of convergent expectations. I referred to this as "coordination," and I tested, by a questionnaire mailed to some sixty friends and colleagues, whether people could coordinate when their interests were identical—"pure coordination," I called it—and then whether they could coordinate when their interests diverged, as between alternative choices but they had to choose identically to succeed at all.

Actually, I was led to this inquiry not through an interest in tacit bargaining but in the belief that the phenomenon I was looking at was crucial in arriving at agreement in explicit bargaining. I had observed that the results of bargaining were often a convergence on some solution that had become "mutually expected," often on some salient outcome qualitatively distinct from most alternatives, or reflecting some precedent or tradition. (Splitting fifty-fifty is an example.) I thought a demonstration that people actually could intuit their way to a common expectation in the tacit case would establish the psychological phenomenon that I was trying to describe. I evidently succeeded in persuading my audience that the tacit case was real; I'm not sure that my original major point was similarly appreciated.

Evidently both the "Essay on Bargaining" and the tacit bargaining article (which appeared as "Bargaining, Communication, and Limited War" in the inaugural issue of the *Journal of Conflict Resolution* [March 1957], which Kenneth Boulding edited) can be construed as game theory. At the time I composed them I didn't know enough game theory to appreciate that. The idea of commitment, whether to an unconditional or a conditional choice, can be construed as reducing selectively some of one's own payoffs in a matrix; a coordination problem can be portrayed as a matrix in which all the payoffs are zero except in a diagonal where they are all equal. According to the Nobel Committee, I must have been doing game theory without knowing it.

One result of my "Essay on Bargaining" was that people at the RAND Corporation saw it, and I was invited to spend summer 1957 at RAND. Several people at RAND were working on the theory and practice of "limited war"—that is, a non-all-out war—of which Korea was the outstanding example. I had already become interested, as my focal point article indicated even in its title. I left RAND thinking I'd do some work on the subject.

Then—fall 1957—R. Duncan Luce of the Harvard psychology department and Howard Raiffa of the Harvard Business School published *Games and Decisions*, and my education began. It was not only a superb introduction to game theory, it was a comprehensive survey of the subject. I spent at least a hundred hours over it—probably two hundred. I learned how to formulate most of what I was doing or wanted to do with the help of matrices. I had never published a matrix, never used a matrix to order my own thoughts. At last I had a versatile tool that could expand my capabilities.

Let me digress here with a comment I've often enjoyed making. I begin by posing the question, What is the greatest invention in all of mathematics? I answer, =. (The equals sign.) It supports the equation, which allows one to manipulate data in an orderly fashion, preserving the equality. What is the greatest invention in all of business history? Double-entry bookkeeping (the equivalent of an equals sign). What is the greatest invention of macroeconomics? National accounts—quadruple-entry bookkeeping. What is the greatest invention of game theory? The payoff matrix. These are all accounting frameworks. They allow an orderly presentation of quantitative data and a framework for manipulating the data. There would be no way to explore how many relations there could be between two parties without matrices, no way to identify all those situations in which it is an advantage to go first or second—situations in which one party, or both parties, or neither can usefully make a threat, or a promise, or when a threat will work only when coupled with a promise. I don't expect real game theorists or mathematicians to agree with me, but I like the concept of an "accounting framework," which the equation, or the matrix, or the double-entry, or quadruple-entry system is.

Armed with what I'd learned from Luce and Raiffa, I took my family to London from February to September 1958. There I enlarged on what I'd done in those two "game theory" articles, this time taking advantage of matrix notation. I was under the impression that the kind of game theory that I was doing was relevant to all kinds of situations that formal game theory was somewhat aloof from. I quote the introduction to what I produced during our stay in London.

On the strategy of pure conflict—the zero-sum games—*game theory* has yielded important insight and advice. But on the strategy of action where conflict is mixed with mutual dependence—the non-zero-sum games involved in wars and threats of war, strikes, negotiations, criminal deterrence, class war, race war, price war, and blackmail; maneuvering in a bureaucracy or in a traffic jam; and the coercion of one's own children—traditional game theory has not yielded comparable insight or advice. These are the "games" in which, though the element of conflict provides the dramatic interest, mutual dependence is part of the logical structure and demands some kind of collaboration or mutual accommodation—tacit, if not explicit—even if only in the avoidance of mutual disaster. These are also games in which, though secrecy may play a strategic role, there is some essential need for the signaling of intentions and the meeting of minds. Finally, they are games in which what one player *can* do to avert mutual damage affects what another player *will* do to avert it, so that it is not always an advantage to possess initiative, knowledge, or freedom of choice.

I went on to propose that we disaggregate non-zero-sum, recognizing that the coordination game was the limiting case opposite to the zero-sum, and that it might be called the zero-difference game, and we needed another name for those in which the conflict and common interest were embedded.

I actually had the temerity to subtitle my article, which appeared as a whole issue of the *Journal of Conflict Resolution*, "Prospectus for a Reorientation of Game Theory." With the exception of a few friends like Howard Raiffa, I don't think I converted any game theorist to my "reorientation," but in psychology, sociology, even anthropology, and political science, scholars tended to be comfortable with my kind of game theory.

I then spent a year at RAND, September 1958 to September 1959. I learned and produced a lot. It was my first introduction to classified information about nuclear weapons and my acquaintance with the foremost theorists on nuclear issues: Bernard Brodie, William Kaufmann, Albert Wohlstetter, and Herman Kahn. Wohlstetter had just finished his article, published the following January in *Foreign Affairs*, "The Delicate Balance of Terror," establishing the crucial criterion for a deterrent force—namely, that it be invulnerable to attack—and arguing that U.S. strategic forces were not. By fall 1958, Eisenhower and Khrushchev had agreed to an international conference on "Measures to Safeguard against Surprise Attack"; five Eastern and five Western nations were engaged, and the five Western—Canada, France, Germany, the United Kingdom, and the United States—met in Washington to prepare.

A U.S. team led by Jerome Wiesner (later President Kennedy's science adviser), and including Wohlstetter and me and two dozen outstanding scientists, assembled in Washington. By this time a high-level government committee had been meeting and had concluded—influenced by the Gaither Committee report of a year earlier—that the problem of surprise attack was *the* problem of nuclear war. Without the prospect of achieving surprise in an attack on the adversary's retaliatory capability, no initiation of war could be attractive.

During the six weeks of preparation—I did not follow the delegation to Geneva, since I had three small children in Santa Monica—I was asked to make a presentation. I had done a "Proposal for a Special Surveillance Force," and presented the idea that it made sense to have Soviet observers in Washington and at various U.S. military bases, and U.S.

observers in Moscow and at various military bases, who could reliably identify themselves on secure communication lines, and report such activities as evacuation of governments from capitals or the absence of such evacuations. At the time, everybody appeared to believe that such communication existed, and all I was proposing was people to use the communications. Three years later, I discovered that there were no such secure direct communications between Moscow and Washington; I'll come to that shortly.

It was during the six weeks prior to the Geneva conference that I wrote "Surprise Attack and Disarmament," the first article to identify publicly that arms control should have as its most urgent focus arrangements to preclude successful surprise attack. Paradoxically, that meant making strategic weapons, not people and economic assets, secure against attack. It was published in 1959 in the *Bulletin of the Atomic Scientists*, a major journal at the time concerned with nuclear dangers. This was probably the most valuable and influential pure-policy article I ever published.

Also at RAND I got an idea—it just sprang into my head while I was musing about something else—that I named "The Threat That Leaves Something to Chance." In my work on threats, I'd always argued that a threat required a commitment—a threat, I argued, was always painful or expensive to carry out, something the threatener would not be motivated to do, otherwise it was just a "warning"—and to allege that one would "probably" indulge in painful or expensive retaliation, as in "come one step closer and maybe I'll shoot you," left open the clear choice not to. But I saw, in this epiphany, that one could maneuver into a position in which there was a risk of mutual harm that was not altogether under one's control.

I use tailgating as an example. If somebody gets his front bumper eighteen inches from my rear bumper, he threatens to kill us both unless all goes well. He will surely use all his skill to make sure nothing goes awry, but at that short interval something can go wrong and we both suffer. The threat is "probabilistic." The same thing occurs when one "buzzes" an airplane to make it change course or land; one gets close enough that all one's skill cannot absolutely guarantee that nothing will go wrong. Later I used the example of President Kennedy's putting a navy quarantine around Cuba during the crisis of 1962: the Soviets knew that any military response carried some risk that though the last thing either party wanted was war, things might erupt into war that neither intended. I even argued that sometimes the purpose of initiating a crisis might be to create a situation that carried the risk of unintended expansion.

As my year at RAND closed, I put some of my work into a book. Submitted to the Harvard University Press, it was accepted (maybe because I was already on the Harvard faculty) and published in 1960. I called it *The Strategy of Conflict*, the same title I'd used for my journal-size article in the *Journal of Conflict Resolution*. It has had a good career, recently boosted by my Nobel Prize.

In September 1959, I joined Harvard, half in the Department of Economics, and half in the Center for International Affairs. At the center I taught, with Henry Kissinger, a seminar on foreign policy; in the department, I shared a seminar on international economics and taught a seminar on defense economics.

For several years, most of my research and publication was in nuclear arms control and weapons policy. In spring 1960, I presented a paper to a conference organized by the American Academy of Arts and Sciences, "Reciprocal Measures for Arms Stabilization," the first suggestion I know of that arms accommodation needn't be a matter of formal treaties. It was published in *Daedalus*, the organ of the academy (and I was agreeably surprised in 2005, when an anniversary issue was published with fourteen selections of the previous fifty years and my article was among them.) An example of "informal," or tacit, arms control was the Soviet response to the Kennedy-Johnson administration's insistence that NATO be prepared to defend without nuclear weapons. The Soviets denied, even ridiculed, the notion that any war in Europe could be anything but nuclear; simultaneously they invested hugely in "conventional" forces, especially aircraft, that would have been redundant, even useless, in a nuclear European war.

For summer 1960, the Twentieth Century Fund financed a "summer study" of arms control. Some twenty of us spent two months at a resort owned by MIT; another twenty showed up for a day or a week. I had earlier visited Yale and met a graduate student, Morton Halperin, who so impressed me that I offered to finance his dissertation for a couple of years at the Harvard Center; I then suggested he join the summer study as rapporteur, and he did. At the end of the summer he and I decided to write a book together, reflecting the consensus that the group had reached.

Meanwhile, the MIT Center for International Studies and the Harvard Center for International Affairs had organized a joint center on arms control that met every three weeks for dinner and discussion. Halperin and I managed to write enough to provide a chapter at just about every meeting, for discussion and criticism. By December, we had a book that had been thoroughly discussed by a select group of academics (and a few non-academics), and the Twentieth Century Fund arranged for a printer to do a six-week printing job, and we had copies just about the time that John F. Kennedy was inaugurated. The fund gave us something like a hundred copies, which we circulated within the federal government.

Meanwhile, McGeorge Bundy of Harvard, who had been in our arms control group, had become national security adviser to the president; Jerome Wiesner, a member of the group, had become the White House science adviser; Walt Rostow, a member, had become assistant secretary of state for policy planning; Henry Rowen became deputy assistant secretary of defense for international security—he was a RAND colleague whom I had attracted to Harvard; Abram Chayes of Harvard Law School, another member of our group, became general counsel to the Department of State; John McNaughton of Harvard Law School became, at my suggestion, deputy assistant secretary of defense for arms control, and though he'd not been a member of the group, he knew us all and had the little Schelling–Halperin book to bring him up to date. As you can see, this was quite a potentially influential group, all of whom had been part of a study group on arms control.

In 1961, John J. McCloy was named the White House adviser on disarmament. He set up eight committees; I was named chairman of one on "War by Accident, Miscalculation, and Surprise." We were the only one of the eight committees concerned with how war might happen and what might be done to prevent it. We made several recommendations, of which one was destined to become famous. It was here that I learned that there was no provision for any reliable contact between the president and the Kremlin. At a time when I could direct dial my mother three thousand miles away to wish her happy birthday, Kennedy had no way to get in touch with Khrushchev.

We recommended what later become known as the "hotline." Henry Owen, a member of my committee, was in the Department of State and resolved to make the hotline happen. Eventually he persuaded Soviet diplomats that the hotline was their idea, and so it came about. Finally, in 1963, Cyrillic alphabet teletypewriters were delivered to the Department of State and Department of Defense with direct land-line connection to their counterparts in the Kremlin, and every day something like "the quick red fox jumped over the lazy dog" got transmitted in both directions to make sure everything was working.

Here I interject a brief note. In 1959, I was persuaded to write an article on the subject of "accidental war," with the suggestion that I introduce it with a review of recent fictional accounts of nuclear war. I did, and reviewed *On the Beach* by Nevil Shute, *Alas Babylon* by Pat Frank, and *Red Alert* by Peter Bryant. I was so impressed by the latter as superior to any professional analysis I'd seen that when Stanley Kubrick saw my article reprinted in the *Observer* of London, he approached the author, whose real name was Peter George, and brought him to the States to do a screenplay. They spent an afternoon and evening with me, trying to bring the story into the missile age—there were no missiles in the original *Red Alert*, published in 1958—and in the end, Kubrick decided to do it as a "nightmare fantasy" and called it *Dr. Strangelove.*

In spring 1961 Lincoln Bloomfield, with whom I had established the Harvard-MIT arms control seminar, and I invented a new kind of game. There had been a few foreign-policy games, at RAND and elsewhere, usually with individuals playing "roles"—that is, secretary of state (foreign minister) or defense, senator, etc. We composed two teams, a blue (U.S.) team and a red (USSR) team, with no role-playing. The whole team was responsible for reaching decisions, and both were instructed not to second-guess what a U.S. or USSR leader or government would do, but to attempt to reach the best possible outcome for the United States or the Soviet Union.

Each team was given a "scenario" that presented a crisis at a date in the near future—near future so that teams didn't need to be given hypothetical future events—and was to produce a decision document indicating what actions it would take immediately or in response to what the other side did. A "control" team then matched the decisions of the two teams, and extrapolated the scenario to take account of what they had indicated they would do unconditionally or conditional on the other team's actions. They were given this extrapolation, and repeated the process. And again. It went on for two days, fifteen hours a day, and usually there were four or five iterations. The control team made a final extrapolation, and all three teams conducted a postmortem examination.

We experimented in Cambridge, Massachusetts, with a crisis involving a Soviet invasion of Iran, and all the participants were enthusiastic. Later, on the fourth of July, I was in Washington on my way to RAND for the summer and had dinner at the home of Charles Hitch, who had been my host at RAND earlier and was now the senior assistant secretary of defense. The other guest was Walt Rostow, who had headed the control team of that Iran game in Cambridge. We talked about it, and Hitch and Rostow suggested that instead of going to RAND for the summer, I should stay in Washington and develop a game involving Berlin, which was currently the crisis de jour. I said I was committed for the summer, but I'd spend it at RAND developing a "Berlin game."

At RAND, I recruited Allen R. Ferguson to be my partner in developing the scenario for a Berlin game. We recruited a blue and a red team from RAND personnel, Ferguson and I were the control team, and we ran the game for a sequence of four or five iterations. Everybody judged the game a success—"success" measured in how much he or she had learned about crisis management. So in September Ferguson and I told my good friend Harry Rowen, deputy assistant secretary of defense for international security, that we were ready for the real event.

Teams were recruited from the Department of State, the Department of Defense, the CIA, the Department of the Treasury, and the White House, and included my Harvard colleague Henry Kissinger; we all went to Camp David for a long weekend; everyone got thoroughly engaged. At the postmortem, the red and blue teams were astonished at how poorly they had "read" each other's actions and intentions. The misunderstandings were especially impressive because they were not Russians and Americans misreading each other but real-live Americans of similar backgrounds.

The players went back to their agencies with enthusiastic reports, and the game was replayed two weeks later with the same scenario and different personnel. Again the players were impressed with what they learned, especially about how preoccupied both sides were with what they thought they were "signaling" about their intentions. In both those games, the crisis tended to subside, and the control team had to invent some irritants to keep the game going.

Ferguson and I had thought that a major concern of both the red and blue teams would be strategic nuclear forces. We had even consulted two generals from the Strategic Air Command about plans for dispersal in a crisis or how to respond to ambiguous warnings of a Soviet attack. But in none of the games did strategic forces ever play a role. And as I mentioned, crises tended to peter out unless the control team introduced some stimulus.

That last point intrigued me, and I believe I can explain it. Usually a team, blue or red (i.e., Americans playing Americans, or Americans playing Russians), contained a variety of opinions on what to do, how aggressively to behave, and how violently to react to what the other side was doing. The decision, embedded in the team's document forwarded to the control team, was invariably a compromise between the more and the less aggressive or assertive members. (Each team had seven members.) And the compromise took a particular form: do immediately and unconditionally the milder actions under discussion, and be ready to escalate dramatically if the other side becomes too aggressive. The result was that what each side saw was the immediate actions, the milder actions; they didn't see what the other side had in reserve. Each felt that its decisions were a combination of milder and stronger actions, without realizing that the other side would see only the milder part of the mix. As both sides displayed the mild responses, with the more violent kept in reserve, each side found the opponent to be less aggressive than the opponent felt. The interaction was thus to ease the crisis. In the postmortem, each team felt its resolve had been underestimated by the other side.

I conducted half a dozen such games. After the first one was reported a success it was easy to recruit high-level players, usually at the assistant secretary level. The last game I conducted involved four simultaneous crises in Africa and Latin America. The participants included the chairman of the Joint Chiefs of Staff, the commandant of the Marine Corps, the director of the Budget of the United States, the attorney general of the United States, and comparably senior people from the Department of State and the CIA. When it was over Robert Kennedy, the attorney general, thought we might use the format for exploring racial crises, especially desegregation crises at schools and universities, and promised to talk to his brother about it. That was Halloween 1963; three weeks later the president was assassinated, and Robert Kennedy's plan fell through.

During the 1960s, nearly all my work was on nuclear weapons policy. I was invited to offer a seminar series at the Institute for Defense Analyses in Washington, DC, and gave eleven weekly lectures that after an eight-month sojourn at the Institute for Strategic Studies in London, became a book, *Arms and Influence*, published by Yale University Press in 1966. I began the preface as follows:

One of the lamentable principles of human productivity is that it is easier to destroy than to create. A house that takes several man-years to build can be burned in an hour by any young delinquent who has the price of a box of matches. Poisoning dogs is cheaper than raising them. And a country can destroy more with twenty billion dollars of nuclear armament than it can create with twenty billion dollars of foreign investment. The harm that people can do, or that nations can do, is impressive. And it is often used to impress.

The book has had a good career, still selling after forty years, and a handsome Chinese edition appeared in 2007 from the Military History and Translation Division of the Ministry of National Defense, Taipei. Some of the chapters are "The Art of Commitment," "The Manipulation of Risk," "The Idiom of Military Action," and "The Dynamics of Mutual Alarm."

In May 1970, on the U.S. invasion of Cambodia, I led a group of Harvard faculty to call on our former colleague in the White House, Henry Kissinger, to declare our loss of confidence in President Nixon's conduct of the war and our cessation of relations. My interests took a turn to other subjects.

One was racial segregation. I was invited to spend a summer at RAND to produce a chapter for a book on racial discrimination. I investigated the concept of "tipping point" in a chapter, "A Process of Residential Segregation: Neighborhood Tipping," published in 1972 in Anthony Pascal's *Discrimination in Economic Life*. I also toyed with the idea that people might, with very little preference for being among their own kind—racially, linguistically, by rank, by gender, by income class—choose neighbors in a way that could lead to severe segregation, much more than met any needs for "like" neighbors. I boarded a plane without anything to read and began experimenting.

I made a line of pluses and zeros that I somehow "randomized," and postulated that every plus wanted at least half its neighbors pluses, and the same for zeros, and would move to the nearest place that satisfied. The results began to look interesting, and when I got home I experimented with copper and zinc pennies from my son's coin collection, and the results astonished me. A line of coppers and zincs that looks like this:

0+000++0+00++00+++0++0++00++00++00++0+0+00+++0++00000+++
000+00++0+0++0,

when each wants at least four of its eight nearest neighbors to be like oneself, becomes:

00000000+++++++++++++++0000000000+++++++++++++++00000000
00000000++++++.

I then tried a sixteen by sixteen checkerboard with a fifth of the spaces blank (to make movement possible), and placed the zincs and coppers at random, provided them with different motives—how many like themselves among the eight nearest neighbors—and varied the population sizes of zincs and coppers, and with my twelve-year-old son moved pennies until all were satisfied (or until all were as satisfied as the board allowed). I soon realized that I was doing unskilled labor unnecessarily and got a student to teach me Basic; I could then try all kinds of alternative hypotheses, including a desire for neighbors unlike oneself.

The results were fairly striking. I published "Dynamic Models of Segregation" in the first issue of the *Journal of Mathematical Sociology* in 1971, and an abbreviated version (using an eight by eight board for typographic convenience) in my 1978 book *Micromotives and Macrobehavior*. An unexpected consequence was that as I learned about twenty-five years later, I was a pioneer in what became known as agent-based computational modeling.

I concluded that I was fortunate not to know anything about computers when I started this; doing it by hand, I saw processes revealing themselves in a way I could not have seen with the computers of those days, which could compute outcomes but not display the dynamics. (I had an agreeable experience on receiving an honorary degree from Erasmus University, Rotterdam, in 2003. My sponsor, Maarten Janssen, in his seven-minute presentation, had on the screen behind him my eight by eight board with red and green "individuals" who took just seven minutes to migrate into a segregated outcome.)

One chapter in my 1978 book was motivated by my mother's experience in a retirement home. The home, which was reserved for naval and marine officers and their spouses, opened with a good spread of ages; I believe the management, which had plentiful applications, selected with a view to "diversity." But every year every resident grew a year older, unless he or she died, or went into a nursing home elsewhere. To keep a decent age gradient, it was necessary to attract new residents at the lower age level—around sixty or sixty-five. Younger residents were helpful; they had cars, and could drive people to church or the hairdresser. Many younger prospective residents found the place so attractive that they resolved to come back when they reached seventy or so. But when they came back the population had aged and didn't look so attractive. Management thus had a problem; they eventually solved it skillfully, but I mention all this as what got me interested in segregation on what I called a "continuous variable," such as age, income, size, skill, or rank, in contrast to discrete variables like race, language, or gender.

So I built models and found that many organizations had problems comparable to my mother's retirement home. Bridge clubs, tennis clubs, study groups, self-improvement groups, and dining clubs—all were subject to adverse selection that might cause the group progressively to dissolve.

I also, in that 1978 book, developed a diagrammatic analysis of binary choices among large groups of individuals, beginning with the "multiperson prisoners' dilemma" and embedding that in a large set of situations, some of which shared with the multi-person prisoners' dilemma a unique inferior equilibrium, some with happy equilibriums, some with two equilibriums, and eventually a total of some eleven different multiperson binary choice situations. I worked hard at it and was pleased with the results.

The question arises, was that book, *Micromotives and Macrobehavior*, game theory? If so, what makes it game theory?

I didn't think so at the time—it just didn't occur to me—but there were hints in the Nobel Committee's remarks that the committee thought it was. And I see now that everything in that book had to do with individuals' adjustment to or anticipation of the choices of others, and with needs and opportunities for coordination, formal cooperation, or submission to direction or regulation. I included one of my earliest observations:

The man who invented traffic signals had a genius for simplicity. He saw that where two streets intersected there was confusion and lost time because people got in each other's way; and he discovered, probably by personal experience, that self-discipline and goodwill among travelers was not enough to straighten them out. Even the courteous lost time waiting for each other. And some who mistakenly thought it was their turn suffered collision.

With magnificent simplicity he divided all travelers into two groups, those moving east-west and those moving north-south. He put the traffic into an alternating pattern. Nobody needed tickets, or schedules, or reservations to cross the intersection. All necessary instructions could be reduced to a binary code in red and green lights; all travelers within the scope of the plan could see the signals; and a single alternating mechanism could activate both sets of lights. There was no need to plan the day in advance; neither the lights nor the travelers needed to be synchronized with any other activity. Nor was there need for enforcement: once travelers got used to the lights, they learned that it was dangerous to cross against the flow of traffic that was proceeding with confidence. The lights created the kind of order in which non-compliance carried its own penalty. And there was impartial justice in the way the lights worked: unable to recognize individual travelers, the lights could hurt no one's feelings by not granting favoritism.

I've now concluded that this is game theory. Game theory, I find (or choose to define), is very much about *situations*. What is "prisoners' dilemma" but a situation? The logic of choice is central to game theory, but what game theory—again, I'm thinking about the invention of matrices—is often critical for is identifying situations in which choice is somehow puzzling, problematic, or challenging, and in identifying how many distinct situations of a certain kind there may be.

Let me give an example. In the early 1970s, I participated in a twoweek seminar on arms control in Aspen, Colorado. My contribution was to examine "the different motives that can lead two countries to bargain about armaments." I wanted to classify the alternative preferences about possession or non-possession of weapons that arms bargainers could have, and see what kinds of bargains were compatible with different preferences, what understandings and misunderstandings were likely, what the role of ignorance or deception might be, and what bargains might need what kind of enforcement.

I ignored, for simplicity, differences within governments and imputed to each of two governments a strict preference order; I considered only binary choices—to have or not to have the particular weapon (e.g., ABM, biological weapons, weapons in space)—and excluded consideration of capabilities that each might prefer the other to have (such as secure control over weapons, or false-alarm-free warning systems), and considered only weapons that each preferred the other *not* to have. This simplified formulation allowed all possibilities to be contained in a 2 × 2 matrix:

| | | Chooses Column | | |
		Have	Not	
	Have :	a :	c :
Chooses Row		: A	: B	:
	Not :	b :	d :
		: C	: D	:

The payoffs to row are the capital letters, and those to column the lowercase. We can think of the letters as representing four ordinal numbers, say four (best), three (next best), two (third best), and one (least favored). The only restriction on how we place the four numbers—four, three, two, and one—for each of the two parties is that: $B > A$, $D > C$, $b > a$, and $d > c$—that is, that whether one side has it or not, it prefers the other not to. With that restriction we have six configurations of payoffs for row, six for column, and thirty-six possible matrices. They correspond to:

1. We want it whether or not you have it, and prefer *both* have it to *neither* have it

2. We want it whether or not you have it, and prefer *neither* have it to *both* have it

3. We want it if, and only if, you *have* it

4. We want it if, and only, if you *do not have* it

5. We do not want it whether or not you have it, but prefer, *if one* has it, that it be *we*

6. We do not want it whether or not you have it, but prefer, *if one* has it, that it be *you*

I then eliminated four, and combined five and six. I could dream up a weapon to which four might apply, but it is far-fetched; and with four eliminated, the difference between five and six was of no consequence. I gave them names: two I called "YES"; one was "YES!," three was IFF; and five and six consolidated were simply "NO." (Note that YES! means we want it so badly we wouldn't trade it away; YES without the exclamation mark means we want it whether or not you have it, but would prefer we both abstain—probably what people most often have in mind for arms control.)

That left four configurations for each party, or sixteen combinations. Of the sixteen, four are symmetrical. I then considered all sixteen, whether any bargain could be in the joint interest, whether a bargain had to be enforceable, whether a bargain was unnecessary, whether it made a difference if a second weapon was brought into consideration (making either a trade or a coercive choice possible), what misunderstandings could arise to make a bargain unachievable, what commitments might be incurred (e.g., by legislation), and how "bargaining chips" might be useful or mischievous.

I've gone into some detail in order to demonstrate what I mean by game theory having to do with the analysis of situations, and how matrices can be essential to any exhaustive exploration of those situations. An ironic footnote here is that the essay I produced was being published by a journal, which shall be nameless, the editor of which insisted I delete all the matrices. I said nobody could follow the argument without the matrices; he said he'd rather have his subscribers perplexed than intimidated. Out they went, but I shortly published the comprehensible version elsewhere. (It is in my 1984 book, if your interest is arms control as well as game theory.)

Pursuing the idea that my interests were often exogenous, I could mention that I was invited by someone I hadn't known to participate in the 1967 President's Commission on Law Enforcement and the Administration of Justice. The thought was that my experience with "deterrence theory" would make me valuable to the Internal Revenue Service. I got side-tracked into "organized crime," became fascinated—a couple of congressional committees had recently held intensive hearings on the subject—and wrote a report that led to two publications (both in my 1984 book). For several years, I was regularly invited to the annual convention of chiefs of police.

In 1966, I was invited to contribute a chapter to a Brookings Institution book on public expenditure; my topic was how to value lives. I had earlier had an air force Ph.D. student who did his dissertation on government evaluation of lifesaving—for example, when the pilot should bail out to save himself, and when to try to land to save the expensive aircraft. The topic had been my idea, and maybe somebody knew of my interest. Anyway, I wrote what I think was the first notion that lifesaving, in the form of modest reductions in risk to people's lives, might well be valued by how they would respond to opportunities to pay for reductions in risk to their own lives. This has always been controversial: Is a poor person's life worth less than a rich person's? My answer was "yes," if the issue were to require the poor person to pay for the same lifesaving as a rich person would willingly pay for, or to offer the poor person an increment of life safety at public expense when he'd rather have something else. It's still controversial.

Finally, climate change has occupied me for almost thirty years. I answered the phone in 1980, and was asked whether I would receive a delegate from the National Academy of Sciences who wished to recruit me to chair a committee on global warming and climate change. I said I'd heard of the subject but knew nothing; he said he'd like to come talk to me anyhow and buy me a drink. I said OK; he flew up from Washington with a senior staff person; I had my drink and said, again, that I knew little. He said all that was known I could learn in the six weeks before the committee could meet and he'd provide knowledgeable people to teach me. I said OK, spent some weeks learning what there was, had a great committee, and produced a report.

This issue was that President Carter was scheduled to attend a "summit" in Venice, and the German chancellor had put "the carbon dioxide problem" on the agenda. The White House asked the National Academy of Sciences to give a quick answer as to what to do about that item on the agenda. My committee recommended, sensibly, that the thing to do was to get it off the agenda, that the U.S. government was not ready to face the issue.

Congress then passed a resolution asking the National Academy of Sciences for a major assessment of the carbon issue, mainly because the president's program for coal-based liquid fuel would produce a highly carbon-intensive product. Because I'd done something already on the subject, I was naturally on the new committee, which—rather like my experience with drugs on that earlier committee—contained experts in fifteen pertinent scientific fields and one amateur, me. Two years later, I was about the best-educated amateur in the country; I wrote the chapter on the policy and welfare implications of climate change, and from then on never managed to drop the subject. My latest book reproduces three of my many publications on the issue of climate change.

I trust I've demonstrated what I said on my first page: how much of my career, indeed my intellectual life, has been determined by opportunities unexpected and suggestions unsolicited.

I'll close with two observations—one about game theory, and one about policy.

Game theory is usually defined as concerned with how individuals should choose rationally in situations in which the optimal choice for each depends on the choice of another or the choices of others. I have been, I believe, more concerned with how to select a behavior that will *influence* another or others—how to influence others by constraining their expectation of how oneself will act. This has led me to consider the institutional, legal, cultural, sometimes physical circumstances that make it possible to commit and reliably signal promises, threats, negotiating positions, and other kinds of commitments, and to appreciate when inability or disability, even deliberately incurred, may induce the favorable behavior of others. This is still game theory, but with a different slant.

My final observation is that one of my favorite applications of a focal point was in an appendix to my 1960 book. That appendix considered what constraints or restrictions on the use of nuclear weapons might ever become appealing, or compelling, and it concluded, via focal point analysis, with an analogy to the non-use of gas in the Second World War, that the only constraint likely to be stable would be absolute non-use. During the Eisenhower administration, both the president and his secretary of state repeatedly spoke of the "taboo" against the use of nuclear weapons, and the need to "break down this false distinction" (between nuclear and other weapons.) The official U.S. position was that nuclear weapons "must now be treated as in fact having become conventional."

In contrast, President Johnson in 1964, when asked about nuclear weapons in relation to Vietnam, said, "Make no mistake. There is no such thing as a conventional nuclear weapon. For nineteen peril-filled years no nation has loosed the atom against another. To do so now is a political decision of the highest order." The taboo survived the Korean War, the war in Vietnam, the war in the Falklands, the Yom Kippur War of 1973, and the hugely demoralizing war of the Soviet Union in Afghanistan. In each case, one party in the war had nuclear weapons.

For more than sixty years, since August 1945, no nuclear weapon has been used in conflict. My current interest, in the second half of my eighties, is to encourage appreciation of the value of that taboo for the next sixty years. That was the subject of my Stockholm lecture in honor of Alfred Nobel.

Thomas C. Schelling
Awarded Nobel Prize in 2005. Lecture presented April 18, 2007.

Date of Birth
April 14, 1921

Academic Degrees
A.B., Economics, University of California at Berkeley, 1944
Ph.D., Economics, Harvard University, 1951

Academic Affiliations
Associate Professor of Economics, Yale University, 1953–57
Professor of Economics, Yale University, 1957–58
Professor of Economics, Harvard University, 1958–90
Professor of Economics, John F. Kennedy School of Government, Harvard
    University, 1969–90
Distinguished University Professor, Department of Economics and School
    of Public Affairs, University of Maryland, 1990–2005
Lucius N. Littauer Professor of Political Economy, Emeritus, Harvard
    University, 1990–present
Distinguished University Professor, Emeritus, Department of Economics
    and School of Public Affairs, University of Maryland, 2005–present

Selected Books
National Income Behavior, 1951
International Economics, 1958
The Strategy of Conflict, 1960
Strategy and Arms Control, 1961 (with M. Halperin)
Arms and Influence, 1966
Micromotives and Macrobehavior, 1978
Thinking through the Energy Problem, 1979
Choice and Consequence, 1984
Strategies of Commitment and Other Essays, 2006

Edmund S. Phelps

Amid the "Theory Wars" in Twentieth-Century Economics

Any account of my evolution as an economist must narrate my early struggle to depart from the scientism and determinism of the neo-Keynesian school—repairing as best I could their omission of expectations, learning, and knowledge creation—only to find myself bypassed by a new classical school founded on a belief in "rational expectations." In the next decades, I struggled against the scientism and determinism of the new classical school—emphasizing their omission of Knightian uncertainty, Keynesian indeterminacy, and Hayekian discovery. Then I was rescued by fervent supporters and an august body from domination by the neo-neoclassicals, and am called "revolutionary." This biography will be tightly focused on that story line.[1] It is, I would say, a part of the story of twentieth-century economics.

Background

When I was a student of economics—from my first course in economics at Amherst College in fall 1952 to my doctorate at Yale in spring 1959—I could see that some fundamental departures in economic theory had taken place in the interwar years of the twentieth century. I sometimes went into the stacks of the library at Amherst to watch the sparks fly in the debates between Friedrich Hayek and John Maynard Keynes in the early 1930s. They were the pioneering architects of a modernist economic theory. Frank Knight, in his 1921 book *Risk, Uncertainty, and Profit*, had argued that what we now call *Knightian uncertainty* was endemic in market economies—a kind of uncertainty in which we *do not know* the quantitative probabilities to attach to each of the known contingencies or even what all the possible contingencies are. The same year,

Keynes in his *A Treatise on Probability* sought to model aspects of how a rational person responds to such uncertainties. But it was Hayek, from his *Monetary Theory and the Trade Cycle* (1928; Eng. ed., 1933) to *The Pure Theory of Capital* (1941), and Keynes, with his *The General Theory of Employment, Interest, and Money* (1936), who began a movement to take account of Knightian uncertainties in macroeconomic models of investment and employment.

I noticed that both Hayek and Keynes showed awareness of *incomplete information* in real-life market economies. Keynes pointed out the "uncoordinated" character of decisions in real-life market economies. Hayek had the vision that in advanced economies and especially creative ones, where novelty and evolution are occurring, each manager and employee possesses little "information" about how the myriad goods are produced (i.e., the formulas), and what the cost of producing each would be. Their information is mostly specialized to one or a very few products. Hayek makes the process of "coordination" of these participants' individual activities in the face of such *private information* a cornerstone of his theory.

I also noticed that both Hayek and Keynes brought *imperfect knowledge* into their models—an even more radical step. Hayek built on the idea that faced with uncertainty, producers and investors may make mistakes in the directions of their investments, with consequences for both employment and growth. (Later, in the 1960s, he built on the uncertainty faced by innovators about the reception of prospective users to a new product or new method.) Keynes in the same decade built on the idea that the visions of entrepreneurs are unobservable, and even if they were observed, entrepreneurs' responses would not be subject to a known probability distribution. Keynes's reference to the "animal spirits" of entrepreneurs conveys the thought that entrepreneurs may exhibit spontaneity and perhaps innovativeness in their investment decisions. Entrepreneurs might take their cue from share prices, but the stock market was flakier than entrepreneurs, basing its current valuations on some fashionable but "flimsy" notion of what was driving the economy, and what would be the next thing.

But by the end of the 1950s, I saw signs of a retreat from this modernism. One sign was that the animal spirits driving investment demand were banished as a source of instability in the Keynesian system. James Tobin in 1955 built a neo-Keynesian model in which investment demand is a sort of residual, not a causal force: if consumption demand should drop, some of the employed move over to producing more of the capital goods; the market for houses and other capital goods willingly buys the additional output. If they were not to do so, interest rates would sag and the prices bid for capital goods would lift up above the opportunity cost of their production, leaving opportunities for a pure profit—a free lunch—by producing capital goods at an infinite rate. (This was the "Q-theory of investment.") Succeeding models provided for rising marginal costs in the capital goods industries. If prospects dimmed for future profits from new investments, the valuations put on having additional units of the capital good would drop, which would reduce production activity and employment in the capital goods sector. Thus, the animal spirits were caged and tamed. Autonomous individuals acting on their individual insights, hunches, and originality could not be a prime mover, sparking fluctuations. It was only changes in *fundamentals*, such as changes in prospects for future profit, which could drive movements in investment activity.

Neo-Keynesians next dissented on the matter of the average money wage. In Keynes's thinking, the wage possessed an element of indeterminacy—it could, for example, hang too high for a time or go into a shuddering descent. Yet the short-run models by John Hicks and Paul Samuelson in 1939 (and the latter's influential 1948 text *Economics*) went so far as to treat the money wage as a constant. A modification by A. W. Phillips in 1957 hypothesized a stable relationship between the rate of wage inflation and the level of unemployment, to be dubbed the Phillips curve by Samuelson and Robert Solow. This had the implication in the Keynesian model that the wage level would gradually adjust to a shift of "aggregate demand" until it had forced the resulting unemployment rate back to its long-run resting place. (So if investment demand is weakened, interest rates must drop as required to prop it back in order to restore [un]employment.) Thus, there exists in this model an equilibrium level—in the expectational sense—that is determinate, being determined by the height of the Phillips curve.

Almost the last remaining entry point for uncertainty was closed in the 1955 growth model by Solow. The basic model offered insights into the effects of slower population growth, but economists took greater interest in extended versions of the model showing effects of slower technical progress. Although it is doubtful it was Solow's purpose, the growth model described the complete determination of the economy's path over the indefinite future: the course of the capital stock, output, consumption, and the corresponding wage and interest rates. This is all driven by a "forcing function" that takes the course of technical progress to be exogenous to the economy, to be free of Knightian uncertainty, and to be known by all participants when they make their decisions. (It is true that one could ask the model what the implications are of a change from one path of technical progress to another. But do the prevailing expectations for technical progress change the same way? Where are the uncertainties in any real-life generation and implementation of technical progress?)

Putting People In

It was with this background that I began my career in economic research. Of course, I did not see immediately or simultaneously all or even most of the things that were unsatisfactory about this new development in economic theory. But having read Hayek's *Prices and Production* (2nd ed., 1935) and Keynes's *General Theory*, I could sense that the neo-Keynesian research, though intriguing and possibly useful in some ways, had utterly abandoned the modernist emphasis on incomplete information and imperfect knowledge in favor of some new method or methodology with which I was not at all comfortable. Instinctively, as Keynes would have said, I understood that the neo-Keynesian models, in abstracting from these things, inadvertently left no role for humans to play. There could be no beliefs as distinct from what is true, no expectations as distinct from what is or will be, no mental stimulation and challenge, no problem solving, no creativity, and no discovery. I remember having a good laugh when Robert Summers, my first statistics teacher at Yale, told the anecdote, which may be apocryphal, of the earnest young student reaction to the formal model the lecturer had just laid out: "But sir, where are the *people* in that model?"

My first efforts to put "people" into the models lay in the area of productivity growth. At Amherst, I had heard more than once the motto that education teaches us to learn. (The thesis, which referred to college education, is associated with Alexander Micklejohn, who was in fact president of Amherst College for a time in the 1920s.) So on hearing my friend and Yale colleague Richard Nelson arguing one day that a farmer would be better able to learn which fertilizer is best for him if he had a college education—I thought of Micklejohn, and of my mother's brothers and sisters who ran the family farm in downstate Illinois, all of whom had gone to college. When I proposed an algebraic model different from Nelson's, he kindly invited me on board to do another version with him. (But he refused to scrap his own model.) My idea was that the best-practice technology in a country would approximate to the best-feasible technology at a *faster rate* the higher the proportion of the economy's participants having a college degree. This proposition has stimulated volumes of research, with a certain amount of confusion (possibly extending to me).

Next, I aimed to develop a model in which technical progress does not occur exogenously at the hands of explorers and scientists who do it without regard for costs and possible revenues. Technical advances require people. In the view I took for the sake of simplicity, it requires technical researchers (and only them). This model too yielded some refreshing results. It turned out that according to the model, the explosion of the population in the nineteenth century must have had something to do with the burst of technical progress from 1870 to 1940. I want to add that this framework is still too narrow, since it overlooks the creation of commercial ideas by businesspeople. (It is commonly said that the big new ideas come from technical people, while the little, "incremental" ideas come from businesspeople, of whom there are a huge number. But I am not persuaded that science generates the preponderance of big ideas and business the little ones.)

I thought these two papers were big steps away from the mechanical approach of the Solow model. That does not mean, though, that we cannot find promising ideas in the Solow model; it does mean that we can develop and work with richer models in which some real-world aspects of the innovation process are present.

My next efforts to put people into models lay in the area of employment and inflation dynamics. For me, the Phillips curve could be neither theoretically acceptable nor empirically reliable, since it took no account whatsoever of what may happen to various *expectations* when monetary policy or a banking development pushes up or pulls down the inflation rate. My 1967 paper arguing that "disinflation" requires the monetary authority to drive down "expectations" of inflation, and my 1968 paper on "money-wage dynamics" and "labor-market equilibrium," were the seminal papers out of which the others sprung. My 1969 paper outlining my "islands parable" had an important influence—too much in some respect, as it took attention away from the incentive-wage theory developed in the 1968 paper. The *Microeconomic Foundations* volume of 1970 signaled the arrival of a micro-macro movement in economics.

Return of the Determinists and Rationalists

The heading for this section recalls the panicky titles of the old horror movies. In fact, it has been a little frightening and not a little disheartening to see virtually the entire economics profession rushing to embrace the rational expectation axiom of neo-neoclassical economics like lemmings in a suicidal jump into the sea.

At Carnegie Mellon, just after giving a paper, I met for the first time Jack Muth, who told me of his paper on what he called "rational expectations." Of course I was intrigued by it. In my 1966 book *Fiscal Neutrality* I had explored the case of "perfect foresight" (rational expectations without any probabilistic element), though with skepticism and not exclusively. I collaborated with John Taylor on a 1977 paper in which rational expectations were used, and I adopted the premise again in my 1978 paper on "disinflation without recession." It was intellectually interesting—even fun. I still think back once in a while to some theoretical results I obtained with rational expectations.

I want to add that the probabilistic aspect that the neo-neoclassicals introduced added to understanding, with or without the rational expectations. My theory implied that, say, employment bulges during a war because wages do not go up enough to prevent it, since wage setters are slow to realize that wages at their competitors have increased as fast as their own. The probabilistic models implied that wages do not go up enough because wage setters take the probability that the war will go on at least another period to be less than one. (This is related to Milton Friedman's distinction between temporary and permanent disturbances.) The rational expectations premise carried the idea to an extreme, implying that the *expected value* of employment in the upcoming period, after wages are set, is equal to the *natural* level (or if there are hiring costs, some natural path back to the medium-term natural level).

But the theory of rational expectations—the idea that the knowledge of every participant about how the economy works could with some generality have converged to something that is complete and right, at least roughly so—seemed surrealistic to me and likely to be dangerously wrong in some contexts. I kept in mind my 1959 doctoral dissertation in which I pointed out that to test a hypothesis statistically, we have to specify one or more auxiliary hypotheses; you can't test in a vacuum, with no model whatsoever. If one or more of the latter are bad hypotheses, we may obtain statistical results that cause us to accept the hypothesis when in truth it is false; it would have been rejected had we embedded it in entirely correct auxiliary hypotheses. Some of the "knowledge" we think we have is a "house of cards" that will collapse if and when the right statistical test is performed. (I would add that Roman Frydman published in 1981 a paper with a formal argument that the individuals in a market economy will not tend to converge to one model: if perchance they had all been following one model, individuals, one after another, would sooner or later try out departures from that prevailing model— even if it were the right model by some miracle. Another discussion of the fallibility of human knowledge appears in a 1986 paper by James Heckman and Richard Robb.)[2]

In the 1981 conference that Roman Frydman and I organized, and the ensuing 1983 conference volume *Rational Expectations Re-examined: Individual Forecasting and Aggregate Outcomes*, my paper started from the point that a participant in the economy will not adopt the "rational expectation" derivable from the model to which he or she subscribes if it is believed that most or all of the others in the economy are basing their expectations on a different model. It is only in very special cases, I have found, that the models converge to one model after some amount of evidence has been observed.

So I conclude that rational expectations are not rational at all.

My Structuralist Models

With my 1994 book *Structural Slumps*, which developed out of *The Slump in Europe*, which Jean-Paul Fitoussi and I published in 1988, I may seem to have overcome my distrust of so-called rational expectations. After a shift in the parameters of the model—a structural shift—I suppose that the economy follows a "perfect-foresight path" until the next structural shift comes along. This looks like rational expectations but it is not. In the rational expectations methodology, there are a given set of possible "regimes," and there is a probability of each regime that is known to all participants. So from time to time, the economy jumps from one regime to another according to some matrix of transition probabilities. In such a model, people constantly give proper weight to the possibility that at any time, the economy may move on to another of the other designated regimes. What I had in mind was something different: after a regime is over, it will never be revisited, and people have no idea what the next structural shift might be like. Business life is just one damned thing after another.

In the 1990s, work with Hian Teck Hoon and Gylfi Zoega, who had done so much to get *Structural Slumps* off the ground, developed fully an idea that may not have been entirely persuasive in that book or the earlier Fitoussi-Phelps book. The proposition was that an increase of, say, investment demand, in causing a real exchange rate depreciation overseas, would offer firms selling abroad greater protection from import competition, and thus lead them into the temptation to contract their output supply to domestic customers, and therefore to drive up their profit margins and contract their employment. This result provided the useful lesson that different macro models often have opposite implications: the Keynesian model predicting expansion as a result of the depreciation, and the structuralist model predicting contraction to result. Practitioners must have a wide range of models under their belt in order to appreciate the richness of possibilities and view their situation with the appropriate uncertainty.

The Costs of Neo-neoclassicism

You may question whether, in fact, the long dominance of neo-neoclassical thinking has had any serious practical cost. I believe it has.

There is no question that "financial engineering" has brought benefits. It has improved the matching of investments to the needs of savers and extended financing to the smallest grains of sand in the economy. (The word *granular* is apt to turn up here.) Yet since August 2007 up to this writing in April 2008, the financial sector has been in near paralysis. In my judgment, this failure is the result of a sort of misfeasance on the part of the leaders at many of the investment banks. Much of this management failure, I believe, can be laid to a dearth of understanding of applicable economics. And some of that ignorance or obliviousness is the result, in turn, of the shortcomings of the neo-neoclassical models used on Wall Street for purposes of "risk management." A paragraph from a piece of mine in the *Wall Street Journal* of March 14, 2008 (with minor edits and an additional point in brackets) suggests some of the failures:

Subprime lending and the securitization of debt were innovations that, it was believed, offered the prospect of increased homeownership. But "risk management" was out of its depth here: It had no past data from which to estimate needed valuations of the novel assets; [it appeared to suppose that diversification would eliminate systemic risks, including the Knightian kind;] it did not allow for possible macroeconomic swings; and it took inadequate account of the system effects when unknown numbers of financial companies enter the new business all at nearly the same time.

I have come across a catchword that nicely captures most, if not all, of what I was saying: *strategic vision*. The term has been used recently in discussions of what has gone wrong at some investment banks by both Luqman Arnold, chief of UBS in 2001, and Leo M. Tilman, senior strategist at Bear Stearns.

Dynamism

The most awful thing about determinism and the idea it inspires, rational expectations, is that they preempt all originality and thus leave no role for creativity in the business world—basically, this world. If everything were determinate or knowable, and it were in fact known by now, then there would be nothing yet to discover or invent. There would be nothing about which to be creative; nothing to create.

This doctrine is not only an affront to humanism, from the ancient Greeks to the present time. It is pretty obvious that it is very bad economics.

In reply, the neo-neoclassicals might suggest that innovators only seem to be prime causes of innovative forces; that, in reality, the conceptions of individual innovations are governed by a selection mechanism based on probability distributions, which are so detailed and granular that we cannot in practice estimate them. Schumpeter's great 1911–1912 book *Theorie der wirtscharftlichen Entwicklung* (*Theory of Economic Development*, trans., 1932) has that flavor, as do the avowedly "Schumpeterian" models by Philippe Aghion and Peter Howitt. That theory looks to be untestable, even metaphysical. Even if it were true or could be true in some cases, most of us appear to share the sense of having *free will*— to be able to choose a life of challenge and creativity in preference to a more passive, safe sort of life—and having *powers of imagination*—to have ideas that no one else has thought up, ideas that are contingent on our imagining. And many societies structure the economy for innovativeness because they desire it. It would be a pity, perhaps disastrous, if we lost that sense of autonomy.

In the view I have taken in several papers and lectures in the present decade, such as my 2002 Munich lecture and my 2005 lecture at the International Economic Association World Congress in Marrakech, the American economy and a few other national economies, defined as a structure of institutions and attitudes, are *mechanisms* for the generation—always with lots of unknown probabilities—of novel commercial ideas. As a result, the American economy can be seen as driven by the occurrence of such ideas, and much of its activity revolves around their financing, development into workable products, marketing, evaluation by prospective end users, and if they get that far, commercial adoption and final acceptance. (This is a straightforward elaboration and articulation of what Hayek called the "discovery procedure.") I have been using the word *dynamism* to refer to the *power* or *propensity* of the economy to generate novel products that are commercially success-ful—thus, the fertility and aim of the economy in producing new ideas. (Think of some value-weighted index of the discoveries per year over some long span as measuring this dynamism. Of course, there are many pieces of circumstantial evidence of an economy's dynamism.) As I see it, this mechanism is the essence of *capitalism*.

I have suggested that this system, where it is well functioning enough, infuses the workplace, the capital market, and the shopping place with an unprecedented character. The workplace becomes a locus for mental stimulation, problem creation and problem solving, intellectual growth, and "fun" too (as Janos Kornai and, more recently, Bill Clinton inter-jected in conversations I had with them). The capital market becomes a place where entrepreneurs try to communicate the nature of their project, and where angel capitalists, venture capitalists, and other financiers draw on their private knowledge in deciding which one, if any, to back and how to structure their support. The shopping place becomes a locus for exploring the array of novel products for sale and judging which ones would be worth buying. All this makes the activities of people in the business economy engaging and rewarding.

In contrast, as I have argued in various papers, the *corporatist* economies, at any rate those in continental western Europe and Latin America—from Paris to Moscow and from Mexico City to Buenos Aires—have far less dynamism than do the relatively capitalist systems of the United States, Canada, and perhaps South Korea and Sweden; and less than Ireland and the United Kingdom. There is evidence for that inference in data on the number of innovations (which must be some-what subjective), the turnover of firms in the "top fifty," the weight of young firms in the economy, and the brain drain from the European continent to Silicon Valley, Dublin, London, Stockholm, and other meccas for enterprise and innovation.

Inclusion and the Good Economy

Starting with a Paris lecture in summer 2006 and my Aristotle lecture in 2007, my thesis has been that problem solving, exploration, and intellectual growth—the attributes to which I referred above—are, for most if not all people in any country, *essential* for self-realization, self-actualization, or self-discovery; and that this experience or development is the essence of the *good life*, as humanist philosophers have proposed, from Aristotle to Dewey and Rawls, and from Cervantes to Nietzsche and Henri Bergson. Further, since a good economy must serve the good life, these attributes must be essential to the *good economy*.

We are not talking about single-agent economies, of course. People differ in their advantages, innate and acquired. This brings to mind the matter of *economic inclusion*. What reason is there to value widespread inclusion? In part, it is that a society can more cheaply mitigate poverty among those not included by helping them to help themselves—by making productive jobs available to them, rather than through the dole. (This is pure Adam Smith.) In part, it is because we think that justice requires sweetening the share they get of the gain or "surplus" produced by their collaboration with others in the business economy. (This is pure John Rawls.) But inclusion is also valued because it would be terribly unjust to watch the disadvantaged come up against difficulties qualifying for or gaining access to the procedures for inclusion without our trying to do something about it, since inclusion *in an economy of dynamism* is, for most people, a hugely important gateway, if not the only gateway, to self-realization. For a great many, this inclusion is the *only* avenue to self-realization (in all or most dimensions) that they can hope to find. To lack any inclusion in business life is a kind of death.

I have argued in my Nobel Prize lecture, published in 2007, that we do not need to *choose* between inclusion and dynamism. It may very well be that continental Europe kept taking state and community measures to push up inclusion—and solidarity—until it damaged its already questionable dynamism. I argue that, in general, introducing institutional structures for greater dynamism, however, does not only serve the self-realization of the more advantaged. Such structures are job creating, and in pulling up employment as well as self-support and respect among the disadvantaged, serve to increase self-realization among the disadvantaged as well. Economies without dynamism cannot be just.

Reversal of Fortune

While happily embarked in new directions with the work on structuralism between 1985 to the mid-1990s, the work later in the 1990s on inclusion and the work in the 2000s on dynamism, I was aware that I had again left the mainstream—and the mainstream showed no sign of following me.

I will always be grateful for the long collaboration over this period of Hian Teck Hoon and Gylfi Zoega, who risked slowing their advancement in committing vast blocks of time to our projects.

I was extremely lucky also to have frequent exchanges over these years with Roman Frydman, Amar Bhide, and Richard Robb. Once Roman and I started up the Center on Capitalism and Society at Columbia in early 2001, the four of us were soon to become the hard core of the center.

It also helped that I was able to keep in touch with kindred spirits stretching back to Richard Nelson and Sidney Winter from my Yale and RAND days, Robert Pollak and Karl Shell from my time at Penn, Guillermo Calvo and John Taylor from my first decade at Columbia, and several Europeans whom I saw regularly, such as Jean-Paul Fitoussi and Luigi Paganetto.

In the 2000s, however, my standing and visibility shot up, first when named a distinguished fellow of the American Economic Association in 2000, then with the massive *Festschrift* conference in my honor that was organized by Philippe Aghion, Roman Frydman, Joseph Stiglitz, and Michael Woodford. The Nobel Prize in fall 2006 brought a renewed recognition of my research stretching from the 1960s to my differences with the new classical school in the 1980s.

With the Nobel Prize, I find myself with a platform that is more amazing than I could have imagined. I have had the opportunity to speak about my distinctive views all over the world. This has kindled the hope that the new theories I constructed in the past two decades and the new dimensions I have tried to introduce into economics will yet win a hearing among economists. Fortunately, I am joined by a band of likeminded economists, and we will make every effort to persuade the profession of the merits of our views.

Notes

Photograph of Edmund S. Phelps by Ramin Talaie.

1. Four earlier memoirs are "A Life in Economics," in *The Makers of Modern Economics*, ed. Arnold Heertje (Aldershot, UK: Elgar, 1995); "The Origins and Further Development of the Natural Rate of Unemployment," in *The Natural Rate of Unemployment: Reflections on 25 Years of the Hypothesis*, ed. Rod Cross (Cambridge: Cambridge University Press, 1995); "Recollections of My Past Research in Economics," Beijing Technology and Business University, June 2005;

"Becoming an Economist," in *Les Prix Nobel 2006* (Stockholm: Nobel Foundation, 2007). These documents and some other data, including my curriculum vitae, are on my personal Web site, available at http://www.columbia.edu/~esp2.

2. The reference is James Heckman and Richard Robb, "Alternative Methods for Solving the Problem of Selection Bias in Evaluating the Impact of Treatments on Outcomes," in *Drawing Inferences from Self-Selected Samples*, ed. Howard Wainer (New York: Springer, 1986).

Edmund S. Phelps
Awarded Nobel Prize in 2006. Lecture presented April 9, 2008.

Date of Birth
July 26, 1933

Academic Degrees
B.A., Amherst College, 1955
Ph.D., Yale University, 1959

Academic Affiliations
Assistant Professor of Economics, Yale University and Member, Cowles Foundation, 1960–62
Visiting Associate Professor of Economics, Massachusetts Institute of Technology, 1962–63
Associate Professor of Economics, Yale University and Member, Cowles Foundation, 1963–66
Professor of Economics, University of Pennsylvania, 1966–71
Professor of Economics, Columbia University, 1971–82
Professor of Economics, New York University, 1978–79
McVickar Professor of Political Economy, Columbia University, 1982–present
Director, Center on Capitalism and Society, Earth Institute, Columbia University, 2001–present

Selected Books
Fiscal Neutrality toward Economic Growth, 1965
Golden Rules of Economic Growth, 1966
Microeconomic Foundations of Employment and Inflation Theory, 1970 (with A. Alchian, C. Holt, et al.)
Inflation Policy and Unemployment Theory, 1972
Studies in Macroeconomic Theory, Volume 1, *Employment and Inflation*, 1979
Studies in Macroeconomic Theory, Volume 2, *Redistribution and Growth*, 1980
Individual Forecasting and Aggregate Outcomes: "Rational Expectations" Examined, 1983 (ed., with R. Frydman)
Political Economy: An Introductory Text, 1985
The Slump in Europe: Open Economy Theory Reconstructed, 1988 (with J.-P. Fitoussi)
Seven Schools of Macroeconomic Thought: The Arne Ryde Lectures, 1990
Structural Slumps: The Modern Equilibrium Theory of Employment, Interest, and Assets, 1994
Rewarding Work: How to Restore Participation and Self-Support to Free Enterprise, 1997
Enterprise and Inclusion in the Italian Economy, 2002

Eric Maskin

When I went to college, I had no intention of becoming an economist. In fact, I scarcely had any idea at that point what economics was all about. I was a mathematics major in college, and I studied such things as group theory and analysis with some superb but occasionally rather eccentric math professors. To give an example, I once bumped into my real variables professor, George Mackey, in the hallway. We talked for a while, and at the conclusion of our chat he asked me what direction he had been going in when we met. I was a bit startled by the question, but I indicated the direction, and he said, "Good. That means I must have had lunch already."

Notwithstanding such odd episodes, I found mathematics a very attractive subject, and I might well have stayed a mathematician had I not wandered almost by accident into a course in economics that the great economist Kenneth Arrow was offering on the economics of information. I didn't know who Arrow was at the time, and I certainly didn't know what the economics of information was, but I thought the class should at least be informative. Arrow's lectures were improvisational. He appeared to have thought up what he was going to talk about on the way over to the lecture room from his office, and sometimes not even then. But in addition to being improvisational, they were inspirational. The list of topics was a bit of a hodgepodge. There was some information economics, as the name of the course suggested. There was some team theory, there was a unit on planning procedures, there was a discussion of moral hazard and adverse selection. But the highlight of the course, and the part that changed my life, was Leonid Hurwicz's work on mechanism design theory. Leo shared the 2007 Nobel Prize with Roger Myerson and me for mechanism design, but he was the founder of this field, and Roger and I simply followed in his footsteps.

I found the course so riveting that I decided to switch out of math and into economics. I did a Ph.D. with Ken Arrow as my supervisor, and a lot of my early work was on mechanism design. And before too long, Ken had introduced me to Leo Hurwicz in person. One of my first research projects was a collaboration with Leo and the economist Andy Postlewaite.

I'll try to provide a one-paragraph definition of mechanism design, but the best way to understand what the theory is aiming at is through examples, so I will spend more time on those. Here is the short definition: mechanism design is the engineering part of economic theory. Most of the time in economics we take existing economic institutions and either try to predict what outcomes they will give rise to (although that's especially hard) or look back on past outcomes and try to understand why they occurred. This is the so-called *positive* or *predictive* part of economic theory. But what I am personally most interested in—and what mechanism design concentrates on—is just the opposite. We first identify what outcomes or goals we want to achieve, and then we work backward and ask what institutions or mechanisms or procedures could be designed to achieve those goals. If possible, we also try to describe what form these institutions will take. This is the *normative* or *prescriptive* part of economics. It's a much smaller part of economics than the positive part, but it's the part I like best.

Here's an example that's likely familiar from our own domestic experience. Let's imagine there's a parent—a mother, say—who wants to divide a cake between her two children, Alice and Bob. If you've ever done this in your own family, you know that it's absolutely critical to divide the cake so that each child is happy with the piece he or she gets. That means Bob should think he's got at least half, and Alice should think *she's* got at least half. If we achieve this goal, then we say we have a *fair division*. You'll know, if you've tried this at home, that not getting a fair division is a catastrophe. So the mother certainly wants to get it right.

How does the mother do this? If she knows the kids see the cake the way she does, then there's a very simple solution. She just takes a knife and cuts the cake exactly equally in her view, and gives each child a piece. Because the kids see the cake the same way, they both realize they each have half, and that's the end of the story.

But what if Bob or Alice sees the cake differently from their mother? In fact, this is what inevitably happens in any real home. The mother might think she has divided it exactly equally, but Bob will probably think that his piece is smaller than Alice's, and Alice will think her piece is smaller than Bob's. The problem is that the mother doesn't have enough information to achieve a fair division by herself. She, in effect, doesn't know what division is fair. Hence the mechanism design question: *Is there an indirect way of proceeding that will generate a fair division, even though the mother herself doesn't know what is fair?* It turns out that this is a very old question.

If you've read or heard Bible stories, you'll recognize that the question I've posed is exactly the same as the one Lot and Abraham faced when they were trying to figure out how to divide up grazing land between the two of them; it's the same question of fair division. This question, then, goes back at least a couple of thousand years, and as usual, the Bible doesn't just pose the question, it provides an answer. Here is the translation of the answer into "cake."

The mother should have one of the children (say, Bob) divide the cake in two, and have the other child (Alice) choose which piece she wants for herself. Very simple. Why does it work? It works because it exploits Bob's incentives to divide the cake equally. This is the crucial word in mechanism design theory: *incentives*. When Bob cuts the cake, he has a strong motivation—a strong incentive—to divide the cake so that in his eyes, the pieces are equal. Why? Because if one of the pieces is bigger, he knows Alice will take that one. So he will try to cut the cake in such a way that, whichever piece Alice takes, he's happy with the other one. By cutting the cake exactly in half, Bob will be assured of at least half. And Alice is assured of half because she gets to choose the piece she prefers. Thus, the divide and choose procedure—the mechanism from the Bible—solves the mother's problem.

Cutting a cake is a relatively simple problem, but one rich enough to exhibit some of the key features of mechanism design. First, the problem arises because the mechanism designer (the mother, in this case) doesn't have enough information to know which outcomes are best (which outcomes are fair, in this case), so she has to proceed through a mechanism. In effect, the mechanism (the divide and choose procedure, in this case) has the participants, through their actions, generate the information needed to identify the optimal outcome. But there's a complication: the participants (Alice and Bob) couldn't care less about the mother's goal. *She* wants to achieve a fair division, but Alice and Bob just want more cake. So the mechanism has to take into account that their goals are not the same as the mother's. To use the jargon of the theory, the mechanism must be *incentive compatible*, that is, compatible with Alice's and Bob's objectives.

Before going on to the next example, I'll look at how mechanism design evolved over time. As we've seen, some elements go back thousands of years. But the subject really took off with the writings of the utopian socialists in the United States and, especially, Britain in the nineteenth century. These writers were disturbed by the unpleasant side effects of capitalism, such as income inequality and the destruction of the environment. They thought capitalism could be much improved on, and they tried out various alternatives. The alternatives didn't turn out to work in practice, but they generated some interesting ideas.

A more immediate precursor of the modern theory of mechanism design was a famous debate that took place in the 1930s and 1940s, now called the planning controversy. There were two major figures on each side of it.

On one side were Oskar Lange and Abba Lerner, who argued that, in principle, central planning had to be better than the free market. They reasoned that, at worst, planning could replicate the outcomes of the market, and moreover, it could correct the market's failures. On the other side were Friedrich von Hayek and Ludwig von Mises, who denied that central planning could ever succeed. Indeed, Hayek and Mises held that only a free market could generate prosperity.

This controversy went on for many years. It was important and drew lots of attention, but it had some shortcomings. In particular, none of the crucial terms, such as "central planning" and "free market," were ever defined; they were invoked without being assigned clear-cut meanings. Moreover, the four principals in the debate did not have the technical apparatus we have today, such as game theory and mathematical programming, to express themselves in unambiguous and precise terms. That's where Leo Hurwicz came in.

Leo was inspired by the planning controversy but frustrated by its vagueness. In his two landmark papers (Hurwicz 1960, 1972), he defined all the important terms with formal precision. He also showed how to use modern tools to obtain sharp answers to the questions debated in the controversy.

The follow-up literature to the planning controversy, much of which was inspired by Hurwicz's work, has produced a consensus view that, in some particular circumstances, Hayek and Mises were correct that the market is the best mechanism. But to reach that conclusion, it is essential that those circumstances obtain. In particular, there must be large numbers of buyers and sellers, thus eliminating monopoly power. It is equally important that there be no significant externalities. An *externality* is created whenever I do something that affects your consumption or production and I don't take this effect into account (for example, people don't usually consider the traffic congestion they generate when they drive their cars). When both these circumstances hold, the market mechanism cannot be bettered. But when either circumstance (large numbers or no externalities) is violated, then typically a mechanism that improves on the free market can be found. That is an important lesson of mechanism design theory.

By coincidence, in the same year that Hurwicz produced his first general paper on mechanism design, an equally important paper by William Vickrey appeared (Vickrey 1961). It was on a particular mechanism that has come to be known as the Vickrey mechanism or the Vickrey auction. Vickrey was later recognized for this work with the 1996 Nobel Prize in Economics, which he shared with James A. Mirrlees.

The Vickrey mechanism was one of the first specific mechanisms developed in the modern era using modern tools. It's simple, clever, and practical—it solves some important real-life problems (even more important than cutting a cake fairly!).

My second example of mechanism design uses the Vickrey mechanism in its solution. We are essentially all participants in the telecommunications revolution; we communicate now using cell phones or iPads or similar digital devices. This revolution was made possible because governments around the world (starting with the U.S. government) in effect privatized the airwaves. That is, large chunks of radio spectrum that had been in the public domain were transferred to the private sector so that telecom companies could use them more effectively.

Let's look at a simple example of such a privatization. Let's imagine that a government wants to transfer the license to use a particular band of radio frequencies to one of several telecom companies interested in this license. And let's assume that the goal of the government is to put the license into the hands of the company that values it the most. That seems like a natural goal because this company is going to create the most value for society. If the license goes to this company, economists call the outcome *efficient*.

The problem is that the government doesn't *know* which company values the license the most, so it doesn't know the efficient outcome. What can it do? The simplest thing would be to ask each company, how much do you value the license? But if you think about this mechanism—and the companies would certainly think about it—you'll see that it would not work very well: companies will grasp that their chances of getting the license go up when they state higher values, and so they have a strong incentive to exaggerate their values. But if all companies are exaggerating, how is the government to identify which company really does value the license the most? This rather naïve way of proceeding is not likely to work very well.

The government could try something bit more sophisticated: it could ask each company to make a bid for the license. A bid is a statement of how much the company is willing to pay. The government could then award the license to the highest bidder and have the winner pay its bid. That sounds more promising than the first mechanism, but it's not going to work either. The reason is that now companies have exactly the *opposite* incentive. In the first mechanism—whereby the government simply asks companies the value they place on the license—the companies will exaggerate. Now the companies have an incentive to *understate*. Why is that?

Put yourself in the shoes of one of these companies. Say you are Telemax. Suppose the license is worth $10 million to you. Will you bid $10 million? If you *do* bid $10 million and you win, you'll be getting something worth $10 million, but you will be paying $10 million. On net, you will have a profit of zero. There's no point in winning if your resulting profit is zero. This means that Telemax is going to bid *less* than $10 million. It's going to understate. Doing so reduces its chance of winning, but at least if it *does* win, it will get a positive profit. Yet if all bidders understate, then once again there is no guarantee of identifying the company that really values the license the most. So this mechanism doesn't work either, and we face the question, is there a way of reconciling the opposing forces at work in these two mechanisms? That is, can we find a mechanism that achieves the perfect compromise between overstating and understating?

That is where Vickrey came in. The answer is yes, we can, and Vickrey showed how to do it in his 1961 paper. The solution is remarkably simple. Once again, the government has each company make a bid for the license. Once again, the government awards the license to the company that makes the highest bid. But instead of paying its *own* bid, that company pays the *second* highest bid. For example, if there are three bidders and one bids $10 million, one bids $8 million, and one bids $5 million, then the $10 million bidder will win, but will pay only $8 million, since that's the second highest bid. In this mechanism, I claim that bidders have the incentive neither to overstate nor understate. They will bid *exactly* what the license is worth to them.

Why won't they understate? Well, if Telemax understates, it gains nothing, because it doesn't pay its bid anyway. Suppose the license is worth $10 million to Telemax and it bids $9 million instead. If the second highest bid is $8 million, Telemax will pay $8 million whether it bids $10 million or understates the value. So it doesn't benefit from the understatement. Furthermore, understatement runs the risk of losing the license altogether. Say Telemax bids $7 million but some other company bids $8 million (the bids are sealed, so Telemax doesn't know this). Then Telemax will lose to the other company. Yet if it had bid what the license is actually worth to it ($10 million), it would have won and made a nice $2 million profit ($10 million − $8 million). Telemax never benefits from understating and, worse, it could be harmed by doing so because it might end up losing altogether.

Telemax also doesn't have an incentive to overstate. If it bids $12 million and the second highest bid is $ 8 million, it still pays $ 8 million. So it doesn't gain anything by overstating. Furthermore, it runs the risk of overpaying. If some other company comes in at $11 million, then Telemax may win with a bid of $12 million, but it will regret doing so: it will pay $11 million, more than the $10 million the license is worth to it. So Telemax won't overstate.

The only thing left is for Telemax to bid exactly what the license is worth to it. But if all companies bid exactly what the license is worth to them, then the winner will be the bidder with the highest value, which is what the government wanted to achieve in the first place. So Vickrey's simple but clever mechanism solves the problem, and for that reason it forms the basis of the mechanisms that governments around the world have actually used.

One attractive property of Vickrey's mechanism is that when a company tries to figure out how much to bid, it doesn't have to worry about what other bidders are going to do. Bidding its true value in the mechanism is optimal independent of others' behavior. Unfortunately, there are many settings where the Vickrey mechanism does not apply and this attractive independence property is lost. That brings me to a final example, which is slightly more complicated than the two previous ones. It's an energy example.

Imagine there is a society with two energy consumers, and let's bring back our friends Alice and Bob to play these roles. There is also an energy authority whose job it is to choose the form of energy that Alice and Bob are going to consume. Let's suppose there are four possibilities: the authority can choose gas or oil or nuclear power or coal. But it can choose only one of these because the technological cost of providing more than one form of energy is too high. Naturally, what the authority wants to do is to choose an energy source that is good for Alice and Bob, that comports with what they want. The problem is that the authority doesn't know what they want.

To make matters simple, let's assume there are only two possibilities for what Alice and Bob may want; I'll call them the two *states of the world*. In one state, Alice and Bob don't care very much about the future; they care mostly about their current consumption. That's state one. In state two, they care a lot about the future and not so much about their current consumption. What do the two states mean as far as energy goes?

Let's imagine that Alice cares mostly about convenience: how convenient it is to consume energy. That means that in state one, where current consumption is weighted heavily, she likes gas the most (because it's the easiest to use), then oil, then coal, with nuclear power down at the bottom because it's very cumbersome to use.

On the other hand, if state two is the actual state—remember, Alice knows which state is the true one but the authority doesn't—then Alice puts nuclear power at the top (because she anticipates that in the future, technical advances will make nuclear power much easier to use)—then gas, then coal, with oil now at the bottom.

Bob, on the other hand, cares mostly about safety. In state one, where the present is important, he likes nuclear power the most (because he thinks it is the safest), then oil, then coal, with gas at the bottom because he's afraid of gas explosions.

But if Bob cares mostly about the future, then nuclear power goes to the bottom of his list because he's worried about the long-term problems of getting rid of nuclear waste. Oil, on the other hand, goes to the top. I summarize Alice's and Bob's rankings in table 1.

The energy authority would like to take into account both Alice's and Bob's preferences, and to choose a source that is a good compromise between these preferences. That suggests that in state one, oil would be a good choice. Although Alice likes gas in state one, Bob doesn't like gas at all. So gas is not a good compromise. Nuclear power is not a good compromise because Alice hates nuclear power, and coal is not a good compromise because both Alice and Bob prefer oil to coal. That leaves oil as the right choice in state one.

For similar reasons, gas is a good choice in state two: nuclear power is not good because Bob doesn't like it, oil is not good because Alice doesn't like it, and both Alice and Bob prefer gas to coal. So the energy

Table 1

State 1		State 2	
Alice	Bob	Alice	Bob
Gas	Nuclear	Nuclear	Oil
Oil	Oil	Gas	Gas
Coal	Coal	Coal	Coal
Nuclear	Gas	Oil	Nuclear

Table 2

		Bob	
		Left	Right
Alice	Top	Oil	Coal
	Bottom	Nuclear	Gas

authority would like to choose oil in state one and gas in state two, but it doesn't know which is the actual state. So how can it proceed?

The obvious thing would be to ask Alice and Bob each to say what the state is. But we notice from table 1 that Alice always prefers gas to oil; she prefers gas to oil in both states. So she's going to say state two even if state one is the actual state because that will raise the chance that gas is chosen (if the authority thinks that state two is the actual state, it will choose gas). For exactly symmetric reasons, Bob is always going to say state one because he always prefers oil to gas. So, if the authority directly asks the two consumers about the state, Alice will say state two, Bob will say state one, and the authority will have no idea what the actual state is.

We need to do something more sophisticated, and I suggest that the mechanism shown in table 2 is the solution.

This mechanism is a game in which Alice can select either the top or the bottom row as her option and Bob can select either the left or the right column. The selections are made simultaneously. The outcome of the mechanism is given by the intersection of their selections. For example, if Alice selects the top row and Bob selects the left column, the outcome will be oil.

What happens if this game is played? To start, Alice's and Bob's behavior will depend on the state. Let's suppose first that state one is the actual state. If Alice predicts that Bob is going to select the left column, then she will ensure that oil is chosen if she selects the top row, and she'll induce nuclear power by selecting the bottom row. This means that, if she predicts Bob will select the left column, she will opt for the top row because in state one, Alice prefers oil to nuclear power. Furthermore, Bob *will* select the left column because no matter what Alice does, he is better off with the left column in state one. For if Alice selects the top row, then Bob has a choice between oil (left) and coal (right). But he prefers oil to coal in state one, and so will select left. If Alice selects the bottom row, then Bob has a choice between nuclear power (left) and gas (right). Since he prefers nuclear power, he again will select the left column.

In the language of mechanism design, Bob selecting the left column and Alice selecting the top row is a *Nash equilibrium* in state one. It is a configuration of actions that is best for each participant, given what the other is doing. Indeed, it is the *only* Nash equilibrium in state one, and so it is a good prediction of what Alice and Bob will do (if they think things through). Furthermore, these selections lead to oil being chosen in state one, which is exactly what the authority wants. Reasoning in a completely symmetric way for state two (the logic is the mirror image), we now expect Alice to select the bottom row and Bob to select the right column. Thus, the predicted outcome in state two is gas (which is also what the authority wants).

Thus, in either state, our little mechanism achieves the energy authority's goals, even though the authority does not know the states itself and even though Alice and Bob couldn't care less about the authority's goals. We say that this mechanism *implements* the authority's goals.

So, I have introduced three examples—cake, telecom, and energy—and for each I've produced a mechanism that implements the designer's goals. However, it might plausibly be argued that I have specially constructed these examples so that the goals could be implemented. And so far I have said nothing about how someone could *find* an implementing mechanism other than by making an inspired guess.

These concerns prompt two general questions. First, is there a systematic way to determine whether a goal is implementable or not? (In the three examples, the goals were implementable, but I could have introduced other examples in which they are not.) Second, if the goal is implementable, is there a surefire way to find a mechanism that does the implementing?

Those were the questions I struggled with many years ago. I won't say how long it took to find a solution; let's just say it was a long time.

But finally, in a 1977 article (published as Maskin 1999), I was able to determine that the answer to both of these general questions is yes. There *is* a way of determining whether goals are implementable, and furthermore, there is a way of constructing mechanisms that do the implementing. I'll forbear from explaining now why the answers are yes. But you can read the paper if you are interested.

Mechanism design theory has been around for a long time; it's been fifty years since Hurwicz's and Vickrey's landmark papers. And the subject remains lively, in part because new potential applications keep coming along and renewing researchers' interest in the field. I'll mention two applications for the future.

One is climate change. This is a global mechanism design problem. We're now in agreement—there is scientific consensus—that not only are temperatures rising but humans are responsible for it by having released greenhouse gases such as carbon dioxide into the atmosphere. The obvious solution to curtailing climate change is to reduce our emissions of these gases.

But there is a conflict between that global goal (which we can agree on) and the individual goals of the countries of the world. Countries are also interested in making sure their economies thrive, and unfortunately, reducing greenhouse gas emissions is economically costly: it requires developing new technologies, or shutting down factories, or reducing output, all of which are expensive. So, each country would like the other countries to reduce emissions, but would prefer not to do so itself. How do we solve this conflict of goals? One way is through an international treaty in which countries pledge to reduce emissions, if other countries do the same. But designing an international treaty on greenhouse gas emissions is a problem in mechanism design. We don't have the solution to that problem; it remains to be found. But one day it will be found.

One last big application for the future: I don't have to remind anyone that we're in the middle of a financial crisis now—I hope it's the middle, rather than the beginning—but I am certain we will be out of it someday (though I'm not making a prediction about when). At that point, we must confront the question of how to prevent such a crisis from happening again. We have a good idea of what went wrong: it was a failure of regulation. Banks had the incentive to take on enormous debt and risk because the possible bad consequences of that debt and risk fell primarily on other people. In such circumstances, it is the job of the regulators to constrain banks, but such constraints were not in place in the years leading up to the crisis. The construction of a regulatory system that actually works is, again, a problem in applied mechanism design. It would be wonderful if some who are economics students today were involved in cracking that one, too.

References

Hurwicz, L. 1960. Optimality and informational efficiency in resource allocation processes. In *Mathematical Methods in Social Sciences*, ed. Kenneth Arrow, S. Karin, and P. Suppes, 27–46. Stanford, CA: Stanford University Press.

Hurwicz, L. 1972. On informationally decentralized systems. In *Decision and Organization*, ed. C. McGuire and R. Radner, 297–336. Amsterdam: North-Holland.

Maskin, E. 1999. Nash equilibrium and welfare optimality. *Review of Economic Studies* 66:23–38.

Vickrey, W. 1961. Counterspeculation, auctions, and competitive sealed tenders. *Journal of Finance* 16 (1):8–37.

Eric Maskin

Awarded Nobel Prize in 2007. Lecture presented April 21, 2009.

Date of Birth

December 12, 1950

Academic Degrees

A.B., Mathematics, Harvard University, 1972
A.M., Applied Mathematics, Harvard University, 1974
Ph.D., Applied Mathematics, Harvard University, 1976

Academic Affiliations

Research Fellow, Jesus College, Cambridge University, 1976–77
Assistant Professor of Economics, Massachusetts Institute of Technology, 1977–80
Associate Professor of Economics, MIT, 1980–81
Overseas Fellow, Churchill College, Cambridge University, 1980–82
Professor of Economics, MIT, 1981–84
Professor of Economics, Harvard University, 1985–2000
Visiting Overseas Fellow, St. John's College, Cambridge, 1987–88
Louis Berkman Professor of Economics, Harvard University, 1997–2000
Visiting Professor of Economics, MIT, 1999–2000
SK Professor, Yonsei University, 2009–10
Visiting Fellow, I.A.S., Hong Kong University of Science and Technology, 2010–present
Visiting Lecturer in Economics, Princeton University, 2000–11
Albert O. Hirschman Professor of Social Science, Institute for Advanced Study, Princeton University, 2000
Adams University Professor, Harvard University, 2012–present

Selected Books

On Time: Lectures on Models of Equilibrium, Churchill Lectures, 1994
Social Security Reform, the 1999 Lindahl Lectures, 2002
Taxation, Incomplete Markets and Social Security, the 2000 Munich Lectures, 2002.
Saving Social Security: A Balanced Approach, 2004, rev. ed. 2005 (with Peter R. Orszag)
Reforming Pensions: Principles and Policy Choices, 2008 (with Nicholas Barr)
Pension Reform: A Short Guide, 2010 (with Nicholas Barr)

Joseph E. Stiglitz

We live in an era in which we strive to explain, systematically and scientifically, the world around us. But we also strive to understand the creative process. It is difficult to explain how that process works. How do our ideas come about?

Those of us who are credited with having made advances in understandings, even breakthroughs, do not fully understand how they arise and get developed. So I welcome this long-standing endeavor by Trinity University to expand our understanding of the creative process by sharing some of my own reflections and experiences, joining a long list of distinguished colleagues who have done so.

This is a moment that should give much of the economics profession pause. The world is in the worst economic crisis of the last three-quarters of a century, and our profession bears more than a little responsibility. When medical doctors take up their profession, they sign the Hippocratic Oath, whose clauses include *primum non nocere*, "First, do no harm." We sign no such oath, but had we done so, many within the profession would have found themselves in violation.

Much of the blame lies with market fundamentalism, the belief that markets and market participants are fully rational, that markets are efficient and self-correcting, and quickly so. These beliefs undergirded the deregulatory movement that played such an important role in giving rise to the financial crisis that began in 2007. It is testament both to the power and the inadequacy of these views that, relying on them, so many failed to recognize that a bubble existed, until it burst. Even when they might have admitted that bubbles were possible, market fundamentalists thought it would be easier and less costly to clean up the mess after a bubble broke than to try to prevent one from forming. These kinds of flawed ideas, which economists expressed in both academia and in the public arena, supported the policies that have brought so much suffering to so many.

Ideological wars linked to policy battles have long played an important role in economics. They energized my graduate studies at MIT,
which was then engaged in a fierce battle with the Chicago school,
headed by Milton Friedman and George Stigler. This was in the early
1960s, a period of real foment in America.[1] It was the Kennedy period
—a period when, to paraphrase JFK, people were asking not what the
country could do for them but what they could do for their country.
That was followed by a period of intense turmoil having to do with the
Vietnam War.

I was doing my undergraduate and graduate studies at that time, and
within academia, these battles get distilled in a particular way. The
Chicago school, politically very conservative, called for a minimal role
for government. The Cambridge school in the United Kingdom—people
like Joan Robinson and Nicholas Kaldor—carried on the mantle of John
Maynard Keynes on the left. Of course, there was a range within each
of these institutions—the intellectual battles within Cambridge, UK, were
perhaps as intense as any of those between Cambridge and Chicago.
These battles played a large role in my intellectual development. But
clearly, that can only be part of the explanation of the processes that
formed my thinking, since many others were subjected to the same
education.

My upbringing and early schooling were also very important. I grew
up in the steel town of Gary, Indiana, on the southern shores of Lake
Michigan. Gary and the upper Midwest in general were in much better
economic shape during my childhood than they are now, but it was still
not the kind of background that would normally be thought of as an
advantage for a future academic. For my intellectual development,
however, it was extremely formative, in several senses. Gary was founded
in 1906. A hundred years later it is in deep decline. Its course essentially
traced that of the industrial period of America. No one growing up in
this town—emblematic of the rise and fall of industrialization in America—could believe that markets were an unmixed blessing. I saw the
darker side—and darker not only because of the pollution (which was
often invisible)—but also because of the obvious economic and social
costs: periodic unemployment, labor strife as workers struggled to get a
fair share of the benefits that increasing productivity was bringing to the
country, rampant discrimination, and urban decay.

I also benefited from a public school system with dedicated teachers
working under the educational philosophy of John Dewey. This system
helped make America's melting pot work by bringing together disparate

groups and teaching them vocational skills (I learned how to be both a printer and an electrician) and life skills (I learned to type as fast as any secretary), as well as the usual academic subjects. Work-study-play was the educational philosophy. I can't fully describe the sense of dedication of my teachers, how they helped shape my thinking and my approach to learning. When I was in sixth grade, a number of them decided there was little point to my studying with the rest of the class, especially mathematics, at which I excelled from a young age. And so until I took advanced calculus in college, what I learned was almost totally self-taught. I suppose this made me not very sympathetic to students who want to be spoon-fed. But more important, it encouraged the habit of mind of figuring things out for myself.

One of my major extracurricular activities was debating. Each year there was a national topic that was debated. The one that sticks in my mind was reforming America's agricultural policies. I found the economics and politics fascinating. I thought what we were doing then was wrong. I formulated what I thought was a set of policies that would be much better at reducing the risk facing farmers, and at lower cost to taxpayers. These were issues I would come back to in my theoretical work,[2] during my years as chairman of the Council of Economic Advisers,[3] and I would write about them in my work on globalization. I am shocked at how little progress we've made in the half century since I debated these issues. It seems as though time has stood still. I still believe my thinking from those high school debates would make sense today.

In the context of my upbringing, I should also mention my parents and the way they conveyed a sense of values. They were very engaged in political discourse, but not in politics. Within our extended family there was a range of views that went from Jeffersonian Democrats who focused on competition policy to New Deal Democrats. They were all within the Democratic family. Even the most economically successful—and there were some that were very well off—believed in the importance of unions and collective bargaining, in fighting for fairness for workers.

My father was born in 1903 and in many ways was a role model for how people can adapt to the quick changes in social mores that America was going through in the 1950s, 1960s, and 1970s. My mother (who had gone to the University of Chicago) did not get the conservative economic disease from going there. She had picked the University of Chicago because during the Great Depression, it was the cheapest place for her to go. She decided later on that she wanted to go to graduate school to get the qualifications that would allow her to teach in elementary school, and my father took up new roles in sharing household duties, which for someone of his generation was quite revolutionary.

I also owe to my parents (my father in particular) my ability to serve in government. A problem for many wanting to serve in the Clinton administration was that, when they were vetted, it would turn out they hadn't paid Social Security taxes on their household help. When I was growing up, my father had told me that you should always pay Social Security taxes for anybody who works for you, because many of these people were poor people and particularly in need of help in their retirement. That's why we have the Social Security Administration. So he was one of the generation for whom Social Security (which started in the mid-1930s) was very important. Today, Social Security benefits are too often taken for granted.

My father believed that one should pay the Social Security taxes for one's employees not just because it was the law but also because it was the right thing to do. So I had done so for those who had worked for me—and was able to surmount this hurdle, which had proved an obstacle for so many others.

Like most teenagers, I asked my parents what I should do when I grew up. They said, "Money's not important. You should never do anything for money." (For a future economist, this was a particularly interesting perspective, and especially so since so many of those in the economics profession seem to believe money drives the world.) My parents' view was that one should use one's mind and be of service in one way or another. Their perspective was something I always remembered as I made decisions later in life.

I will skip forward a little to Amherst College, a small college in New England—at the time there were about a thousand male students. One of the reasons I went to Amherst was that my guidance counselor worried that someone coming from Gary, Indiana, would not be adequately equipped to deal with large schools like Harvard, Yale, or Chicago. She thought a small, nurturing community was what I needed, and that Amherst would enable me to live up to my potential.

When I went to Amherst, I was very well prepared. I could give testimony to the quality of America's public education system, at least at that time. Amherst shaped me in more than one way, and I have tried to do what I can to repay it.[4] Amherst, like Trinity University, is a liberal arts school, and I thrived there. At the time, it had what was called the core curriculum. We had almost no choices in the first two years. (One of the few schools that still have a variant of this kind of core curriculum is Columbia.) We could choose which foreign language we would study, and we had also a choice of which "hard" science to study. It was very intense. Everybody had to take calculus, physics, English, history, and humanities.

One of the aspects of that kind of liberal arts education is that it focuses on teaching—very much in a Socratic style, small classes where the teachers would ask questions—which encouraged a questioning spirit, including a questioning of established theories. I think that's one of the most important elements of the creative process, and one of the most important for democratic processes as well. There is no such thing as an established authority. It is really important that our students should question what we say. I try to encourage such questioning in my classes. My teachers at Amherst also stressed that what matters is not so much the answers but how you frame the questions. If you can ask the question—frame the question—in the right way, then it's just a technical matter to figure out the answer. Much of what we did was focused on figuring out what it means to frame the question right—how to frame the questions in ways that give meaningful answers.

What I learned at Amherst stuck with me and affected my thinking and my research years later, as I was doing my work in the economics of information and globalization. For example, my development of the theory of screening was informed by my study of Plato and the notion of Platonic ideals. So, partially obscured by the mathematics, behind the theory of screening were some fairly deep philosophical ideas.

Another example: One of the world history courses I took was concerned with the encounter of civilizations before the expression "clash of civilizations" was fashionable. We studied in particular the encounter between the West and Asia, mainly in the nineteenth century. It was an encounter that was not handled very well. The Western powers engaged in conflicts with China called the Opium Wars. We went to war to make sure that China kept its markets open to our sale of opium. It sounds a little strange now. The problem was that China produced a lot of things that we wanted—like china tableware—and we produced nothing that China wanted. So all we could do was go buy opium in Afghanistan, transport it to China, get them addicted, and make the middle-man profits that made this whole global balance of trade work out. When you try to understand why some people in Asia are less than enthusiastic about what we call market access or opening initiatives, they have memories of what that means, and may not view it as positively as those in the West do. This is an example of some of the understandings I brought to the discussion when I started working at the World Bank that many other people who hadn't had that kind of liberal arts education didn't bring to the subject.

When I was at Amherst, I was very focused on my academic studies, but that was also when I began to be more active in political life. I was elected to the college's Student Council and eventually became its president. But I was always a little bit of an agitator, interested in making changes. At the time, around 93 percent of the students at Amherst belonged to fraternities. But I thought fraternities were a bad idea. I belonged to one, too, but I still thought they were divisive and undermined the sense of community that was so important, especially at a small college like Amherst. And so I began a campaign to abolish fraternities. It succeeded, though only about ten years after I left.

These and other initiatives I undertook were not always popular. There was a recall motion, which I defeated, and a fight with "the press" (the student newspaper). It was certainly not boring.

There were a number of other initiatives we undertook. In the 1960s there was still segregation in the South. I led a small group from Amherst to go down there and engage in pushing the desegregation agenda. We were unaware of the dangers in this kind of endeavor—several people did die, though thankfully, none from Amherst.

I had been a physics major at Amherst. I was attracted to the beauty of mathematics and the way it helped explain reality in some deep and fundamental sense. But I also took a number of courses in economics. We had some fantastic teachers—some of them were analytic, some were very policy-oriented, and all of them were very exciting in their own way.

When I was doing physics, I also got very interested and involved in environmental issues. I was a bit ahead of the time, I suppose. One of the branches of physics I was interested in was oceanography. I spent a summer working at Woods Hole Oceanographic Institute. One of the most exciting and enjoyable parts of that summer was going out on the ocean on a ten-day expedition. In much of my later work I've been involved in work on environmental economics. I was on the IPCC (the Intergovernmental Panel on Climate Change) and one of the lead authors of the 1995 *Report*. (The IPCC shared the Nobel Peace Prize in 2007 with Al Gore.)

There was a moment in the spring of my junior year when—and I can't quite explain why—I decided I wanted to become an economist instead of a physicist. I thought I could make use of the analytic rigor of economics to have some impact on the social problems that were really my passion.

This was still an era of informality, and what happened then likely could not happen today. My professors told me, "If you're going to major in economics, there's no point in staying at Amherst. You might as well just go on and get a Ph.D." One of them got on the phone, called up Paul Samuelson at MIT, and said, "We have somebody that you should take, and can you find some money for him?"

Going to MIT after my junior year meant I would not get a degree. I had this (you might say) risk-taking view. I had the view that degrees were just symbols, and that if you did good work, you didn't need those symbols. Why did I need a B.A. degree anyway? I would just go ahead and become an economist without a degree. So I went to MIT without an undergraduate degree and no understanding that I would ever get one. (Amherst decided to grant me an undergraduate degree after one year at MIT, so I could graduate with my class, and later gave me an honorary doctorate. And a couple of years later, I got a Ph.D., so it all worked out in the end.)

At MIT I again had some absolutely fantastic teachers. Several of them are represented in this lecture series: Franco Modigliani, Ken Arrow, Bob Solow, and Paul Samuelson.

I mentioned earlier the battle MIT had with Chicago, and the Chicago school's view that markets work perfectly, leaving no role for government policy. The problem was the models that we were being taught at MIT actually were consistent with the Chicago school's view. The neoclassical models we were taught (supply = demand, etc.) implied that markets worked perfectly. I knew those models were wrong because I had seen unemployment; I had seen so many things that were inconsistent with the neoclassical model. One thing that really motivated me in my research was my recognition as a first- and second-year graduate student that what my teachers were telling me had to be wrong—even if I didn't yet know what was wrong. Then an active debate began with some of my classmates on what was wrong. Many things were wrong—let me make that clear—but the question was, what was the pivotal thing that was wrong?

For instance, it was assumed there is perfect competition. We all know that's not right, but you could not explain the problems of unemployment with imperfect competition. You could explain some aspects of the distribution of income, you might be able to explain inequality, but you could not explain business cycles. But I was interested in explaining the fluctuations in the economy and the persistence of unemployment. I was trying to figure out which of the assumptions was responsible for these phenomena, and why the models we were being taught could not account for them.

Within the group of people at MIT, I was very much in the center of the political spectrum. There were many classmates who were far to the left of me. There were people who insisted on bringing in Marxian economics, and much more radical departures from the neoclassical models that were at the core of what we were being taught. There was much discussion of "power relationships." At the time I was unconvinced by these approaches.

In the end, the assumption that I became convinced was wrong and that was at the center of the failure of neoclassical economics was that of perfect information. What was interesting about the assumption of perfect information was that if you looked at one of the standard treatises of modern economics, Gerard Debreu's *The Theory of Value* (the analytic workings behind much of what students are taught), he never lists any assumptions about information. And the reason he doesn't is because the assumption of perfect information was so ingrained in his way of thinking he wasn't even aware it was an assumption. I think this is true more generally: Quite often we are not aware of the really important assumptions we make because they are so ingrained in our way of thinking.

The other assumption that was very important is the assumption of rationality—that people are perfectly rational and have well-formed preferences. This is also an ingrained assumption, and it's clearly a bad one. When I look around, it's clear to me that many people are not rational. In fact, when I look at the Chicago economists, they are irrationally committed to the assumption of rationality. So to me it was obvious that those of my colleagues who were wedded to market fundamentalism were so irrationally committed to the hypothesis of rationality that nothing I could say would ever change their minds. It was a religion, not a matter of science. So I focused on those things where I could change their minds, and I thought it was obvious they couldn't really believe everybody has perfect information. I narrowed my research strategy to the simple hypothesis that people have imperfect information but have rational expectations about the world. I assumed all the assumptions of rationality my colleagues had always made but changed one little assumption, and that was the assumption of perfect information. This was a change that nobody, not even they, could disagree with.

This is an idea that has profound consequences. Let me try to briefly describe the evolution of the idea. The first idea was a very simple one—like most ideas, it began very simply and then got elaborated and made more precise. It began with the metaphor of an egg sorter. Some eggs are bigger and some eggs are smaller. If you go to the store and the price is the same for all of them, you want to get the biggest egg for the price you have to pay. It's more efficient (for the farmer or retailer, more profitable) to sort eggs by size, and to sell the larger eggs at a higher price. This provides incentives for farmers to have hens that lay bigger eggs.

I realized that the same principles apply in other markets. When you look at a set of people whom you might hire or a set of products you might buy (such as eggs), you realize there are large differences within the set. At any given wage, you want the most productive worker; at any given price, we want the best product.

The basic idea was that there are very strong incentives on both sides of the market to try to identify who is more able or who has better projects or who is less risky. And this is so on both sides. If I am more able, I have an incentive to convince someone that I am more able because that will drive up my wage. And if I am an employer, I want to try to figure out who the best employees are. This sorting out was a concept that had no role in economics before (even though a lot of the activities of markets are really about sorting) because it was assumed that there was perfect information.

I discussed this basic concept of sorting with my MIT classmate George Akerlof in 1965 (who was to share the Nobel Prize with me thirty-six years later). Two years later, I went to Kenya. I was still quite young—about twenty-six. I was asked a question by the government there: "How much should we invest in education?" And that raised the question, what is education doing? At the time, the standard answer was, "It's improving skills." (This was called human capital.) Another part of the story was, "It's getting credentials." One of my friends in Kenya at the time, Gary Fields, had developed a theory of credentials and how credentialing works. He had made some assumptions that were not consistent with economic equilibrium. Here was a policy question. Fields had provided an analytic framework, but there were some inconsistencies in it, or at least departures from standard equilibrium theory that were unsettling. That led to the development of a number of my ideas that formed the center of my work in the economics of information, in particular the theory of screening.

Another example of how trying to explain or understand what is going on around you can help inspire new theories also occurred while I was in Kenya. In that country (as in the urban areas of so many developing countries) one could observe massive urban unemployment. There was no question of unions, no question of minimum wages, causing the unemployment. Even when there was a minimum wage, it was not enforced. You couldn't blame government or the unions for the unemployment, and the question was, why were wages evidently at levels above market clearing? There had to be an economic explanation, an economic theory. That led to the development of an idea called the efficiency wage hypothesis, which held that the productivity of workers was affected by the wage.

Now, there had been within development economics an analogous idea, based on nutritional concerns: paying workers better led to better nutrition and thus more productive workers. And, thinking about the world of developed countries, I started thinking about how the wage might affect the profitability of firms, as a result of the quality of the labor force firms could hire or the incentives of workers to work or their morale or the turnover rate. Efficiency wage theory helped explain why wages might be above the market clearing level: it paid firms to pay higher wages than they had to in order to get workers.

It also became clear that there was a link between efficiency wage theory and the theory of screening that I was simultaneously developing. One reason that it paid to pay high wages was that higher wages led to an improvement in the quality of the labor force—something that would not have happened if one had perfect information. This is an example of how one theory is linked to the next, and through this linkage each of the theories gets further developed.

It was clear by that point that this approach revolutionized how one thought about labor markets and capital markets, in a quite precise way. I then started thinking about the various mechanisms by which one might sort and screen, such as self-selection mechanisms, examinations, and so forth The mathematics of these theories is extraordinarily complex and—interestingly—not yet sorted out. Many of the problems that I raised forty years ago have still not been fully solved.

The most important idea to come out of this line of research was some work I did about a decade later with my colleague at Columbia, Bruce Greenwald. One of the principal ideas in economics—certainly one of the most influential—is Adam Smith's invisible hand. That is, individuals in pursuit of their self-interest are led, as if by an invisible hand, to the well-being of society. It's the basic idea behind the belief in a market economy. Adam Smith formulated this idea in 1776. But he didn't prove it; it was just a conjecture, but people took it seriously for a long time.

Arrow and Debreu (who were awarded the Nobel Prize for their work) laid down a specific model, trying to identify a set of assumptions under which the invisible hand hypothesis was true. One of the things that Bruce and I did was to show that the reason the invisible hand often seemed invisible was that it wasn't there. In fact, in general, market economies are not efficient. There are almost always interventions by government that could lead to everybody in society being better off. One of the critical assumptions in Adam Smith was that there was perfect information and a complete set of markets—you could buy insurance against every risk, including the risk, for instance, that your house price might go down. We showed that markets are not efficient whenever these imperfections exist in the markets—and they are pervasive in every economy. They are not caused by government intervention; they are inherent. This was a theoretical result that had very profound policy implications: it was a very strong attack on market fundamentalism, the notion that there was a presumption in favor of unfettered markets because they were necessarily efficient.

I finally achieved what I had set out to do: I had come to understand what was wrong with the models we had been taught. At first this was unsettling to many economists, especially those devoted to "free market" economics. A number of the Chicago school economists tried to refute it. Whenever you have a model like this, you can never be sure you did not make a mistake. All humans are fallible. But in thirty years, no one has found a mistake in the math. Sometimes you make hidden assumptions (such as the hidden information assumptions I mentioned earlier in Debreu's theory of value), but no one has found a hidden assumption that invalidates the results. So it really does provide a very strong counter to the notion that is still very prevalent in American mythology about efficient markets.

Another response to these ideas has been that theoretically it's a nice result, but empirically it is not relevant. That's a hard thing to prove one way or the other, but the recent crisis points to the markets not working very well. That episode of markets not working well is obviously "empirically relevant." Similarly, the episodes of great depressions and great recessions, with the associated episodes of mass unemployment, happen often enough that one has to conclude that "market failures" are empirically relevant.

The final response to this analysis is that yes, markets are inefficient, but government is worse. Now, what's interesting about that response is that it entails economists (in saying that) becoming political scientists. It is a statement not about our economic system but about our political system. Those who make such claims are arguably worse as political scientists than they are as economists. There are subtleties in political analysis that those who make claims about the inevitability of government failure do not go into. They neither establish the result empirically nor show it theoretically. Certainly, at least some governments have historically done a credible job in correcting market failures. Even if government is imperfect, outcomes are better than they would have been in the absence of government intervention.

This brings me to the last topic I want to engage, the evolution of my ideas about another set of issues I have been involved with my whole academic life, namely, macrostability issues, which are very germane to the current crisis. The first question I have already discussed: Is the economy efficient? The results show that in general, the markets are not efficient; there are interventions that can improve the efficiency of the markets. The massive waste of resources in the run-up to the global recession of 2008–2009 and its aftermath (the massive misallocation of resources before the crisis, the massive underutilization of resources after the crisis) should be proof enough of the inefficiency of unfettered markets. The theories that I helped develop provide at least part of the explanation for these failures.

The second question is the following: Are the markets stable? The assertion of people like Alan Greenspan is "Yes, they are stable. We don't have to intervene." If the markets get off course, they are self-correcting—and self-correcting fairly rapidly—so we don't have to steer the economy.

Now, the obvious response to those beliefs is, what about the Great Depression? Didn't that happen? That was a long time ago—certainly before most of us who are writing today were alive—so the assertion is that that was ancient history. We're so much smarter today than those people in the 1920s were; we would never do anything as stupid as they did!

What is remarkable is that historically, people have always thought that way; people have always thought they were smarter than the previous generation and incapable of making the same mistakes. In the history of capitalism there have been bubbles, and the bubbles have inevitably burst. There have been these kinds of booms and busts over and over and over again. Of course, each time those involved in the creation of the bubble believe it is different from the past. Every episode is different—the world is always different—but what is remarkable is how similar they all are. We even had a stock market bubble in 1999, less than a decade before the housing bubble. If you look at bubbles, their structure, and what gives rise to them, they are remarkably similar.

This was a question that was very much on our minds in the 1960s, when I was a graduate student, only thirty years out from the Great Depression. We were still interested then in trying to understand why there were economic downturns. Back then, there were models of business cycles—multiplier = accelerator models—that went out of fashion partly because if these periodicities were detectable, rational behavior would be expected to undermine them—so they weren't sustainable. (I've already expressed my skepticism about economists' excessive focus on rationality.)

One of the worst aspects of these economic fluctuations is the high levels of unemployment associated with the downturns. The actuality runs counter to a major hypothesis of Chicago-style economics and its particular models, that demand equals supply—for everything.

But if demand for labor equals supply of labor, what does that say about unemployment? According to that mode of thinking, there's no such thing as unemployment. What does demand = supply mean when 9.8 percent of Americans are unemployed, as is the case now?[5] How does the Chicago school interpret that stubborn figure? They say that the unemployed are really just enjoying leisure. They're getting a little bit of an early vacation. But when most people go on vacation, they are happy. If you look at most of the people who can't get a job, they're not enjoying a vacation. The Chicago school would say this is not a problem for economists; it's a problem for psychiatrists. The unemployed should all go see a psychiatrist and try to understand why they aren't enjoying their leisure. But my own view is this is really quite an absurd view of economics and what's going on today.

This was not the only unsatisfactory aspect of the standard paradigm. To get equilibrium in these models required a full set of markets extending all the way out to infinity, and a natural question to ask was, what would happen if markets extended out only for a thousand years—or a hundred years, or twenty years? One of the results we showed was that you could have perfect foresight for any arbitrary period into the future and still get bubbles. There is an intrinsic dynamic instability, and to avoid it, markets have to extend out infinitely into the future in economic modeling. That was an insight that somehow got lost in the debate over the subsequent years.

Another question we asked was, what would happen if you don't have instantaneous adjustment of wages? The supply-and-demand model says that wages always adjust right away to get the economy to the point where demand equals supply. Again, that assumption is not credible: adjustments do not happen instantaneously. One of my earliest papers with George Akerlof showed that with reasonable adjustment processes, one can actually get regular, cyclical fluctuations. Another study, with my teacher Robert Solow, showed that with reasonable adjustment processes to wages and prices, one could get longlasting unemployment, as real wages adjust very slowly.

Still another strand of work showed that one could even retain the assumption of rational expectations but change another assumption, that of individuals who are infinitely alive, and get not just cycles but an economy that never settled down to any equilibrium.

The bottom line that I want to convey was that over the past forty years, a wealth of work has rejected the notion of markets as self-regulating, stable systems that converge smoothly to an equilibrium. There were some peculiar models (people infinitely alive, with more than rational expectations, single-individual economics, and so forth), but these were constructed worlds that are not the world any of us live in. And yet these models became the predominant paradigm, rejecting all the theory and empirical work on the other side that questioned both the assumptions and the conclusions of these analyses. That says something about the discipline of economics itself.

There were, of course, strong policy implications of these analyses. Policy became the servant of some special interests, those who benefited from the absence of good regulations (including many in the financial sector.)

In a way, I was lucky to be chief economist of the World Bank when the East Asia crisis struck, because it served to test some of the ideas about macroeconomic stability that I had developed in the preceding twenty years. The disparity between my views, which recognized that market economies could be both inefficient and unstable, and those that were then dominant at the IMF and the U.S. Treasury not surprisingly gave rise to quite a bit of controversy. Those who had advocated the simplistic market fundamentalist models basically said a crisis cannot occur. And responding to a crisis that can't occur obviously poses some problems. We got into some intense policy debates. I believe that the policies that were foisted on the countries of East Asia by the U.S. Treasury and IMF made the crisis worse; it made the downturns deeper and longer lasting than they otherwise would have been.

The interesting thing is that, on the whole, the economics profession didn't learn the lessons of the East Asian crisis. I wrote about it a great deal, and I continued to do some research on the subject. But because we didn't learn the lessons of that crisis, we've had the crisis that began in 2007.

Let me just conclude with this thought. Economics is a complex and absolutely fascinating subject.

As I think about that spring afternoon when I went for a walk in a New England forest and decided to become an economist rather than a physicist, I am reminded of a Robert Frost poem about two roads that diverged in a yellow wood. I wonder what might have happened I had I taken the other road.

Notes

Since the lecture at Trinity, some information has been updated in footnotes, or changed for clarity, but most references to chronological events have been left as is. I have retained the informal tone of the lecture.

1. I graduated from high school in 1960, went to Amherst from 1960 to 1963, and then attended MIT from 1963 to 1965. I spent a year at Cambridge in 1966, and then I started teaching at MIT and Yale.

2. In 1981 I wrote, with David Newbery, *The Theory of Commodity Price Stabilization* (Oxford: Clarendon Press of Oxford University Press; New York: Oxford University Press).

3. From 1995 to 1997, during the Clinton administration.

4. I served on the Amherst Board of Trustees for twelve years.

5. The unemployment rate in the United States would peak at 10.0 percent in October 2009.

Joseph E. Stiglitz
Awarded Nobel Prize in 2001. Lecture presented September 30, 2009.

Date of Birth
February 9, 1943

Academic Degrees
B.A., Amherst College, 1964
Ph.D., MIT, 1967

Academic Affiliations
Assistant Professor of Economics, MIT, 1966–67
Visiting Professor, Department of Economics, University of Canterbury,
Tapp Research Fellow, Gonville and Caius College, Cambridge, 1966–70
Christchurch, New Zealand, 1967
Assistant Professor, Cowles Foundation, 1967–68
Associate Professor, Cowles Foundation, 1968–70
Nairobi (under Rockefeller Foundation Grant), 1969–71
Professor of Economics, Cowles Foundation and Department of
    Economics, Yale University, 1970–74
Visiting Fellow, St. Catherine's College, Oxford, 1973–74
Professor of Economics, Stanford University, 1974–76
Drummond Professor of Political Economy, Oxford University, 1976–79
Oskar Morgenstern Distinguished Fellow and Visiting Professor, Institute
    for Advanced Studies and Mathematica, 1978–79
Professor of Economics, Princeton University, 1979–88
Professor of Economics and Senior Fellow, Hoover Institution, Stanford
    University, 1988–2001
Stern Visiting Professor, Columbia University, 2000
Professor Emeritus, Hoover Institution, Stanford University, 2001–
University Professor, Columbia Business School, the Graduate School
    of Arts and Sciences (Department of Economics) and the School of
    International and Public Affairs, Columbia University, Present

Selected Books
*An Economic Analysis of the Conservation of Depletable Natural Re-
    sources*, prepared for the Federal Energy Administration, 1977 (with
    P. Dasgupta, G. Heal, R. Gilbert, and D. Newbery)
The Theory of Commodity Price Stabilization, 1981 (with D. Newbery)
The Economic Role of the State, 1989
*Peasants versus City-Dwellers: Taxation and the Burden of Economic
    Development*, 1992 (with R. Sah)
Whither Socialism?, 1994
Globalization and Its Discontent, 2002
The Roaring Nineties, 2003

(continued)

Toward a New Paradigm in Monetary Economics, 2003 (with Bruce Greenwald)

An Agenda for the Development Round of Trade Negotiations in the Aftermath of Cancun, prepared for the Commonwealth Secretariat, 2004 (with Andrew Charlton)

Fair Trade for All, 2005 (with Andrew Charlton)

Making Globalization Work, 2006

The Three Trillion Dollar War: The True Cost of the War in Iraq, 2008 (with L. Bilmes)

The Selected Works of Joseph E. Stiglitz, Volume I: Information and Economic Analysis, 2009

Freefall: America, Free Markets, and the Sinking of the World Economy, 2010

Mismeasuring Our Lives: Why GDP Doesn't Add Up, 2010 (with J. Fitoussi and A. Sen)

The Price of Inequality: How Today's Divided Society Endangers Our Future, 2012

The Selected Works of Joseph E. Stiglitz, Volume II: Information and Economic Analysis: Applications to Capital, Labor, and Product Markets, 2013

Paul Krugman

This is actually a very tough assignment. The question is *how do you talk about yourself without coming across as pretentious and full of yourself?*, and the answer is, *There probably isn't any way to do that.* I'll try to mix a bit of personal history with a bit of life philosophy (or, anyway, economics research philosophy) and see if that works.

Back in 1976, when I was in grad school, the grad students at Harvard and MIT in economics combined to put on a special program celebrating the bicentennial of the publication of Adam Smith's *Wealth of Nations*, in which we had Jerry Goodman—who wrote and did TV under the name of Adam Smith—dress up in a frock coat and wig to portray the actual Adam Smith. We also got various people to give humorous speeches about Adam Smith. One of them was Alan Blinder (who is now my colleague at Princeton). He gave a list of reasons why Adam Smith could not have been a great economist. They included things like not knowing a lot of higher math, not growing up in the New York suburbs, not being Jewish, and so forth. The point of this story is that I have a very boring background (the exact standard background for an American economist of my generation). The next generation is very different—it has a lot of Asian Americans, and other non-standard-issue economists.

I grew up on Long Island, in the suburbs, on the Babylon line of the Long Island railroad, went to John F. Kennedy high school—nothing interesting! I spent my time not studying very hard but doing okay, and reading a lot of science fiction novels. In particular, I loved the novels of Isaac Asimov, and especially his classic Foundation novels, which (if you haven't read them, you should) were written around 1940. They are about how at some point in the distant future—when galactic civilization is headed for collapse—the psycho-historians, who are mathematically inclined social scientists, with their theory of society, plan the rescue of galactic civilization and in the end save the day. In my teens I wanted to be one of those guys, and economics is as close as you can get to that in today's world.

At first I didn't know that. I went off to college thinking I wanted to do history. And I still love history—I love to read it—but it turned out I didn't have the temperament. Doing history requires an awful lot of nitty-gritty research, and while economics requires research, nitty-gritty research is not my style. Also, history is primarily about what happened. You can talk in the last chapter of your book about why it happened, but it is mostly about the *what* and not the *why*. I wanted more of the *why*. So I gravitated toward economics and had one of those really lucky breaks—the kind of lucky break you find behind the life story of anyone who has done well in his or her career. In my case, I had a really good instructor who taught a really good course (Bill Nordhaus, at Yale)—a special course on the economics of natural resources. I took it, and stumbled onto a good term paper topic for the course. I found some international data on the price of gasoline and on gasoline consumption, and put it together, and said, "Actually, you know, it looks like gasoline demand *is* affected a lot by the price."

On the strength of that paper, I was hired to work for Bill Nordhaus as a research assistant between my junior and my senior year. I spent most of that summer camped out in the geology library at Yale, doing research on energy for his big paper that year, and discovered that I loved doing it. That is, I discovered that doing research was my thing—that economic research was *really* my thing. So that went well, and I got a recommendation from Bill Nordhaus and went to grad school. The point I'm trying to make is that it was good that there turned out to be something I both enjoyed and was reasonably good at, but it was crucial that I lucked into meeting the right person at the right time.

I went off to MIT and raced through, finishing in three years, because I wanted to get out into the world (although you could argue I never have, given the kind of life I have). At MIT I figured out again what style of research suited me. I again lucked into finding another great mentor, this time the late Rudi Dornbusch, a great international macroeconomist at MIT—some would say the most influential international macroeconomist of the past thirty years or so. He was a great teacher and a great inspiration because of the way he worked.

Rudi had a personal taxonomy of economic researchers. He said that researchers can be divided into pigs and goldsmiths. Pigs are people who jump into a subject and wallow around, and that can constitute good research. Goldsmiths are people who produce very finely crafted little things. Both are good—Rudi described Larry Summers as a fearful pig, which was praise! (Larry is amazing—a kind of juggernaut; I'll come back to that later.) I was a goldsmith, which was a little surprising because I am not an organized, neat person in ordinary life. If you ever visited my office at Princeton, you'd see it always looks as if a concussion grenade just went off. (I've received a couple of citations from the fire marshal.) I would also like to say there are some people whose office appears to be a total mess, but they can always find just what they need. I am not one of them.

It turned out, however, that I loved and was pretty good at producing little models. What do I mean by model? This is where we get into what research is about. There are various ways to be a good economist. Doing painstaking empirical work (working with, especially uncovering, data, or producing data) is a very important style, and some people are terrific at it. My colleague, Alan Krueger, has done fantastic work on labor markets in part by finding natural experiments you can look at. There are people who do deep theorizing, who work with proofs and theorems and get at very broad principles, and that's important. The style I've always liked, however, is the fairly small conceptual framework that is informed by real-world data and events but that offers a great way to approach the problem, resulting in an "Aha!" moment. It doesn't have to be a mathematical model (though that's by and large what we do); it could be a real-life story with broader implications.

For example, one of the models I've always thought tremendously important is the Capitol Hill Babysitting Co-op. This was a real-life situation, created by about a hundred and fifty couples in the 1970s who had young children and arranged to swap babysitting so as to save money. The co-op operated on a coupon system. Coupons were issued to all the members, each coupon representing a half hour of babysitting time, and when one couple babysat for another, they would exchange the appropriate number of coupons: The couple whose baby was "sat" would give coupons to the couple that was babysitting. (This story, by the way, was published in the *Journal of Money, Credit and Banking*.) It turned out that people wanted to keep some coupons in a drawer, in case they wanted to go out several nights in a row, and the number of coupons people wanted to hold was more than the number of coupons that had been issued. So members of the babysitting co-op were reluctant to go out because they wanted to accumulate more coupons, and that meant there were fewer opportunities to babysit and earn more coupons, which made people even more reluctant to go out. So the babysitting co-op fell into a recession. Obviously, the world is a lot more complicated than that, but this real-life story gets at the fundamental idea of how it is possible to have not enough demand in an economy. That's the kind of issue that opens my mind and gives me a framework for thinking about a problem.

I eventually discovered I was not too bad at doing this myself, and I had another lucky break in 1976. Bob Solow, the great MIT economist, gave a short course just for fun on topics he was interested in, and one was about the new models of monopolistic competition—models of markets that are not like supply and demand, but where everybody is a little monopolist. And there was an outgrowth of new ideas about how to model this that took place in the mid-1970s, with Mike Spence, Joe Stiglitz, and Avinash Dixit all producing little ways to think about this.

I took that course and came back from it; it was fun, but it bounced around in my head a bit. After I had left for my first teaching job, it came together in my head that this was a way to think about international trade. This would be a gadget—a way to think clearly about what happens when countries specialize in different products because there are advantages to producing each product on a large scale. I was at a loss my first year out of grad school—I wasn't sure what I was doing—and I went to talk with my old mentor, Rudi Dornbusch, to try out a few ideas I had. When we got to talking, I described the idea of doing something for international trade. He said, *"That's the one to work on."* I went back and started working on it some more, and it all fell into place. The more I worked on it, the clearer it got. It was one of those things where the solution was not intuitively obvious until I had done the math. Then it became obvious, and I could figure out a way to do it in plain English afterward. If you're interested, the *American Economic Review* paper that came out of these thoughts—one of their top twenty papers of the past century—was called "Scale Economies, Product Differentiation, and the Power of Trade."

At that point I realized I was developing a style, so I wrote up my rules for research about twenty years ago. Let me give you my four rules for research: listen to the Gentiles; question the question; dare to be silly; and simplify, simplify!

By *listen to the Gentiles,* I mean *listen to people who are not of your tribe.* In economics, there is a lot of work that is not coming from mainstream research; there are a lot of ideas floating around out there. This was especially true in international trade circa 1980. There was a very powerful, standard way to think about international trade, and then there was a counterculture. These counterculture types were saying it is not comparative advantage, there is something else going on. What about imperfect competition? What about the claim that countries export products not for which they have especially favorable supply conditions but for which they have large domestic markets?

All this was floating around, and it was mostly dismissed because people didn't know how to think about it. But once you had some alternative mathematical models—some alternative tools—you could go back and think about these things again, and all of a sudden a lot of that counterculture began to make sense. Ever since, I have said if there are people outside the core—people who are not a part of the standard way of thinking about something—don't assume they're completely wrong. What have they got that we might be missing? That was true for international trade, it was true for economic geography, and it has been true for issues like macroeconomics and financial crises. Just because people are heterodox doesn't mean they're right, either—sometimes someone from mainstream economics comes across as a crank, and he *is* a crank. But you want to listen and think about it. Is there some way in which what these people are saying makes sense?

Question the question: Often, you want to ask whether the question people are asking is the right one to ask. In international trade, a lot of people thought what a model of trade had to do was predict who produces what. That turned out not to be a good question to ask in the context of those models because the models suggested there could be a lot of randomness. The question we *should* be asking is why countries produce different things. Then the model could say it might be a small historical accident that determines what the country produces. But the point was to back up.

The real question is not *why does the United States produce wide-body jet aircraft* but *why is the production of wide-body jet aircraft concentrated in just a few places in the world?* That turned out to be an easier question to answer—and the one that people wanted answered. Today, if you were to ask, *Why did we have a major world financial crisis going nuclear on September 15, 2008?*, I don't know if we would ever be able to answer that question. We ask the question, *Why do modern economies seem to be subject to periodic financial crises?* (as opposed to the specific date and the specific way it happened), and that is a much more answerable question. So see if there is a question that you can answer that is interesting!

Dare to be silly is my third principle. There are always two tempta-tions. One is the temptation to think you always have to be realistic in that what you write has to be a description of the world as it really is (which is impossible because the world is insanely complex, and you have to abstract some things), and the other is the somewhat different temptation to believe that what you are doing has to be technically dif-ficult. In economics there is a strong tendency to believe if the problem does not involve hard math, it can't be real work. That is clearly not right.

Something like the babysitting co-op is a very abstract, stylized, simple story that doesn't use any math at all but tells you something important. In general, finding something that is simple is more important. It doesn't have to be hard. Some of the best economics I have seen is actually very simple, but simple in a way that is sophisticated: *What is it we really need to think about here, and how do we do it?*

In fact, let me use this occasion to put in a good word for Milton Friedman. I don't agree with everything Friedman advocated, but he pro-duced a lot of great economics. His key insight into the value of flexible exchange rates was a spectacular example: he compared flexible rates to daylight saving time. Rather than have everybody change their work schedule, we just move the clocks back.... That's a comparison that's incredibly simple and yet very powerful.

Last, *simplify.* If you are doing this kind of analysis, you always want to think, "What am I putting into this story that doesn't need to be there?' Always strip it down to as few moving parts as you can.

Those are the four rules, and I have adhered to them throughout my professional life. After the international trade work, which took about six years, I realized I should be talking about economic geography, too. But that was the *listen to the Gentiles* principle. A lot of people compare the way things are within countries—why are some regions more densely populated than others? Why did the fact that in 1817, if you were going to try to build a canal from the East Coast to the Great Lakes you pretty much had to go up the Hudson River, lead to a situation in which New York is still the largest American city some one hundred sixty years after the canal ceased to be relevant? Very similar underlying economics led me to modeling the geography of economies within countries instead of between countries. I suddenly realized that international economists had been doing economic geography all their lives without realizing it. How do we formalize that?

Now, what you should know about international economics is that it is a very divided field. That is, there are two kinds of international economics. There is real trade (why do countries produce what, where?) and there is international macroeconomics (roughly speaking, what determines the value of the euro?). These two divisions require two quite different sets of tools, and by and large they involve different and often mutually hostile sets of people. Only slightly joking, the real trade people think the international macro people are flaky and ad hoc and often don't make any sense at all, and the international macro people think the real trade people are boring and dull and occupied with minor technical issues of no significant interest. And by and large, both sides are right. Oddly, however, I have always done both, and have felt very comfortable with both sides. A wonderful paper by Rudi Dornbusch, Stanley Fischer, and Paul Samuelson, published in 1977, that redacted one hundred seventy years of economics in one go, bridged the real and the monetary sides. When I saw that, I said, "*Hey, both sides make sense,*" so I've always done that.

In my first couple of decades as an economist I published several papers on currency crises—I actually invented the academic literature of currency crises in grad school—but the real place where that came together and became my big preoccupation was with the Asian financial crisis of 1997–98. If you look at economists focusing on current events, you see a big difference between those of us who were involved in the Asian crisis and those who were not. For many people in the international field, the crises in Indonesia and Thailand and Korea—and also the slide of the Japanese economy into a long stagnation—were a huge wakeup call. The monsters of the Great Depression have not gone away— they're still here! Look at the people who were closest to being right about the current crisis. For example, Nouriel Roubini forecast some aspects of the crisis. He earned his spurs working on the Asian crisis in the late 1990s. And I got very involved with it as well.

The book *The Return of Depression Economics and the Crisis of 2008* is a much revised reissue of a book called *The Return of Depression Economics,* which I published in 1999. The revision was inspired by the Asian crisis and basically said, *This could happen to us.* When you looked at the problems that had occurred, both the high-speed financial crisis that had happened in places like Indonesia and the prolonged, seemingly intractable slump in Japan, these were not the result of specifically Asian problems. Watching Asia led me to rethink what I thought I knew about macroeconomics. It led me to worry that something like that could happen to us. And then I reissued the book in 2008 when it *did* happen to us. It still remains an important guide.

I've been vocal about the financial crisis and its aftermath partly because I looked at the Asian crisis in 1998, and have worried ever since that we could get caught in something like the kind of trap that Japan was caught in. When it hit, I said, *Here it is. We have to move effectively to deal with this*, and we didn't, and haven't. I think Ben Bernanke is doing the best he can under the circumstances, but my former departmental chairman (now demoted to running the world), is being referred to as "Bernanke-san." It really is amazing how much worse we're doing than the Japanese did.

I wrote a little model in 1998 called "Japan's Trap," which has been my guide to everything. That was one of the best papers I ever wrote. By the standards of economic modeling, it's ridiculous, just a couple of equations and a few diagrams, but it's got the story that you need. There are some elaborations, which I've been working on, that you need, but what I said about Japan turned out to be an alarmingly good guide to the United States over the past five years.

In the last few years I have become known as a public intellectual. I started writing nontechnical economics in 1982, when I was on the staff of the Reagan Council of Economic Advisers, a nonpolitical position. Marty Feldstein, who was the chairman, brought a couple of whiz kids from Cambridge, Massachusetts, to work with him on the staff. Among the junior economists was Greg Mankiw, and he also brought in two people who were senior economists, me and the other guy, Larry Summers.

A funny story: Larry and I were charged with writing the 1983 Economic Report to the President, and Larry's sections were, ah, somewhat lacking in tact. (An old saw says that people grow worse as they grow older because they become more like themselves.) So I ended up taking over the writing—I was good at the euphemisms. You don't say "*union wages are too high in the steel industry*," you say "*prices and wages in some U.S. heavy industries are probably excessive in an integrated world economy*," or something like that.

After that, I took to writing more popular economics. I wrote a couple of well-received articles for *Foreign Affairs* in the early nineties and then got hired to write for *Slate*, in its early stages, and then got a second gig at *Fortune* (also writing once a month), and I was having a ball doing this stuff. Finally, the *New York Times* approached me in 2000. They said, "*We have all these people writing about the Middle East*, and nobody cares about the Middle East anymore, so we need somebody *to write about the economy.*" They had apparently gone through their list of people who knew economics and were not terrible writers (already a very small set), and there I was.

How do I juggle these roles? First of all, the logistics. It turns out that anybody who does policy-oriented international economics has to be not quite human in some dimension. So Larry Summers is a juggernaut—he gets not just himself but *teams* of people moving in ways I can't imagine. Jeff Sachs is a cyborg. He can take forty-eight hours flying without sleep to get to Outer Mongolia, and this is literal, and step right off the plane into meetings. I don't have any of those things ... but I do write faster than anybody. So I can actually handle doing a column for the *Times.*

When I was hired we were in the middle of the dot-com bubble, and I thought I would be writing interesting stories about the new economy. Instead, it turned out to be a pretty bitter political environment. I caught on to that earlier than most people. I'm not a proper journalist (I don't know how to pound the pavement or do interviews with important people), but I do know some things that most of the people in this journalistic venture don't know (arithmetic), and I know how to read statistics, and so sometimes I make the *Times* nervous, but I do get to weigh in on the debate. Surprisingly, a lot of the rules for research actually apply pretty well to writing columns, too. Listen to the Gentiles—don't accept that whatever passes for Washington conventional wisdom is necessarily right. Quite often the crazy people are crazy, but sometimes they are entirely right. There have been some amazing incidents when you could see that a particular line became accepted—nobody who was anybody was going to challenge it—and yet if you took a real look at it, the facts were pointing entirely against that. Just to mention the biggest of those: in 2002, if you asked "*What evidence do we actually have that there are weapons of mass destruction in Iraq? Is there any evidence?*," it turned out there wasn't. So I was one of those people who said, "*There is not a case for this war,*" which wasn't economics, but it was the same style of thought that lay behind the economics.

Now we are in the crisis, and it is still going on, and we are *not* responding to it effectively. It's terrible, but it's actually good for column writing—and also for economics. I'm coming up on fifty-eight years old, and people at my age do not do a lot of fundamental research anymore. Even Paul Samuelson had slowed down a lot by the time he was my age. But I have been doing some real modeling work—with Gauti Eggertsson of the New York Fed—because it is interesting. It's horrible, but it's interesting, and there is a lot to be done. I've had a pretty satisfying career, and I'm trying to do what I can to make the world a less bad place. Mostly, I'm just wondering, how does this work out? This is the nightmare that has haunted economists for seventy-five years, and now it's come true. What do we do now? I will keep on trying my best to do something about it.

Paul Krugman
Awarded Nobel Prize in 2008. Lecture presented February 2, 2011.

Date of Birth
February 28, 1953

Academic Degrees
B.A., Yale University, 1974
Ph.D., MIT, 1977

Academic Affiliations
Assistant Professor, Yale University, 1977–80
Visiting Assistant Professor, MIT, 1979–80
Associate Professor, MIT, 1980–84
Professor, MIT, 1984–94
Professor, Stanford University, 1994–96
Professor, MIT, 1996–2000
Professor, Princeton University, 2000–present

Selected Books
Market Structure and Foreign Trade, 1985 (with E. Helpman)
Exchange Rate Instability, Lionel Robbins Memorial Lectures, 1988
Market Structure and Trade Policy, 1989 (with E. Helpman)
The Age of Diminished Expectations, 1990
Geography and Trade, 1991
Currencies and Crises, 1992
Peddling Prosperity, 1994
Development, Geography, and Economic Theory, 1995
The Self-Organizing Economy, 1996
The Accidental Theorist, 1998
The Return of Depression Economics, 1999
The Spatial Economy, 1999 (with M. Fujita and A. Venables)
Fuzzy Math, 2001
The Great Unraveling, 2003

Peter A. Diamond

The title of this lecture series suggests that I try to decipher the process of my change from the time I took my first economics class as an eighteen-year-old math major to my present self as a seventy-two-year-old public policy analyst and public policy–oriented economic theorist. Perhaps a better title would be "My Memory of My Evolution," for I have no diaries, no notes; just working papers and published papers, and memories. I have identified five phases in the evolution of my approach to being an economist: student (first economics class, 1958), applied mathematician (first research, 1960), teacher (first publishable lecture material, 1964), the "what's wrong with economics" phase (first research, 1965), and policy analyst (first detailed analysis, 1974). These were not separate phases but overlapping, as I expanded my repertoire of interests and methods.

My first economics class as that eighteen-year-old math major was a yearlong introductory class at Yale in 1958–59, taught by Charles Berry. It was my first exposure to economics, for I had had no exposure to discussing or analyzing economies or economic policies before that. While my father checked stock prices daily, there was no sign to me that he was interested in the economy that lay behind the stocks, and no discussion of the economy or economic policy at the dinner table. Stocks held no interest for me, apart from a short period between the time I was given shares in a single company for my bar mitzvah and the time that stock became worthless. The gift came from a neighbor who was a stockbroker, making the experience particularly salient.

I didn't look closely at stock prices again until nearly 2000, when asked to do so by the Office of the Actuary of Social Security, at a time when I was much involved in the policy process around Social Security. Starting in the mid-1990s there were lots of proposals with a similar theme of investing in stocks, through a trust fund or through individual accounts. The Office of the Actuary had the problem of projecting stock returns as part of projecting Social Security finances. I was commissioned to write an essay addressing the question of what stock market rate of return they should use in the projection, given their projection of the workings of the economy. The essay appeared in the *Social Security Bulletin* (2000). It turned out to be a very lucrative assignment. As I studied the determinants of stock prices in general, not just of individual stocks, and looked at the bubble happening at the time, I kept adjusting my retirement portfolio. When my study started, my 401k was 95 percent stocks. By the time I completed the report, it was down to 35 percent stocks, somewhat before the bubble broke.

Phase 1: Student

I want to begin a year before that first economics class, with the start of my college education. I was obliged to name a major. I chose to name electrical engineering. I had no idea what the major really was, or what a career in the field entailed. I was required to name a major. I thought that engineering paid well, that I had been good at math and science in high school, and that I needed a subject that did not require being able to work with my hands. Partway through my freshman year, I learned a little about what the subject entailed, and promptly thought to change my major. Stepping back from my first decision, starting over in choosing a major, I chose the subject I liked best and did my best in— mathematics. Not that I had any idea of what a career as a mathematician might entail, either. This choice surprised the graduate student who had shown me a graduate electrical engineering text with its unattractive (to both him and me) mathematics. Choose what you like and do well still seems a good rule of thumb for an undergraduate.

In my second year at Yale, I took a yearlong class in real analysis from Shizuo Kakutani in which I learned how to do a rigorous mathematical proof. I took one-semester classes in probability and number theory, both taught by Oystein Ore, and I took the yearlong introductory economics class from Charles Berry as a seminar, not as part of a large introductory class. I have no memory of how I chose that class; I suspect I needed to fulfill a social science requirement, but that would not be a full explanation. While I enjoyed the class and was good at it, at its completion, I had no intention of taking any more classes in economics. The following summer I was an actuarial trainee at Metropolitan Life, which did not catch my interest and did not add much to my understanding of what a mathematician might do for a living.

For my third (and last) year at Yale, I planned to take three yearlong math classes in order to complete the major—the senior seminar, which was devoted to game theory (yes, I did read every word of von Neumann and Morgenstern)—and two graduate classes, in topology and abstract algebra. And I planned to take a second year of French. Beyond those four classes, I was shopping for something interesting. Several famous possibilities were being offered by visiting professors instead of the usual faculty members, which left me at loose ends. For advice, I turned to Charles Berry, the faculty member I had become most friendly with. He suggested that I take the yearlong intermediate theory class for economics honors majors, taught by Edward Budd. Not knowing how academe worked, I was a little surprised to be let in, as I was not an economics major. My pleasure in the fall microeconomics class started my serious consideration of economics versus mathematics—not that I knew what economists did for a living, either.

This class increased my interest in economics enough that I ended my study of French and registered for the graduate mathematical economics course taught by Gerard Debreu. The class was based on his newly published *Theory of Value* (1959). Debreu was an outstanding teacher, *Theory of Value* was an outstanding text, and I remained unsure in what direction to go for graduate work. I remain grateful to Debreu for this early and thorough grounding in general equilibrium theory, which has stood me in good stead, shaping my thinking about economics. The class was also taken by several of my math major classmates. Although I have no idea of the source, something was pushing us math majors collectively away from math. This push affected my friends Dick Beals, who tried economics and then returned to math, and Dave Krantz, who became a psychologist. (I have wondered whether Dick's outcome might have been different had he tried economics at MIT instead of Harvard.) I applied to graduate school in both economics and mathematics while trying to make up my mind.

Phase 2: Applied Mathematician

I do not know which teacher (or teachers) provided the information that led to an offer of a job as a summer research assistant for Tjalling Koopmans in 1960. I was hired to help with the mathematics as he continued to work on infinite horizon preferences. When Koopmans asked me to produce an example of a function satisfying certain conditions, I thought it might be a lot easier to consider a whole set of functions—a class of functions—that would satisfy these conditions rather than cranking one out. The class of functions I provided led Koopmans to reorient his research plan, giving this class of functions a central role. And he promoted me to co-author for my first publication (Koopmans, Diamond, and Williamson 1964). I have always viewed Koopmans as a splendid economist and a splendid person, and so as a role model for doing economics and relating to people.

I had no idea when doing the analysis that the class of functions would make for interesting economics. I was just avoiding what I thought would be tedious calculations. It has been interesting to be on the other side of a similar experience. At one point I gave a graduate student RA a math assignment—something to crank out—and he came back with an answer that was so interesting it became a short paper in the *American Economic Review* (Aura, Diamond, and Geanakoplos 2002). As when I was the RA, Saku did not realize how interesting his calculation was. An important part of maturing as a researcher is figuring out what is interesting in what you have stumbled across. In general, it is important to figure out what problems have stronger possibilities of turning up something interesting. I do it as a theorist, but of course, the same thing is true with empirical work. One needs to ask whether the answer to the question being researched is likely to be interesting. If you just come up with an answer nobody's interested in, it may not have been a good use of your time.

I applied to graduate schools in both math and economics, and then settled on the MIT Math Department. My initial plan was to take micro- and macroeconomics and complex and real variables, and to decide at the end of the year which subject was better for me. A beauty of the American educational system is its enormous flexibility. But the complex variables class conflicted with both micro and macro, and I needed a different plan. I dropped complex variables, planning to make it up in the summer if economics didn't hold me. Given the imbalance in classes, the math graduate registration office (GRO), represented by George Thomas (author of the best-selling calculus book I had studied), thought I should be advised by the Economics Department. Thomas straightforwardly transferred me (along with my fellowship) to the Economics Department. There was no paperwork for me to fill out—he put my file in an envelope, handed it to me, and told me to walk across campus and hand it to the economics GRO, Bob Solow. Bob promptly added the statistics and economic history classes to my fall load.

I enjoyed the economic theory classes and didn't enjoy the real variables class (and I was better at the economics). My reaction to the real variables class was that it was about proving the same theorem about integration and differentiation again and again, in steadily more general settings. I had no interest in the generalizations, perhaps because I was ignorant of what could be done with greater generality that couldn't be done otherwise. On the other hand, for me, economics was all about new models for different phenomena. That is indeed what I've been devoting my career to—trying to focus on how to capture insights into the complex things that are happening—so it was an easy decision. After the fall semester, I was committed to economics; my experimentation had ended after one semester. The Math Department still had to pay the second semester of my fellowship.

I was still approaching economics research as an applied mathematician, as I had as Koopmans's RA. That is, my focus was on finding math to use on well-defined economics questions. Browsing in a pamphlet of theorems about matrices, I saw one that would provide a result on *tâtonnement* convergence to general equilibrium, a theorem that I had not seen in the literature. I took it to Frank Fisher, who was giving a reading class to Steve Goldfeld and me at the time—basically an exploration of potential thesis topics. Frank hadn't seen the theorem either, and we immediately headed for Paul Samuelson's office. Paul went straight to his bookcase, pulled down a conference volume, and opened it to a chapter by Lionel McKenzie. It had exactly the theorem I had in mind. While I had lost a potential thesis chapter, I felt that I was in very good company.

As I finished my classwork and started working on my thesis, I continued working in the applied mathematician mode. Over the summer (1962, spent at RAND Corporation), I looked at the same problem I had worked on with Koopmans, examining properties of infinite horizon preferences, but using a different mathematical structure. The resulting analysis became my job market paper and landed me a job at Berkeley. With that paper done, I read the Yale thesis of T. N. Srinivasan, with whom I had driven around the country after we had shared an office at the Cowles Foundation while I was working for Koopmans. I had an idea for solving a problem he didn't get to in his analysis of growth theory. So this was his problem and my answer—I was still an applied mathematician at work.

These first two thesis chapters were finished before September was over. I cockily asked my thesis supervisor, Bob Solow, how many theorems it took to complete a thesis. He said a year's worth. But I promptly hit a wall and had no ideas for the compulsory third essay. Early in the spring semester, Solow gave me a book to read by W. E. G. Salter (1960), *Productivity and Technical Change*, which analyzed the falling costs of production for a firm as a result of technical progress. I recognized that the structure could be inverted and turned into a growth model, and I was off and running on my third essay, including an extension of the one-sector model to two sectors. I finished just in time for a June degree. Again, I was reacting to something I had read, finding a way to use math on well-structured questions.

Phase 3: Teaching

Following a summer at the Council of Economic Advisers, working for George Perry, I became one of the four new assistant professors at Berkeley who started in September 1963. Hiring was organized by Andy Papandreou, shortly before he left for a political career in Greece. There are three Nobel Prizes among the four of us. In 1963–64, Berkeley was a perfect place to be a young theorist. The junior faculty interacted all the time, and became close friends. Dan McFadden, Bernie Saffran, and Sid Winter were particularly important for me, both personally and professionally. For part of the fall I shared an office with Olly Williamson, and we played handball each week. And the senior faculty were supportive of us.

I didn't know it at the time, but I was about to start phase three of my evolution—with research driven by the process of teaching. I taught the graduate micro-macro sequence (one semester of each) jointly with Tibor Scitovsky. But key for me was a yearlong undergraduate public finance class for majors, which had a prerequisite of intermediate theory. Since the students had had intermediate theory and we had all year for the class, I could develop the material systematically and thoroughly, with enough time to start with foundations.

Of course, I drew on the public finance class I had taken at MIT, taught by E. Cary Brown. We had worked all the way through the recently published *The Theory of Public Finance* by Richard Musgrave (1959). It is an outstanding book, written by an outstanding scholar. Musgrave's approach was to put public finance on a general equilibrium footing (as had happened to international trade theory). This was important for my intellectual development and complemented the general equilibrium orientation I had learned from Debreu. This background played a central role in my later work on optimal taxation.

As I read about different topics for class, I did not want just to teach the articles or book chapters; I wanted to figure out my take on the topics. This started a phase transition as material prepared for class evolved into a good paper. I attribute this success to the circumstance of preparing carefully for a class of sharp, attentive students. And it meant I was thinking about the economics, not just applying math. In the spring, preparing to lecture on the public debt, I read the relevant writings of James Buchanan (*Public Principles of Public Debt: A Defense and Restatement*, 1958) and Modigliani ("Long-Run Implications of Alternative Fiscal Policies and the Burden of the National Debt," 1961). These were very different in both focus and modeling style. I realized I could construct a model that addressed the distributional issues central to Buchanan's analysis and the economic growth issues central to that of Modigliani. The model started as a handout to the students in this undergraduate class, and then became my 1965 paper on the public debt. I have continued to prefer developing my own materials rather than teaching the contents of existing papers. While many people worry about the time needed for teaching taking away from the time for research, my experience was that they reinforced each other. Indeed, the times when my research went most slowly occurred when I did little teaching.[1]

Berkeley was great for me for more reasons than just good teaching and research opportunities. First on the list was meeting my wife, Kate (real name Priscilla Myrick), who was a student at Berkeley law school when I started teaching economics. I was teaching public finance, and she found taxation to be her least favorite class. Nevertheless, we married in 1966. In Berkeley I witnessed the 1964 start of the student uprisings with the Free Speech Movement. I saw repeated mistakes made by the Berkeley administration, and watched the same mistakes repeated by university administrations across the country. I was part of a faculty that was trying to help, but not succeeding much.

The teaching phase of my research continued until I stopped teaching in 2010. Before turning to the start of phase four in the summer of 1965, let me mention two later examples of research coming from lecture preparation. My return to MIT in 1966 meant teaching graduate public finance for the first time. The standard analysis of the deadweight burden of taxation was the model of Al Harberger ("The Measurement of Waste," 1964). But I didn't like it; thinking that it didn't show consistent underpinnings. So I worked up a different approach using the expenditure function, which was a hot new tool at the time. While this eventually became part of a joint paper with Dan McFadden (Diamond and McFadden 1974) combining my analysis of the burden of taxation with his analysis of the evaluation of lumpy investments, both using the expenditure function, the impact for me came much sooner.

As I was teaching this topic to graduate students at MIT in 1966–67, having put the analysis on the blackboard, I had the thought that it might be interesting to see what kind of tax structure would give the least possible deadweight burden in the economy, while raising the amount of revenue needed, using only linear taxes on transactions. I walked out of the classroom, down to my office, and immediately started writing down the calculation. And I was launched onto optimal taxation and the aggregate efficiency theorem. Shortly after arriving at Churchill College, Cambridge, for the next summer, I presented the optimal taxation results I had developed. That the expenditure function is defined in terms of prices, not the quantities consumed, was critical for the next step. Jim Mirrlees came up after the seminar and pointed out that by being in price space, my model of a one-consumer economy could be used as a start on analyzing a many-person economy. That is, with prices the same for all households, the welfare, demand, and supply functions were interpretable as coming from a many-person economy. We started working together on optimal taxation that summer and had essentially finished our first paper by the end of the summer, which we then presented at Econometric Society meetings that fall. The paper was not published until 1971 for a variety of reasons, including the absence of the Internet. Collaboration at a distance was slow, with the compensation of the value of spending time together, which we did repeatedly.

Jim and I have completed a dozen papers together and have had something in progress (sometimes very slowly) ever since, even today. The success of this collaboration reflects a number of factors, including our having perhaps the ideal distance between the ways our minds work. Our thinking has been similar enough that communication has been quick and thorough, but our different approaches to things make me suspect that much of this would not have happened had we been working separately. (One of our rare miscommunications opened up an issue neither of us had recognized.) This collaboration has been a joy.

When trying to work out something new for class, I'm showing students the research process as it is happening. This approach is exciting, but it is very hard on the students. Some of them love it; some of them hate it. But it works for my getting into new research. In time, having thought a lot about a subject and found a way of teaching it that I like, I am no longer exposed to many new issues. That doesn't stimulate my thinking, and it also results in a tendency to get rather boring in class.

After hitting diminishing returns from teaching taxation, and having trouble making it exciting for students, that topic was passed to my public finance colleagues, and I returned to teaching pensions. Years later I was asked to cover optimal taxation again, because of the department's teaching needs that year. The mathematics used to analyze the optimal income tax, following Mirrlees, was very complex. I thought to give the students a simple example and looked for an assumption about the economy that would make the calculation simple enough to make it easy to see some of what was involved in the optimization. The assumption I chose to explore was that there were no income effects in labor supply, which followed from having preferences linear in the single consumption good in the model. While not fully realistic, as people do change in response to some income changes, it is also not too far off because those changes are often small and slow (apart from triggering earlier retirement for some). I set to work cranking out the optimum in this case, and found that it greatly simplified the problem. That simplification allowed a lot of insight into some of what matters when trying to decide on marginal income tax rates.

The results were so interesting, and so suggestive of insights that would be relatively robust, that I assumed I was merely rediscovering what must have already been in the literature. I was surprised to discover that was not the case, and the result was that the handout I had made for the students became the basis for another paper in the *American Economic Review* (1998), which ignited a literature drawing inferences, particularly on how high the marginal tax rates should be on the very top earners. It is something that I continue to write about, and, by the way, the number is a lot higher than what we have now.

Phase 4: What's Wrong with Economics

Now I jump back to 1965. Among the pleasures of an academic career are the visits to other places, for short times and, especially valuable, for long ones. My first year of leave was 1965–66. Frank Hahn organized the opportunity for me to be an Overseas Fellow at Churchill College, Cambridge. Talking economics with Frank lived up to expectations. At Cambridge, I gave a series of four lectures on the economics of uncertainty (my first venture into teaching that subject) and had the experience of tutoring outstanding undergraduates—you can imagine the pleasure of meeting weekly with Tony Atkinson and Geoff Heal. But I no longer had my usual teaching load.

The summer of 1965, just before leaving for England, was the beginning of phase four, of my doing research built around what struck me as inadequacies in economics. From Debreu I had acquired a thorough understanding of a model in which the present and the future are treated exactly the same, as comes with the assumption that markets are complete. With no costs to creating or using markets and a complete list of the states of nature, all plans for the future are made and coordinated before anything actually happens in the economy. I thought the range of insights one could gain were limited because markets are incomplete and because we deal with the future very differently from the way we deal with the present. I have thought of the complexities of what happens over time as the source of one of the real holes in a lot of economics. What particularly interested me was creating models that avoided the completeness of the coordination of agents that happens with complete competitive markets.

Later, I found a quotation from Alfred Marshall revealing that I was on the same page as he, a passage in which he refers to the "element of Time" as "the centre of the chief difficulty of almost every economic problem" (Marshall 1948, ii.) I tried to bring out this perspective on the importance of how time is modeled in the Churchill Lectures I gave in 1993, which were published in 1994. While the book was a mixed success, I thought the cover I had chosen was right on target—Harold Lloyd hanging from the hands of a clock far above street level as an image of a theorist grappling with the modeling of time. It is very hard, and you're dangling without a net.

The point of the kind of theory work I do is to get insights—insights about how the economy works and, in my case, insights mostly about policy. The idea is to capture a piece of an issue, and to capture it in ways so that you learn something that you can carry over when you think about many of the pieces, which you need to be doing when addressing concrete policies. Again, I found a link to Marshall:

It [is] necessary for man with his limited powers to go step by step; breaking up a complex question, studying one bit at a time, and at last combining his partial solutions into a more or less complete solution of the whole riddle.... The more the issue is thus narrowed, the more exactly can it be handled: but also the less closely does it correspond to real life. Each exact and firm handling of a narrow issue, however, helps towards treating broader issues, in which that narrow issue is contained, more exactly than would otherwise have been possible. With each step ... exact discussions can be made less abstract, realistic discussions can be made less inexact than was possible at an earlier stage. (Marshall 1948, 366)

And if a model developed for one question is useful for answering other questions, that is a bonus.

Central to my responding to the concern about differences between the present and the future was the idea that an awareness of uncertainty changes the way you think about the economy. Economic agents are always trying to work things out, in this way different from the standard model of consumers, which comes with a list of what the consumer can buy and a list of prices, so that the maximization of utility follows directly. My concern about trying to capture the effects of uncertainty per se led me to stay away from including asymmetric information in the models I analyzed.

In the summer of 1965, before heading for England, I decided to model different ways of allocating resources with incomplete markets. I was not focused on any particular aspect of actual institutions, but just planned to write down a bunch of models and then see what might come of it, hoping to recognize something worth pursuing. The very first model I wrote down had linear restrictions on how uncertainty was dealt with. Recognizing its potential value, my first venture into analyzing incomplete market equilibrium in 1965 became a paper on the stock market (1967). A continuing attempt to extend that model into more time periods contributed to my lack of research productivity while on leave for 1965–56, as did the absence of regular teaching while at Churchill College.

My next foray into changing basic theory started from the absence in the Arrow-Debreu theory of a mechanism or process by which an economy achieves its equilibrium allocation. In the 1960s there were ongoing analyses of processes that might converge to competitive equilibrium, with a focus on equations for price adjustment based on excess demands and supplies at tentative prices (referred to as *tâtonnement*). Rather than asking whether a process could be found that would converge to a standard competitive equilibrium, I decided to look for the allocation to which a plausible process would converge. This led first to my 1971 paper, which applied search theory to a retail market.

I set up a model of price adjustment in which each firm sets prices each period, and consumers don't know all the prices that are out there. To find out a price in this simple model, you visit a store, and that uses some resources. You can think of it as time; you can think of it as utility or money. If you want to see whether a different store has a better price, you've got to pay—excuse the expression—a "search cost" to go to another store. It turned out this process had a rather stunning result. Not only did it not go to a competitive equilibrium, it went to what would be a monopoly price if all the firms colluded and worked together. It did that because, if I have a customer in my store and I know there's a cost to checking the price elsewhere, then my price can be a little bit higher than elsewhere by less than that cost, without triggering a departure to shop elsewhere. So I have a little bit of market power, but that's true of every store. Each store, taking advantage of that little bit of market power, contributes to a dynamic process that results in stability only when at the monopoly point. At that point, nobody wants to raise the price, even though they can. They just don't want to.

Of course, I did not think of this result as directly applicable. Rather, it was both a start on a form of dynamic modeling and a claim that the issues raised by search had important consequences, not minor ones. The paper was followed by models exploring equilibrium with alternative patterns of information about prices, as well as empirical studies of the presence of a distribution of prices for identical goods. Particularly noteworthy were the work of Butters (1977) and of Burdett and Judd (1983).

What I wanted to do next was to push into other settings, and eventually to get a model of the economy as a whole in order to consider Keynesian issues. The desire for a microeconomic foundation for macroeconomic analyses was shared by a number of economists at the time, although the thinking varied considerably as to what they thought it might lead to. What would it take to have a model of the economy as a whole, in which all transactions involved some of these costs? There are costs to trying to sell things, as well as costs to trying to buy them. But only after a decade of working on the same thing again and again did I get to the point of modeling the whole economy (1982).

The retail price paper came from thinking about a very concrete setting. I was looking for another concrete question that would lead to new modeling of events happening over time. I thought that by taking law classes, I would be exposed to many legal problems, and perhaps I would find one or some that would have time-dimension issues that did not fit standard modeling. Those cases might then provide a basis for developing the next model to work on. I completed three of the first-year classes at Harvard Law School, doing one class per year. (I then took the income taxation class with Stanley Surrey.) We lived in Cambridge at the time, and I walked to class. Walking to class doesn't leave much uncertainty about the length of time to get there. Yet I found I was getting to class quite early. Why was this happening? And then I realized: I was so happy to be sitting in this classroom, with no responsibility for teaching it.

Well, the research plan didn't work. I did write some law and economic papers, but none of them connected to why I took law classes, and none of them would show up on a list of the papers I felt best about. My next attempt to move the process forward was to choose a question that made no sense in an Arrow-Debreu setting. The goal was to affect my thought processes, not necessarily to find anything interesting. The resulting paper ("Welfare Analysis of Imperfect Information Equilibria," 1978) fit the bill. It altered my thought processes while not containing much of interest.

I then took to thinking in terms of a process in real time (and using a Poisson process, as I had seen Dale Mortensen do). Ironically, this resulted in a law-and-economics-related question, the effects on overall efficiency of alternative rules for breach of contract (jointly published with Eric Maskin, 1979, 1981). But, as I recall, the question fit the modeling approach, rather than vice versa. Then I moved on to modeling the labor market (1981, 1982a), and then the entire economy (1982b). And in work with Olivier Blanchard, I went from examining steady states to looking at the cycle, particularly the Beveridge curve, on which I am still working.

There is a nice little story about the way the mind works that is connected with finally producing a model of the whole economy. The summer I wrote that paper—I don't remember now whether it was '81 or '80—Kate and I were sharing a house on Wings Neck, Cape Cod, with our good friends Sid and Georgie Winter. Sid, a distinguished economist, had been an assistant professor with me; he was at Berkeley when I arrived, and we have been friends ever since. We were sharing a rented house on a point extending into Buzzards Bay, where there was a loop I could walk, and I think better walking. (I talk better standing still.) I would walk this loop and try to think about why I couldn't get a workable version of the model I had in mind for the entire economy. It was just too complicated. It wasn't working. I finally decided to describe how I was stuck to Sid. I knew that he was a terrific economist; I thought that he would react, we would have a good conversation, and I would get something out it. Completing yet another loop around the point, I saw Sid come out of the house as I was coming up the driveway. So I focused on formulating in my head how to explain to him where

I was in my thinking. The mental process—maybe it parallels the teaching-research links that I have talked about—was trying to explain to Sid where I was stuck. Formulating my problem for Sid, I got unstuck before a word came out of my mouth. I had a simplification that seemed likely to work, and went back into the house and started writing down a model. The slow, hard work was done; it was then just a matter of sorting it out. Sid had not said a word, but I couldn't have done it without him.

Phase V: Policy Analyst

My activity as a policy analyst started in 1974. While continuing to do basic research, I have been involved in policy discussions and analyses, primarily about public pensions. Pensions have been the subject of a series of enjoyable collaborations, with Bill Hsiao, Peter Orszag, and Nick Barr. In 1972, the Social Security benefits schedules were overhauled to include automatic adjustments for inflation, but they were not indexed properly. The Social Security Administration was aware of this but did not consider it important. The year 1972 was a bad time to have indexing that would rely on continuing mild inflation not to explode in cost. With Social Security costs projected to explode, Congress was told of a need for reform. First, Congress wanted to check whether it would have to do something about it. Bill Hsiao was asked to form a panel to answer whether the expenditures were growing too rapidly, as the Office of the Actuary had said. At the recommendation of Paul Samuelson, Bill approached me, and I joined the Panel on Social Security Financing, consulting to the U.S. Senate Finance Committee.

Our answer to whether there was a need to change the indexing was yes. Then came a request to Bill to form a panel to lay out the issues that lay ahead in accomplishing reform, because this called for a significant, fundamental change in the way benefits were constructed in the system. This wasn't just tinkering with the parameters. And I joined that panel and became part of the debate that led to the 1977 Social Security reform.

Our consultant panel prepared a report that both Ways and Means and the Senate Finance Committee wanted (Report of the Consultant Panel on Social Security to the Congressional Research Service, August 1976). Now I was involved in recommending policy, involved in exploring the multiple aspects that matter for putting together a policy analysis that reflected many issues that seemed important.

I got caught up in Social Security for two reasons. First, it matters: the Social Security Administration and its programs matter a great deal for a lot of people, and trying to get them to function well is important. And second, as with teaching, thinking about policy has fed my basic research. The prime example was addressing the question of what should determine how much bigger monthly benefits should be after a delay in the start of benefits. I was aware of no theory beyond using the actuarial equivalent for the average person. Jim Mirrlees and I set to work to develop a theory of what ought to be done, drawing on the role of insurance with asymmetric information about job opportunities (our first paper was published in 1978, and work is ongoing). The dynamic nature of choosing a time to retire led us to find (but not name) the inverse Euler condition.

In addition to a focus on Social Security in the United States (which led to a series of articles and a book with Peter Orszag in response to seeing the report of the commission appointed by President Bush), I have studied and written about public pensions in a sizable number of countries, including Australia, Chile, China, France, Germany, Italy, the Netherlands, New Zealand, Spain, Sweden, and the UK. The work on China led to two books with Nick Barr (and another one in process). Both collaborations have been a source of great pleasure from the writings and real satisfaction from the outputs.

I am not sure Nick and I would have launched into the first book had we seen this passage from Honoré de Balzac, "It is as easy to dream a book as it is hard to write one." On the other hand, we have not learned to stop, even as we had this experience.

Pensions have been a perfect topic for me. They fit well with my public finance theory interests and with my social concerns. I have given many talks on economics, particularly on Social Security, which has remained a hot topic in the United States for a long time. I have ended some of those talks with a quotation from Franklin Roosevelt's second Inaugural Address, January 20, 1937, which I saw carved on a wall at his memorial in Washington, D.C.: "The test of our progress is not whether we add more to the abundance of those who have much; it is whether we provide enough for those who have too little."

Notes

1. For more on how valuable teaching has been for my research, and for the diverse ways I approached finding and choosing topics to work on, see Giuseppe

Moscarini and Randall Wright, "An Interview with Peter Diamond," *Macroeconomic Dynamics* 11 (2007): 543–565 (doi:10.1017/S1365100507060403), and my "My Research Strategy," in *Eminent Economists II: Their Work and Life Philosophies*, ed. Michael Szenberg and Lall Ramrattan (New York: Cambridge University Press, 2013).

References

Aura, Saku, Peter Diamond, and John Geanakoplos. 2002. Savings and portfolio choice in a two-period two-asset model. *American Economic Review* 92 (4): 1185–1191.

Buchanan, James. 1958. *Public Principles of Public Debt: A Defense and Restatement.* Homewood, IL: R. D. Irwin.

Burdett, Kenneth, and Kenneth L. Judd. 1983. Equilibrium price dispersion. *Econometria* 51 (4):955–970.

Butters, Gerard R. 1977. Equilibrium distributions of sales and advertising prices. *Review of Economic Studies* 44:465–491.

Debreu, Gerard. 1959. *Theory of Value: An Axiomatic Analysis of Economic Equilibrium.* New Haven, CT: Yale University Press.

Diamond, Peter A. 1965. National debt in a neoclassical growth model. *American Economic Review* 55 (5):1126–1150.

Diamond, Peter A. 1967. The role of a stock market in a general equilibrium model with technological uncertainty. *American Economic Review* 57:759–776.

Diamond, Peter A. 1978. Welfare analysis of imperfect information equilibria. *Bell Journal of Economics* 9 (1):82–105.

Diamond, Peter A. 1981. Mobility costs, frictional unemployment, and efficiency. *Journal of Political Economy* 89:798–813.

Diamond, Peter A. 1982a. Wage determination and efficiency in search equilibrium. *Review of Economic Studies* 49:217–227.

Diamond, Peter A. 1982b. Aggregate demand management in search equilibrium. *Journal of Political Economy* 90 (5):881–894.

Diamond, Peter A. 1998. Optimal income taxation: An example of a U-shaped pattern with optimal marginal tax rates. *American Economic Review* 88 (1):83–95.

Diamond, Peter A. 2000. What stock market returns to expect for the future? *Social Security Bulletin* 63 (2):38.

Diamond, Peter A., and Eric S. Maskin. 1979. An equilibrium analysis of search and breech of contract: I. Steady states. *Bell Journal of Economics* 10:282–316.

Diamond, Peter A., and Eric S. Maskin. 1981. An equilibrium analysis of search and breach of contract: II. A non-steady-state example. *Journal of Economic Theory* 25:165–195.

Diamond, P. A., and D. L. McFadden. 1974. Some uses of the expenditure function in public finance. *Journal of Public Economics* 3 (1):3–21.

Harberger, Al. 1964. The measurement of waste. *American Economic Review* 54 (3): 58–76.

Koopmans, Tjalling C., Peter A. Diamond, and Richard E. Williamson. 1964. Stationary utility and time perspective. *Econometrica* 32 (112):82–100.

Marshall, Alfred. 1948. *Principles of Economics*. 8th ed. New York: Macmillan Co.

Modigliani, Franco. 1961. Long-run implications of alternative fiscal policies and the burden of the national debt. *Economic Journal* 71:730–755.

Musgrave, Richard. 1959. *The Theory of Public Finance*. New York: McGraw-Hill.

Report of the Consultant Panel on Social Security to the Congressional Research Service. 1976. 94th Congress, 2d Session. Washington, DC: U.S. Government Printing Office, August. http://www.ssa.gov/history/reports/hsiao/hsiaoIntro.PDF.

Salter, W. E. G. 1960. *Productivity and Technical Change*. Cambridge University, Department of Applied Economics, Monograph No. 6. New York: Cambridge University Press.

Peter A. Diamond

Awarded Nobel Prize in 2010. Lecture presented April 17, 2013.

Date of Birth

April 29, 1940

Academic Degrees

B.A. Mathematics, summa cum laude, Yale University, 1960
Ph.D. Economics, MIT, 1963

Academic Affiliations

Assistant Professor, University of California, Berkeley, 1963–65
Acting Associate Professor, University of California, Berkeley, 1965–66
Overseas Fellow, Churchill College, Cambridge, 1965–66
Associate Professor, MIT, 1966–70
Professor, MIT, 1970–88
John and Jennie S. MacDonald Professor, MIT, 1989–91
Paul A. Samuelson Professor, MIT, 1992–97
Institute Professor, MIT, 1997–2011
Department Chairman, MIT, 1985–86
Visiting University College, Nairobi, 1968
Visiting Hebrew University, Jerusalem, 1969
Visiting Nuffield College, Oxford, 1969
Visiting Balliol College, Oxford, 1973–74
Visiting Harvard University, various years
Visiting European University Institute, 1992
Visiting University of Siena, 2000

Selected Books

*A Search Equilibrium Approach to the Micro Foundations of Macroeco-
nomics*, 1984
On Time: Lectures on Models of Equilibrium, Churchill Lectures, 1994
Social Security Reform, the 1999 Lindahl Lectures, Oxford, 2002
Taxation, Incomplete Markets and Social Security, the 2000 Munich
Lectures, 2002
Saving Social Security: A Balanced Approach, 2004 (with Peter R. Orszag)
Reforming Pensions: Principles and Policy Choices, 2008 (with Nicholas
Barr)
Pension Reform: A Short Guide, 2010 (with Nicholas Barr)

Lessons from the Laureates: An Afterword

A goal of the Nobel Economists Lecture Series at Trinity University has been to enhance our understanding of the link between biography, especially autobiography, and the development of modern economic thought. Each of the twenty-three lectures, organized around the theme "my evolution as an economist," provides source material for this endeavor.

The purpose of this afterword is twofold. The first section identifies common themes as well as some disparate views expressed by the laureates in describing their development as economists. Among these are the importance of real-world events, coupled with a desire for rigor and relevance; the critical influence of teachers and scholars during the laureates' formative years; the need for scholarly interaction and a lively intellectual environment; and the role of luck or happenstance in their lives. Most, but not all, of the laureates view their research program as having been largely unplanned, evolving through the marketplace for ideas and taking form as a coherent body of thought only after the fact. There are exceptions, however. In summarizing these themes, we rely heavily on the words of the laureates, taken from their Trinity University lectures.

The second section assesses the difficult question of whether or not biography is important for understanding the development of modern economic thought. Ultimately, we cannot provide a definite answer to this question. One can neither observe nor simulate in any methodical fashion the appropriate counterfactual—how economic thought would have developed absent these individuals and their particular life histories. The inability to answer this question in a definitive way, though, does not imply that it should be ignored. These twenty-three essays provide ample source material for reasoned speculation on the significance of biography in the evolution of economic thought.

Common Themes and Disparate Voices

Few individuals begin life expecting or desiring to be an economist. This same generalization holds true among Nobel economists. The laureates came to economics through the influence of particular teachers or scholars, because of the intellectual challenge and rigor of economics, or because economics was perceived as relevant for addressing real-world issues. Several of the laureates cite their favorable reaction following exposure to formal economics. Four examples follow:

Rare is the child, I suspect, who wants to grow up to be an economist, or a professor.... Cutting my teeth on *The General Theory*, I was hooked on economics. Like many other economists of my vintage, I was attracted to the field for two reasons. One was that economic theory is a fascinating intellectual challenge, on the order of mathematics or chess. I liked analytics and logical argument.... The other reason was the obvious relevance of economics to understanding and perhaps overcoming the Great Depression and all the frightening political developments associated with it throughout the world.... Thanks to Keynes, economics offered me the best of both worlds. (James Tobin)

In the first semester of my sophomore year I took required courses in accounting and microeconomics. The former was, in reality, bookkeeping—and mindless bookkeeping at that. I loathed it. But microeconomics had everything: rigor, relevance, structure, and logic. I found its allure irresistible. The next semester I changed my major to economics and never turned back.... Thus my first stroke of luck. I sometimes break out in a cold sweat thinking about what might have happened had I taken a modern accounting course and an institutional economics course. (William Sharp)

My choice of Colorado College was more eventful than I could have forecasted.... In my junior year, I took a readings class in economic growth from Ray Werner.... We read Ricardo, Smith, and Arthur Lewis.... The professor also loaned me his copy of Paul Samuelson's *Foundations of Economic Analysis* (which I still own) to read as an extra bonus.

Samuelson's *Foundations* had a major impact on me. It demonstrated to me that economics could be as rigorous and empirically relevant as physics.... At the same time, it showed that economics had empirical content through the theory of revealed preference. I saw a counterpart in social science to the hard science I had experienced in Oppenheimer's classroom. Lewis's *Theory of Economic Growth* appealed to my liberal arts training.... My junior year readings class led me to decide on economics as a career.... I could have my science and my social science too. (James J. Heckman)

I relished the unbending rigor of mathematics, physics, and engineering, but then, as a senior, I took an economics course and found it very intriguing—you could actually learn something about the economic principles underlying the claims of socialism, capitalism, and other such "isms"? Little did I know, but I was intrigued. Curious about professional economics, I went to the Caltech library, stumbled on Samuelson's *Foundations of Economic Analysis,* and later that year, von Mises's *Human Action.* From the former, it was clear that economics could be done like physics, but from the latter there seemed to be much in the way of reasoning that was not like physics. I also subscribed to the *Quarterly Journal of Economics,* and one of the first issues had a paper by Hollis Chenery on engineering production functions. So economics was also like engineering. I had not a hint then as to how much those first impressions would be changed in my thinking over the decades to follow. (Vernon L. Smith)

The desire for relevance is an important theme in the lectures. As indicated in the earlier quotation from James Tobin, for the older generation of Nobel laureates it was the Great Depression that triggered an interest in economics. Tobin, as well as other laureates, makes this point forcefully:

Keynes's uprising against encrusted error was an appealing crusade for youth. The truth would make us free, and fully employed too…. Economic knowledge advances when striking real-world events and issues pose puzzles we have to try to understand and resolve. (James Tobin)

Yes, 1932 was a great time to be born as an economist. The sleeping beauty of political economy was waiting for the enlivening kiss of new methods, new paradigms, new hired hands, and new problems. Science is a parasite: the greater the patient population the better the advance in physiology and pathology; and out of pathology arises therapy. The year 1932 was the trough of the Great Depression, and from its rotten soil was belatedly begot the new subject that today we call macroeconomics. (Paul A. Samuelson)

Soon there will be no more active economists who remember the 1930s clearly. The generation of economists that was moved to study economics by the feeling that we desperately needed to understand the depression will soon have retired. Most of today's younger and middle-aged macroeconomists think of "the business cycle" as a low-variance, moderately autocorrelated, stationary, stochastic process taking place around a generally satisfactory trend. That is an altogether different frame of mind from the one with which I grew up in the profession. (Robert M. Solow)

Although the Great Depression is long past, the desire for relevance remains crucial among Nobel laureates. Edmund S. Phelps characterizes his research as a response to a prevailing orthodoxy that lacked relevance, leaving too little room for realistic human behavior and uncertainty. For example:

But having read Hayek's *Prices and Production* (2nd ed., 1935) and Keynes's *General Theory,* I could sense that the neo-Keynesian research, though intriguing and possibly useful in some ways, had utterly abandoned the modernist emphasis on incomplete information and imperfect knowledge in favor of some new method or methodology with which I was not at all comfortable. Instinctively, as Keynes would have said, I understand that the neo-Keynesian models, in abstracting from these things, inadvertently left no role for humans to play. There could be no beliefs as distinct from what is true, no expectations as distinct from what is or will be, no mental stimulation and challenge, no problem solving, no creativity, and no discovery. (Edmund S. Phelps)

Gary S. Becker is one of several laureates who looked for relevance with respect to social issues:

During my senior year at Princeton, however, I was losing interest in economics and began to think that I should go into something else. Economics seemed excessively formal to me.... Economics appeared incapable of helping me understand the issues in which I had an interest: inequality, class, race, prestige, and similar issues that were important for society.... I remained unhappy—unhappy by what seemed to me a disconnect between what economists would talk about in textbooks and elsewhere and what I wanted to talk about....

[At Chicago] Milton Friedman became the greatest influence of any individual on my development as an economist. Attending his graduate course in price theory was just exciting, and I would eagerly wait for that course to come twice a week.... Here I saw economics as a tool and not simply as a game played by clever academics.... [Friedman's course in price theory] showed me what I thought was not possible. You can do economics and do it in a rigorous way and nevertheless talk about important problems. (Gary S. Becker)

The above quotation from Becker shows how Milton Friedman opened his eyes to the relevance of economics. Most who were students at the University of Chicago mention the charismatic importance of Friedman in their lives. Personality matters. But none of the Nobel laureates, even Friedman, is more renowned for his personality than for his scientific work. Becker is far from alone in recognizing the influence of a great teacher or a particular individual. Myron S. Scholes, James M. Buchanan, Edward C. Prescott, and Eric S. Maskin are among the others:

McMaster turned out to be a fortuitous choice. Because it was such a small school, Professor McIver, a University of Chicago graduate in economics, worked closely with me in my studies. He directed me to read and understand the work of many classical economists, including the more contemporary teachings of Milton Friedman and George Stigler.... Because of my enjoyment of economics and my planned return to business, I decided on business school, not law school. Although my family wanted me apply to other schools, such as Harvard, I wanted to go only to the University of Chicago, where Stigler and Friedman were teaching and conducting research. (Myron S. Scholes)

I am not a "natural economist" as some of my colleagues are, and I did not "evolve" into an economist. Instead I sprang full blown upon intellectual conversion, after I "saw the light."... I was indeed converted by Frank Knight, but he almost single-mindedly conveyed the message that there exists no god whose pronouncements deserve elevation to the sacrosanct, whether god within or without the scientific academy. Everything, everyone, anywhere, anytime—all is open to challenge and criticism. There is a moral obligation to reach one's own conclusions, even if this sometimes means exposing the prophet whom you have elevated to intellectual guruship. (James M. Buchanan)

With this collaboration, I understood the comment he [Lucas] made after I defended my dissertation. He was telling me to use dynamic economic theory to model aggregate phenomena. With this collaboration I became a Bob Lucas student and an economist. To return to the theme of this lecture, Bob Lucas is the most important person in my development as an economist. Having been at the right place at the right time was another stroke of luck.

The principle guiding my research is the importance of theory interacting with measurement. I came to the conclusion that there was no hope for the approach being used in macroeconomics of empirically searching for the policy invariant laws of motion of the economy. I had read the Lucas critique. Something else was needed. Given this, I stopped teaching what was then called macroeconomics and began using dynamic equilibrium models to study aggregate economics as practiced by Bob Lucas. (Edward C. Prescott)

Notwithstanding such odd episodes, I found mathematics a very attractive subject, and I might well have stayed a mathematician had I not wandered almost by accident into a course in economics that the great economist Kenneth Arrow was offering on the economics of information. I didn't know who Arrow was at the time, and I certainly didn't know what the economics of information was, but I thought that the class should at least be informative. Arrow's lectures were improvisational. He appeared to have thought up what he was going to talk about on the way over to the lecture room from his office, and sometimes not even then. But in addition to being improvisational, they were inspirational. The list of topics was a bit of a hodgepodge. There was some information economics, as the name of the course suggested. There was some team theory, there was a unit on planning procedures, there was a discussion of moral hazard and adverse selection. But the highlight of the course, and the part that changed my life, was Leonid Hurwitz's work on mechanism design theory. (Eric S. Maskin)

Tobin emphasizes the important role played by his graduate school professors, but suggests that much of this learning occurred outside the classroom:

I see in retrospect that our professors left most of our education to us. They expected us to teach ourselves and learn from each other, and we did. They treated us as adult partners in scholarly endeavor, not as apprentices. I am afraid our graduate programs today try too hard to convey a definite and vast body of material and to test how well students master what we know. (James Tobin)

Nearly all the laureates identify a particular work environment, usually but not always a university economics department, as a critical factor in their evolution as an economist. George J. Stigler, Lawrence R. Klein, and William F. Sharpe are particularly emphatic on this point:

So to understand the conditions under which modern work in economics has emerged, one must look at the conditions of training and work of the modern scholar. Those conditions are no substitute for creativity, but they have become an indispensable condition for creativity to be exercised....

There is good reason for believing that economics is a social science in quite another sense from the indisputable one that it concerns itself with mankind in social relationships. It appears also to be a social science in the literal sense that it is a science in which it is difficult to do creative work if one is not in a congenial intellectual environment. (George J. Stigler)

A truly exceptional group of people was assembled in Chicago during the late 1940s. I doubt that such a group could ever be put together again in economics. From our closely knit group, four Nobel laureates have emerged, and two others came from the next bunching of Cowles researchers—partly at Chicago and partly at Yale. We worked as a team and focused on a single problem—to put together an econometric model of the American economy (a second attempt after Tinbergen's of the 1930s)—using the best of statistical theory, economic theory, and available data. After about four or five years of intensive research built up around this theme, the team dispersed to new openings in academic life. (Lawrence R. Klein)

The RAND [Corporation] of 1956 was a truly unique organization.... Employees were free to work any hours they chose, within wide limits. Office doors were open, intellectual discussions on the most wide-ranging topics were de rigueur, and everyone was expected to spend one day per week on research of strictly personal interest.

Those were heady days. Some of the key work in systems analysis, operations research, computer science, and applied economics was being done at RAND. One of our first computers was designed by John von Neumann. George Dantzig was working on linear programming. Some of the most illustrious academics served as consultants. Everyone was on a first-name basis. If ever there was a place for one interested in practical theory, the RAND Corporation in the 1950s was it. (William F. Sharpe)

A common theme in the laureates' lectures is the role of luck. The emphasis on the role of luck no doubt stems in part from the general tone of humility expressed in many of the lectures. Obviously, a combination of brilliance and hard work is a necessary though not sufficient, condition for being awarded a Nobel Prize. The laureates often use the term "luck" to mean the unpredictability or unplanned path through which their career evolved. Each can readily imagine some alternative turn taken early in life that would have set them on an altogether different path. Friedman, Becker, and Paul Krugman make this fact explicit:

I have been enormously impressed by the role that pure chance plays in determining our life history.... As I recalled my own experience and development, I was impressed by the series of lucky accidents that determined the road I traveled. (Milton Friedman)

I soon realized that much more was needed.... There were no foundations for the theory of investment in human capital.... I set about trying to sketch out a small set of foundations to give the work theoretical content.... I had no vision at all of what this would lead to. Once again, here is an example of the role of luck.... I was amazed and then greatly excited when I began to realize that this framework could integrate scores of observations and regularities in individual earnings, occupational differences in earnings, and employment. (Gary S. Becker)

Doing history requires an awful lot of nitty-gritty research, and while economics requires research, nitty-gritty research is not my style. Also, history is primarily about what happened. You can talk in the last chapter of your book about why it happened, but it is mostly about the *what* and not the *why*. I wanted more of the *why*. So I gravitated toward economics and had one of those really lucky breaks—the kind of lucky break you find behind the life story of anyone who has done well in his or her career. In my case, I had a really good instructor who taught a really good course (Bill Nordhaus, at Yale)—a special course on the economics of natural resources.... So that went well, and I got a recommendation from Bill Nordhaus and went to grad school. The point I'm trying to make is that it was good that there turned out to be something I both enjoyed and was reasonably good at, but it was crucial that I lucked into meeting the right person at the right time....

At MIT I figured out again what style of research suited me. I again lucked into finding another great mentor, this time the late Rudi Dornbusch, a great international macroeconomist at MIT—some would say the most influential international macroeconomist of the past thirty years or so. He was a great teacher and a great inspiration because of the way he worked. (Paul Krugman)

One area where there is not a consensus among the laureates is how research programs are developed. The above passage from Becker shows that he had little idea what eventually would develop from his early forays into human capital theory. Many of the laureates likewise insist that their research was not part of any grand design or vision but rather evolved within the highly competitive marker for ideas. Buchanan, Samuelson, and Krugman are exemplars:

I recognize of course that my own research-publication record may be interpreted as the output of a methodological and normative individualist whose underlying purpose has always been to further philosophical support for individual liberty. In subjective recall, however, this motivational thrust has never informed my conscious work effort. I have throughout my career and with only a few exceptions sought to clarify ambiguities and confusions and clear up neglected pockets of analysis in the received arguments of fellow economists, social scientists, and philosophers. To the extent that conscious motivation has entered these efforts, it has always been the sheer enjoyment of working out ideas, of creating the reality that is reflected finally in the finished manuscript. (James M. Buchanan)

Repeatedly I have denied the great-man or great-work notion of science. Every drop helps, the old farmer said, as he spat into the pond. One does the best one can on the most pressing problem that presents. And, if after you have done so, your next moves are down a trajectory of diminishing returns, then still it is optimal to follow the rule of doing the best that there is to do. Besides, at any time a Schumpeterian innovation or Darwinian mutation may occur to you, plucking the violin string of increasing return....

Scientists are as avaricious and competitive as Smithian businessmen. The coin they seek is not apples, nuts, and yachts; nor is it the coin itself, or power as that term is ordinarily used. Scholars seek fame. The fame they seek ... is fame with their peers—the other scientists whom they respect and whose respect they strive for. (Paul A. Samuelson)

At that point I realized I was developing a style, so I wrote up my rules for research about twenty years ago. Let me give you my four rules for research: listen to the Gentiles; question the question; dare to be silly; and simplify, simplify. (Paul Krugman)

Thomas C. Schelling notes that the direction of his research was shaped in no small part by suggestions and requests from others.

The second, related impression is that nearly everything I've done was stimulated by opportunities I didn't seek but came to me, and many things I've done, including some of the things I'm most satisfied with, I did at the suggestion of somebody else or as a result of some unsolicited invitation. (Thomas C. Schelling)

Douglass C. North, Franco Modigliani, James Tobin, and Peter A. Diamond are four laureates who describe a more methodical course. One knew where he was headed early on, one attempted to run counter to whatever was currently in fashion, one states that he consciously aimed for the big problem of his day, and one drew his research ideas from teaching.

I knew where I was going from the day I decided to become an economist. I set out to understand what made economies rich or poor because I viewed that objective as being the essential prerequisite to improving their performance. The search for the Holy Grail of the ultimate source of economic performance has taken me on a long and certainly unanticipated journey, from Marxism to cognitive science, but it has been this persistent objective that has directed and shaped my scholarly career. (Douglass C. North)

As I contemplate my contributions, I find one unifying thread: a propensity to swim against the current by challenging the self-evident orthodoxies of the moment, be it that the classics are altogether outdated, or that the rich must save a larger fraction of their income than the poor, or that debt financing is cheaper because the interest rate on high-quality debt is lower than the return on equity.... I would love to be able to continue to play that role. But I don't want to think too much about where I am going. I just like to let things come and be ready to jump in where there is excitement. (Franco Modigliani)

The most important decisions a scholar makes are what problems to work on. Choosing them just by looking for gaps in the literature is often not very productive and at worst divorces the literature itself from problems that provide more important and productive lines of inquiry. The best economists have taken their subjects from the world around them. (James Tobin)

As I read about different topics for class, I did not want just to teach the articles or book chapters; I wanted to figure out my take on the topics. This started a phase transition as material prepared for class evolved into a good paper. I attribute this success to the circumstance of preparing carefully for a class of sharp, attentive students. And it meant I was thinking about the economics, not just applying math.... I have continued to prefer developing my own materials rather than teaching the contents of existing papers. While many people worry about the time needed for teaching taking away from the time for research, my experience was that they reinforced each other. Indeed, the times when my research went most slowly occurred when I did little teaching. (Peter A. Diamond)

Important breakthroughs in economics do not occur in a vacuum. Some of the major developments in economics are likely to have occurred in much the same fashion absent the contribution of a particular economist. Other contributions are more distinct—very much shaping the future path of economic literature in that area. For other work, its precise contribution to economics evolves over time. These alternative possibilities are evident in the following passages:

Multiple discoveries are in fact very common in science.... Developments in related fields with different motivation help one to understand a difficult problem better. Since these developments are public knowledge, many scholars can take advantage of them. It is pleasant to the ego to be first or among the first with a new discovery. However, in this case at least, the evidence is clear that the development of general equilibrium theory would have gone on quite as it did without me. (Kenneth J. Arrow)

Further work led to "Expectations and the Neutrality of Money" ... finally published in the *Journal of Economic Theory* in 1972.... The paper contained a careful and explicit construction of a theoretical example of an economy in which the motives, opportunities, and information of every economic actor was unambiguously spelled out. Expectations were rational. In this setting, as in Friedman's AEA address, there was no long-run trade-off between employment and inflation. Yet the model also implied the kind of correlations between employment and inflation that were then widely interpreted as hard evidence that such trade-offs did exist. I felt I understood for the first time both why Friedman and Phelps were right in arguing there was no long-run trade-off between unemployment and inflation and why econometric tests continued to reject this "natural rate" view.

Working out this example took me to the limit of my technical skills and beyond: it was not easy reading, nor had it been easy writing.... It is easy for me to see the influences of Phelps, Rapping, Prescott, and Cass in this paper, but the combination was new and striking: no one else was doing macroeconomics this way in 1970. The paper made my reputation. (Robert E. Lucas, Jr.)

The question arises, was that book, *Micromotives and Macrobehavior,* game theory? If so, what makes it game theory? ... I didn't think so at the time—it just didn't occur to me—but there were hints in the Nobel Committee's remarks that the committee thought it was. And I see now that everything in that book had to do with individuals' adjustment to or anticipation of the choices of others, and with needs and opportunities for coordination, formal cooperation, or submission to direction or regulation.... I've now concluded that this is game theory. Game theory, I find (or choose to define), is very much about *situations*. What is "prisoners' dilemma" but a situation? The logic of choice is central to game theory, but what game theory—again, I'm thinking about the invention of matrices—is often critical for identifying situations in which choice is somehow puzzling, problematic, or challenging, and in identifying how many distinct situations of a certain kind there may be. (Thomas C. Schelling)

The "lessons from the laureates" identified in this section provide considerable insight into the intellectual process through which ideas in economics, and no doubt other disciplines, develop and evolve. One cannot come away from these lectures without an appreciation for the critical role of teachers, the intellectual environment, the search for rigor and relevance, and the role of happenstance in the evolution of modern economic thought. Contained within these lessons is at least the suggestion that biography matters. It is to this topic that we turn.

Does Biography Matter?

Do the autobiographies presented at Trinity University since 1984 reveal anything of scientific significance? Would our understanding of the laureates' pathbreaking achievements be incomplete without these stories of their intellectual journeys, as told in their own words?

The phrase "as told in their own words" is important. For in the Trinity lecture series each author is the living subject, providing an "oral history" of his own "evolution as an economist." Of necessity, time constraints force the scholars to present their glimpses into the past in a much abbreviated form. What they choose to reveal and not reveal is of their own choosing. But in the case of autobiographical data, the voice and image of the living subject are before us in a way not possible in biographies written by others. There is a sense of immediacy in these personal histories that typically is not to be found in more impersonal narratives of their lives. It is likely that the more influential of these economists will inspire biographies written by others long after these subjects have passed from the scene. Absent direct contact with these laureates, the biographers will find it difficult to capture the uniquely idiosyncratic perspective that only autobiography can offer. For that reason, future biographers might find the Trinity lectures providing invaluable insights for their work.

When the lecture series was organized in 1984, it was thought that a larger purpose was to supply crucial source material for a theory of scientific discovery. After thirty years, it is fair to ask whether the rationale has been in any significant sense justified. Do these autobiographical accounts reveal a connection between an economist's life and his or her intellectual achievements?

Certainly the lectures make obvious some links between environment and subsequent intellectual development. The traumatic impact of the Great Depression led several future laureates to identify economics as their intellectual discipline of choice. But this evidence for the role of biography hardly suffices. After all, the most casual observation would lead one to expect that experience affects choices. Does the study of the lives of the laureates do nothing more than confirm what everybody knows? Or can we say something about the extent to which the very substance of their contributions is a reflection of the individual lives they have led?

The last question is complex and can be answered only through the careful study of the autobiographies themselves. In that way, we become observer-participants in the lives of the speakers, focusing not only on what they explicitly reveal but also on any inconsistencies and self-deceptions in their narratives. Yet in doing so, the authors of this afterword must assume the role of biographers themselves, as distinct from the autobiographers-subjects of the lecture series. Autobiography is, of course, a subset of biography. Nevertheless, it forms a crucial part of the archive from which biographical data are drawn. The autobiographies provide valuable material from which we, as biographer-editors, try to reach a deeper understanding of the connection between the lives led and the pathbreaking work achieved. If we can accomplish this task, the larger purpose of the lecture series will have been realized.

In the introduction to this volume we asserted that "these autobiographical essays reveal psychological truths—perhaps hidden from the subjects themselves—that an especially perceptive reader will discern." The autobiographical elements give us some tantalizing glimpses into the imaginative and creative minds of these scholars, insights that only autobiography could provide. Below we offer some examples.

The link between autobiography and subsequent intellectual development is made explicit in James J. Heckman's essay. As Heckman recounts his childhood,

My father fell victim to company politics and suffered various demotions and lateral transfers throughout his career.... He urged me at an early age to enter a profession where I could develop an independent reputation and avoid the politics of the bureaucracy of middle managers that he had experienced. I took his message to heart and decided early on to enter a profession where I could make my own mark independent of the good will of any superior and where I would never have to be a company man. (James J. Heckman)

His father's career also took his family to towns in the border South and West, where "I saw firsthand the last vestiges of the Jim Crow system of racial discrimination. Its protocols and intrinsically demeaning effects on all participants fascinated me."

Also critical for Heckman was his early faith, being raised in a tradition of fundamentalist Protestant Christianity. "As a young child, I fervently embraced the faith of my parents and by age eight, I was a child minister giving sermons on Sunday evenings introduced by a motto taken from the New Testament, 'A little child shall lead them.' It was expected that when I became an adult, I would be a minister.... My deep religious belief led me to read and study the Bible very closely. I committed vast passages of it to memory." But Heckman's faith did not survive.

By my early teenage years ... I began having doubts.... I began to notice inconsistencies in the Bible, and as I read more broadly in science and philosophy, I came to question the literal interpretations of creation and other aspects of the fundamentalist Christianity with which I was raised.... The intolerance, bigotry and unwillingness of most of the elders in my church to discuss ideas left me deeply dissatisfied. I found that I was unable to accept authority qua authority, a trait that has characterized me ever since.... At the same time, I learned early to live off my own intellectual and emotional resources. (James J. Heckman)

Heckman ends his essay by summarizing his approach to economics:

Economics is useful only if it helps to explain the economy and solve practical problems. It produces wise policy advice when it is anchored in data and potentially dangerous advice when it is not.... Good answers to these questions require good theory and econometrics.

Anchoring my own research in serious empirical analysis has protected me from the fads that plague the profession and has given me the autonomy and independence I have always craved.... This is my way of following my father's advice of being independent and developing an independent reputation and my way of avoiding appeals to authority in any form—whether mathematical or divine—that motivated my early break with organized religion. (James J. Heckman)

For Heckman, the lessons of his childhood experience not only made the choice of economics and empirical inquiry irresistible but also helped frame his personal and intellectual approach to his career within economics.

Joseph Stiglitz observes the impact on his thinking of the Midwest locale of his childhood and the guiding principles learned from his parents.

My upbringing and early schooling were also very important. I grew up in the steel town of Gary, Indiana, on the southern shores of Lake Michigan. Gary and the upper Midwest in general were in much better economic shape during my childhood than they are now, but it was still not the kind of background that would normally be thought of as an advantage for a future academic. For my intellectual development, however, it was extremely formative, in several senses. Gary was founded in 1906. A hundred years later it is in deep decline. Its course essentially traced that of the industrial period of America. No one growing up in this town—emblematic of the rise and fall of industrialization in America— could believe that markets were an unmixed blessing. I saw the darker side—and darker not only because of the pollution (which was often invisible)—but also because of the obvious economic and social costs: periodic unemployment, labor strife as workers struggled to get a fair share of the benefits that increasing productivity was bringing to the country, rampant discrimination, and urban decay....

I also owe to my parents (my father in particular) my ability to serve in government. A problem for many wanting to serve in the Clinton administration was that, when they were vetted, it would turn out they hadn't paid Social Security taxes on their household help. When I was growing up, my father had told me that you should always pay Social Security taxes for anybody who works for you, because many of these people were poor people and particularly in need of help in their retirement. That's why we have the Social Security Administration. So he was one of the generation for whom Social Security (which started in the mid-1930s) was very important. Today, Social Security benefits are too often taken for granted.

My father believed that one should pay the Social Security taxes for one's employees not just because it was the law but also because it was the right thing to do. So I had done so for those who had worked for me—and was able to surmount this hurdle, which had proved an obstacle for so many others. (Joseph E. Stiglitz)

Thomas Schelling is widely recognized for developing the idea of a focal point (sometimes called a Schelling point). Although he cannot recall precisely how the idea developed, he is certain it arose out of his early life experience.

Again, I happened to run into Kenneth Boulding outside the Yale Cooperative Store in New Haven one afternoon.... I told Ken that there was one topic I'd wanted to include in the article that I couldn't get a grip on, and I tried to express what it was. I couldn't be explicit or else I'd have been able to deal with it in the article. Boulding said something to me—I've never been able to reconstruct what it was—that clicked in my brain and revealed what it was I was trying to formulate. Just one sentence on a sidewalk in New Haven and I had the grasp I needed. His suggestion—actually it wasn't a suggestion, just a hint of some kind—led me to the idea of a "focal point," and the concept of tacit bargaining and its influence on explicit bargaining.

I mention here an experience in my development of the focal point idea. I spent summer 1940 driving from San Diego to New Hampshire and back with two college friends. Somewhere I stopped so one of the other two could buy some crackers and peanut butter. A policeman made me move on; I tried to go around the block but was frustrated by one-way streets, and when I got back to where I'd let him out, he wasn't there. (Not seeing me, he had gone looking.) I went around again, and there he was. As we drove on, eating crackers and peanut butter, one of us said, "You know that could happen. Suppose we got separated in a strange city. How would we find each other?" ...

After supper—we were sitting out around a campfire—we compared solutions. We had all gone to the same place.... The one location in some city that was unique to us was the general delivery window of the main post office. Every city had a main post office, and every main post office had a general delivery window where one could show up and ask if there was anything for Schelling.... That experience was still vivid when I needed a focal point to concert expectations. (Thomas C. Schelling)

Vernon L. Smith's essay focuses on the lessons learned from his childhood experiences in Kansas. In this passage, he contrasts the vibrancy of city life, characterized by impersonal exchange, with an earlier farm life and personal exchange.

In 1934, my father returned to the Bridgeport Machine Company [in Wichita] for alternate week half-time work and subsequently full-time work. This was fortuitous, as we lost "ownership" of the farm to the mortgage bank.... We were returning from the farm world of personal exchange through the trading of favors to a world of impersonal exchange through markets. More, but far from all, of our needs would be met from store-bought goods, and that world would gradually be emerging, reinvigorated, from the Great Depression....

Wichita and farm life were separated by location, by intellectual and economic activity. The city had homegrown a surprising breadth of prominent business life. Beech, Stearman, and Cessna Aircraft, the Coleman Lantern Company, Dold meatpacking, and the Fred Koch, Jack Vickers, and other petroleum companies provided tangible initial evidence of the machinery of markets, specialization, and globalization. Bold independent actions by Coleman, Cessna, Beech, Koch, Garvey, and many others instilled a midwestern sense of freedom and entrepreneurship. (Vernon L. Smith)

Intriguing glimpses into these private realms can be illustrated as well by the example of Robert E. Lucas, Jr., although here the link is not made explicit for the reader. Lucas begins his memoir with a reminiscence of his mother, who worked as a commercial artist drawing newspaper ads for a clothing store. He tells us that she took him and his two siblings (at ages six, four, and three) to an apparel shop in downtown Seattle where she received the items that were to be advertised by the store the following week. His recollection of this early childhood experience is told in vivid detail:

> She would take the three of us, at ages 6, 4, and 3, all of us struggling to keep up with her clicking heels, on the half-mile walk to the bus and then on the long bus ride downtown to the McDougal's store. There we would sit still while she handed over her drawings from last week, discussed her assignments for the week to come, and put the articles to be advertised into a shopping bag.... At home, she took out a dress, shoes, and a belt from the shopping bag. She hung the dress up on a hanger near the drawing board, in the living room of the shabby house we rented during the war, and put the accessories in front of her, at the top of the board. She set out her paints—pure white, glossy black, elegant grays—and her tiny brushes, and as I watched there came into being on paper a confident and attractive woman, stylishly dressed in what I had seen as nothing more than an ordinary dress, limp on the hanger. (Robert E. Lucas, Jr.)

Lucas's creative work for which he is admired by his peers and which earned him his Nobel is his construction of ingenious theoretical models of the economy that brought a refocusing of the way economists think about the world. In his own words, he gives his opinion of why he values mathematical modeling: "It is a method to get to new levels of under-standing of the ways things work.... It is this struggle to capture behavior in tractable models that leads us deeper into the economics of market transactions and forms the progressive element in economic thought." Just as the ordinary dress on the hanger was transformed into a stylishly dressed woman at the artistic hands of his mother, so too would his own model building bring us to new levels of viewing and understanding the welter of confusing data that make up the macroeconomy. Lucas's choice of subject matter to open his lecture is surely a way of leading his audi-ence into a significant area of his being. We are allowed to see him as the observant little boy who had watched with astonishment as his mother skillfully used paints and tiny brushes to transform something ordinary and mundane into something beautiful.

What are we to make of this unexpected story? Surely this: long before Lucas had a conscious interest in economics, he had cultivated an eye for bringing new ways of seeing the evidence before him. This tale of innocence and wisdom was surely a crucial episode in his life. The story offers grounds for conjecture about the value of autobiographical details in bringing us to understand at least some part of the creative process.

Another example linking autobiography and one's intellectual approach is that of Milton Friedman. Yet here we attempt to draw a perhaps unconscious link that the author has not drawn. Friedman made it respectable for economists to question the efficacy of Keynesian policy; he resurrected the quantity theory of money and placed in on a secure footing; and he championed the private market economy at a time when intellectuals who did so were often subjected to ostracism in respectable academic circles. Few would doubt that we are all richer for his having become an economist. But why did he enter graduate school in economics? Initially, Friedman had planned to choose mathematics because he liked the subject. The Great Depression was under way, though, and Friedman was intrigued by what he called "the paradox of great need on the one hand and unused resources on the other." Moreover, making the decision process more difficult, he had offers of financial aid from two universities—one for the study of mathematics at Brown, and the other to study economics at Chicago. The final decision came down almost to the toss of a coin. Economics and the puzzle of the Great Depression won out. In his autobiographical lecture he attempts to explain his choice. To do so he quotes Robert Frost's famous poem, "The Road Less Traveled":

Two roads diverged in a yellow wood,
And sorry I could not travel both
I took the one less traveled by.
And that has made all the difference. (1–2, 19–20)

And yet reference to the Frost poem does not seem appropriate in his case. During the Great Depression, when Friedman entered college, economics was not the road "less traveled by." To the contrary, it was among the most popular of majors. He said he chose economics because of its relevance to the issues of the day, as with so many others of his generation. But this leaves us with a mystery. What is the relevance of Frost's poem? Why did he quote it?

Perhaps the choice of the poem reveals something about Friedman that was hidden from him when he quoted its words. Even if entering economics during the Great Depression was not really taking the road less traveled, nevertheless Friedman's subsequent career persistently took him along untrampled pathways *within economics*. Was this a conscious decision? For in his attempt to answer questions posed by the Great Depression, Friedman stood apart and almost alone. He rejected the Keynesian solutions that the overwhelming majority of the profession had come to accept. Friedman lived long enough to see many of his ideas become the consensus view of a younger generation of economists. Because he was different, he attracted attention: his persuasive powers, style, and charisma did the rest. For Friedman, the road less traveled indeed "made all the difference."

From the other side of the spectrum of political economy, another economist, Joseph E. Stiglitz, also draws inspiration from the same Robert Frost poem in pondering his choice of a career in economics.

As I think about that spring afternoon when I went for a walk in a New England forest and decided to become an economist rather than a physicist, I am reminded of a Robert Frost poem about two roads that diverged in a yellow wood. I wonder what might have happened had I had taken the other road. (Joseph E. Stiglitz)

In the end, the case for biography generally, and autobiography in particular, is a strong one. To believe that biography is *essential* for understanding economics and the evolution of economic ideas admittedly requires a leap of faith. We simply are unable to meaningfully compare the current state of economic science to what might have existed under some reasonable counterfactual. That being said, the twenty-three lectures in this volume provide strong evidence that biography matters. We have seen how the most important developments in modern economics did not spring out of the air randomly but were intimately related to the laureates' backgrounds, intellectual environments, interactions with teachers and colleagues, desire for relevance and rigor, and competition in the marketplace for ideas. For individual laureates, the road traveled was sometimes the result of happenstance and sometimes not. Following the laureates on their intellectual journeys not only makes for fascinating reading but also enriches our understanding of the development of contemporary economic thought.